nfonteyn. 9 Loort Pant. Baffecourt 10 Vrouwen Vertreck. 11 Guarde joperix et Meribl 12 Stallingen

WILLIAM'S MARY

QUEEN MARY.   WISSI

Mary II when Princess of Orange

ELIZABETH HAMILTON

William's Mary

A BIOGRAPHY OF

MARY II

TAPLINGER PUBLISHING COMPANY

NEW YORK

First published in the United States in 1972 by
TAPLINGER PUBLISHING CO., INC.
New York, New York

Library of Congress Catalog Card Number: 78-164583

ISBN 0-8008-8248-2

SECOND PRINTING

To ANDREW *and* SUSANNA

CONTENTS

LIST OF ILLUSTRATIONS

ix

ACKNOWLEDGEMENTS

I SHOULD LIKE TO THANK for their courteous help the staff of the Bodleian Library, the British Museum Manuscripts Room, the London Library and the Warwickshire County Library, particularly Mr Champion. I am indebted to Mr Robert Mackworth-Young, Librarian at Windsor Castle, Mr E. K. Timings of the Public Record Office, Mr H. M. G. Baillie of the Royal Commission on Historical Manuscripts, Mr T. S. Wragg, Librarian and Keeper at Chatsworth, Professor Potter and, in Holland, Dr E. Pelinck of the Koninklijk Huisarchief, Mrs M. A. P. Meilink-Roelofsz, Mr Fox and Miss van den Berg of the Algemeen Rijksarchief, Mr van Kretschmar of the Iconographisch Bureau, Mr L. J. van der Klooster of the Rijksbureau voor Kunsthistorische Documentatie, Dr A. M. Luyendijk-Elshout of the Rijksmuseum voor de Geschiedenis der Natuurwetenschappen at Leyden, Mr van Groningen of Leyden University Library, Mr H. Hardenberg and Mr J. A. van Hasselt. I should like to thank Arnoud and Elizabeth Waller for their hospitality, and Tom and Iola Symonds for putting me up at Edensor Vicarage.

Extracts from the account book of Mary II and from the notebook of James, Duke of York, are printed by gracious permission of Her Majesty the Queen, and letters at Chatsworth by permission of His Grace the Duke of Devonshire. I am grateful to Earl Bathurst for permission to quote from family manuscripts, to Sir William Dugdale for allowing me me to use the description of James II's visit to Coventry in 1687 from Sir John Dugdale's *Heraldic Notebook*, and to Mr M. F. Farr, the Warwickshire County Archivist, for drawing my attention to it.

I acknowledge my indebtedness to all those whose published work is listed in the bibliography and particularly to Mary II's more recent biographers—Miss Nellie M. Waterson, Miss Marjorie Bowen and Miss Hester Chapman—as well as to Mr Stephen Baxter and Dr Nesca A. Robb for their studies of William III.

On the home front, the Bainses, 'Huckie', and, appropriately enough, three Marys—Mrs Wills, Mrs Olorenshaw and Miss Eckert—have all indirectly contributed to this book as has Mrs Lamerton. My husband, as always, has been tolerance itself, and has assisted me greatly with translations and transcripts and his careful reading of the manuscript.

The author of this book received financial assistance from the Arts Council of Great Britain in 1969–70.

NOTE

DURING the lifetime of Mary II, England was ten days behind the Continent where most countries had adopted the new style of dating. To avoid the clumsiness of quoting both dates throughout, events which took place in England are dated according to the Old Style and those on the Continent according to the New Style.

Notes at the end of the book are given according to page references.

CHAPTER I

DAUGHTER OF YORK

IN 1649, when Charles I was executed—or murdered as they preferred to call it in Stuart circles—his elder sons were already living in safety on the continent. Their mother, Henrietta Maria, daughter of the late King Henry IV of France, had been entrusted with the task of guiding them in every matter except their religion. She was a forceful woman who enjoyed having her sons dependent on her, especially for money, but Charles, now nineteen, and James, three years his junior, were not prepared to submit to her domination. At the first possible moment they left Paris for Jersey, the only part of the lost kingdom which remained open to them. There, surrounded by the dregs of Cavalier England, and living on credit with a semblance of grandeur, they kept their mother well out of their counsels, and continued to do so even when they were forced to return to France.

In spite of, or perhaps because of, the maternal supervision, the exiled King and his brother soon broke free from all constraint, in the moral as well as the political sphere. Only a few months after his father's death, Charles became the father of a son by Lucy Walter, the daughter of a down-and-out Royalist. This child, James, later Duke of Monmouth, grew up to be handsome and charming, and his father always nursed an extraordinary fondness for him. The mother, 'this beautiful strumpet' as Evelyn called her, was however, abandoned by the young King in 1651 following his remarkable escape after the battle of Worcester. In England he had encountered people, men and women, so loyal that they had risked their lives for him, and it was a shock for him to find that in the meantime, whilst he had been away trying to regain his crown, his mistress had casually proved unfaithful. All the same, in spite of this disillusionment, more seedy amours followed. Running into debt wherever he went, and calling down the wrath of Cromwell on any nation that harboured him, Charles soon began to find himself coldly received in most of the courts of Europe.

The young King might have expected to find a welcome in the Netherlands where his sister Mary, the Princess Royal, had married William II of Orange, Stadholder of the United Provinces. But William had quarrelled with the States, particularly with the powerful state of Holland, and when, in 1650, he had died of smallpox and the Princess Royal had given birth to a son, William, a few weeks after his death, there were many people who were determined to show the new Prince of Orange that the Stadholdership was not a hereditary title. It seemed no more likely that William would become Stadholder of the States than that his Uncle Charles would ever occupy the throne of England. In the Netherlands, the House of Orange was in disfavour, and as for the Princess Royal herself, the Dutch had never liked her. They found her proud and haughty, a typical English snob, while she nursed what one observer called 'une aversion horrible pour la Hollande'. All she cared for was her own family and she demonstrated her affection by lending her brothers considerable sums of money to help finance their ill-conceived plots to retrieve the crown. It was to her house at Honselaersdyck near the Hague that James had first come after his escape from England, and to her that Parliament sent over in 1653 her youngest brother, Henry, Duke of Gloucester. She showed far more affection for this boy than she did for her own son and wept bitter tears when their mother, Henrietta Maria, demanded to have him with her in France. William was a stunted, delicate child, his only good feature the lustrous eyes which he had inherited from the Stuarts. Some reports said he was slightly deformed and certainly his health was precarious—he suffered from asthma, fainting fits and violent headaches.

It was Edward Hyde, the late King's loyal counsellor, who, in the course of a two years' embassy at Madrid, persuaded the King of Spain to let Charles set up his court in the Spanish Netherlands. Although Hyde was only forty-one at the time of Charles I's execution, the young exiled King looked on him as an elder statesman. He had been what was in those days termed 'a private gentleman' who had abandoned a legal career for politics, and, by his own intelligence and hard work, had risen above his Wiltshire parentage and found his way into the King's inner counsels. Moderate, with a deep respect for the constitution, Edward Hyde had alienated many of Charles I's more rabid supporters and as a result had been relegated to the post of guardian to the Prince of Wales, whom he had accompanied into exile. Before he left for Spain, charged with the task of begging help for his new master, he had brought over from England his wife and four children for fear of reprisals, and had settled them in a house at Antwerp, where they lived frugally during his absence.

Mrs Hyde was no great beauty but she was a good wife with whom Hyde was able to live 'very comfortably in the most uncomfortable times'.

During the years of exile she had to endure long periods of separation, but she bore without complaint the task of bringing up her daughter and three sons on a meagre income eked out with presents smuggled over from friends in England. The Princess of Orange, who was always ready to help an exile, granted her a rent-free house at Breda which at least eased the financial situation. Hyde had taken on a depressing task as Chancellor of a non-existent Exchequer, and he soon became the target for crowds of clamouring, penniless expatriates. Though jovial and witty, he had an air of intellectual superiority which, coupled with the aggressive assurance of the self-made man, did not appeal to the inbred courtiers who made up Charles's shabby entourage. Nor did he invariably find favour with Henrietta Maria, who was jealous of the influence he wielded over her son.

In 1654 Charles visited Spa, not so much to take the waters as to find an excuse for enjoying the company of the Princess Royal who joined him there. They had been there no more than a month when an outbreak of smallpox forced them to move at short notice to Aix-la-Chapelle, leaving behind one of the Princess's maids of honour who had contracted the disease and who subsequently died. The Princess was anxious to fill the vacancy as soon as possible, before her mother, who always liked to interfere, should try to suggest a candidate. People said that Hyde's daughter Anne might prove suitable, and the Princess liked the idea, for she knew that Hyde had been a faithful friend to her father and brother. The Chancellor, granted a rare spell of leave during the royal visit to Spa, was with his wife in Breda when a member of the King's Bedchamber arrived with the proposal that Anne should enter the Princess's service.

Hyde's reaction was not all at favourable. He was under no illusions about the dangers to which young and innocent girls were exposed at court, and he was unwilling to deprive his wife of her only daughter—her one comfort in a dreary existence. Nor had Hyde any desire to call down the wrath of the Queen Mother on his already much-battered head. To his surprise, however, his wife took the opposite view, and in this she was backed up by Dr Morley, an exiled divine who was in the habit of staying with the Hyde family for protracted periods on the pretext of helping with the children's education. In Hyde's words, Morley was 'a gentleman of very eminent parts', but he had failed to gain promotion so far on account of his unfortunate tendency to make sharp answers in 'accidental discourses'. Once he had told an earnest country gentleman who had wished to know what tenets were held by the Arminians, that they held all the best bishoprics and deaneries in England. Morley was also what Hyde called 'a wary director', which was perhaps why, when he counselled acceptance of the Princess's offer, the Chancellor was persuaded to agree against his better judgment.

At the Princess's court Anne Hyde proved to be a great success. She soon became Mary's favourite, and Elizabeth of Bohemia, the exiled 'Winter Queen' and sister of Charles I, doted on her as if she were her own daughter. Anne had inherited her father's wit and intelligence, she was handsome rather than pretty and well-built, with a hand that was fine, white and fat, as Pepys noted at a later date when he kissed it. According to Gramont, there was nobody at the Hague capable of putting her in the shade, and her striking looks caused comment when she played the part of a shepherdess in one of the court masques. Unlike her father she was also gifted with tact, a quality which she displayed on a famous occasion when the vivacious little Princess Palatine, Elizabeth Charlotte, better known as Liselotte, enquired of her cousin William the identity of the lady with the 'furious' nose—it was his mother, the Princess, who was suffering from a heavy cold. Anne Hyde diplomatically shuffled the children out of the room and played games with them in the bedchamber, where they rolled about on a Turkish carpet.

In 1656 there were rumours that the Princess of Orange intended to marry again. Her mother would have liked to see her firmly tied up with Louis XIV, who was at this time casting an approving eye on Olympia Mancini, one of Mazarin's nieces, so she invited her to Paris. The Princess was met between Péronne and Cambrai by her brother James and a crowd of courtiers who accompanied her to the Palais Royal. We do not know whether it was here, outside the gates of Paris, that the Duke of York first noticed his sister's maid of honour, Anne Hyde, but the Princess stayed in France for nearly a year, so there were plenty of opportunities for further meetings. There were fêtes and parties of every description, and although the Princess did not find herself a husband, she was in no hurry to return to Holland or to the small son she had left behind. She finally left on receiving a message that William was seriously ill, but dallied for a further month or two at Bruges when she discovered that her son's illness had turned out to be measles and was not likely to prove fatal.

At this stage in his career James, Duke of York, was probably happier than at any subsequent time. He was serving with the French army and the active life suited him; he was of a more 'stirring nature' than the easygoing Charles, who was averse to action and to business—he only wrote letters on a Friday, if at all. James did not get on well with his mother, who found him obstinate and difficult, and kept him short of money; but amongst his fellow officers he was liked and respected. He was good-looking in the Stuart mould, with a fair complexion, heavy curls and a doomed expression, but he lacked his brother's wit and was completely without a sense of humour; intelligent ladies found him insufferably dull. Where women were concerned, though far less fastidious than Charles, he was just as susceptible, and it was not long before he became enamoured of Anne Hyde. She had, as he put it himself, 'wit and other qualities capable of surprising a heart less inclinable to sex than was that of his Royal Highness in the first warmth of his youth'. The romance might have died after the Princess's return to Holland, but soon after this Charles wrenched his brother away from his niche in the French army and made him live at Bruges in the Spanish Netherlands to help cement the alliance with Spain. Here the Duke found himself in very changed circumstances. Nobody looked up to him, he had less money than ever, and he was soon quarrelling with Charles, who disliked his choice of servants. The Stuart cause had never looked more hopeless. A Royalist rising planned for the summer of 1659 had been betrayed before it could take place. James had set out in high spirits from his sister's court, hoping to be among the first to embark for England, but he had slunk back to Brussels a disappointed man. He was penniless, his credit had run out, his clothes were shabby, and Anne Hyde, with whom he fancied himself to be in love, was resisting his advances. He had tried, as Burnet put it, to make her 'comply with his desires', but she continued, tantalizingly, to withhold her favours, a situation to which he was unaccustomed.

It was during this period of gloom that the Duke accepted an invitation to become High Admiral of Spain, a post that was welcome if only because it was likely to bring in some money. And since Anne Hyde refused to give him satisfaction until he married her, he entered into a secret contract at Breda in November 1659, after which she gave him all he desired.

Soon afterwards, the climate of opinion in England began to change rapidly. Disenchantment with the Commonwealth spread so quickly that General Monck, the Cromwellian commander-in-chief in Scotland who had undergone a change of heart, met with no resistance when he marched down from Scotland. In London, the City fathers joined with him in demanding a 'free' Parliament which, when elected, opened negotiations with Charles. The Duke of York could now forget about the Spanish navy. The English fleet came over to Holland and welcomed him as its own Lord High Admiral—a post to which he had first been appointed at the age of four and a half. Sir John Grenville arrived with £50,000 for Charles, £10,000 for James, and £7,000 for Henry, Duke of Gloucester, all in a portmanteau. Offered ready cash, the tailors of the town soon ran up new suits to mark the occasion. Charles set sail for England in May 1660; he was given such a send-off that anyone would have thought he was King of the Dutch. When he entered the Hague in state, the Duke of York and the Princess of Orange travelled in the royal coach which was joined by seventy-two others, each drawn by six or eight horses. The Duke took on his knee his nephew and future son-in-law William, who was now ten years old, a serious-minded and precocious child.

The English fleet was anchored at Scheveningen, and the sand dunes on the shore were thick with people waiting to watch the departure. The Princess went on board the King's ship with her son, and parted from her brother with great emotion. All night long the wherries went from one great ship to another, carrying those who had gone out to wish goodbye to their friends. The moon was full, the wind favourable, the sea calm, and there was not a cloud in the sky. A hundred or so brave ships went across the channel, sailing before the wind, with the sound of trumpets and other music to help them on their way. Monck met the King on the shore with five thousand gentlemen; when the General knelt to kiss the King's hand, Charles embraced him, and called him a true friend.

The route to London was lined with people, and the capital was so crowded that there were not enough lodgings to go round. This was a satisfactory beginning, but the King soon had to face many problems. Few of the friends who had joined him in exile could boast of any political experience of the kind required to deal with a Parliament that could give or withhold the money needed to pay off the army, compensate those who had suffered in the civil war, and meet current expenses. And the King was not inclined to be parsimonious. Once restored to his throne he reacted vigorously against the poverty of exile, indulging in a glittering round of pleasure.

Edward Hyde was appointed Lord Chancellor. He was the King's chief counsellor—one of the most important men in the country. His daughter Anne was now a desirable match, and one noble family, observing that her father had reached a position of status and power, was already making an overture. Before long Hyde wrote to the Princess of Orange asking her to release his daughter from her service. Hyde apparently knew nothing of her earlier entanglement, although it was common knowledge in some circles on the continent that the Duke of York regarded her with affection. The Duke, however, was no longer a penniless exile dependent on his mother. He had an income of his own and was next in line to the throne: he could look for a wife among the most eligible princesses in Europe. His love for the ample Anne was already on the wane, and he began to wish he had never become involved with her. In Holland she had seemed outstanding, but here, in a country 'so fertile in loveliness' as Gramont termed it, her charms looked a trifle faded. She informed the Duke on her return to England that she was bearing his child. He could have done without this embarrassment, and his cronies agreed that it would be farcical to tie himself for life to the daughter of a petty lawyer.

A group of the Duke's friends—Berkeley, Arran, Killigrew and Talbot —undertook to extricate him from his difficulties by the simple expedient of casting doubts on Anne's reputation. Gramont gives a résumé of the plot with a number of vivid if apocryphal details. Arran recalled an occasion in the gallery at the court of the Princess of Orange during a game of ninepins; the maid of honour had pretended to feel unwell and the Earl had done his best to help by cutting her laces, 'to lend the theory that she was suffering from an attack of the vapours a certain colouring of likelihood'. He had gone on from there to offer her further consolation. Talbot described an episode in the Chancellor's study—that gentleman being conveniently absent at a cabinet meeting—when in the excitement of the moment he and Anne had spilt a bottle of ink over a despatch four pages long, a crime which they had blamed on the King's monkey. Others boasted of 'protracted and favourable audience', and Killigrew capped them all by alleging that he had given her satisfaction in a certain closet constructed above the water 'for quite another end than relieving the pangs of love'. Nobody could dispute this, since, as he said, only three or four swans had been witnesses of his good fortune.

Anne Hyde resisted all these attacks with typical firmness and she stubbornly denied that there was any truth in them. The Duke at last had to admit that he was cornered, and decided there was nothing else to do except to tell the King—which he did, according to Hyde, in floods of tears. The King was naturally surprised, particularly as the Chancellor, with whom he was in close contact every day, had never mentioned the matter and was apparently ignorant of his daughter's follies. Southampton and Ormonde, the Chancellor's close friends, were sent to break the news to him and to observe his reactions. If he was play-acting, he put up a convincing performance. He declared that he would turn his daughter out of the house as a strumpet and never see her again; he said he would far rather see her as the Duke's whore than as his wife, and he declared that he would ask the King to convey her to the Tower and have her head cut off.

The Chancellor's behaviour, some thought, was worthy of an ancient Roman. Southampton, however, wondered if he had gone mad since he

was suggesting such extraordinary remedies. When the King arrived on
the scene, he found the Chancellor looking red-eyed and furious; he was
leaning against a wall and appeared to be bursting with some kind of
pent-up emotion. The King looked at him 'with wonderful benignity',
and advised him to compose himself in order to decide on the best course
to take. Hyde protested that he would never presume on the King's good
nature to the extent of allowing his daughter to marry the Duke; he knew
well enough that had he done so, people would not have been slow to
accuse him of plotting the marriage in order to consolidate his own position. He went home in a rage and told his wife to keep Anne in solitary
confinement in her own room, a heavy punishment for a gregarious girl
who was already attracting a great deal of company. After spending a restless night, Hyde went to see the King who reproved him for acting with
so much precipitation.

The Duke, it appeared, was offended by the Chancellor's attitude, and,
in defiance, he managed to find a way into Anne's chamber where he
stayed 'whole nights', in the father's indignant phrase. The secret marriage
contract was then produced and this was examined, on the King's orders,
by various bishops and judges, who reported that according to the law of
the gospel and the law of England, the Duke and Mistress Hyde could be
legally termed man and wife.

Later, James alleged that the Chancellor had played his part very
cunningly, softening the King in a matter that could only be to his own
advantage. Otherwise, James believed, his brother would never of his own
accord have agreed to recognize a marriage to which all his friends, and
even the menial servants, were unanimously opposed. It was always
Charles's failing, Evelyn said, to be managed by crafty men, and at this
time Hyde was the King's oracle. Looking back on it, James felt that he
himself had pursued an honourable course in the face of much advice to
the contrary, 'chusing rather to undergo the censure of being frail in
promising than of being unjust in breaking his promise'. Probably the
more likely story was that James begged his brother to extricate him from
his difficulties, but that the King simply told him he must 'drink as he
had brewed'. To ensure that there was no further argument the couple
underwent a marriage ceremony on September 3, 1660. Charles Stuart,
Duke of Cambridge, the first of Anne Hyde's eight children, was born on
October 22. The King sent several ladies 'of known honour and fidelity
to the Crown', to be present at the birth. Dr Morley, Anne's tutor in
exile, now Bishop of Winchester, also hurried to her side. He stayed with
her throughout her labour, asking her, in the intervals between her

sharpest pangs, and sometimes when they were upon her, such pertinent questions as, 'whose the child was of which she was in labour?'—to which she firmly replied, 'the Duke's'.

The scandal was kept secret for several weeks, but rumours soon began to circulate. Elizabeth of Bohemia, James's godmother, was incredulous. She had heard a story that when Anne was at Breda, and ten weeks gone with child, she had told Dr Rumph that she felt ill because she had eaten too much fish that Lent, and she asked him for some medicine to carry it all away. The physician had innocently given her some 'good strong purges and vomits', but when he started letting blood in her foot, he guessed her secret and refrained from further treatment. The Winter Queen's theory was that if Anne had really been married, she would not have attempted to rid herself of the child.

Nobody, least of all Hyde, relished the idea of telling the Queen Mother the news. Both she and the Princess of Orange were coming over to England to congratulate Charles on his restoration. The Princess arrived to find the whole court in mourning for her brother Henry who had just died of smallpox. Everyone was dressed in long cloaks and even the servants were in black. She was then told about the Duke's marriage, which shocked her deeply, especially as she had always given the girl so much trust. The Princess refused to stay in the same room as her new sister-in-law, and the whole affair cast a gloom over her visit. She went into partnership with the Queen Mother, and they both did what they could to sabotage the marriage. Henry, in general 'the best natured youth that could be', had been just as vehement, saying, before he was taken ill, that Anne 'smelt so strongly of her father's green bag that he could not get the better of himself, whenever he had the misfortune to be in her presence'.

The Princess of Orange had not been in England for long before she too fell sick. At first they thought it was 'measells and the purpells together'; later smallpox was diagnosed, and by Christmas she was dead, a tragedy which, as Evelyn reported, 'wholly altered the face and gallantry of the whole court'. William of Orange was only eleven years old when his mother died. 'I'm too young to do very much,' he said, in his sad way, when they told him the news.

Although nobody was pleased when they heard the identity of the new Duchess of York, such criticism as there was gradually died down. Even the Queen Mother, on Mazarin's advice, made up her quarrel with the Chancellor, who had now been created Earl of Clarendon. She realized that there was more chance of settling her debts if she could bring herself to

regard her daughter-in-law with a loving eye. And the friends who had tried
to blacken Anne's reputation were now forced to recant. 'The Duchess
of York,—there she stands,' the Lords Falmouth and Ossory were told.
Berkeley flung himself at her feet begging forgiveness, and she coolly gave
him her hand to kiss. Except when incapacitated by pregnancy, the Duchess
entered into court life with a dignity which made people forget her Wiltshire origins. 'It is as if,' wrote a Frenchman at the court, 'she were of the
blood of Kings, or of Guzman at the least, or Mendoce.' Even her husband
had to admit, in his pompous way, that 'what she wanted in birth was so
well made up by other endowments, that her carriage afterwards did not
misbecome her acquired dignity'. She was majestic and managing, and
gave such an air of grandeur to everything she did that she might have
been born to her high rank, instead of achieving it by a mixture of luck
and good management. She was witty—in this respect she certainly
outshone the Duke—and also had the gift of gathering round her men
and women of merit. But her new position brought out a domineering
streak in her character, and she was to be seen sitting at the Duke's
council table as if she was trying to be Queen Elizabeth. She had a good
business head and kept a careful watch on the accounts, crossing out
wages or prices if she thought they were too high; though thrifty where her
staff was concerned, she kept five thousand pounds a year for her own
private use and had a fine collection of jewellery. Pepys though she was a
plain woman, and said maliciously that she was very like her mother, my
Lady Chancellor.

In February 1661, the Yorks' son, Charles Stuart, died at the age of
four months, which was as well, for if he had lived his legitimacy would
always have been in question. In any case the Duchess was soon expecting
another child, and on April 30, 1662, at one in the morning, she gave
birth to a daughter, Mary—'at which I find nobody pleased,' Pepys
observed. Being a girl and therefore undervalued, Mary managed to
escape the attention of well-meaning doctors, and it could have been for
this reason that she grew up to be a reasonably healthy child, pretty and
graceful, with her father's complexion, heavy curls and dark, lustrous eyes.
A year later, when a son was born to the Duke and Duchess, he had a far
better reception. There were crowds of coaches waiting at the gate of
St James's Palace as people called to present their compliments.

The unwanted Princess was brought up in an atmosphere of plenty at
St James's and at the house at Twickenham which her grandfather,
Clarendon, had given the Yorks as a wedding present. In her earliest years
her father was acquitting himself well as Lord High Admiral, for although

he was humourless and inclined to nag his brother, he was efficient when given a task that appealed to him. When England went to war with Holland, his bravery at sea was acknowledged even by those who as a rule had little good to say about him. He was not naturally affectionate, but he had a happy relationship with his elder daughter; sometimes Pepys saw him playing with her as if she were an ordinary child rather than the daughter of a Royal Duke, and she remained his favourite until she was grown up.

Apart from her father's approval, however, the Lady Mary's childhood contained few of the ingredients of happiness. There was little love between her parents; although in the early days they made some show of affection in public, which was thought to be slightly shocking in a married couple—they were seen kissing and leaning upon one another at a performance of *Claracilla* by Killigrew—yet as time went on it became evident that her father loved her mother just as much as any man loves a wife who he is sure has trapped him into marriage. The Duke appeared to be quite frightened of his wife, which was surprising, considering their inequality of rank, but less so considering the Duchess's character, for she was a hard, pleasure-seeking woman, singularly lacking in maternal feeling, or in any kind of soft feminine emotion. Sir John Reresby, who had a charming habit of keeping a snake in a small box of bran, noticed that when he produced this reptile suddenly, the maids of honour all shrieked with fright, but the Duchess took it into her hands without any fear at all. She dominated her husband in everything, even helping him with his memoirs, which was an advantage as his own style was turgid and dull. 'In all things but his cod-piece [he] is led by the nose by his wife' was how Pepys summed it up. Inconstancy was his only outlet, but, as Burnet put it, 'he was not very nice in his choice'. He went through his maids of honour so fast that they themselves speculated as to whose turn it would be next. Most of his mistresses were so ugly that the King was of the opinion that they had been given to him by the priests as a penance. In 1662 he was smitten by the fair, blue-eyed and tiny Lady Chesterfield whose husband incurred the Duke's displeasure by hurrying her off to the country. When his wife had measles, James slept in his study in a bed delightfully hung with red velvet, and this came in useful on other occasions. The Duke made a habit of sleeping with the Duchess and afterwards walking down the matted gallery to his study where he would find his current mistress waiting for him. When Lady Denham died at the age of twenty and there were rumours that she had been poisoned, the Duke was fond enough of her to be really upset, and he declared that he would never have a public mistress again. Not that he ever kept this good resolution; there was Lady Carnegy, whom he fell for the very next year, and Frances Jennings and Arabella Churchill, to name but a few. Years later when he was in Dublin in 1690 during the Irish campaign, it was rumoured that he was carrying on there with what Liselotte described as two 'frightful scarecrows'.

In all this the Duke could have been said to be following his brother's example. Evelyn admitted that the King brought in a 'politer way of living', but he complained that this soon led to luxury and 'intolerable expense'. In general there was a decidedly permissive attitude towards promiscuity among the great, but all the same there were some who believed that the King's mistresses weakened his judgment. He found it difficult to refuse them anything, so that they used up all his money to the detriment of those who had served him faithfully in the past and deserved a reward. His marriage to the Infanta of Portugal, Catherine of Braganza, did little to alter his habits. The Portuguese Queen was small, with a pretty figure, languorous eyes, and protruding teeth. She spoke English charmingly, with quaint phrases, and as time went by she unbent a little, and was seen to hug the King and to gallop to meet him on the road. Naturally enough she did not approve of the presence of Lady Castlemaine, the King's mistress, who had been given apartments too close for comfort, and was the most well off of all the 'concubines and catell of that sort' as Evelyn termed them. Lady Castlemaine's rooms far outstripped the Queen's in extravagance, and she was richer in jewels than the Queen and the Duchess of York put together. She went about accompanied by a little black boy and put on a great many airs and graces, hectoring the King mercilessly. Pepy's cousin Roger found her very handsome, but thought it a pity she could not be as good within as she was fair without. The Queen soon discovered that the only way to keep even a vestige of the King's affection was to ignore his amours. He made no attempt to hide them; he dallied publicly with Mrs Stewart, Lady Castlemaine's successor, and walked in and out of her room so openly that the sentries would ask each other, 'Is the King above or below?'

The Queen brought with her to England six hideous attendants, headed by a 'supplementary monster', as Gramont called the duenna. Their enormous old-fashioned farthingales did not appeal to the English courtiers, who also found their 'Portugal musiq' excruciating; it was performed on pipes and harps, accompanied by what were, in Evelyn's opinion, 'very ill voices'. The Duchess of York, on the other hand, had a genius for attracting interesting people, and her court was far more worth while visiting than the Queen's. In another respect, too, she was more successful. Catherine was not, as they termed it in those days, a fruitful lady. Although in the early days of her marriage there were rumours that she was with child—it was said that the coachmen had been ordered to ride very gently though the streets—it soon became clear that she did not conceive very easily and that if she ever did so it was unlikely that she would give birth to a living child. The Duchess, for her part, was producing children almost at the rate of one a year. In 1664 she had a daughter, Lady Anne, followed by two boys in 1666 and 1667. And as any hope of Catherine producing an heir receded, so the York children grew in importance. This fact made some people uneasy, owing to the current and well-grounded belief that the Duke had a secret and unshakeable sympathy for the Catholic Church. The Duchess also was not above suspicion. So, as her parents pursued their inexorable course towards Rome, Lady Mary was, on the King's instructions, put under the guidance of Protestant tutors. They taught her that Catholicism was the most wicked influence in the world.

In 1666, the year of the plague, the royal family was forced to leave London to avoid the risk of infection. The King took this opportunity of sending the Duke and Duchess on a good-will tour in the north of England. The visitors were not altogether welcome, as there was always a fear that they might bring the plague with them in their train, and anyone who showed the slightest sign of sickness was sent off at once to the pestilence house. All the same, the Duke spent an enjoyable time hunting and indulging in other pastimes, while the Duchess held her court and received the ladies of noble families. They were well treated at Woburn—'an excellent and capacious house'—and at Lord Banbury's they were entertained with a breakfast table laden with sweatmeats and fruit. It was during this tour that the Duchess, by way of taking her revenge on the Duke for all his infidelities, conducted a mild flirtation with Henry Sidney, a member of the Duke's Bedchamber, and one of the most handsome young men of his time. He seemed to be very much in love with her, and she did not discourage him. The Duke took exception to her behaviour with all the self-righteousness of the male libertine who, for once, finds himself wronged. A fierce quarrel took place, and for a while James appeared to be more docile. Both he and his brother made themselves popular by their personal bravery during the Fire of London, but later that year he was as unfaithful as ever, and Pepys reported that he had become a slave to his new whore, Denham.

The following year, it was rumoured that the Duke had another mistress, Mrs Middleton. He was at sea from April to June, which suited him, and he finished his active spell with a glorious victory over the Dutch. On the less fortunate side, two of his sons died within a few months of each other. Added to this, the Duchess's father, Clarendon, was being elbowed out of the King's counsels by jealous rivals. Charles had warned his brother that Clarendon would be laid aside before Parliament met, and gave him the task of breaking the news to his father-in-law. On the night of the Chancellor's fall there was gloom at St James's. The Duke and Duchess dined alone and seemed very melancholy. Parliament's reaction was violent and there were threats of impeachment. Clarendon was advised to go abroad, and he went at once, leaving behind his costly palace where he had only recently sat in the garden—in a wheel chair because of his gout—watching the gates being set up and other finishing touches. Clarendon died in exile and was never to see his grandchildren or the Duke and Duchess again. But in any case his relationship with his daughter had been steadily deteriorating. He thought she was being too extravagant, and her leanings towards the Catholic Church greatly distressed him. Her marriage with the heir to the throne had on the whole been a hindrance rather than a help, for however hard he tried to appear impartial, his political enemies always accused him of arranging matters to the benefit of his own family. One of the charges levelled at him was that he had engineered the King's marriage knowing that Portuguese women tended to be infertile, it was even said that he had arranged for Catherine to be given a drug to make her incapable of producing any heirs who might stand in the way of his own grandchildren.

After Clarendon's disgrace it was noticed that people paid the Duchess far less respect than before. In an attempt to keep in the King's circle she even went so far as to pay her court to Lady Castlemaine: she indulged in an extravagant social round, started hoarding jewellery and began to eat compulsively. In fact, Lady Mary's parents were not a pretty sight. The fatter her mother grew, the leaner her father became, the result, many people hinted, of distempers contracted in the course of his many love affairs. Burnet believed that he infected his Duchess, which accounted for the sickliness of her children, six of whom died in infancy, and also for the gout and eye trouble suffered by Anne and, to a lesser extent, by Mary. The children were, in Burnet's opinion, nothing but 'dregs of the tainted original', although James's bastards tended to flourish, lacking the over-intensive care from well-meaning doctors whose medicaments were calculated to throw the toughest infants into convulsive fits.

In spite of her strange childhood, Lady Mary was growing up gracefully. On April 2, 1669, Pepys wrote, 'I did see the young Duchess, a little child in hanging sleeves, dance most finely, so as almost to ravish me her ears were so good.' Anne was the more delicate of the two sisters and in her early childhood her eyesight was so bad that she had to be sent to her grandmother in France to see whether the French doctors could find a cure for her trouble. Her mother spoilt her, feeding her on titbits until she became as fat and round as a little ball. The girls were perhaps too young to notice that their parents were alienating all their friends and relations as they progressed steadily towards Catholicism. Once their father had been, as he expressed it himself, 'the darling of the nation'. He had risked his life for his country, and it was in his honour that New Amsterdam had been re-named New York when it was captured from the Dutch in 1664; but now his open preference for the Church of Rome made everyone forget his achievements in the sphere of naval operations. In 1669 he was, to use his own words, 'more sensibly touched in conscience, and began to think seriously of his salvation'. He sent for Father Simmonds, a learned Jesuit, who said baldly that nobody could be received into the Catholic Church unless they were prepared to absent themselves from the Anglican communion. Knowing the difficulties this could create for his brother, James tried to obtain a special dispensation from the Pope, on the grounds that his case was singular, but he found that the Catholic doctrine took no account of expediency. So he continued in an uneasy atmosphere of deception which offended against his candid nature.

The King also had Catholic leanings, but knew better how to hide them. Had he given any public expression of his religious tendencies, he would have offended Parliament, whose approval he needed if there was to be any hope of improving his chronically unhealthy finances. From time to time he made some half-hearted attempts to cut down his expenses; he even reduced his diet for a short while in 1663, allowing himself and the Queen only twelve dishes per meal—a great sacrifice. But the only real hope of solving his monetary difficulties was to accept subsidies from France, and Louis XIV did not hand out money without some conditions attached. The most important of these were that Charles should declare himself a Catholic and should also undertake to restore the whole of England to the faith. Financial dependence on France meant in addition that England would have to pledge herself to oppose the Protestant Dutch and enter into war on the side of Louis XIV.

In May 1670 the Duke and Duchess of York went away to Dover with the King, leaving their children in London. Charles and James were meeting there their favourite sister, Henrietta, Duchess of Orléans, 'Minette', ostensibly for a family reunion; but in fact the Duchess had brought over the French King's terms, and a secret treaty was signed which included the Catholic clauses. For those who were left behind in London it was lonely and quiet. 'The parks look very thin, the King and Duke not being there, and the Queen's chapel strange, when she is praying at Dover,' wrote one of the York retainers, adding 'I hope your sweet Highness will soon return to the little children'.

The Duchess of York cared more for her own soul than she did for the welfare of her offspring. In 1669 she joined the Catholic Church, although she blatantly denied that she had done so. For a long time she had been remiss in attending prayers and the Anglican sacrament, but she had let this be attributed to bad health. She did not surrender her pleasures so easily. In 1669 she and James gave a house-warming party at their mansion in Deptford; since the builders were behind schedule as usual, the guests had to sit on the floor playing parlour games, for example 'I love my love with an A'. In spite of her grotesque obesity the Duchess could still outshine everyone with her wit, and even Lady Castlemaine was put in the shade on this occasion, but her health was deteriorating fast and over-indulgence was turning her into a massive and revolting figure. On March 30, 1671, just a month before her eldest daughter's ninth birthday, she went out to dine with the Burlingtons at their house in Piccadilly. Shortly after returning home, she was taken ill and almost immediately fell into her death agony.

The Duchess asked her husband to insist that nobody should be allowed to talk to her about controversial subjects. Lord Cornbury, her brother, who was a violent Church of England man, refused to come near her, but Laurence Hyde, apparently ignorant of her conversion, came hurrying along with Blandford, who had succeeded Dr Morley as the Duchess's spiritual mentor. The Duke met them in the drawing room and gave them the Duchess's message, but Blandford, went into her room, 'made her a short Christian exhortation suitable to the condition she was in' and managed to avoid a direct clash by asking vaguely if she continued in the truth. Even in her last extremity, the clever Duchess had the presence of mind to be non-committal. 'Truth, truth,' she moaned, and at that Blandford tactfully departed. When the Duke asked her if she still knew him, she replied 'Aye', and called out 'Death is very terrible'. Her illness was accompanied by 'many uncomfortable circumstances' and she died in excruciating pain. Margaret Blagge, afterwards Mrs Godolphin, the Duchess's pious maid of honour, watched her mistress's end with a mixture of pity and horror. Unloved and unlamented, the Duchess died like a poor wretch, as the maid of honour put it. Her 'stately carcase' was in such an advanced state of decomposition that it could not be put on view, and it was tossed and flung about without reverence or respect. 'What is this world, what is greatness, what to be esteemed, or thought a wit!'—these were Margaret Blagge's thoughts on the subject.

Neither the Lady Mary nor her father attended the Duchess's funeral, which took place in the Henry VII Chapel at Westminster. Neither of them was heartbroken; the child had seen little of her mother, and probably found her repulsive when she did. As for the Duke, he was for a while without an anchor. Surrounded by huge and rather fierce dogs, including a hound called Mumper, he lived mostly at St James's, neglecting his lodgings at Whitehall with their fine view of the Thames. Within a few months of their mother's death, two more of the Duke's children, Edgar and Catherine, were dead, leaving Mary and Anne as sole survivors, motherless, familiar with death, watched over by Protestant tutors and a Catholic father, second and third in line to the throne and, innocent and childlike though they still were, taking up a position now at the very heart of the Protestant–Catholic controversy of the time.

CHAPTER 2

AN ARTIFICIAL DAY

MANY EYES were focused on the two small girls at St James's Palace. The King feared for their future, for he understood far better than his brother how much his countrymen dreaded the prospect of a Catholic succession. James's obstinacy was a legend—'you know my brother, he is as stiff as a mule,' the King remarked on one occasion, and he also talked about '*la sottise de mon frère*'. The Duke possessed all the inflexibility of the stupid man; as Buckingham put it, 'the King could see things if he would, the Duke would see things if he could'. Charles said, prophetically, 'he will lose his kingdoms through his religious zeal, and his soul through his unsightly wantons, because he has not even the niceness to like them beautiful'. The King, fortunately possessing that instinct for situations and personalities which James entirely lacked, was alive to the dangers of allowing the Ladies Mary and Anne to remain within their father's Catholic orbit. There was no doubt that the Duke would have found it hard to resist the temptation of bringing them up in the Church which he himself, with impolitic ardour, had decided to embrace.

If their father had been prepared to keep his conversion to himself, the two girls could have been brought up normally in London, but the King felt he must make some gesture in order to reassure the nation. It was considered an unforgivable sin that the heir to the throne and the son of a 'Protestant martyr' should be guilty of apostasy. 'What the consequence of this will be God only knows, and wise men dread' was how Evelyn put it. To avoid any possibility of the Duke's influencing his daughters the King declared them children of the State; a separate establishment was prepared for them at Richmond House, and they were provided with a governess, Lady Frances Villiers, and two Anglican chaplains, Dr Lake and Dr Doughtie. So long as everyone could be assured that they were saying their prayers in the Anglican manner, and receiving a daily dose of Church of England dogma, nobody was concerned about the rest of their education. It mattered little if they had no Latin nor Greek, nor if their spelling was lamentable. Nor did anyone complain if they whiled away their time playing ombre, bassett and whist, for such pastimes kept them away from the dangerous game of religion and politics.

Colonel Edward Villiers, wife of Lady Frances, had been appointed housekeeper at Richmond soon after the restoration. He was keeper of the park, the lodges and the game, and he was also responsible for the wardrobe, the gardens and green belonging to the house, which had suffered a great deal of damage during the civil war and in the years before the Restoration. In the days of Henry VIII and Queen Elizabeth the Palace had known much gaiety. Well away from the wickedness of the court and breathing the clean country air, the girls lived an uneventful life, wandering in the deer park, playing cards, and indulging in a 'bellyful of discourse' with the other young ladies who had been picked as suitable companions. The six Villiers daughters formed the nucleus of the establishment, and other girls, such as Frances Apsley, Sarah Jennings and Anne Trelawny, were added to their number. In this girls' school atmosphere, in the dilapidated rooms of the old Palace, which were enriched by the voluptuous works of Titian, Raphael, Rubens and Giorgione, the Lady Mary and her friends poured out their hearts on quires of paper with crows' quill pens; they danced, sang and drew, and succumbed to occasional bouts of illness with all the attendant remedies—blistering, bleeding, leeching, taking physic, followed by possett drink 'to make it work'. The girls also learnt French, although it seems that they did not make any startling progress. Anne was frankly lazy, but Mary was more conscientious and showed far more aptitude than her sister in every subject including dancing. The French master, Peter de Laine, found her docile and willing. Mr Gibsone, only three and a half feet tall, and married to a wife of similar height who bore him nine normal children, was appointed as drawing master. He had started his career as Henrietta Maria's official dwarf, but had since made his name as a miniaturist. Lady Mary liked and trusted him and she proved to be a talented pupil in the subject. Mrs Langford, the children's nurse, was also on the staff, in spite of the fact that she was Catholic; and they were allowed a small quota of dressers and laundresses, with one page of the backstairs between them.

The Duke sometimes came down to Richmond to enjoy a few days' hunting, and he was allowed to have his daughters to stay with him at St James's fairly frequently. Throughout the summer of 1672, accompanied by Mumper, he was away with the fleet off Dogger, doing his best to entice the wily Dutch Admiral, de Ruyter, to come out and do battle. The King's pro-French leanings had involved the English in another war with the Dutch, a conflict that was viewed without enthusiasm in some Protestant circles. But at least it kept the Duke of York out of the public eye for a few months, which was a relief to the King, who found his open Catholicism a distinct embarrassment.

In his matrimonial affairs the Duke displayed his usual lack of tact and good sense. To the King's amusement he was only too anxious to embark for the second time, which was astonishing in view of his first experience. But the King was less amused when his brother announced his intention of marrying Lady Bellasyse, a seventeen-year-old widow of little beauty and no royal blood whatsoever, a quite unsuitable choice, even though she was of the Protestant faith. 'It is too much,' the King exclaimed, 'that you have played the fool once, it is not to be borne, and at such an age!' To extricate the royal suitor was no easy matter. He had already been indiscreet enough to make a written proposal, and this was not retrieved until Lady Bellasyse had taken a copy which she did not scruple to show to all her friends.

Having saved him from a second disaster, the King impressed on his brother the need to unite himself with a wife of royal blood and political importance before his fallible eye led him to the nearest plain woman of ignoble birth. James then sent the Earl of Peterborough, loaded with an inconvenient cargo of jewellery worth twenty thousand pounds, to scour the courts of Europe for a likely candidate. Burnet observed that the Duke was often 'led by his amours to objects that had no extraordinary charms', but he stipulated that his bride must be beautiful, which the King found another cause for jest. What need of beauty in a wife, when a husband became so used to her face that he ceased to notice it after a few weeks? Beauty in mistresses was another matter, but this also James apparently failed to appreciate.

One day in the autumn of 1673 the Duke of York paid his daughters an unexpected visit. Mary was then eleven, and Anne only eight years old. 'I have provided you with a playfellow' was how he broke it to them that he had married by proxy a fifteen-year-old Italian princess, Mary Beatrice d'Este. Peterborough had taken his instructions seriously; 'you will find this young princess to have beauty in her person, and in her mind, to be fair tall, well shaped and very healthful', he wrote glowingly. Mary Beatrice was also well educated, far more so than her step-daughters, and she could speak several languages fluently. There was one drawback— she was a Catholic, and a very fanatical one too. Not that this worried the Duke of York, on the contrary, but he had been displeased when the young girl at first resisted Peterborough's proposal and announced her firm intention of entering a convent. It had taken some forceful letters from important Catholics, including the Pope himself, to persuade her that she must balance the interests of sky and earth, and realize that the good of the Catholic Church was more important than her *quieta privata*. The Pope pointed out to her that she would be better employed producing Catholic heirs in England than worshipping God in her home town of Modena.

The delay made James impatient. Naturally he was anxious to make the acquaintance of his unknown bride and to introduce her to his daughters; it was also important that the marriage should be consummated before the opening of Parliament, for he knew too well what that body would have to say about his marriage to a Catholic. Messages were sent urging the bride to leave at once and to travel as fast as possible, wasting no time on the way. Duchess Laura of Modena, the Princess's mother, who insisted on accompanying her daughter in spite of strong hints that it would be far more advisable for her to stay at home, found it hard to understand the English attitude. Her daughter was closely connected by family ties to the Pope—this was surely a recommendation. She wasted valuable time in Paris introducing her daughter to King Louis, and it was while they were there that she heard all about the *parliamento infuriato*. James's hope that his bride would arrive before the opening of Parliament had not been fulfilled, and there was an uproar when Members discussed the Duke's latest alliance. It was not surprising that while she was still in Paris, Mary Beatrice, in a fit of nerves, was struck down with a 'lousnesse' as James described it.

At last, in November, the Duke set off to meet his bride. Having heard so much about her beauty, he was in a state of pleasurable expectation, but not many others shared his elation. Few gentlemen were courageous enough to accompany him, and the Italians in Mary Beatrice's train were shocked when he met her on the sands of Dover with a complete lack of ceremony and only a handful of retainers. The couple did not go up to London immediately and, as James put it with customary bluntness, the bride was 'married and bedded that same night'.

The Duke's daughters, waiting at St James's, may have seen the angry glow of bonfires that were lit in protest against his marriage. On the night of their step-mother's arrival at Dover, youths carried through the streets of the City an effigy of the Pope which was burnt on one of the bonfires. But some of the excitement had died down by the time the newly wedded couple arrived at Whitehall. They were met by the King and the principal nobility on the river. Most people felt in anything but a welcoming mood; they would all have much preferred a plain Protestant to a pretty Catholic.

All the same, when she arrived, it was difficult not to be impressed by Mary Beatrice's beauty and grace, and by what the King of France had described as her rare virtues.

James was palpably pleased with his new acquisition. Peterborough noticed with approval that she had taken possession of his heart as well as his arms. The attraction was not, however, mutual, and the new Duchess had a disconcerting habit of bursting into tears whenever she looked at her husband. He was, after all, over twice her age; his good looks were tinged with decadence, there was a cruel expression about his mouth, and he tended to stammer, especially when nervous. 'I cry often and am unable to rid myself of melancholy,' she told the Mother Superior of the Convent of the Visitation at Modena. The English court seemed overwhelming, even a little shocking, and she felt far more at home with her two step-daughters than she did with the more sophisticated ladies who waited on her. She was scarcely more than a child herself, and not by any means past enjoying a game of blind-man's buff. Mary and Anne found her gay and humorous once she had recovered from her homesickness, and not nearly so serious about her religion as they might have expected. Their different faiths made no barrier between them and, much to the dis-appointment of the French, the Duchess made no attempt to influence them or persuade them to join the Catholic Church. Dr Lake, their chaplain, reproved them when they played cards with her on a Sunday, telling them that it was not 'expedient'. The habit grieved his Puritanical heart, for Sunday card-playing was to him a Catholic sin, copied from Queen Catherine.

As soon as her mother, who had made many difficulties, finally returned to Italy, Mary Beatrice began to feel much better; she even seemed to find her husband attractive. 'He has the holy fear of God and loves me very much,' she admitted. She appreciated the fact that he was 'firm and steady in our holy religion'—just the very reason why he was so unpopular with everyone else.

The King was as kind to his new sister-in-law as he always was to his two nieces. He was well-mannered, affable and polite—'the civilest person that can be to those that are civil to him' in Elizabeth of Bohemia's opinion. He could always be relied upon to utter a quotable remark, usually proceeded by the exclamation 'Odds fish'. Although none too scrupulous about repeating stories to those who had heard them before, his flippancy often proved a welcome antidote to James's over-seriousness. His Queen was less amenable, for she was jealous of the Duchess's youthful beauty and her ability to attract admiration even amongst the Protestants.

It was due partly to Catherine's jealousy, partly to Charles's wisdom, that Mary Beatrice was not granted the public chapel she had been promised before she came to England, she had to content herself with worshipping privately at St James's.

Very soon Mary Beatrice had a miscarriage, but it was not long before she was pregnant again, and she was too far gone in the autumn of 1674 to join in the revels which the King was planning for the opening of the festival season. Sarah Jennings, subsequently Duchess of Marlborough, in later years reminisced about the 'pretty entertainments and romantic amusements' which helped to pass the time away for the Lady Mary and her companions, and the most memorable of these was performed in early December of that year, when the King decided to commission a masque in which his nieces were to be the principal performers. There were plenty of precedents. In the time of James I when the masque tradition had reached a crescendo of magnificance, noble men and women of the court had given glittering performances, the whole story leading up to the arrival of the silent masquers who invited ladies in the audience to dance. In 1618 Charles, Prince of Wales, Mary's grandfather, had taken a leading part. But that was nearly half a century ago, and although there had been so-called court masques since the Restoration, the tradition was moribund and there were no writers and designers of the calibre of Ben Jonson and Inigo Jones to give it new life. The symbols and *iconologia* of that earlier age were half forgotten. Civil war had destroyed the close-knit quality of the court audience, with its shared experience and ideals, and its focus in the monarchy. The century had seen the rise of a Puritanism that frowned on the extravagance of royal entertainments. The re-established monarchy was a precarious institution, watched over by a disapproving Parliament; the King had no heir, his brother was a hated Catholic, and the cold eye of Newton's science was casting its light over the crowded imagery of earlier times. All the same, the Lady Mary, still only at one remove from the throne, made a graceful pretext for some kind of show, an end-of-term entertainment to prove to her friends and relations that she had not been wasting her time at Richmond. She was already being talked of as one of the most eligible and charming ladies in Europe.

Dryden, the most admired of contemporary poets and dramatists, was the obvious choice of author, especially as he held the post of Poet Laureate. But his talents were set aside owing to literary feuds, and John Crowne, a protégé of the Earl of Rochester, was called out of obscurity and given the task of providing a vehicle for the histrionic talents of the Lady Mary and her sister. Although naturally gratified, he had to admit that he

was as overwhelmed 'as shepherds and herdsmen . . . of old, when from
their flocks they were called to prophesy to kings'. Lured on by the promise
of a generous lump sum, Crowne set off with the pious hope—which was
hardly fulfilled—that he would find inspiration in the glorious work to
which he had been called. It would have been better if he had shrunk
back into his former shades.

Crowne was an easy and amiable character, better known for his habit
of wearing a stiff white cravat than for his literary talents. He had been
bred up in Nova-Scotia in a non-Catholic community, which was to his
advantage, but he had later broken away from the strict life of a plantation
and the stark parental influence, and had come over to try his luck in
London, writing plays for the King's and Duke's players who were always
short of material. The invitation to write a court masque could be
described as his first break-through, but he was unable to take full advantage of the opportunity for the whole affair was dismally rushed. Kings do
not always appreciate the fact that works of art take longer to prepare than
a state banquet. Crowne modestly admitted that his genius was not really
equal to the task he had been set, but he did plead that the result might
have been better if only he could have been given time to 'ripen his
conceptions'. He was told to find a suitable subject for seven characters
and to report back in a few hours when he had made his choice. A quick
look through the book of Ovid provided him with what at a cursory
glance struck him as the ideal theme. Not until too late did he realize
that his chosen Calisto, had suffered, in the original story, the fate well
known to be worse than death; he had, in his own words, undertaken the
task of writing 'a clean, decent and inoffensive play' on the subject of
rape. His inspiration was hampered from the start by the delicacy of the
situation; 'the bullets were to fly.' he complained, 'but give no report,'
and the arrows had to be pared until they were thin enough 'to pass
through nice and delicate ears without wounding 'em'.

Given a month to complete the work, Crowne found himself setting
out with 'a brisk dullness, writing quick, but flat'. He admitted that anyone looking for a superlative piece was in for a disappointment for
'when it was in the womb . . . [it] was squeezed and hindered of its due
growth'. The ladies of the court, when they were in possession of the script,
quite failed to appreciate the need for hard work and the mastery of
technique. Even after twenty rehearsals they seemed to be making little
progress. Their voices were too feeble and their dancing far too amateurish
to satisfy a critical audience.

The main part of Calisto went to the Lady Mary, with Anne cast as

Nyphe, her friend. Margaret Blagge was chosen to play Diana. Unlike most young girls she found acting a vain and unenviable occupation. 'Would you believe it,' she wrote 'there are some that envy me the honour (as they esteem it) of acting in this play, and pass malicious jests on me!' Psecas, the envious nymph, was played by Lady Mary Mordaunt, the spoilt and wilful only child of the Earl of Peterborough. The Countess of Suffolk, the King's daughter by Lady Castlemaine, played Juno, Sarah Jennings was cast as a god, and among the attendant nymphs was Carey Frazer, daughter of Charles II's prime physician—'the maddest fool alive' according to Evelyn.

Rehearsals went so badly that at one time it looked as if the whole performance would be called off, but it was decided to supplement the 'quality' with professional singers, including Mrs Davies and Mrs Knight, with whom the King had been in the habit of taking his repose twice daily. They insisted on more rehearsal time, and Mrs Betterton was called in to coach the amateurs. After this everything began to 'go on mightily', much to the disappointment of Miss Blagge who had been praying that the play would be cancelled. Each day, when she could spare the time from her books of devotion, Evelyn heard her part, and as the great event approached he found her in a permanent state of tears and trepidation.

The evening of December 2 arrived. The cast was assembled, dressed in a glitter of gauze and stars. Diana and her train were fitted out with bows and arrows, and Margaret Blagge carried twenty thousand pounds worth of borrowed jewellery. The audience was scarcely less magnificent, no expense had been spared on the scenery, the music was superb and the whole had been prepared with such extravagance that some onlookers felt it was quite overdone in view of the King's precarious finances.

The evening opened with the graceful Mrs Davies revealed leaning on an urn. She was playing the part of the river Thames which was by tradition given to a man, but she considered herself the best singer and had thrown a fit of temperament until Crowne succumbed and let her start the proceedings. 'I know of no sexes in lands and rivers,' he wrote philosophically, deciding henceforth not to trouble himself with the *hic haec hoc* of his trade. The composer, Mr Staggins, had set the second song for a treble voice, which gave Mistress Davies the chance to warble both the first speech and the reply to it.

After this propitious opening, the nymphs and shepherds arrived to dance a saraband with castanets, which was one of the easier dances well within the compass of the amateurs. When they had finished, the stage was given over to the dazzling Duke of Monmouth, the King's favourite son, whose talents as a dancer so far outstripped all the others that nobody was considered good enough to partner him. He was the idol of all the ladies of the court who were attracted by his magnificent carriage and 'the astonishing beauty of his outward form'. There were some people who hoped that the King would produce proof of a marriage to Lucy Walter and thus legitimize his son, who, though not as clever as he was handsome, was at least a Protestant. The King had married him to a rich but dull heiress, Anna Scott, daughter of the Duke of Buccleuch, but he was tired of her already, and his cousin Mary and her friends were fascinated by the rumours and scandals which were associated with his name. His latest attraction was Frances Needham, a member of the York set, and it was Sarah Jennings who took it upon her to tell Monmouth's Duchess, although they were all sworn to secrecy. Anna of Buccleuch took the revelation 'mightily to heart', but such lapses could easily be forgiven in so good-looking a man by everyone except his wife.

The Sea Gods and Tritons who next appeared, with a Temple of Fame, and trumpets, paid tribute to the King, at whose feet they strewed crowns and trophies:

Genius :   But stay! What wonder does my spirit seize?
              [Turning to the King and Queen]
              See! Here are both the great divinities!
Thames :   The God and Goddess too of this blessed isle.
              Chaste beauty in her aspect shines,
              And Love in his does smile.

After this tactful comment, the quite irrelevant prologue was over. Carpenters arrived to set the scene for Arcadia, and the plot was set in motion. It took place throughout one 'Artificial Day', and began when Jupiter descended to a 'half-burnt world' which was suffering from the aftermath of a heatwave, and kindly set the rivers running, clothed the withered fields with grass, and brought new leaves to the trees. While engaged on this work, he was struck down by love for Calisto, one of the nymphs in Diana's train. Mercury was in the same condition having fallen for Psecas:

Jupiter :   See! Something swiftly darted by my sight.
              Was it a nymph, or sudden glance of light?
Mercury :   . . . See! See! to yonder grove she's gone!
              There like a glittering star in night
              She tempers all the shades with light.

After this build-up Calisto herself appeared, and the gods retired to hide themselves in a convenient near-by cloud, and thereafter to chase their quarry in a pattern of pursuit, confusion and misunderstanding. To avoid the embarrassment of a rape, the author had decided to make Jupiter assume the shape of Diana and to woo Calisto in that guise, though the nymph was distressed by the unnatural advances of her mistress, and had to admit that 'a fiery blushing' flamed about her face. She was puzzled, and hazarded the theory that Diana 'of some accursed plant did rashly taste' which made her call out for help in verse that is a fair example of Crowne's style:

> She raves, I to the nymphs for aid must call,
> Or she will do some horrid act I fear,
> Help, help my goddess is distracted here.

And so it went on through the artificial day, from rosy morning to the golden dusk of evening, with a creaking plot and faded imagery, with dances for basques and shepherds, songs for Sylvia, and scornful nymphs defying a host of militant Cupids. Jupiter, on his return to heaven—his wife having appeared on earth to retrieve him—was uncertain what to do with Calisto, since he could not take her with him, and did not wish to leave her in Arcadia. He finally decided on a 'middle region', and asked her to accept the small dominion of a star.

Calisto and her sister appeared in triumph beneath a canopy supported by Africans. The final song complained of the injustice of removing two young girls to heaven before they had been given a chance to taste the pleasures of love.

Soon it was all over and the cast was back in the tiring-room. For the young actresses it was an evening to remember. As they had waited in the wings for their turn to appear, they had laughed and flirted with the gallants, all except Margaret Blagge who had spent her spare time sitting apart and reading a book of devotion. And there was an unfortunate incident which cast a gloom over the glowing aftermath of Arcadia. In the crush as the play ended, somebody had snatched from Miss Blagge's dress a diamond worth £80 belonging to the Countess of Suffolk. The stage was swept, a search was made, but it was not found. Other borrowed jewels were hastily returned to their owners, and the Duke of York made good the loss to pacify the distracted Margaret Blagge, who was now confirmed in her belief that theatricals were the work of the devil. The critics, as always, were 'nibbling at everything they could catch', but the principal performer, Lady Mary, called forth nothing but praise. '[She] spoke to the eyes and souls of all who saw her,' wrote Crowne admiringly. She had grown tall and slender, with a clear complexion, almond-shaped eyes and dark curls. Mary's cousin, William of Orange, who that autumn had brusquely refused a secret offer of her hand in marriage, may have learnt something, from eye-witness accounts of *Calisto*, of the value of that prize he had rejected.

CHAPTER 3

AURELIA

IN THE NEW YEAR OF 1675 the birth of the Duchess of York's child was imminent, and this important event was awaited with apprehension by the Protestants and with pleasurable expectation by the Catholics. Mary Beatrice herself was in good health and continued to live a normal life. One evening early in January she sat up playing ombre with the Duchess of Monmouth until eleven o'clock, having dined well. In the morning she heard two masses, and it was after lunching with her two step-daughters that she felt her first labour pains. With enviable speed, and without complications, the Duchess gave birth to a daughter. So swift was the birth that many ladies of the court, who had fully intended to be there, were unable to arrive in time; the Queen hurried over from Whitehall in case the child should prove to be a son, and no doubt felt a certain satisfaction when she heard that it was not. The King kissed the Duke of York with great affection, and James himself, though disappointed, was pleased to know that his wife could produce children with such ease. He despatched a message to William of Orange, telling him the good news and hinting that since all had gone so well on this occasion there was a good chance of male heirs in the future.

The young Duchess had her daughter christened at once in the Catholic faith, a mistake which the King hastily rectified. A public christening was held and the Anglican service was attended by the baby's two step-sisters; Lady Mary was one of the godmothers and the child was christened Catherine Laura, in honour respectively of the Queen and her Italian grandmother. The King's tact saved the situation on this occasion, but he was unable to stem the tide of James's growing unpopularity which was the direct result of his open Catholicism. The French, who had always regarded James as the one man they could trust and who was really *inébranlable*, now began to realize that he had his drawbacks. His behaviour was setting the whole of England against France, a fact that alarmed the French Ambassador and his agents. The English believed that a man who was prepared to risk losing a throne for his conscience, was so fanatical that he would never rest until he had turned the whole country Catholic. The King might be bound by the Treaty of Dover to bring together the two Churches, but he saw to it that this clause was kept secret, and as usual he had no difficulty in finding ingenious excuses for failing to keep his promise. The Pope was old; surely nobody would wish the King to precipitate a papal heart attack by mentioning that if the Anglican Church were to be brought back into the Catholic fold, some dispensation would have to be made for married clergy?

Aware now of James's unpopularity, the French turned their attention to his Duchess. They gave her jewellery and promised to obtain a Cardinal's hat for her uncle Rinaldo. But Mary Beatrice's tender years made her unconcerned with such wider issues. She was more in sympathy with the childhood world of her step-daughters than the complicated sphere of diplomacy. It was noticed that she and the Lady Mary had become close friends, and it was probable that the York daughters now spent more time in London and less at Richmond. The Duchess often needed a little comforting, for her husband, thought by Italian observers to love her *tenerissimamente*, was not cured of the habit of paying his respects to Arabella Churchill and other ladies. 'In two or three years men are always weary of their wives and look for a Mrs as soon as they can get them,' was his daughter Mary's cynical comment to Frances Apsley. Ironically enough the Duchess had by now completely conquered her aversion for the Duke, and she loved him enough to be saddened by his lapses. In the spring of 1675, when he went on a prolonged visit to Newmarket, Mary Beatrice's lady in waiting, the Countess Lucrezia Vezzani-Prateroni, noticed that she looked melancholy, especially at certain times of the day. The Countess hoped that on his return on April 7 he would put everything right by ensuring that there would be a longed-for Prince the following year. Mary Beatrice's only consolation at such times was the lively companionship of her two stepdaughters, a particular comfort to her when in October of that year her baby died after a fit of convulsions.

Lady Mary did not appear in any more plays, although her sister took the part of Ziphares in Nathaniel Lee's *Mithridates*. Perhaps the King felt that she was too valuable a pawn in the political game to be put too often in front of the public eye. He took her, with the Queen and her father, to dine at the Lord Mayor's feast at the Guildhall, but as a rule she was kept well out of sight and only allowed up to London to visit her stepmother privately. The Prince of Orange might have rejected her once, but there was plenty of time for him to change his mind, and so she had to be kept, tantalizingly, as a lure and a peace counter, away not only from Catholic influences, but also from the court gallants. It was a strange position for an adolescent girl, and all the more unhealthy since she was passionate by nature and had from the start been starved of mother-love. She had no real place in her father's life, and she must have known that as soon as Mary Beatrice had children of her own, these would take up the first place in the Duchess's affections.

Deprived of male company just at the time when she should have begun to take an interest in the opposite sex, Lady Mary found no emotional outlet for those feelings which were aroused by her readings in the superficial literature of her day. She identified herself strongly with the lovesick heroines she met in books—'poor unhappy I sat reading of a play, my heart ready to break,' she recorded. Her father realized, too late, the dangers of such light reading, and in his *Papers of Devotion* he gave a warning to educationists of the future:

You as have young persons under your charge should not let them read romances, more especially the women kind, 'tis but loss of time, and is apt to put foolish and ridiculous thoughts into their heads.

Living an isolated life, with nothing to occupy her mind except the gossip of the court, it was not surprising that Lady Mary became a prey to 'foolish and ridiculous thoughts'. In her stage role of Calisto she had blushed when wooed by one of her own sex; in real life she fell unashamedly in love with another girl, Frances Apsley, nine years her senior, the beautiful daughter of Sir Allen Apsley, keeper of the King's hawks, and a York retainer of long standing. Correspondence which lay for many years in a leather box amongst papers of the Bathurst family at Cirencester were thought for a long time to be letters from Mary to William, but later research revealed that the adored 'husband' was Frances Apsley, who later married Sir Benjamin Bathurst. Sometimes sitting up until she was too sleepy to write any more, sometimes dashing off a few lines before the morning lessons began, Mary directed a stream of letters at the object of her affection. 'You shall hear from me every quarter of an hour if it were possible,' she wrote, or, 'all the paper books in the world would not hold half the love I have for you my dearest, dearest, dear Aurelia'. She signed herself 'Mary Clorine', and learned attempts have been made to discover the work which inspired the names the two girls used in their fantasy world. There is an Aurelia, but no Clorine, in Dryden's play *An Evening's Love*, in which the plot turns on the discovery by some Spanish girls that Englishmen are not, after all, the cold 'northern beasts' they have been led to expect.

Sometimes, out of the welter of barren cliché, the poetic jargon and the incantatory appeals to the 'dear, dear, dear, dearest' Aurelia, come a few earthy epithets, standing out vividly against this anaemic background. 'There is nothing in this heart or breast, guts or bowels, but you shall know it,' she wrote, and at one point even offered to be Aurelia's 'louse in bosom', an act of devotion that would seem to be slightly bizarre in a nymph of Diana's train. There is a passage famous for its startling bathos:

[I am] your humble servant to kiss the ground where you go, to be your dog in a string, your fish in a net, your bird in a cage, your humble trout.

The letters which Mary wrote later in her life reveal considerable literary talent, but at this stage her style lacked discipline, and indeed she had no faith in her own powers of expression. 'Do not expect from me,' she told Aurelia, 'a letter like your own this morning, for I am sure Mr Dryden and all the poets in the world put together could not make me such another.' Yet for all their lavish sentimentality, the letters illuminate Mary's character, revealing the emotional instability of a child deprived of her full quota of parental love, and a Latin temperament inherited from the Medicis through her grandmother, Henrietta Maria, as well as from her father. James, in spite of his stubbornness and lack of humour, was an emotional man, prone to indulge in fits of weeping at moments of crisis. And Mary's moods swung between ecstasy and despair:

I myself am one while killing myself with sighs, another time I kill myself with joy for her. All I know is so confounded together the good with the ill, the ill with the good. I don't know what to make of it, but now a melancholy qualm comes over my stomach, and oh I tremble to think the ill will overcome the good.

Her father's blatant promiscuity and his growing unpopularity, her early acquaintance with death, which had carried away her mother and so many of her frail brothers and sisters, all this had made her understandably pessimistic, and her passion for Aurelia became the one stable factor in her life.

The letters went to and fro, carried by Mr Gibsone, the dwarf drawing-master. Nobody else was trusted with the precious missives; to send them by a footman would have been far too dangerous. It seems that at first the older girl was flattered by her royal friend's admiration, but later became embarrassed by her effusions and began to adopt a more discouraging attitude. Frances even went so far as to play the two sisters off against each other, for after taking part in *Mithridates* Anne too was struck down by Aurelia's charms. Frances gave Anne a coveted cornelian ring, while Mary looked on, with a breaking heart. Her letters, Mary's 'onely bliss', became less and less frequent, and the 'dear handwriting' was seldom seen. 'Your not writing me in so long time, what do you think, it would make an unbelieving atheist whose heart were as hard as stone repent and turn Christian,' wrote the desperate girl. And it was worse still when Aurelia's family moved house. She was to be seen then only on Sundays and holidays, and on 'grave' visits when she arrived accompanied by her mother. Even when she came to church she did not vouchsafe a word:

O have some pity on me and love me again or kill me quite with your unkindness for I cannot live with you in indifference, dear dearest loving kind charming obliging sweet dear Aurelia, remember all your vows and protestations and though you made them when you were in love yet let um bind tho' you do not love me so well as you used to do.

Mary Clorine was so frenzied that she began to take risks, and one day she was nearly caught. Sarah Jennings, with her striking good looks and domineering temperament, was already playing an important part in the lives of the two York sisters, and they trusted her enough to let her carry their letters to Aurelia. On this occasion they were in a hurry, and Mary asked Sarah to seal Anne's letter while she dealt with her own. They had carelessly left the door open, and Lady Frances Villiers, perhaps noticing that something furtive was going on, walked into the room to take a closer look. Mary, on her own admission, blushed as red as fire, but she was resourceful enough to run up to her governess and ask her how she liked her new mantle. Lady Frances replied by asking what she was doing in her closet at this time of the day, and Mary, lying desperately, said that she had brought Mistress Jennings in to admire her stepmother's portrait, while Mistress Jennings, for her part, was demonstrating a new way of sealing a letter. 'She is very ingenious,' said Lady Frances sarcastically.

It is probable that Mary's guardian had grown suspicious. A similar correspondence which Anne had been conducting with Mistress Cornwallis had already been intercepted, and the Duke and Duchess of York had been understandably shocked by its passionate outpourings. Miss Cornwallis, as a result, left the court rather suddenly, although some said this was because Sarah Jennings had denounced her as a Catholic. Mary had so far avoided discovery, but Lady Frances was evidently on her guard.

The Duke could have done without any extra anxieties, for his determined Catholicism was already making life difficult. He was still flaunting his beliefs in a way that was calculated to bring the whole family into disrepute. In April 1676 he made it clear that he did not intend to go to any more Anglican services. He accompanied the King to the door of the church and then turned away at the last moment. His Duchess described this as '*una generosa risolutione*'; others could have put it differently. Nothing else was talked about in the whole town, and the King felt he had had enough of his brother's moral courage. In particular, the King did not wish William of Orange to receive an unfavourable impression. It was true that this dour young prince had turned his back on Mary's charms, but all the same he was in his twenties now and must soon think about settling down. There were rumours that he was doing up his houses and buying pictures and furniture. It was most important that he should not be in any doubt about Lady Mary's doctrinal allegiance and so, early in 1676, the King appointed Henry Compton, Bishop of London and brother to the Earl of Northampton, as spiritual mentor to the Duke's daughters.

Henry Compton was famed for his zeal in opposing Papists. He had started his career as an army man and was not ordained until he was over thirty. His rise in the Church had been rapid, as he was not afraid to speak out against popery in general and James in particular. 'The churchyard for the dead, the church for the living' was his motto; he was sincere and practical in his religion, and, as an ex-guardsman, he was not afraid to press home his attack. His appointment as religious adviser to the children of the man he most disliked in the world put him in an excellent strategic position.

Dr Lake and Dr Doughtie had been doing their best; they had given the two girls meticulous instruction in the Anglican dogma, had said prayers with them every day, and had taught them to observe the appropriate saint's days—these included January 30, the anniversary of their grandfather's execution, when they dressed up in black and spent the day fasting and weeping. Dr Doughtie's pupils were not above having a secret joke about his 'Mrs', but in general the two divines had been successful in keeping their charges on the straight and narrow Anglican path. It needed a man of Compton's calibre, however, to tackle James on the subject of his daughters' confirmation. He was not a distinguished theologian, but he was bold enough to enjoy crossing swords with a papist. Before long the world knew that the Lady Mary had been confirmed in the Anglican faith and this was bound to increase her value in William's eyes. But as the year went on, curious eyes began to note another fact which could, on the contrary, decrease her worth as a bride. That summer it became evident that Mary Beatrice was expecting another child, and Lady Mary's fate as future heir to the throne hung on the sex of the infant. But at the end of August, to the relief of all good Protestants, the Duchess presented her husband with a daughter. The Duke assured her that this mattered little. He seemed quite unaware that he was responsible for the growing hatred of papists which was subjecting his fellow Catholics to considerable persecution; laws, normally overlooked, were being implemented and goods were being confiscated.

If Lady Mary knew anything of the intricacies of her father's religious embroilments, it is probable that at this time she wasted little thought upon them, and that she was unaware of anything or anybody except Aurelia. Life at court bored her; 'St James is so dull as to afford no news dear husband', she wrote to Frances; 'now Windsor may shake hands with it for I have drained it so dry in my last letter, I have none left for this.' She would have taken no interest, had she known of it, in a correspondence even more diffuse than her own, which was going on between Temple, the Ambassador in Holland, and William of Orange together with his advisers. Her name was now mentioned in the same breath as strategic towns in the Netherlands, such as Condé, Valenciennes and Tournai. For months there had been growing rumours that William would soon be coming to England to claim his bride.

During the summer of 1677 William sent his friend Bentinck to prepare the ground, and in the autumn he came over to England himself. Mary was too busy brooding over the graceful female form of Frances Apsley to show any flicker of interest in her cousin's arrival. He had not been in England since she was eight, and the visit he had made at that time could hardly have been termed an unqualified success. The King found him somewhat prim, and had made him drink hard, knowing that he was not usually in the custom of imbibing liberally; they had told him the next morning that in his drunken state he had broken the windows of rooms belonging to the maids of honour, and might even have entered their apartments 'had they not been timely rescued'. But he was seven years older now; he had shouldered many responsibilities and was respected by his countrymen, who had made him their Stadholder.

Mary was introduced to her cousin when he came up to London, having first visited his uncles at Newmarket. She found herself looking down on a man who was four inches shorter than herself, with a slightly hunched back, a hooked nose and an asthmatic wheeze. He might be the hero of the dykes who had saved his country from the French by inundating the approaches to the north, but to someone who had a cousin of such dazzling looks as Monmouth, and a 'husband' such as Frances

Apsley, he could only be a creature of little interest, one of those cold northern beasts dreaded by the Spanish ladies in Dryden's play.

A few days later, her father, who had been dining at Whitehall, came back early to St James's. He went along to his daughter's apartments and took her into her closet. He then told her that she was to marry William of Orange, the small, unromantic man who had no place in Arcadia, who was a stranger in Mary's world, and who was to take her away almost immediately to a foreign country, away from her father and step-mother, her sister and the adored Aurelia. The shock of this news brought on a 'melangcolie qualm' worse than any she had known before. She broke down immediately and wept for a day and a half without stopping.

CHAPTER 4

THE PRINCE

THE YOUNG MAN who had made such a sudden and unwelcome intrusion into Lady Mary's life had been tantalizing his uncles for some years. As he was only half their age, they refused to admit that he was more than a match for them in the diplomatic game. The King underestimated his nephew's qualities, and insisted on thinking of him as a mere boy who could be patronized and lured on with the promise of a pretty wife. And James could hardly be expected to like a Calvinist who had been impudent enough to refuse an offer of his daughter's hand in marriage. As for William, he had little desire to be dependent on, or beholden to, his English uncles, and for a long time he appeared to be in no hurry about 'the disposal of his charming self in wedlock'. James's Catholicism he disliked, and, like many of his countrymen, he distrusted Charles for his endless compromises and his tiresome flirtation with the French. Ever since the Restoration, the King had been playing his evasive game, and the more he played it, the more complicated it became. To avoid a conflict was wise, but to shift his ground so many times in the process was to lose the confidence of everyone who had to deal with him. There were occasions when he would have sacrified any principle or any person in order to obtain a money subsidy from France generous enough to make him independent of his hated Parliament.

Towards the end of 1674, at the time when the ladies of the court were busy with their performance of *Calisto*, Arlington and Ossory had been sent over to suggest a marriage between William and Mary. Sir William Temple, who knew as much about Dutch affairs as any other Englishman, could have told them that they had chosen the worst possible moment. Though he himself had always been on good terms with the Prince, this year he had found him preoccupied and unapproachable, always ready to give the excuse that he did not know where he would be at a certain time. Arlington, accompanied by a large train and all his family, was forced to land at Middelburg owing to bad weather. M. Odyck, the Prince's kinsman, entertained the lords and ladies at his wife's house in Zeeland, 'which was quite unfit to receive persons of so great quality' in the opinion of William Blathwayt, who was one of the party. After a hazardous journey along the inland waterways, in which at least one frigate went aground and the main party had to borrow Odyck's private yacht, the visitors were accommodated at the Hague and the Prince came in from Honselaersdyck to meet them. There were various dinners, suppers and private audiences, and a visit to the French church, when Lord Arlington was accompanied by the Prince. 'In a word,' Blathwayt reported, 'they are as much together as the Prince's business will give him leave; His Highness remains in very good humour, and yesterday there was a health drunk *au bon voyage de son altesse*, and mention made of his inclinations.' Temple had raised the question of a marriage with Mary when he had seen the Duke of York just before leaving England. James had deigned to smile and had said cryptically, 'You do not know how far a young man's desire may go.'

It soon became evident that William's desire did not go very far at all. He was too busy fighting the French to give his mind to such a subject, and was in any case of the opinion that all thought of matrimony should be put off until the end of the campaign. A more diplomatic ambassador might have made some progress, but Arlington had adopted a patronizing attitude, talking to William 'too much in the strain of a governor'. Temple reported that he behaved as he might have done when dealing with a child, and anyone would have thought that he had taken himself for the Prince of Orange, and the Prince for my Lord Arlington. William simply told him shortly that he did not think any wife would like the noise of war, but Ossory's despatch reporting William's refusal was badly worded and sounded like a snub. As a result, the Duke of York was extremely offended.

In any case, the war was not likely to last for ever, and meanwhile William kept an open mind. Lady Mary was not the only eligible young woman in Europe. In Holland they tended to be disparaging about her pedigree; after all, her mother had been no more than the Princess's maid of honour and some thought that as a result William's claim to the throne of England was more convincing than hers. There was also a general belief that because James was diseased, none of his children by Mary Beatrice would survive. Such considerations made William at various times think he could ignore Mary and ally himself with the widowed Queen of Poland or a Danish princess. In any case the planning of his campaigns was far more important to him than the claims of conjugal love.

Temple, who had been recalled from the Hague in 1670 because he was at that time considered too conciliatory towards the Dutch, was sent back in 1674 with instructions to further a treaty between France and Holland. The Pensioner of Holland had told him that he did not know of anyone who would not agree with the idea. 'Yes,' said William when Temple passed this on to him, 'I am sure I know one, and that is myself, and I'll hinder it as long as I can.' Two years later, however, peace talks were begun at Nimeguen, though ridiculous arguments about precedence threatened to prevent any serious negotiations. Temple had to take a house there, which, with the necessary outhouses, cost him £1,600 a year, the one compensation being that the air was considered drier and more healthy than the damp atmosphere at the Hague. Temple arrived at Nimeguen on the ferry, which was large enough to take his two coaches, fourteen horses and a wagonload of trunks, but the horses were so frightened by the canonn which were fired to mark his arrival, that he nearly ended up in the river.

Although the peace negotiations were slow and unproductive, they prompted William to think seriously of matrimony, but when he asked permission to visit England, his request was not granted. James was still smarting from the wound inflicted by William's previous refusal of his daughter's hand and King Charles had swung and was recommending that there should be no wedding until peace had been completed. He found it convenient to hold Mary out as a bribe in the hope that William might become more amenable. James had come to the conclusion that he would rather marry her to the Dauphin.

The United Provinces were no more enthusiastic about the match than William's uncles; this was due to their distrust of Charles and their disdainful attitude towards Mary's social status and lack of dowry. But William was not afraid to act independently when it suited him. In January 1677 he summoned Temple to Honselaersdyck and, as they walked together in the garden, William asked if he could speak to him as a friend 'or at least as an indifferent person, and not as the King's ambassador'. He asked some pertinent questions which revealed a level-headed and human approach unusual in Princes of the time in search of a wife. Without affectation he told Temple that Mary's fortune and circumstances were less important to him than her character. The kind of wife considered desirable in most courts would not suit him at all. For one thing he knew that he himself would be none too easy to live with, and therefore it was important to find a mate gifted with the right temperament, for as he put it 'if he should meet with one to give him trouble at home, it was what he should not be able to bear, who was like to have enough abroad in the course of his life'. Temple was well armed with political arguments. He

reminded William that the match would put him 'one degree nearer the
crown, and to all appearance the next'. He did not know a great deal
about Mary's character, but he had always heard his wife and daughter
speak very highly of 'what they could discern in a Princess so young'.
Her education was not anything to boast about; she knew nothing of
Latin and Greek, but she had been kept well away from the licentious
atmosphere of the court and, most important of all, she was a well-
indoctrinated Protestant. The Prince seemed well pleased with what
Temple could tell him, and he asked Lady Temple to go secretly to England with messages for the King and the Duke. Bentinck followed in the
summer to make further representations. It was stated that *son altesse*
wished to make a little tour of England after the seasonal cessation of
hostilities.

Bentinck found Charles in a favourable frame of mind. Some said he
revelled in the thought of forcing a hard and Calvinistic son-in-law onto
his tiresome brother. He granted William permission to visit England,
while assuring Barillon, who had just arrived in London as French
Ambassador, that Bentinck's visit was of no importance at all; William
had 'only a mind to talk to him'. Fettered as he was by the Treaty of
Dover, the King was forced into duplicity, but his nonchalance did not
deceive Barillon who guessed only too well what William had in mind.
The Frenchman did his best to whip up opposition by persuading
Charles's French favourite, Louise de Kéroualle, Duchess of Portsmouth,
to use her influence, and the Duke of York to exert his—not that he wielded
much. Charles told Barillon that the French ought to approve of the match;
with typical casuistry he said it would show the English that although
their King wished to be friendly with France, it did not necessarily follow
that he wished to turn his country Catholic—which people would insist
on believing in spite of all his denials.

For William himself the marriage was a gambler's throw. Unpopular
as he now was in Holland, a wedding with James's daughter could prove
the finishing stroke, provoking the States to conclude a peace without him.
Nor would it necessarily bring the English throne any nearer, for the
fruitful Mary Beatrice was expecting another child, which could well
prove to be the long-awaited son. There was even a danger that he might
alienate the English opposition party which up to now he had wooed very
successfully, for, in marrying the King's niece, he could be accused of
putting himself under court influence. The French would obviously be
against it, not to mention the girl's father. As for the girl herself, nobody,
of course, thought of telling or consulting her.

William had hoped that the summer campaign would prove successful enough to lend him extra strength at the conference table, but he was disappointed. The French remained unbeaten and as truculent as ever. A good peace looked remote, but this did not deter William from pursuing his prize in England. In October he wrote to Arlington saying that he was awaiting with great impatience the arrival of the yachts which were to take him over. He knew that the King and the Duke were at Newmarket and he was anxious to have a word with them there before they returned to London. While he waited for Ossory to bring the boats he did some shopping, buying paintings by Rubens and Brueghel and continuing the improvements he had begun in some of his palaces. At Dutch army headquarters they were openly discussing Mary's charms.

After a rough crossing, William landed at Harwich and went post-haste to Newmarket 'like a hasty lover' as Temple put it, perhaps with some exaggeration. He asked Temple for an introduction to Arlington's rival, Danby, who had recently 'run into the ill will of the people' and was looking for some means of regaining his popularity and of ingratiating himself with the Protestants. William was determined to conclude his matrimonial arrangements before entering into any talks about the international situation; he did not want the States to think that he had accepted a bad settlement for his country in order to gain a good one for himself. His uncles on the other hand were enjoying the October meeting and were in no hurry to settle anything. The King, still judging William on his own standards, treated him as if he were a young man who 'wanted a wife as much as he did a mistress, and would be brought to anything for a fair bedfellow'. But William, who was not afraid of his wicked uncles, could afford to be firm. His agents had been working hard to gain support among the English Protestants and this enabled him to hint to the King that he had enough friends in England to place him in a strong position; furthermore he had Danby on his side.

The story was that Danby primed his 'creatures' to put the King in a good humour before he himself arrived to broach the fateful subject. During the course of the conversation he casually mentioned that a great many friends had been saying lately what a good thing it would be if Mary were to marry William of Orange. He knew the King well enough to guess that he would be too idle to find out if this were true. Charles said he knew that his brother would never agree to such a thing, and Danby replied, 'Maybe not, unless you take upon you to command it.' When others reminded the King that he had promised he would never dispose of his nieces without their father's consent, and that James could well withhold that consent now, the King broke out with his usual oath, 'Odd's fish! He must consent.'

William visited the Duke of York with a view to bringing up the subject he had scrupulously avoided until now. He said that he wished to talk about the affair which was the chief reason for his coming to England and which was 'to desire that he might have the happiness to be yet nearer related to him by marrying the Lady Mary'. The Duke replied with his usual pomposity that 'till they had treated and brought to ripeness the public affair of war and peace, it was not proper that a discourse upon any other matter should take place'. The Prince of Orange urged, the Duke remained firm, 'and so the visit ended'.

Temple had been afraid that the whole affair would break down when the King insisted that the match could not be concluded until after the peace, and William was so annoyed by Charles's 'punctilio' that after supper one day Temple found him in a black temper; he had made up his mind, he said, to stay in England for only two days longer. At the same time the King was amused because his nephew refused to commit himself irrevocably until he had seen the lady in question. This Charles found a quite unnecessary piece of 'nicety'.

On arriving in London, the Prince met Lady Mary, and whereas she was unimpressed by his appearance, he was so pleased with hers, and so sure that he could see in her 'all those signs of such a humour as had been described to him upon former enquiries', that he was ready to go ahead with his plans without further delay.

The Duke was still in a bad humour after his interview with William. He was further enraged when his brother told him blandly that he had given William permission to broach the subject of the marriage, and he told Charles stiffly that 'he could have wished his Majesty had been pleased to have acquainted him before with his mind'. The King refused to enter into a quarrel and said that he would speak of the matter another time. A few days later, having given James time to simmer down, Charles talked to him quietly about the advantages of the match, though the Duke always maintained that he never gave his consent.

The next day, the Duke was sent for to the Council Chamber, where the Council was sitting. The King told the assembled meeting about William's intention of entering into an alliance by marrying Lady Mary, and said that he himself was ready to consent as he believed that the match would unite the family and please the nation. At this the Duke realized he had no alternative but to agree. He declared his consent in a formal speech, adding that he always acted in the interest of the security and peace of the nation, that he hoped he had now given a sufficient testimony of his right intentions for the public good, and that he believed nobody would now be able to say that he wanted to alter the government, 'for, whatever his opinion in religion might be, all he desired was, that men might not be molested merely for conscience sake'. He also assured the Council that he would not hinder anyone from educating his children in the Church of England, which caused 'general joy' among his hearers. William was then called in and the King said to him, 'Nephew, it is not good for a man to be alone; I will give you a helpmate for you,' adding a piece of wise, if not altogether disinterested, advice. 'Remember,' he said, 'love and war do not agree very well together.'

The Council decided that the wedding should proceed, and the Lord Treasurer worked hard drawing up the necessary articles which were produced after only three days. The Prince, by express, sent the States General of the United Provinces an account of his proceedings, saying 'that in consideration it had been their earnest desire and request to him, to see him married, when he had well weighed the reasons that induced him to it, in a conformity to their wishes and desires and the tranquillity of their state, that he had conceived he could not do better, than to address himself to the Princess Mary. The King and Duke had condescended to him in his request and proposals, and therefore thought it requisite to give their Lordships an account of it that he might the sooner return to them'. William also asked that his wedding present of £40,000 of jewellery should be dispatched at once; he had not brought it with him, for fear of looking too conspicuous.

Lady Mary's reaction to his suit, though unflattering, probably did not surprise him; she was not the first young lady to take one look at him and shy away. In any case nobody took the slightest notice of her distress. The day after her father broke the news, at five o'clock, the Council came in a body to congratulate her, and the Lord Chancellor made a speech. Later the Mayor and Aldermen came in their turn, followed by the Civilians of the Doctors Commons. There was another speech from the Recorder and a visit from the African Company. Among the common people there was great rejoicing. Everyone seemed pleased except the bride herself and the French King. Montagu, the British Ambassador, said he had never seen Louis more upset. 'I always knew the journey would end in this,' he remarked grimly. Barillon, fat, sly, and small, felt that he had had enough of Charles's sophistry—he had been forced to swallow a great deal of cant about furthering the Catholic cause by marrying the royal niece to a Calvinist, and he felt that he would be wiser in the future.

While the Prince waited for news from Holland, there was a succession of ceremonies and celebrations, including a visit to the Lord Mayor's Show, a rather nervy occasion as there had been a threat to assassinate the King as he stood on the balcony at the Angel. A suspicious-looking man was actually arrested in the vicinity, but instead of carrying 'a fatal engine' under his cloak, he was found to be holding nothing more lethal than a large rule, as he was a carpenter by trade. The Prince went incognito with the 'royalties' to revels at Lincoln's Inn. The bride's trousseau was ordered in Paris, but although the City disapproved of this, it gave a magnificent banquet at the Guildhall on October 29 in honour of the betrothal. The King with his brother, and the Lady Mary with her sister and future husband, travelled by barge, and those carrying the mayor, sheriffs, aldermen and city companies, were decorated with banners bearing the arms of the different guilds. When they arrived they were treated to a sumptuous feast of venison, roast beef pies, jellies, cakes and custard.

Opinions about William's character differed. Temple, who knew him well and had seen him in his own surroundings, considered him 'a most hopeful prince', gifted with an agreeable humour, plain good sense and that application to business which was so singularly lacking in his Uncle Charles's make-up. The French Ambassador in Holland, the Marquis de Pomponne, had found him wise, gentle and civil, with a grasp of affairs well beyond anything one would expect of a man of his age. But although one observer kindly reported that at the court of England he behaved himself 'like a general, as well as under his canopy of peace, as he doth under that of war, and is an active dancer on the ropes', many were repulsed by his remote, abstracted air, and found him prim and bad-tempered. He never shone in company, lacking what Temple described as 'that kind of wit which is neither of use to oneself nor to anybody else'. He liked hunting, but otherwise appeared to be impervious to the normal pleasures of life. He took no notice of women, and lived a well-regulated existence, always retiring to bed at ten o'clock, which the King found very amusing. Thanks to his Calvinistic upbringing, he disliked swearing, and detested trivial conversation or 'whipped cream' as it was called. Another peculiarity to English eyes was that he preferred cock ale to any kind of wine. Among the overdressed gallants at the English court this stunted, pallid, sober man looked strangely out of place. He had earlier survived an attack of smallpox which had permanently affected his health; his main disability was a chronic cough which came on in hot candlelit rooms. On horseback he looked reasonably impressive, but on the ground, in a crowd, he attracted attention only by his ugliness. His best features were his dark, silky hair and his large and lustrous eyes, but one lady observer, ignoring these points called him 'the plainest man ever seen and of no fashion at all'. This was perhaps a trifle unkind, as his clothes were ordered in Paris, even if they were black in colour and simple in cut.

The Prince was quite smitten with his cousin's beauty and grace, although habit and temperament had taught him to hide his feelings so that few people realized how pleased he was. He went on looking as sombre as ever and he certainly did not have the appearance of an avid bridegroom. The bride continued to look utterly miserable. With her father and step-mother—who was due to give birth to her child at any minute—she sat and wept whenever there was a spare moment, and sometimes they went on in unison for three hours at a time. Mary was particularly distraught at the thought of leaving her stepmother, and the Prince was not prepared to put off the evil hour of departure for a moment longer than necessary. He was in a hurry to get back to the Hague to prepare, of all unromantic things, his military budget.

So, as soon as word came through of the States' approval, a ceremony was hastily prepared. The wedding jewels had not yet arrived from Hol-land, but this was a minor detail. On the Prince's birthday, November 4, the marriage was solemnized in Lady Mary's bedchamber, between eight and nine in the evening. The Bishop of London was called in to officiate as the Primate was ill. William had met Compton once before, on his previous visit to England; then he had been Canon of Christ Church and had sat beside William during a church service at Oxford and helped him to follow the unfamiliar proceedings. The Prince now insisted that such an important moment in his life should not be spoiled by elaborate ceremony nor carried out in the midst of a hot and curious crowd which would probably have precipitated a fit of coughing. Only the closest relations were allowed to be present, and the atmosphere was hardly hilarious. William, as usual, looked serious, Mary was on the verge of tears, Anne was unwell, and James was feeling gloomy about parting with his daughter and anxious about his wife. The King, who gave his niece away, was, how-ever, as irrepressible as ever. He urged Compton to hurry on with the service in case the bride should be gifted in the meanwhile with a step-brother; it would not do, he said, for William's hopes to be disappointed until after the ceremony. When the Prince put down some coins with the words 'all my worldly goods I thee endow', the King advised his niece to gather them all up and put them in her pocket, 'for 'twas clear gains'. At eleven o'clock, which was well past the bridegroom's bedtime, the couple withdrew to bed, and the King, unable to resist a joke at the expense of his old-womanish nephew, drew the curtains with a flourish, and the words, 'Now nephew to your work! Hey! St George for England'.

The wedded pair had to be up early in the morning to receive the Mayor and the Aldermen who came this time to wish them joy of their marriage. William presented Mary with the jewels which had arrived just a day late. In the evening—it was Guy Fawkes night—bonfires were lit and bells pealed out in celebration. In Edinburgh, the conduits flowed with wine, and the town cross was decorated with an arbour bearing hundreds of oranges. The Prince presented Mary with a small ruby and diamond ring which she always treasured. 'It was the first thing he ever did give me,' she wrote years later when she put it away after one of the stones had been lost.

Even jewels were not enough to cheer the Princess at this moment. The prospect of parting from everything and everybody she loved was weighing on her, and a further cause of unhappiness was the fact that Frances Apsley was unwell; she had not been able to sleep at all 'for the noise of the clocks'. An epidemic of smallpox which had been raging outside the Palace had now spread to the court, and soon it was confirmed that Lady Anne, who had been sickening for several days, had the disease. On November 7 Protestant jubilation, which had been running high since the marriage, was tempered by the news that Mary Beatrice had given birth to a small but lively boy, Charles, Duke of Cambridge. He was christened the next evening, not by Bishop Compton, who would gladly have strangled any York son at birth, but by Dr Crewe, Bishop of Durham, the only cleric who had been brave enough to officiate at the Yorks' wedding ceremony. William now had the galling experience of standing godfather to the child who had for the moment removed his hopes of succeeding to the English throne. This even raised French spirits, and brought Mary Beatrice the congratulations of the Pope.

Although one observer thought that William's pretty lady looked at him with satisfaction, there was little doubt that she was still feeling miserable and rebellious. 'The Prince is a very fond husband, but she is a coy bride, at least before folks' was one observation. William's sullenness and 'clownishness' were universally noted, though it was not surprising if he felt anxious and depressed, with the growing danger from smallpox which his wife had never had. When they went to the play together they never looked at each other once: the Prince might well have echoed Jupiter's words in *Calisto*—'I'll give my empire for a smile, a look.' Before long they were having their first row. William, beginning as he meant to continue,

ordered his wife to stop visiting her sister for the time being and urged her
to move away from the infection at St James's and to stay at Whitehall
until her departure. She refused to do so, and it was with great difficulty
that he dissuaded her from entering the sick room.

William found the carefree attitude of the English quite incomprehensible. Dr Lake, who had been told to refrain from giving Anne her daily
ration of prayers, had gone off to warn Compton that her nurse was a
Catholic. The moral danger to which she was exposed caused Compton to
override medical instructions; he ordered Lake to do all suitable minister-
ial offices which were 'incumbent' on him. Lake interpreted this advice in
its widest sense. He preached at Albemarle House, having immediately
before read prayers at Anne's bedside; he then proceeded to christen her
nurse's child, and infuriated William by going straight from the sickbed
into Mary's presence. Lake promised the elder sister that he would
scrupulously look after the spiritual well-being of the younger, reminding
her at the same time that he had been serving her for seven years for the
meagre remuneration of one hundred pounds a year, and asking her to
recommend him to the King and to the Bishop. Expressing the hope that
God would show her favour in the sight of the strange people amongst
whom she was to go, he kneeled down and kissed her gown. Mary thanked
him and promised she would do what she could 'but was able to say no
more for weeping'.

The weather had now turned very cold and the wind was contrary, which
forced William to stay in England longer than he had intended, continuing his inconclusive discussions with the King on the subject of a general
peace. Every day there were arguments and rumours about the question
of the Princess's train. William would have liked his bride to take the
minimum of retainers; he knew that there were plenty of Dutch women
perfectly capable of filling all the necessary posts. But there was a great
deal of rivalry among the young ladies of the English court, and some
jealousy was aroused by the fact that the Villiers family was monopolizing
all the best appointments. Lady Frances was to accompany the Princess
in her old position of governess, taking at least two of her daughters with
her, and her husband was going too as Master of the Horse. Several of the
Richmond girls were selected, including Anne Trelawney, but Frances
Apsley's name was significantly omitted from the list. Sir Gabriel Sylvius,
fussy, ambitious and tiresome, had talked himself into the job of major
domo, and was carrying on a swift courtship with Anne Howard, who had
been named as a maid of honour, with the object of improving his position
still further. Although it was said at first that his new preferment added

WILLIAM'S MARY

48

nothing to her inclination for him, she quickly succumbed to his blandishments, and there was further heart-searching as a replacement had to be found. 'Miss Sedley stands in her room, maid of honour, to the wonder of everybody,' wrote one gossip-monger. The Prince was disgusted by all this undignified jostling for position, and Savile uncompromisingly called the young ladies a collection of 'beggarly bitches all sueing for places'. When John Churchill enquired about the amount of money needed to buy inclusion among the selected few, William told him coldly that places would not be bought and sold at *his* court.

The wind continued easterly, and each day there was more grim news as friends and retainers fell a prey to smallpox. The Princess's train was decimated. Lady Frances became a victim, and Colonel Villiers announced his intention of staying behind to look after her. Mrs White, another of those chosen, was also dangerously ill. A new governess had to be found at short notice, and Henrietta Hyde was among those suggested. The Prince, however, firmly rejected this idea, for Mrs Hyde was the wife of Laurence, afterwards Earl of Rochester, Mary's uncle, and it was not his policy to perpetuate the family influence. He was equally cold when Hyde himself was suggested as Ambassador to Holland, for the same reason, though the King said he thought there was 'a great difference between an uncle and the wife of an uncle'.

On November 15 a ball was held to celebrate Queen Catherine's birthday. The Princess dressed up in all her new jewellery, but even this apparently did not cause William to give her a second glance. He was preoccupied with the thought of departure, for the wind had veered and he was determined that he and his wife would leave immediately afterwards. As soon as the ball was over he told the Princess to prepare herself for the journey. At about eight o'clock all the family came to kiss her hand and take their leave, but no sooner had she finished this ordeal than she was told that the wind had veered again, and it was not until November 19 that it was back in a favourable quarter.

At nine o'clock on that morning, William and Mary boarded a barge at Whitehall steps with the King and the Duke and 'several other persons of quality'. The Princess was weeping piteously. She was leaving behind a sister whom she might never see again, for Anne had not yet passed the crisis, and might well never recover from the disease that was taking so many others to the grave. Frances Apsley's father was dangerously ill, and so there had been no opportunity of bidding farewell to Aurelia. The Queen tried to comfort her, reminding her that she too had been sent to a foreign country, to a husband she had not even seen, but the Princess was inconsolable. 'Madam,' she said, 'you come into England; but I am going out of England.'

The King and the Duke accompanied the Prince and Princess as far as Erith where, after a farewell dinner, they went on board the yacht *Mary* and did not disembark until they were in sight of Gravesend. Then they took their leave, the Duke, it was said, in a very bad humour. The yacht was one of the most beautiful ever seen in England; it was magnificently gilded and furnished. Once his uncles had departed, William urged the captain to press on quickly, but the weather was deteriorating steadily. The wind was now so unfavourable that at the end of the day they were no more than eight miles out, and everyone was being seasick with the exception of the Princess who happened to be a good sailor. The 'beggarly bitches' were now in a position to regret their shameless place-hunting. Most of them had parted from relations who were either dying or already dead. The Villiers sisters had left their mother on the point of death, Anne Trelawney had a father and uncle mortally ill and, as far as they were concerned themselves, they probably did not care whether they lived or died. The Prince would undoubtedly have preferred it if they had stayed with their expiring relations. He had no wish for his wife to be hedged about with querulous Englishwomen, and as it turned out most of them were to prove nothing but a worry and expense.

The English captain advised the Prince to turn back, but William pressed him to continue. He had seen too much hysterical weeping in the royal barge to relish the thought of a second parting. But at last the captain said that he refused to cross the North Sea in such a gale, and he landed the Prince and Princess at Sheerness, where the Governor offered them hospitality. The King sent a message asking them to return to London, but the Prince could not face the thought of the journey in such rough weather, and in any case wished to remain nearer the coast so that they could re-embark as soon as the weather improved. Most of the party was left on the yacht and the Princess was accompanied by just one dresser and Lady Inchiquin, her lady in waiting, while the Prince took with him his friends Bentinck and Odyck and Count Horn. The next day they moved on to Canterbury where they put up at the inn. Nobody had any ready money or plate, and Bentinck was forced to beg a loan from the Mayor and Corporation, who found the request so unusual that they refused to lend anything. At this Dr Tillotson, the Dean, who happened to be in residence at the time, hurried over to the inn and not only offered to lend all his own plate as well as some he had borrowed, but also produced a good number of guineas, and suggested that the party should be his guests at the Deanery, which was large and roomy. The Prince accepted the money and plate with gratitude, but refused the offer of accommodation, some said because he wanted to make the most of his discomfort in order to put his father-in-law in a bad light.

During his short stay in Canterbury, William cultivated Tillotson's friendship and also held a small court, receiving some of the local gentry, especially those, it was rumoured, who were antagonistic towards the King's policies. Meanwhile the wind had dropped and the yachts were becalmed at Gravesend with all the luggage still on board.

At the first indication of a fair wind the ships were brought round to Margate. William of Nassau, Odyck and other of the Prince's relations were alarmed to see that the weather had turned very stormy, and they thought the King should have sent some men-of-war for his niece and her husband, rather than trusting them to the fast but frail-looking yachts that had been put at their disposal. It was decided that the Prince and Princess should travel in separate ships, the *Mary* and the *Catherine*, and William was able to watch his wife's being tossed and buffeted by the waves. He must have wondered whether having snatched her away from the menace of smallpox he was not now going to lose her to the deep. And at this stage, it could have been a relief to Mary to see her unwelcome husband vanish under the waves.

Eventually the yachts carried the Prince and Princess safely through the storm. They arrived off the Dutch coast only to be told that the rivers were iced up. If they had hung about waiting for the Maas to clear, the wind might have veered and blown them back to England more rapidly than they had come. William, for one, was not prepared to face this indignity, and he gave orders that the boats should be anchored off the small fishing village of Ter Heyde, and the passengers rowed ashore. The weather was so bad that the coaches waiting to meet the travellers were unable to get within four miles of the village 'and so his poor princess was fain to walk that in a frost' as one English writer put it. The Princess was more fit to face this marathon than her ladies, who had all suffered agonies of sea-sickness. Once the coaches were reached, there still remained a two-hour drive to Honselaersdyck, the palace which had been made ready for the bride's arrival. Late that evening the cortège of coaches drove up the long tree-lined avenue and into the courtyard in front of the palace which was to be her new home.

CHAPTER 5

MARY OF ORANGE

WHEN HE ARRIVED HOME, William was greeted with bad news. The French, taking advantage of his absence, had laid siege to Saint-Ghislain, one of the vital barrier towns guarding the approaches to the Spanish Netherlands. He had come too late to go to its defence, but he sent a message to the Dutch commander, Waldeck, assuring him that his wife would not have prevented him, had his presence been considered necessary, for she was not the kind of woman who insisted on putting her own interests first.

The Prince and Princess spent their first days in Holland quietly, recovering from the journey, and Mary soon began to look more cheerful and to take an interest in the country she had come to. The Palace of Honselaersdyck was set in the flat country that stretched away to the sand dunes and the sea. The grey stone house, built round a central courtyard, was surrounded by a severely formal garden; beyond the ornamental water which encircled the grounds was the little village of Honselaersdyck, with its church and its typical Dutch houses bordering the canal. The Palace itself was pleasantly mellow and filled with the pictures which William had inherited, as well as some that he had bought himself. Here, in rather less hopeful circumstances, the Princess's father and uncle had come to stay with their sister when they had first gone into exile. Here, if Gramont is to be believed, her mother, when maid of honour to the former Princess of Orange, had played ninepins in the gallery with the Earl of Arran prior to throwing a fit of the vapours. This upstairs gallery was an impressive room, with windows reaching to the ground, pilastered walls, a gilded ceiling and a chimney piece by Rubens of Diana with a hound, a lion and a tiger. It had been just as much a fashion for Dutch ladies to be pictured as the Goddess of the Chase as it was for Mary and her companions, and Amalia of Solms, William's formidable grandmother, could be seen in this guise in one of the Palace portraits.

The outside of the house might be severe and formal in the classical manner, but the interior aimed at a gay and flowing, Rubens-like effect.

Honselaersdyck was a summer house, a *recreatif zomerblief*, and the holiday atmosphere was reflected in the light-heartedness of the interior decorations, in the flower festoons, cherubs, and nymphs. In the great gallery, the coving was decorated with groups of figures on a balcony. The illusionist style of painting was imported from Italy, but the figures themselves were copied from homely Dutch models, Dutchmen of heavy build, and ample-bosomed ladies, large but not voluptuous, country people with round faces and protruding eyes, all occupied with domestic tasks. Above the fireplace was a merry musical group conducted by a young man with long hair, and a lute player sat astride the balcony.

These were the kind of people that the Princess was soon to meet, and she took a liking to the Dutch at once, for their honesty and plain dealing appealed to her. Their cleanliness was a relief after the unsavoury atmosphere of her uncle's court, which Evelyn could only describe as 'nasty and stinking', and where the King's spaniel bitches made the air unwholesome, giving suck to their innumerable puppies even in his bedchamber. Sir William Temple had commented on 'the strange and curious cleanliness of the Hague'; once, dining with a Dutchman when he was suffering from a cold, he had spat on the floor in what seemed to him the normal manner, and was surprised to see a 'tight, handsome wench', who was standing in the room with a clean cloth in her hand, bend down at once to mop it up. His host told him it was lucky that his wife was not there, as she would certainly have turned him out of the house for fouling her floor, even though he was the English Ambassador. On another occasion, when 'a strapping North Holland lass' opened the door to a magistrate who had come to see her mistress, she noticed that his shoes were dirty and picked him up bodily, carrying him to the bottom of the stairs, where she pulled off his shoes and put on a pair of clean slippers without saying a word.

If the new Princess responded well to the simplicity and homeliness of her husband's countrymen, she no doubt also appreciated the fact that during the first weeks after her arrival they left her alone, giving her time to get to know the man she had married. She soon found that there was a different side to the grim and very reserved character she had seen in England. William was already mature and seasoned by experience. *Le feindre est défendu mais le dissimuler point*—to feign is forbidden, but to hide one's feelings is not—this was one of the precepts taught him by his tutors. So he had grown up to be far more honest in his public dealings than many of his contemporaries, but he also learnt the wisdom of hiding his feelings except in the society of his intimate friends. When he was with

the few people he allowed himself to like and trust, he was a different man
—humorous, even gay, emotional and full of concern. And the revelation
of this aspect of the Prince's character came to Mary during her first days
in Holland.

The weather brightened and became warmer soon after the Princess's
arrival. William took her on a private visit to the Hague, which was only a
short journey from the palace along the tree-lined avenue into the city.
He showed her the Binnenhof, the grand but rather grim-looking Gothic
building where he had been born, so soon after his father's death into a
room entirely hung with black. It was here in the Stadholder's quarters
that he had spent much of his childhood, watching the comings and goings
of the deputies to the assemblies of the States General and the States of
Holland which shared the building. At one time he had been almost a
prisoner there.

William had, from the start, been the focus of innumerable quarrels
amongst those who wished to dominate his upbringing. His childhood had
been even stranger than his wife's. 'Ce précieux enfant', Huygens had called
him, but there were plenty of people who would have been happy if he had
perished at birth. In infancy he had been brooded over by two jealous and
masterful women, his mother and his grandmother, Amalia of Solms.
Mesdames les Princesses Tutrices, was the formidable title they shared.
Amalia, like Anne Hyde, had once been no more than a lady in waiting
and the daughter of a court official. The elder of the Orange brothers had
picked her out and married her to the younger, Frederick Henry. Like
many people whom good fortune has raised above their station, she was
driven by social ambition, perhaps to cover an insecurity caused by her
own lack of noble birth. It was this ambition that had made her marry off
her son William to the ten-year-old Princess Royal who turned out to
be a hard, unfeeling girl with whom she never ceased to quarrel.

In view of this background, it was not surprising that William grew up
into a priggish and precocious youth. From the start, however, there had
been signs of an unusual strength of character, and as a small child he had
been able to sit with a group of grown-ups, listening to their talk with
almost unnatural stillness and attention. His mentors took his education
so seriously that a document, the Discours sur la Nourriture, was drawn up,
setting out in numbered clauses the principles on which he was to be
nurtured, with many practical recommendations. His tutors were told to
talk to him intelligently, and to discuss with him, from an early age, the
tactics of war. A sensible régime, with plenty of physical exercise and a
well-regulated diet, helped him to overcome his childhood delicacy, and

the general stipulation that he should be kept out of the hands of doctors as much as possible probably saved him when, in 1675, he fell seriously ill with smallpox and was nursed through it by his friend Bentinck with the minimum of remedies.

Like his wife, William had been brought up as a child of State, but for him the circumstances had been far more distressing. He was sixteen when he was told that as he had become a ward of the States of Holland, he would have to part with his governor, Zuylestein, and most of his friends. The States, headed by John de Witt, leader of the Louvestein party, were to take charge of his education. Since the Louvesteiners had always been opposed to the House of Orange, the outlook was not encouraging, and William went to the French Ambassador with tears in his eyes, begging him to intercede for him. But the States were intractable; Zuylestein was dismissed and a Frenchman was appointed in his place, 'like a little spy about him to watch him and all his gestures, words and actions'.

The Louvesteiners hoped to destroy all chances of the House of Orange regaining its former power, but they had reckoned without William's strength of character and without the power of the mob. The United Provinces formed a nation that was a republic but not a democracy. The system had thrown up a ruling oligarchy, and in the provincial assemblies as well as the States-General, the deputies came from a few ruling families of the burgher type, who clung to their privileges as religiously as they sought to deprive members of the House of Orange of theirs. The people as a whole had no more say in government than it would have had under a monarchy, and it could not express itself except through public demonstration. The mob revered the House of Orange as much as the oligarchy reviled it, and proceeded to display its feelings at William's birth in an outbreak of spontaneous rejoicing. A vast crowd gathered for his christening and was kept waiting while his mother and grandmother had one of their customary arguments about the names he was to be given—in the end his mother refused to go to the christening at all since she could not have her own way, and the far more congenial Elizabeth of Bohemia stood sponsor. When, at the age of three, William appeared to the waiting crowd at a window of the Binnenhof in the Hague he was loudly cheered, and there was a popular disgust when, in his eleventh year, he did not take part in the traditional ceremonies of the May carnival, the Kermesse. He was fêted when he visited Haarlem with his mother.

As William grew up it became evident, to the discomfiture of his enemies, that he possessed qualities which fitted him for the role of Stad-holder. He soon proved that he could speak in public, a valuable asset, and in his first speech after he was admitted to the Council he spoke in rousing terms about his august ancestors, William the Silent and his sons Maurice and Frederick Henry, who had helped to lay the foundations of the glorious republic. For those who disliked the narrow ruling cast, William symbolized unity, liberty and the Protestant religion, and he seemed to be the natural, chosen leader of his country. His own merit and behaviour, coupled with the reverence of the populace, had enabled him to rise to power and to save his country from the onslaught of the French. The people began to worship him as a hero, kissing the ground he trod on and the horse he rode.

So, at an early age, William learnt about the wiles of statesmen and the fickleness of human nature. From John de Witt, whose appointment as his governor had caused him so much mortification, he had learnt how to handle the complicated machinery of his country's government, that unwieldy union where each state and city maintained its independence and was able by one negative vote to paralyse the workings of the State. De Witt had been a man of courage, strong will, acute intellect and forceful personality, and the young William had listened to him, played tennis with him, and become his friend. Some people maintained that William condoned the action of the mob when it tore de Witt and his brother to pieces, but this was more likely to have been a personal blow, deeply felt and filling him with disgust. Such experiences, undergone so young, could have accounted for the austere mask which the Prince had assumed, and which Mary had found so repellent in her first encounters with William at the English court.

In 1671 the United Provinces had gone through dark days, and it looked for a time as if the whole nation would succumb to the French attack. As every Dutch schoolchild knows, the situation was 'radeloos, redeloos, reddeloos'—the people desperate, the government senseless and the country beyond hope. It was William who had come forward as a saviour and had stemmed the invading army, but this did not mean that the States as a whole had been behind him ever since. The powerful State of Holland, which included the city of Amsterdam, was always ready to oppose his policies. And his marriage had by no means been greeted with enthusiasm in every quarter. There were many people who feared that the Prince would now come under the domination of his uncles; those who were agitating for a speedy peace at any price had a suspicion that William would be tempted to prolong the war if he could be sure of English support.

And there was always the danger that Mary, like her namesake, William's mother, might prove to be a cold unfriendly Englishwoman who would make no attempt to fraternize with the Dutch. It was also difficult for natives of the United Provinces to forget their fear of royalty. For nearly a century their country had struggled to free itself from the yoke of royalist Spain, under which it had fallen when the Hapsburg Philip the Fair married a princess who became heiress of the Spanish kingdoms. Philip's descendants, growing increasingly Spanish in outlook, had done their best to crush the growth of Calvinism in the northern provinces, and there had been outbreaks of terror and brutality which the Dutch could never forget. An inbred hatred of monarchy and Catholicism made many Dutchmen unlikely to greet with enthusiasm a member of the English royal house, whose father was known to be a Catholic, and whose uncle's religious leanings were also suspect.

For all these reasons, nobody knew how successful an occasion the State entry would prove to be. The date chosen for William to introduce his bride to the people of the Hague was December 14, and the day dawned fine and warm for the time of year. It began badly when William heard that Saint-Ghislain had fallen, but otherwise proved to be an unqualified, and rather unexpected, success. Mary sat beside William in a gilded coach drawn by six piebald horses. Lady Inchiquin sat opposite her, holding on her lap the jewels William had given his bride. Church bells were ringing and guns were firing as they drove towards the Hague, and they were greeted at the gates by twelve companies of burghers, drawn up under their own ensigns. They then crossed over the bridge into the city which was decorated with garlands, and were met by twenty-four young virgins from the public orphanage, all dressed in white, who walked two by two on either side of the coach, singing and throwing under the wheels bunches of fragrant herbs which gave out a delicious scent. In front of the Stadhuis they passed under a triumphal arch adorned with foliage and grotesque work with their coats of arms above two clasped hands. One glimpse of the soft-featured princess, with her large dark eyes, her youthful bloom and charming, virtuous manner, was quite enough to dispel any fears that she resembled William's marble-hearted mother, and the populace was soon roaring its approval.

That evening, when the martial ceremonies were over, there was a magnificent display of fireworks. Pitch barrels had been placed in the streets to feed the large bonfires, some of which had been built in the form of pyramids and castles. The fireworks represented, among other things, a lion, a drake, St George on horseback, fountains, pyramids, flower pots, and triumphal chariots, not to mention Jupiter and Mars descending out of the air. The day finished with feasting, and, to commemorate it, a medal was struck—on one side a portrait of William and on the other, *Mary by the Grace of God, Princess of Orange, Daughter of York*.

The next day, before they had been given time to recover from the celebrations, William and Mary received a delegation from the States-General, and ambassadors and envoys came to offer their congratulations. Among the Princess's wedding presents were 'two of the richest night-gowns as ever came from the Indies' brought over by the Governor of Batavia. In the new year Mary received a succession of letters from the German relations, from Electors, Dukes and Princes, offering congratulations, wishing her '*plus riches Bénédictions, toutes sortes de Bien imaginables*', and the gift of children, and hoping that she and her husband would '*augmenter la gloire de leurs prédécesseurs*'. Frederick William of Brandenburg, who addressed her as 'a dear and well-loved relation', expressed pleasure that his nephew had chosen her above all others, for, he wrote, her high qualities and virtues were well known. Some of the German states sent the plenipotentiaries who were still at Nimeguen to offer congratulations in person. The small principality of Orange, from which William took his illustrious name, situated far away in the south of France not far north of Marseilles, sent a delegation representing the residents of the city, as did all the Dutch states; the Ommelanders, who sent their Pensionary rather later than some of the others, assured her that their good wishes came not only from the mouth—'*ceux sont, Madame, les propres mouvements de nos cœurs.*' Villa Hermosa, the Spanish governor in the Netherlands, sent '*muchos felices*' [sic], and the octogenarian, Constantine Huygens, one of the most faithful supporters and servants of William's family, penned an Epithalamion on the subject of the marriage, in Latin, 'in an hour of leisure caused by a little gout in his feet'.

In England, the aged poet Waller had been one of the few 'sweet singers' to mark the occasion with a rhyme. 'I have not yet seen his verses, but I am promised them before I seal this letter,' Savile told Rochester, 'and then you yourself shall be judge whether the old gentleman stink in the socket or blaze a little yet.' There was a vestige of the poetic fire left in the seventy-five-year-old bard, as his lines show:

> As once the lion honey gave,
> Out of the strong such sweetness came;
> A royal hero, no less brave,
> Produced this sweet, this lovely dame . . .

Orange with youth experience has;
In action young, in council old;
Orange is what Augustus was,
Brave, wary, provident, and bold . . .

Thrice happy pair! so near ally'd
In royal blood, and virtue too!
Now Love has you together ty'd,
May none this triple knot undo!

Early in January, William's 'lovely dame' performed her first solo ceremony. Alone, she was to receive the ladies of the Hague in audience, and
William had coached her in the niceties of his country's etiquette, explaining that although power had long ago passed from the nobility to the
ruling oligarchy, the noblemen still formed a closely knit group of their
own. They had lost their power but not their pride, and they seldom
married outside their own class, even in the good cause of bettering the
family fortunes. Social dignity mattered more to them than political
advantages; they would not even deign to doff their cap to a social
inferior. Some of the burghers, on the other hand, wielded almost un-
limited power in their own states, like Valconier of Amsterdam, who, as
Sidney observed, could turn out or put in anybody he chose: 'What he
saith is ever done without any contradiction . . . yet he walks about the
streets just like an ordinary shopkeeper.' To pander to the snobbery of
the nobles, it was decided that the Princess should only kiss married
women if they were of noble birth, and spinsters if they were related to
William's family.

The ladies of the Hague were evidently in a flutter of expectation, and,
for all the plebeian manners of their husbands, they were not unmoved
by the thought of being received by a real live princess. Great was their
disappointment when they realized that the royal kiss was not for them.
Afterwards many were in tears and some were so upset that they became
quite ill. Outraged officials remonstrated with William, saying that their
wives merited a kiss by virtue of their husband's office, which gave them
the necessary rank. William drily and firmly insisted that office could not
ennoble the holder in any way at all.

This incident aroused fears that the Princess might, after all, be imbued
with typical English snobbery, and some time after her arrival she gave rise
to further criticism. In the Hague two broad streets, called the Voorhout,
formed the centre of the social world of the city. Planted with rows of
lime trees, which were deliciously fragrant when in blossom, with a space
in the centre railed off for pedestrians, the streets provided a focus for all

those who wanted to see or be seen. At midday, or in the evening, there was a gay and sociable parade of people, walking or in coaches, reminiscent of the *passegiata della sera* in modern Italy. The street was not broad enough to take two carriages abreast, and as those who used it vied with each other over the magnificence of their coaches, which were sometimes so large that they had to be drawn by six horses, difficulties could arise if both coachmen refused to give way. There had been a notorious occasion when the Spanish and French Ambassadors had brought traffic to a halt and an international crisis was avoided only when the central barrier was broken down to give the Spaniard a chance to extricate himself without losing face. William himself, as a very young man, had nearly precipitated a similar incident, when he had refused to give way to d'Estrades, the French Ambassador, and had been brought to his senses by his grandmother who had been hastily summoned, and who advised him to follow her back to the Binnenhof on foot. The Princess, driving out one day from the Binnenhof past the Vyver, the rectangular lake or fishpond by the Palace, went on into the Voorhout, foolishly insisting on her right to drive against the stream of traffic. She came face to face with the wife of the Danish Ambassador, who was in no mood to withdraw. This kind of incident, which was inevitably aggravated by Mary's ignorance of the Dutch language, made it difficult to avoid some misunderstandings at first, but it was not long before she was able to correct any adverse impressions. Her own charm and virtue transcended all barriers, and she soon endeared herself to the Dutch by her obvious liking for their country.

In character most of the Dutch were grave and free from levity. Seen in their proper context William's plain manners and simple, dark clothes seemed less prim and Puritanical. A few turns round the Voorhout were enough to show that in this country people were thrifty and unostentatious in their choice of apparel; they dressed without the peacock glitter that was emptying so many English purses. The Dutchman preferred to go abroad in sober black velvet adorned with exquisite lace, and he was more ready to spend his money on beautiful houses and furnishings for his children to inherit, rather than on extravagant and quickly outdated fashions. William was not a rich Prince, for his father and mother had dissipated much of the family fortune in their futile attempts to support the exiled English King and his brother. It was thanks to the financial acumen of his grandmother that William was able to live comfortably, even if he could not afford to be extravagant. William preferred a simple life among friends to any excess of gaiety, and he was too preoccupied with his coun-

try's affairs to have any inclination for lavish entertaining. His health was
another factor which dominated his way of life. He had been ill at ease in
England not only because he disliked the artificiality of court manners,
but also because there was always a danger that the hot atmosphere of
crowds and candlelight might bring on an acute attack of asthma. Having
spent his earliest years surrounded by domineering women, he had reacted
against this state of affairs as soon as he was old enough to regulate his
own life. In manhood he had sought the company of other men, choosing
a few firm friends, and dining with officers of the Hague garrison or
foreign diplomats. His closest friends, chosen for their discretion and
steadiness rather than for their brilliance, were Bentinck, Ossory, Odyck
and Overkirk.

William Bentinck now twenty-eight, a year older than the Prince, had
been appointed as a page when he and William were both children. He
belonged to an old Dutch family, and Temple said he was the best
servant he had ever known in the Prince's or any other private household.
When William fell ill with smallpox, Bentinck nursed him day and night,
even, as tradition has it, sleeping in the same bed as the invalid, for it was
a contemporary belief that anyone catching the disease would take away
the ferocity of the attack from the original sufferer. The Prince said that
in sixteen days and nights of illness, he never called once, but Bentinck
was there to answer him. Trustworthy and a trifle stolid, Bentinck's most
outstanding characteristic was his reddish-gold hair, which in later years
he hid under a peruke.

Both Overkirk and Odyck were sons of Beverweerd, the natural son
of Prince Maurice, William's great-uncle. Of the two brothers, the elder
was the less exciting. Overkirk was of mediocre talent and he lacked great
ambition. His main virtue lay in his absolute fidelity to the Prince. His
younger brother Odyck was more outstanding in every way. A good
speaker, with an air of grandeur about him, he threw himself into work
and pleasure with equal enthusiasm. He had been wise enough to marry
an heiress, and this enabled him to entertain with an *éclat* unapproached
by anybody else at the Hague. The parties he gave had the lavishness that
made people think of their host as a minor sovereign; it was said that he
himself rose at the time when most people were just going to bed, and
although the French underestimated him, thinking that he was entirely
dedicated to his pleasures, William knew his value and entrusted him with
several important embassies. When he was engaged in negotiations, he
was clear headed, a brilliant diplomat, but his family always hoped his
missions would not last long as he spent so much of his own money helping

to make them a success; indeed he had not much to leave to his many children when his life, so '*bizarre et déréglée*', finally came to an end.

The Earl of Ossory was another of William's circle, a member of the 'big four' who had gone with him to England. He also was a relation, if only by marriage, for his wife was one of the Beverweerd sisters. He commanded the six English and Scottish regiments in the pay of the States, and William was devoted to him.

William was certainly a man's man, and it would not have been surprising, in view of his upbringing and the influence of domineering women, if he had developed homosexual tendencies. His modern biographers, and in particular Dr Robb, have shown however, that there is little except rumour to support the long-established theory that he was in any way abnormal.

The Prince's closest friends might well have resented the Princess's intrusion into their bachelor-like existence, but she was tactful enough to refrain from making her presence felt too strongly at the outset; and as they came to know her better, they grew to like her with the same devotion that they lavished on the Prince. Since she had been brought up for the most part in the company of women, the Princess did not find it strange that she was expected to eat in the middle of the day with her ladies, whilst William held his 'business luncheons' with his friends and advisers. He gave as his excuse for this segregation the fact that it would have been unseemly for the Princess to dine with her social inferiors; it is certain that her presence would have cramped their masculine style for their conversation was often indelicate. In the years before his marriage, William had been in the habit of playing cards in mixed company until eight o'clock and then, since it was the custom for women in his country to retire at that hour, he had usually gone on to the house of one of his men-friends, to play there until half-past nine.

The Prince and Princess kept up this tradition—William having spent most of the afternoon in his bedchamber talking business. The Princess was to be 'at home' to certain privileged people who came to play cards or sometimes to dance. After the company had gone, William and Mary were able to retire and have supper together. Knowing that her husband was occupied with affairs of State all through the day, the Princess made a point of avoiding all serious topics, and she considered it her duty to entertain him with chat about more trivial subjects. She was fortunately a vivacious and amusing conversationalist.

During the first few weeks of the year, the Dutch did their best not to trouble William with too much business. This gave him a chance to see more of his wife, and also to indulge in the pleasures of the chase, which was his only relaxation and pastime, and one which he enjoyed far more than anything as sedentary as card-playing. When he was out, Mary, who was no great horsewoman, could remain securely in the Palace, busily answering congratulatory letters, or playing cards with her ladies—which Lake disapproved of, when he heard about it. She fell easily into the new routine, and life in Holland seemed to suit her, for she put on weight and was described by one visitor from England as 'very beautiful withal'. Walter Harris, who later became William's doctor, was of the opinion that there was something in the air and diet which contributed towards the Dutch tendency to put on weight; he also thought that the prevalent plumpness could be due to the fact that Dutch doctors were far more reluctant than their English counterparts to subject their unfortunate patients to constant letting of blood—'an extremity of bleeding little' was how Harris described it.

For the first few weeks, the Princess found scant time to write to her friends, but it was not long before she resumed her correspondence with Frances Apsley. Like any other bride, she could not resist trying out her new name, which she was, however, quite incapable of spelling: 'Mary Oreng' was the nearest she could manage. Frances was slightly overawed by the thought that her old school friend had become 'the greatest princess now alive', and Mary also found it confusing having to write to her first 'husband' now that she had acquired another. Letters from home brought her the news that her infant step-brother, the Duke of Cambridge, had died of smallpox soon after her departure. It was not surprising that he had succumbed to the disease, considering the English carelessness about infection, but it was thought that his death had been caused by his nurse who had tried to suppress the spots rather than drawing them out. He had been a healthy child, who might well have survived but for this misfortune. The Catholics gloomily foretold that no York heir would ever be allowed to live.

Lady Anne, on the other hand, had made a good recovery, though some reports said she was 'well-pitted'. For several days after Mary's departure, James had invented messages from the Princess, pretending that she was still in the Palace, but when she was finally told that her sister had gone without being able to take her leave, Anne bore the news 'very patiently', in her bovine way.

William owned several Palaces besides Honselaersdyck, but they were too distant for the Princess to visit in winter weather. He himself went away to Soestdyck, the nearest of these, for a few days early in January, but the Princess was no doubt overjoyed when on January 7 he drove back into the front courtyard, which, in the winter time, was decorated with ever-green plants in pots arranged along the top of the protecting wall. Although some people were never likely to find out that there was more to William than an uncouth statesman in a mis-shapen body, the Princess had rapidly and rather unexpectedly fallen in love with him. One eulogizer wrote that 'his forehead resembled that of Julius Caesar, his eye that of M. Antoninus the Philosopher, and his nose that of Constantine the Great', which was perhaps carrying it rather far; all the same, his wife evidently saw in him some of these qualities. Young, impressionable, highly emotional and somewhat unstable, the Princess could feel that in William she had found an anchor, and in his informal, orderly court, a home. Before long she had the added happiness of knowing that she was expecting a child.

Both the Prince and the Princess had been carefully educated in the dogma of their own Churches. Triglandus, the Prince's chief instructor, had attended him daily, reading passages from the scriptures and psalms to help give him comfort in adversity—he was to need plenty of that. He was allowed to compose his own prayers to suit the occasion, and he always prayed before a battle; in fact, he was known as 'the praying commander'. The sacrament he took without fail four times a year, reserving three or four days to prepare himself. Mary, naturally religious herself, could appreciate this side of his character, and when they went together to the Dutch established church at the Hague, Protestants everywhere felt that this augured well for the future—everywhere, that is, except in England, where the hierarchy greeted the news with dissatisfaction. Her easy-going chaplain, Lloyd, was recalled, and in his place the Archbishop appointed Dr Hooper, who was charged with the task of ensuring that the Princess should not be contaminated by foreign influences, even though they might be of a Protestant variety.

Thus, although the Princess was believed to be old enough, at fifteen, to marry and bear children for the good of the Protestant cause, she was not considered sufficiently mature to think for herself, or to be allowed to go to her husband's church. For the time being, in any case, the Princess was too busy making new friends and absorbing new impressions to be greatly worried about ecclesiastical variations. And the Prince certainly had far too much on his mind to be concerned with such matters.

The first days of the new year of 1678 may have seemed peaceful enough to the Princess in the seclusion of the palace at Honselaersdyck. She was as yet too inexperienced to interpret the meaning of the messengers who arrived in increasing numbers as the days went by, or to realize the full implications of what it meant to marry a Prince who was also Captain-General of a nation at war. The Prince continued to hear disquieting news from the front, but he kept his anxieties to himself. In February the situation darkened. Ghent and Bruges fell to the French. There was widespread alarm, and even the English were apprehensive. 'The Commons,' wrote Sir John Reresby, 'grew very warm, and began to reflect upon the King's ill councils, that had not advised him to this war sooner.' In England, people could afford to be angry, but in Holland, where only a few remaining fortresses stood between the French and the flat plains of the Netherlands, the sentiment was understandably one of fear. The Commons might talk, and grow indignant, and make nebulous plans, but for the Dutch immediate action was necessary.

One morning in late February, William went hunting as usual. He returned to the Palace and went up to his room without saying a word to anybody. The Princess was startled when a young officer came to take leave of her, saying that he had been sent ahead to the front and that the Prince would be following shortly. On enquiring further, she found out that William had been met by messengers as he returned from hunting, and had been told that the French had laid siege to Namur. Although some of his friends advised him against going to the army—they knew there was little chance of saving Namur and thought he would be well advised to let Waldeck have the mortification of seeing the town fall—he had decided to leave immediately. 'His Highness is pretty sudden in his resolutions,' Lawrence Hyde observed, 'and having once taken them is not easily persuaded to change them.'

William allowed his wife to go with him as far as Amsterdam. It was there that Mary's uncle, Hyde, witnessed, to his surprise, a very tender parting on both sides. The Prince was in remarkably high spirits, which was understandable, since he had found himself a wife so much to his satisfaction—and he was nothing if not fastidious—and now he was going off to his first love, the army. For the Princess it was not easy to appear cheerful. It was true that the Prince had promised he would send for her to come to Breda, a town only fifteen minutes' ride from the front. But this was for the moment a remote possibility; all she had at present was the empty house and the ache of an unfamiliar anxiety.

CHAPTER 6

THE WAR

IT SEEMED INCREDIBLE to the Princess that she was now tasting grief more bitter than any she had felt when wrenched away from her home and family. The only comfort she had was to pour out her feelings to Aurelia and to tell her the things which she would not have dared to reveal to anyone else, even to angels. 'I suppose you know the prince is gone to the army,' she wrote, 'but I am sure you can guess at the trouble I am in, I am sure I could never have thought it half so much. I thought coming out of my own country, parting with my friends and relations the greatest that ever could, as long as they lived, happen to me, but I am mistaken that now till this time I never knew sorrow, for what can be more cruel in the world than parting with what one loves?' Worse, she pointed out, was the fact that this was no ordinary parting, but a war-time separaration, 'so as maybe never to meet again, or to be perpetually in fear, for God knows when I may see him or whether he is not now at this instant in battle'.

The anxious days went slowly by, with little news coming through from. the front. Communications were bad in any case, and William, in his bachelor way, had gone off without giving anybody much idea of his destination. All this made the Princess prepare for the worst. 'I reckon him now never in safety, ever in danger, oh miserable life that I lead now,' she wrote.

Many people were already saying that the time had come to make peace, to bow to the might of France while there was yet time and before sixty thousand well-trained Frenchmen could capture the last of the barrier towns and sweep on into Holland. William, a young general and still inexperienced, was considered mad to fight on with inadequate, ill-equipped forces, and without the help of any strong allies. Each town that fell was another bargaining point for the enemy at the conference table. There had been a widespread hope that when the Prince went over to England he would bring back not only a bride, but also the firm possibility, after discussions with his uncle, of an end to hostilities in the near future. Sophia of Hanover put the matter succinctly, as was her custom:

We are savouring the sweet hope which is given us in the newspapers of a
peace which the Prince of Orange will bring us which he has found with the
deflowering of his wife, although I think this more certain than the other, and
that the peace will likewise be as easily broken, since its ligaments will be no less
feeble and will only serve for a respite.

William himself was under no illusions. He continued to warn everyone
that the French King's word was not to be trusted; he was resolved to
continue the war until his country was strong enough to dictate the terms.
But as one barrier town after the other fell, so the possibility of making a
favourable peace receded and William's reputation as a war-monger
increased. As long ago as 1676 Sophia had been able to write, with some
truth, 'the Prince of Orange is at present more hated than loved', and the
more he tried to contain the organized strength and expansionist greed of
Louis XIV, the more checks the jealous States placed on his power.

In England, Mary's father, in his unbalanced way, had suddenly
changed his allegiance. After supporting the French in everything, he
was now advocating the policy of raising a large army which he himself
intended to take to the Netherlands in support of the Dutch. His countrymen were suspicious; as far as they were concerned, when a Catholic
Duke unexpectedly became eager to lead an army, his motives could be
open to only one interpretation, and they were sure his enthusiasm was
due to a long-term plan of using such a force in times of peace to further
the cause of Catholicism. And as for the King, who could trust him, after
his long record of broken promises? The Dutch were sceptical about his
declared intention of coming to their aid; they feared that it would turn
out to be nothing more than the latest refinement in his flirting game
with France, a screen for yet another attempt to procure subsidies from
Louis. Sure enough, English indignation at the French King's aggression,
slow to awaken, quick to die, soon showed signs of cooling. The grand
army that had been talked about was whittled down until it turned out to
be no more than a token force under the leadership of the Duke of
Monmouth.

The unreliability of the English added to William's burdens, but at that
moment it was of little importance to Mary. All that mattered to her was
that towards the end of March she was able to go south to Antwerp to
meet William. She left immediately after receiving a letter, which gave
rise to rumours in the Hague that William was either sick or dead. The
news of her departure reached him at Mechlin and he set out at once to
meet her. She spent a fortnight at Antwerp, exploring the town and doing
some shopping, under the watchful eye of lady Inchiquin. The freedom

the Prince allowed her was severely criticized by Sir Gabriel Sylvius, who was turning out to be a very officious *hofmeister*. He was an elderly, self-important man, a great lover of gossip, who was always to be seen whispering into the ear of somebody influential. 'The languishing knight', as Evelyn called him, having persuaded Anne Howard to listen to his suit, had brought her over in happy expectation of the honours and favours that would be awaiting her at Mary's court. He was disappointed. The Prince, who was, in Temple's words, 'the sincerest man alive, hating all tricks and those that use them', gave him no encouragement at all, and kept his wife well away from the Princess. So Sylvius was feeling sour and ready to find fault, which he did, with some reason, when he heard that the Princess had inadvertently wandered into the least reputable corner of the town.

After a fortnight the Princess returned to the Hague, but she had only been there a few weeks when the Prince sent for her again. This time she went to Breda. Her pregnancy had by now reached the dangerous stage, around the second or third month, and the journey was ill-timed. She had not been there long when she suffered a serious miscarriage. It was particularly unfortunate that this happened when she was away from the Hague, and when it was unlikely that she could be attended by the doctors whom the Prince would certainly have called in had she been at home. Drelincourt, one of William's medical advisers, for example, was a brilliant gynaecologist and embryologist. The board of the University of Leyden had summoned him from Paris in 1668, though it was not until 1670 that his Dutch was good enough for him to be able to start lecturing to students. His work in anatomy and diseases of the lower abdomen soon became well known, and as he grew more famous, so he numbered many rich and famous people among his patients. In Leyden he entertained lavishly, to the disapproval of the Elders there, who talked disparagingly of the 'infection' of a French atmosphere, for Drelincourt was a Catholic, and some people even thought that he could have been an enemy agent. Had the Princess been at the Hague at the time of her miscarriage, he could have reached her quickly; he probably visited his patients at the Hague by means of the regular Delft *trek* boat, one of the comfortable craft which plied the waterways, serving food on board, and travelling so smoothly that passengers could read a book on the journey. There was also Cornelis Solingen, a well-known surgeon and obstetrician, who practised at the Hague, and whose forceps can still be seen in the Rijksmuseum voor de Geschiedenis der Natuurwetenschappen at Leyden. Either of these doctors, had they been called in, would have probably been skilled enough to give her the treatment which would have enabled her to have more children without further trouble; but it is also probable that there was no very skilled doctor in attendance at Breda.

The miscarriage was a great disappointment, to William and Mary themselves and to their supporters. The Princess received an anxious letter from her father, begging her to be 'more carefuller of herself' in the future. As soon as she was better she made her 'solemn entrance' into the town of Breda, and then the Prince sent her back to Honselaersdyck, for in any case it was hardly wise to let her stay so near the front at this time. Even the Prince had to admit that his country was on the verge of defeat. Ghent and Bruges had fallen to the French all too easily, and everyone saw that unless England could be persuaded to come to the rescue, the Dutch would be unable to stand out on their own. Lawrence Hyde was under no illusions, and he did his best to warn people at home of the danger:

The French are in the very heart of the country, ready on one hand to swallow all, and on the other hand, flattering this state with all the good words and artifices imaginable, that they, I mean the French, may avoid the only thing that can be hurtful to them, a perfect good understanding between us and the Dutch.

The basis of William's talks with his uncles had been that Louis should be forced to surrender the fortress towns he had gained, before peace talks began, but as long as England procrastinated, the French King knew that he could dictate whatever terms he chose. He knew, too, that many of the Dutch were ready to accept defeat and to grasp peace at any price. History has a habit of repeating itself and just like his father before him, William found that the States of Holland, on whom, being so rich and powerful, most of the burden of maintaining an army fell, were only too ready to come to terms with the enemy.

Mary appeared to make a good recovery, and this was helped by the fact that William himself came back from the front in mid-May in order to be present at the vital debates which were going on in the Assembly of the States of Holland. It was a fine, warm May, and Hyde's wife, coming over from England to join her husband, had such a calm crossing that nobody was 'sicker nor more sensible of the voyage than if they had been going from London to Twickenham'. But the Prince had to spend most of his time indoors, attending the sessions of the Assembly which went on late into the evening. All the time he was expecting to be called back to the army, for French troops were massing at a new rendezvous. The situation began to look so black, and the hope of standing up to a French onslaught so remote, that on June 1 the Dutch were forced to seek a truce.

This meant that for six summer weeks the Prince was at home and out of danger. Had it not been war time, he would have taken his wife to visit his country houses, but he was too busy with military affairs to leave Honselaersdyck. All the same, he found time to enjoy some hunting or the occasional game of tennis. It was the Princess's first summer in Holland, and she now had a chance to explore the country to which she had come and to discover its fascination. The spring, as Temple told Sidney, was nowhere more beautiful than at the Hague from April to the middle of June, with the blossom in the avenues and the lime trees in bloom in the Voorhout. While William indulged in more active pastimes, the Princess and her ladies went out in one of the *trekschuyten*, the gilded canal boats with their colourful canopies and fluttering pennants. When she travelled on land, the Princess rode in one of the Prince's coaches, drawn by half a dozen dapple-grey horses, magnificent broad-backed creatures, their harness decorated with orange plumes. The canal boats, however, were by far the most comfortable method of locomotion, and as she drifted gently along, the Princess could admire the gracious houses which bordered the waterways outside the Hague, and the gardens which ran down to the water's edge. Clipped hedges and green obelisks, immaculate parterres, trees in tubs, yew pyramids, statuary and topiary, all these filled the pleasure grounds of the neat houses that could be glimpsed from the boats. The gardens reflected the domestic outlook of the Dutch themselves, and although refugee Huguenots were beginning to import many ideas from France, the grand manner had to be tamed to suit the flat and formal character of the landscape. The Dutch were a seafaring nation and loved to see the pennants fluttering at the masts of boats beyond their garden hedges. The influence of the Orient could be seen in the brilliant colours of the tulips, ranunculus and pinks decorating the formal borders, and travellers were now bringing back exotic plants which Dutch gardeners were learning to cultivate in greenhouses.

There was, however, a certain sameness about the lowlands, with often little except a windmill to enliven the scene; Walter Harris missed the variety of the English landscape, for, as he put it, 'one place has the same aspect and resemblance to another, as an egg is like to an egg'. So the Princess and her train often whiled away the time playing cards, or gossiping about a variety of subjects, or doing their embroidery. Dr Hooper, the Princess's chaplain, considered it a part of his task to extend his protection to the female company on all its pleasant expeditions. He was a rather fussy man who, on account of his premature baldness, was nicknamed 'Father Hooper' by the Archbishops Sancroft and Dolben. They advised him to buy a peruke, even though wigs were as a rule considered too effeminate for the clergy at that time. When the ladies were busy with their embroidery he would read aloud to them, and the Princess sometimes asked him to do so in French. Although his accent, on his own admission, was excruciating, 'she graciously bid him to go on, and she would tell him when he was wrong or at a loss'. Hooper, described by Evelyn as 'one of the finest pulpit men in the country,' was probably more than half in love with his mistress, for she seemed to exert an irresistible, but very proper, attraction over most of her ecclesiastical advisers. Hooper was amazed to find that though she was still only sixteen, her youthful charm was tempered with a thoughfulness for others which one would hardly expect to find in anyone of such tender years. When she attended chapel she was so anxious not to keep anyone waiting that she told Hooper to inform her when the congregation was assembled, and then always came at once. He found that she was fair-minded, had no favourites, and had such an influence over her retainers that 'if she looked but grave at anything said by any of them, there was an immediate silence'.

It is as well that William's opinion of their watery expeditions has not been recorded. One suspects that he would happily have drowned the whole boat-load, with the exception of his wife. The Prince, whose coffers were much depleted by the war, had to keep up a large staff which included pages, foot soldiers, gentlemen servants, kitchen servants and Switzers, as well as many others who 'lived out'. The invasion by English maids of honour put an extra strain on his finances, all the more so as his wife had no income of her own, and as her uncle was apparently in no hurry to pay her promised dowry. In his youth William had managed to rid himself of his hated governors by making life so unpleasant for them by his coldness that they had been only too glad to retire from his service; now he tried the same technique on the English retainers, though these proved even more difficult to shake off. All he achieved was a reputation for rudeness and meanness, for the English observed many examples of what they considered to be his parsimonious behaviour. In addition to paying for her attendants, the Prince had to give his wife an allowance, and her private account book shows that she even let some of this go to people to whom the Prince was already paying a salary. Her nurse, Mrs Langford, 'my mam', was given a thousand gelders a year, which the Princess said she had promised to pay 'whenever I should marry'; and one of the Villiers sisters was given the same treatment. Mary's allowance came to no more than 4,000 gelders, about £4,000 a year, which was little enough for a royal princess, especially as she had to buy all her clothes and jewellery herself and still managed to give a large proportion to charity.

As soon as his master married, William Bentinck began to look about for a wife, and he chose one of the Villiers sisters, Anne, who was the most likeable of the maids of honour. They were setting up house at Sorgvliet, not far from the Hague, and later became, for William and Mary, the most valued of friends. Lady Inchiquin, like Anne, was one of the least troublesome of the English ladies; she served the Princess faithfully without too much self-seeking, although her father, the Earl of Orrery, did take the opportunity of writing from Castle Martyr in Ireland, asking the Princess to take an interest in a play he had written called *Herod the Grate* [sic] which had never been acted. 'I writt this play,' he told her, 'some years since, having observed that every nation had been acted on the English theatres except the Jewish, whose stories afford a great argument for the stage.' The struggling, if noble, playwright, had hopes that if his play on the subject of Herod should prove pleasing, she would take an interest in some of his work 'on sacred things . . . for they will furnish your Highness with subjects, upon which you may exercise your charity, in pardoning ill performances. . . .'

Another welcome member of Mary's suite was the dwarf painter Richard Gibsone who had come out to Holland to continue her instruction in drawing; he helped her to develop her acknowledged talent in miniature-painting. But William made no secret of the fact that he found some of her attendants quite superfluous, and he did his best to ignore their existence. In particular he resented the fact that the English Church in its wisdom had seen fit to provide her with two chaplains, one for her household, and one to supervise her personal devotions. The Anglicans were tortured by the fear that the Princess, having been saved from Catholicism, was now going to fall a prey to the twin danger of Calvinism. The Prince had lent Mary books which, in Hooper's view, were likely 'to incline her to a more favourable opinion of the dissenters, than was consistent with that regard which a person so near the crown ought to have'. Hooper did his best to counteract William's influence by providing her with literature that would give her a better idea of her Church of England obligations. One day the Prince came into her room and found her sitting with Eusebio's *Church History* and Hooker's *Ecclesiastical Polity* in front of her. He was not pleased. 'What!' he exclaimed. 'I suppose Dr Hooper persuades you to read these books.' He might well have thought that such learned works were heavy reading for a fifteen-year-old bride.

In all the controversies that arose in the early days between her husband

and her English household, the Princess steered a tactful middle course. She obviously saw a far more congenial side of his character than they did. It was only his more intimate friends who heard him laugh, and he had built up a defence against those who wished to turn casual contacts into friendship. '*Ik sall zien*', 'I'll see', was one of his sayings, and those closest to him knew that this really meant 'no'. To his favourites he was generous and open, but he undoubtedly did have a parsimonious streak, for it was sometimes said that he underpaid those who served him well. On the whole William fell in with anyone who walked in his own straight paths, and he felt at ease with men of integrity and courage. On the other hand he disliked people who were pompous and wordy. He fitted in well in the Temple household, where he was in the habit of supping twice a week; he was fond of Sir William and Lady Temple, and enjoyed their 'plain manner of eating'. On the other hand, he disliked Arlington, whose sententious letters made his blood boil, and Arlington for his part found William dry and sullen. Men who indulged in what Temple described as 'a forced or squeezed strain of humour' held no attraction for the Prince. He could not wait to escape from tedious company, and it suited him well to sit alone with his wife in the evenings, listening to her lively and harmless conversation. It was thanks to the unsociability which so many people disliked, that Mary was able to enjoy a more private and domestic life than many other princesses of her time. The querulous Sir Gabriel might complain about the *chicheté* which Mary had brought to her husband's court, but apart from the card playing and the plethora of ladies, the Princess had done nothing to bring back the hectic gaiety which the Hague had known in the days of William's great-uncle Prince Maurice, or even in the days of his father, when Elizabeth of Bohemia had lived there with her marriageable daughters.

The weeks of truce passed happily enough for the Princess, but there was an undertone of anxiety during these summer days, for Louis still kept up the siege of Mons. The negotiators hurried to and fro with peace terms, but William reminded everyone that unless the French loosed their hold on this strategic town and furthermore moved out all of the fortresses which were to come under discussion at the peace conference, all talks and negotiations would in the long run prove futile. He was convinced that Louis did not intend to enter into serious discussion until after the fall of Mons, and having gained this prize, he would insist on keeping it, and thus dominating the Netherlands for years to come. The French King was growing increasingly truculent, confident as he was that 'the boastful fisherfolk', as he liked to call the Dutch, were already on the point of surrender. It was reported that he enjoyed saying that the marriage of the Prince and Princess of Orange was a case of 'two beggars being well met'. This incensed the Duke of York, who was sensitive about his dignity. At the moment, James was urging his brother to assert himself more, and to make himself independent of the English Parliament and of French money. In his opinion, the King had no more power than the Duke of Venice, and this was to become one of his favourite sayings in the years ahead, appearing like a refrain in many of his letters.

Pride and over-confidence now caused Louis to make a blunder. The truce ended abruptly when on June 24 he published the most outrageous demands, and stated categorically that he had no intention of releasing his hold on any of the towns he had conquered in the Low Countries. The implications of this new move were clear. In the course of the peace talks, Louis might agree to surrender the notorious towns, but there was no guarantee that he would actually do so. What was even more certain was that the English Parliament and the Dutch Assembly, both of which had a neurotic fear of maintaining armies in times of peace, would vote away the means of enforcing the treaty. Louis would refuse to move from the towns, and nobody would have the strength to make him.

The English were roused to a fury by the French King's behaviour, and Temple was sent over at once to engineer an alliance with the Dutch. Temple was far more popular than Hyde, in fact it was said in Holland that they looked on his coming like the swallow's which brought fair weather always with it. The day after the treaty was signed, William left for the front. He knew that Mons would soon be forced to surrender from sheer starvation, for all food stocks would be exhausted by the end of July. As always, when he was off to active service, he was in a good humour, but the fact that he did not have the resources to play the French at their own game accounted for an underlying melancholy. Sophia of Hanover said this was because, politically, people put 'too much water in his wine'.

The Princess was left alone once again to face loneliness and anxiety. 'There never was so desolate a place as the Hague at this time,' Hyde recorded. But at least she and Anne Bentinck had one consolation—they were both expecting a child. 'I have played the whore a little,' Mary confessed to her first 'husband,' and she added 'because the sea parts us you may believe it is a bastard'. She begged Frances to keep the news to herself, as it could not be 'above 6 or 7 weeks at most'. Her step-mother had been badgering her for 'news', but she did not want anyone else to be let into the secret at this stage.

As William marched on Mons with an army of 45,000 men, the French hastily confronted the delegates at Nimeguen, and told them that Louis would agree to withdraw from the town if peace were signed at once. No one at the peace conference wished to prolong the war, and, taken aback by the sudden ultimatum, the delegates signed, late at night on August 10, a document calling for immediate peace. The next day, William, with Ossory at his side, joined battle with the enemy at Saint-Denis. It was a hard-fought but inconclusive struggle, and it was not until the end of the day that William learned that his country had made peace a few hours before the battle began. His enemies made out that he had actually received a message which he had put in his pocket and chosen to ignore; he could well have been incredulous that his country had acted so precipitately, and without proper consultation with Spain.

In England many people were disappointed that the union with the Dutch had lasted such a short time; they would have liked the chance to teach Louis, 'that proud and potent King', a lesson. The French Ambassador at the Hague, on the other hand, was in an exultant mood; he made an ostentatious display, which included two fountains outside his house gushing wine for passers-by to drink. In 1668 William had marked the end of the war with a *Ballet de la Paix*, in which he himself had played the part of Mercury bringing good tidings of peace and prosperity to the spectators, but this time he took no part in the celebrations.

By August 25 it was generally known in court circles that the Princess was pregnant 'for certain'. The weather at this time was fine and warm, and the Princess stayed at Honselaersdyck, without visiting the Hague, where the Prince's apartments at the Binnenhof were undergoing repairs and renovations. Early in September William went away to visit his estate at Hooge Soeren. He did not take his wife with him; it would have been unwise to risk a second miscarriage. All the same, the Princess was unwell at this time. It was thought that she was suffering from one of the recurrent malarial types of fever which were prevalent in the Low Countries especially during the summer months. Temple, who went to visit William at his hunting lodge, with the good news that Mary's dowry of £20,000 had at last been paid, was able to report that the Princess was better, all of which put the Prince into a good humour; Temple said he had never seen him look 'so bold or so pleasant'.

The Princess was treated with asses' milk and physic, which, as she confessed herself, left her feeling very low. Early in autumn there were rumours of a threatened miscarriage. Her father, who was alarmed by reports of continued ill-health, wrote to warn her of the dangers of too much standing, and Mary Beatrice, who was genuinely fond of her

step-daughter, decided that she would like to go over to Holland to see
the Princess for herself.

England was in the throes of a major crisis following the discovery of a
supposed plot on the King's life, but this had not prevented the royal
brothers from making their usual plans to go to Newmarket. It was not
in the King's nature to deprive himself of his pleasures, and at this time
the Duke made a point of going with him wherever he went; some people
thought that the visit was an 'indecent levity' in the circumstances. The
Duchess believed that her trip abroad would help to rid her of the boredom
she always felt when her husband was away enjoying himself at the races.
She went into the matter and discovered that she could easily go and come
back before the Duke returned from Newmarket; if the wind proved
favourable, the journey would not take more than twenty-four hours from
door to door.

CHAPTER 7

DEAR LEMON

SOME PEOPLE thought they could see political implications in the Duchess of York's visit to the Hague; they believed that Mary Beatrice was being sent as an envoy to make a firmer liaison between England and the United Provinces. Barillon, the French Ambassador in London, was, however, sceptical about this; he inclined to the view that the visit was '*un voyage de pur plaisir*'. The Duchess told her brother in Modena that she was going because her step-daughter, who was four months pregnant, was very unwell and had a great desire to see her, as well as her sister Anne. Mary Beatrice confessed that she loved the Princess as if she were her own daughter, besides, she was very curious to see the Netherlands. The Duke, for his part, was pleased to think of her visiting his daughter, and was also glad that she was to be given a chance to enjoy herself for a few days in these difficult times.

A messenger arrived on September 27 with a letter in which the Duke assured William that the Duchess and Lady Anne would travel incognito, bringing very few people with them. They were anxious to have accommodation as near Mary's court as possible. The 'little company' mentioned by the Duke in his letter nevertheless included the Duchesses of Richmond, Buckingham and Monmouth; Lord Ossory, who had returned to England in September, was also one of the party, but he was always a welcome visitor. Plans had to be made at short notice, and it was decided that the Duchess and her train should be accommodated in the quarters normally occupied by the Hyde and Temple families at the Old Court in the Noordeinde at the Hague. Hyde took the first alternative house he could find, and decided to live there permanently; he said it was the first warm place he had come across since his arrival in Holland—a great improvement on 'the wide Old Court'. William had the apartments refurnished, and the general opinion was that the visit was going to cost him *een stuyvertie*, a pretty penny.

William was subjected to a certain amount of badinage on the subject of his in-laws, and the arrival of the visitors caused a great deal of excitement and speculation. On October 13 everyone was awaiting the boat which was due to arrive at any time, loaded with five or six Princesses and Duchesses. This *'belle troupe'*, as one observer called it, was given an ecstatic welcome by Princess Mary; people commented, in particular, on the affectionate way in which she greeted her sister. Anne had changed little. She was as stolid as ever and not at all abstemious in the matter of food. Lake had made it his duty, the previous spring, to tell the Princess that her sister had received the Holy Sacrament. He had omitted to add that he had been scandalized to notice her help herself to several good gulps of the Communion wine, a characteristic action, but one which put her spiritual mentor in agony in case her father should notice and think her inadequately prepared by her Church of England tutors. The Duchess and her stepdaughter went straight from the waterside to their lodgings in the Princess's coaches, and Mary was carried over to see them in her chair. William arrived back the same evening from Soestdyck. The girls, who were all still in their teens, found that separation had done nothing to spoil their friendship. A new nickname was found for Mary; since her husband was Prince of Orange, she was to be known as 'Lemon'. William went out of his way to be friendly and hospitable. During their stay a troop of strolling Flemish players was performing in the town. The fact that they were there enabled the Director, Jan Baptiste van Fornenberg, to put on his shows without the permission of the Ministers, who cried out more loudly about the Comedy than they did about the greatest sins in the world.

The travellers returned on November 18, arriving back at eleven at night on the same day as the King and the Duke returned from Newmarket, after a slow calm crossing. They seemed pleased, even elated, after their journey. 'I must give you a thousand thanks,' James wrote to his son-in-law, 'from her, and from myself for her kind usage by you. I should say more on this subject, but I am very ill at compliments and you care not for them.' It was a pleasant interlude for the Duchess, who went back to find London, to use her own word, full of *'imbrogli'*. The alleged Popish plot had gained credence on the flimsiest of evidence; in the opinion of many foreigners, the English would believe anything if they were in the mood for it. The fabricated tales of such 'mean divines' as Titus Oates and Dr Tonge had been accepted because James's open Catholicism, his desire to head an army, and his generally unbalanced behaviour had created the right climate. Many were only too ready to believe that Oates's stories were evidence of 'a hellish and damnable design to assassinate the King'. Although Charles was sceptical about the truth of the allegations,

he was too afraid of the force of public opinion to make a stand. He
watched helplessly as one Catholic after the other was implicated, though
at least he defended the Queen when she was accused of intending to
poison him. She might be a weak woman who had 'some disagreeable
humours', but he refused to let her suffer at the hands of false witnesses.

The Duchess's secretary, Coleman, had been arrested just before her
visit to Holland. No evidence came to light to prove that he had been implicated in any plot against the King's life, but it was clear from the letters
that he had corresponded freely with the Jesuits, and in general had
indiscreetly pursued his aim of rooting out 'the pestilent heresy that had
reigned so long in these northern kingdoms'. He was executed in December, and there was '*une grande consternation*' in the Duke's household.
The feeling prevailed that James was lost; he himself was anxious and
sad, and the Duchess feared for his life. In the Lords several influential
peers, and the old enemy, Bishop Compton, called on the King to banish
the Duke from his counsels. There was even talk around the town of
substituting William for James as heir to the throne. A general edict that
no papist was to be allowed within ten miles of the capital ensured that the
Duchess had to part with all her Catholic retainers. There was no *alle-
grezza* for her now; all that had been left behind in Holland where for a
short time she had been able to enjoy herself with her dear Lemon.

William did his best to spare his wife any unnecessary anxiety, and tried
to keep on good terms with her father. He received endless letters from
the prolific James, which were a mixture of references to the weather,
protestations of esteem, concern for Mary's health, and such inept pieces
of advice as 'do not exasperate France that may be of use to you'. All the
same, it is clear from a letter which William wrote to Hyde, that he was
under no illusions about the cause of the troubles in England; he feared
they would get no better unless God should see fit to enlighten '*him* who
I sadly fear will suffer in all this'.

The Prince was anxious about the progress of the peace talks which
were going on as slowly as ever at Nimeguen. Temple reported that the
Imperialist and French delegates were still busy fencing—making endless
closes but always parting again—so that they were no further ahead than
they had been two months before. The French were receding every day
from their original promises; although Maastricht had been evacuated
there were still several disputed towns in French hands, and the English
were being far less pressing than William could have wished. Inevitably
the States of Holland had begun to agitate for the reduction of Dutch
forces, and the Prince, a wiser and more restrained man than his father,

was trying to direct affairs through constitutional channels in ways that he had learnt in the days of de Witt's tuition. He gave up time to eat and converse frequently with deputies from many different towns, and gradually his credit began to increase in his own country. Temple was struck all over again by his good sense and prudence which he now felt were mated with greatness and authority. The States were beginning to realize what a 'rascally peace' they had made, and how right William's advice had proved to be in so many ways.

The cessation of hostilities at least gave the Prince a chance to devote more attention to his property, and to reorganize his estates. The House in the Wood, the small summer Palace near the Hague, where William's grandmother, Amalia of Solms, had spent much of her life, needed little renovation, for Amalia had furnished it richly, with lavish silks and brocades, chimney pieces by Pieter de Post and paintings by Rubens, Van Dyck and Honthorst. Here there were portraits of many of the relations: Mary's grandmother-in-law with her three youngest daughters, all with attendant cherubims, and William II with Mary Stuart, holding hands as betrothed children, the boy looking shy, and his bride, cold and composed even at that early age.

At Soestdyck the painter Lairesse had been engaged to paint pastoral pictures on the wall of the main rooms and in the Prince's bedroom. William also had plans for the extension of his hunting lodge at Dieren to make it possible for the Princess to accompany him to Gelderland the following summer. He had decided to choose as his chief architect Daniel Marot, a French Huguenot whose work was becoming increasingly popular in Holland. Many new appointments were made at this time, and for the head gardener at Honselaersdyck, Charles de Buisson, a list of careful instructions was drawn up concerning the care of plants and paths, orange trees and flowers, and all the pruning and grafting necessary in a big garden. Whenever possible fresh flowers were to be brought into the Palace twice a week. In January 1678 Charles Gerbay was appointed as *chirurgyn* to the domestic staff, with orders to attend to all employees without distinction of quality or sex. Altogether William was giving thought and care to the organization of his own affairs, since public matters were claiming less of his time.

After Christmas exceptionally cold weather set in. Temple had a miserable journey to Nimeguen, where he had to go in order to be present at the signing of the peace treaty. The snowdrifts were ten foot high, there were coaches and waggons on the Rhine, several postboys died on the road and people were walking about with long icicles hanging from their noses. It was unlikely that the Prince would allow his wife to go out in this *'furieux froid'* as Susanna Huygens called it, but her failure to appear in public was beginning to cause comment. The French Ambassador, d'Avaux, was looking for some way of making trouble for the Prince, and he spread it about that the Princess was being kept a prisoner at Honselaersdyck. People now began to remember what an austere 'man's man' William had always been before his wedding, looking upon marriage as a duty, something that he knew 'was a thing to be done at one time or other', and even admitting that he might not be too easy for a wife to live with. How could a man like this ever become the ideal husband? The Princess's apparent melancholy lent colour to these stories, but it is probable that her seclusion and low spirits were due to bad health rather than her husband's unkindness. D'Avaux's calumnies were part of a campaign that had begun as soon as he arrived at the Hague. He made a point of being publicly uncivil whenever he could, and said openly that he had come as Ambassador to the States and not to the Prince.

Rumours soon reached England, and Mary Beatrice was prepared to believe that William was ill-treating her step-daughter, only allowing her out for a walk once a week and making her spend the months of her pregnancy in great loneliness. The Duke was also anxious and he wrote saying that his wife would probably visit the Princess sometime before the birth of her child. Then, to the shock and surprise of all concerned, not only the Duchess turned up at the Hague at the beginning of March, but also James himself. They stayed for a few days before going on to Brussels.

Affairs having reached such a crisis in England, the King had decided to deprive himself of his brother's presence for a while in the hope of bringing down the political temperature. So long as he himself did not have to go on his travels again he did not care whether James was one side of the Channel or the other, but he was prepared to resist to the last any suggestion of excluding his brother from the succession. He did not mind if Parliament wanted to 'pare the nails of a Popish successor', but he would not brook any interference with the hereditary principle.

No rhetoric, Burnet said, would have prevailed on the Duke to leave England, if the King had not told him positively that it was for the best and must be done. James shed many tears at parting, but the King shed none. The Duke and Duchess, accompanied by very few domestics, travelled to Rotterdam, where William gave them an impressive welcome, and then sent them on, in three of his yachts, to Brussels, where the British Resident met them with twenty coaches. The Duchess's intention was to leave again for the Hague almost at once, for both she and the Duke, and indeed everyone else, had grown alarmed about the fact that Mary had gone well over her nine months and yet there was still no sign of a child or indeed any hope of a confinement.

There must have been some very red faces among the doctors at the Palace that spring. At some stage the Prince's physicians, who were amongst the most eminent in the country, had made a wrong diagnosis, and had been too cowardly to disillusion the patient. She had been allowed to make all the usual preparations for the birth of a child, and the nursery had been furnished down to the last detail. So sure had William been that an heir was expected that at Christmas time he asked the States-General to stand sponsors to the child when it arrived; in late February it was reported that he would be returning from a journey to Gelderland where he was supervising alterations to his hunting lodge at Dieren, as in a short time the Princess was 'due to put a little prince into the world.' In spite of these evidences of good faith, William's enemies were soon making out that he had invented the pregnancy to disconcert his rivals. Mary Beatrice was of the opinion that it had been entirely imaginary from the start, while the court gossips were sure that although William shared a bed with one of the most beautiful women in Europe, he had never given her any cause to hope for a child. Sophia of Hanover told her brother that the kind of fever Mary had been suffering from could produce the same symptoms as pregnancy. 'If you remember,' she wrote, 'they bled me for this at Heidelberg and Prince Edward twitted me and said that I had been delivered.' She had also heard that at a large dinner party at the Hague, one of the gentlemen of the company had averred that the Prince would never have any children, and spoke about this 'in such a demonstrative manner that all the ladies looked down at their plates in embarrassment'. Sophia's brother took up this theme in his next letter, telling her that he himself suffered from a certain irritation (he refrained from telling her the cause given by the doctors, for fear of making her look down at her plate out of modesty like the ladies of the Hague). 'I would think,' wrote the Elector Palatine, 'that the Prince of Orange has a far greater need of that particular superfluity with which those people are so anxious to credit me.'

A possible explanation is that the Princess's autumn illness had produced bilious symptoms which could have been mistaken for those of early pregnancy. There had been talk at the end of September of a threatened miscarriage and the Princess could actually have miscarried at that time. It is even more likely that her bad miscarriage at Breda set up an infection which was mistaken for a malarial fever, and which was the cause of permanent infertility. Whatever anyone else might think, the Princess continued to believe that she might be able to bear children; the words of the angel to Zaccharias were in her mind to the end of her life. The fact that she still continued to hope suggests that William did not fail to play his part.

In any case, for the time being, the disappointment and humiliation were extreme. What perhaps made it worse was the fact that in February Anne Bentinck had given birth to her child in a normal manner. The disappointment was a bitter blow, too, for the Orangists, who felt that William himself had been such a miracle, an only son born when, for a fortnight, there had been no Orangist heir. What a relief it had been, too, when he had lived through the smallpox that had proved fatal to his father and mother, and how they had wished to see him in the happy state of being able to perpetuate the race. It had seemed, once, as if God had listened to their prayers and now that he had abandoned them in the end.

The shock of discovering, after all the weeks of expectation and preparation, that she was not to have a child, left the Princess prostrate. In April she had a recurrence of her fever, and it was a very sharp attack, accompanied by an agonizing pain in the hip. This adds weight to the theory that the fever was a result of an infection caused by the miscarriage. Bulstrode, the British Ambassador in Brussels, told Sir Joseph Williamson that he had heard the Princess had suffered three fits of a tertian ague, but that after being let blood she had felt better. This was on April 14, and a few days later her father reported her eleventh ague fit. The 'cold fit', however, was not so long as it had been at first, and he had hoped that she was on the mend. At the beginning of May he wrote to the Prince saying he was glad his daughter had not had an ague for some days, and hoping that once the warmer weather set in, the illness would not recur.

It was summer time now, and the Dutch people were gradually emerging from war-time austerity. In the winter the fashionable world had flocked to see the French comedians who had arrived in the Hague after the end of hostilities, much to the disgust of the local company, which found itself deprived of its regular audiences. The Prince could never enjoy visiting the theatre because the hot atmosphere brought on attacks of asthma, but he encouraged the Princess to patronize both companies and helped out with welcome financial support. To keep the theatres going in the summer season was, however, something of a problem, for as soon as the warmer weather came rich patrons preferred to be outside in the fresh air, strolling in the Voorhout where they could see and be seen. In May the celebrations of the Kermesse provided another distraction, and this year, with the coming of peace, the carnival was more elaborate than it had been for twelve years. The main attraction was a group of tight-rope walkers, in particular a man with a girl of ten years old standing balanced on his shoulders, who ran up a ladder and proceeded to do a dance on the tight rope.

The Princess was well enough to watch some of the festivities from a window at the Binnenhof, and once the Kermesse was over she set off for her first visit to Dieren, where she and the Prince were expected to stay for six weeks. As soon as she had gone the town emptied, and Henry Sidney, who had been sent to the Hague as British Envoy in place of Henry Hyde, found it 'something dismal'.

The journey to Dieren seemed rather long to the Princess, for it took all night to travel from the Hague to Utrecht by boat, but she felt none the worse when she arrived and indeed she told Frances that she believed she had been cured of her 'everyday ague'. Dieren was set in pleasant rolling countryside, well-wooded, with tracts of moorland ideal for hunting. The air in Gelderland was fresher and far healthier than the humid atmosphere in the low-lying lands round the Hague. The alterations to the house which William had ordered during the winter months made it more or less habitable for the Princess, and he planned further extensions to the house and garden, with fishponds and orchards. It remained, even when all the improvements were completed, one of the most unassuming of all the Prince's properties, a small brick house with a little clock-tower in blue and gilt over the very ordinary green front door, which had not so much as a single step leading up to it. Later there was to be a square pond and a magnificent grotto with walks shaded by pleasant arbours, but for the time being it was only a hunting lodge with limited rooms for visitors, a quiet retreat for a young couple who had spent the first eighteen months of their marriage without any respite from the anxieties of war and the claims of State affairs.

CHAPTER 8

SUMMER AT DIEREN

WHEN the Prince was at Dieren he cut himself off completely from all business and devoted himself to the pleasures of the chase. It was Temple who said that William loved hunting as much as he hated swearing. For the first time the Princess saw him in a really carefree mood, enjoying the company of his closest friends. Ossory, whose regiment was scattered, spent much of the summer at Dieren, and Henry Sidney paid his first visit to the Prince and Princess in August. It was he who as Master of the Horse in the York household had, supposedly, fallen in love with Mary's mother. He was, in Burnet's words, 'a man of a sweet and caressing temper, had no malice in his heart, but too great a love of pleasure'. Sylvius, who had been left behind at the Hague, fed the newcomer with stories about William's boorishness; but Sidney soon found that he could discount the Hofmeister's sour comments. At first he was not over impressed with Dieren; he called it an 'ill house', perhaps because there was not room for him to stay there. William had deliberately not enlarged it so as to accommodate all the 'beggarly bitches', who, with the exception of Lady Inchiquin and one or two others, had remained at the Hague, and found great solace in Sidney's company.

William's summer court was informal and friendly. The Prince invited Sidney into his room for a friendly talk the first time he saw him, and asked him a great many questions. Afterwards he went through to see the Princess and gave her some letters. Like everyone else he was struck by her good looks, and he later told her father she appeared to be so well that although she had informed him she was going to the baths at Aix he could not believe she needed any remedies.

The Princess's apparently blooming health was often deceptive, and William had been anxious about her that summer. In June she had suffered further ague fits which had assailed her at regular intervals for nearly a week; she eventually had to submit to a vomit, but still continued to have fits even after this drastic and unpleasant treatment. Her health was being cared for by Charles Drelincourt who, besides being a professor of medicine at Leyden, was also a doctor of divinity; his treatise, *A Christian Defence against the Fears of Death*, had proved to be a best-seller for all its sombre subject. It was probably Drelincourt who recommended that the Princess should drink the waters at Spa and take the baths at Aix.

It was too hot in August to make the journey and the Princess remained at Dieren quietly, doing her embroidery during the daytime—she had spent ninety-five gelders on gold thread in April before leaving for the country—and in the evening supping and talking with the Prince and his closest friends. There is no evidence that he felt any bitterness, or bore his wife any malice for their recent disappointment.

In September the Princess set off for Aix, while William remained at Dieren for the weather was now cooler and perfect for hunting. On her way, at Nimeguen, she dined with Sir Leoline Jenkins, the English mediator at the peace treaty, who had delayed his departure from the town especially to have the honour of entertaining the popular princess. Sir Leoline was the son of a Glamorganshire yeoman and had reached his high position by his own hard work and effort. He was the kind of learned but plodding man whom William disliked, and he had not been invited to join the company at Dieren. According to d'Estrades, the former Ambassador, he was '*un homme peu résolutif*'; worse still, from William's point of view, he was 'set on every punctilio of the Church of England to superstition'. The Princess evidently summed him up accurately at her first meeting, for when Temple and Jenkins were together at the Hague, Temple sent a message to the Princess asking for leave to receive the Communion next day in her chapel. She gave orders to her chaplain to make everything ready, ' "for though I am persuaded" says she "he does not intend it, and by tomorrow will bethink himself of some business or excuse, yet my Lord Ambassador Jenkins I doubt not will be there" '— and she was right.

While Mary was away, the Prince seemed uneasy and distressed. He was anxious about the Bentincks, for Anne had been dangerously ill with an infectious fever, and other members of the family had succumbed to it, though in a milder form. One day, after he had returned to Honselaersdyck, Sidney met him in a passage at the Palace and told him that the King had been taken ill very suddenly—'he was very sick in his stomake'—and that James, to everyone's amazement, had gone over to England to see him. William remained calm, saying that he did not blame him, and adding that had he been in his father-in-law's place he would probably have done the same. It seemed that the Duke's friends had sent alarmist reports of the King's health and had advised him to come at once to safeguard his interests. He went over in disguise in a French shallop, landed at Dover, and, without being recognized, rode post-haste to London, where he spent the night with the Apsleys. By the time he arrived at Windsor, the crisis had passed; it was something of an anti-climax to find the King sitting up in bed shaving. Having, as one of Sidney's friends put it, 'exchanged water gruel and potions for mutton and partridges', Charles, with the help of Jesuit's powder, had averted the crisis which everyone feared so much. 'Good God, what a change would such an accident make! The very thought of it frights me out of my wits,' Savile told Sidney. Foul play was universally suspected, for, as Lady Sutherland put it, 'there is scarce anybody beyond Temple Bar that believes his distemper proceeded from anything but poison, though as little like it as if he had fallen from a horse'.

By the time the Princess arrived back in mid-September, the excitement was nearly over. Sidney met her at Breda and was later joined by the Prince. She began to make plans at once to go to Brussels to see her father as soon as he returned from his visit to England. Her sister Anne and also her half-sister Isabella had been sent out to Brussels in August to help James feel resigned to his exile, although it seems that he had submitted to the idea of a long stay, since he had already demanded his hounds, his hunting coaches, his town coaches, and his hunters. These were all to come over via Dover, the shortest route. He had also asked for such faithful retainers as Lord and Lady Peterborough and Lady Bellasyse, although he was not too fussy about which route they chose to come by. He was always gloomy about the situation in England, prophesying rebellion and reiterating over and over again that his brother had less power than the Duke of Venice. The Duchess tried to be as philosophical as possible about what she called '*nostra peregrinatione*'. She would have liked to fill in the time by going back to Italy for a while, but this was considered unwise and she had to be content with a visit from her mother who thought she had grown rather thin. The only really good piece of news they received was that Oates had fallen ill with jaundice, which all devout Catholics hoped would be 'the first of many just castigations'.

The Prince decided that he would not accompany his wife to Brussels, for, as he said, 'he should be sorry to be clapped up in the castle at Antwerp, which he thinks would be likely enough if he passed that way'. Plans for the Princess's journey were well advanced when some very startling news was received from England. It seemed that the King, on recovering from his illness, had banished his beloved son Monmouth, who was said to be coming over to Holland with Utrecht as his eventual destination. It was now generally known that the Duke of York, rather shamefaced at arriving in England to find his brother looking so healthy, had apologetically said that he would go back to Brussels, or anywhere else that the King liked to send him. But he stayed long enough to persuade Charles that it was unfair to let the Duke of Monmouth remain in England while he himself was sent into exile. Jealousy of his nephew had been smouldering in James's heart for years, and in recent months he had been continually warning his brother of the danger of showing his natural son so much favour. The King was surrounded by knaves and mean-spirited men; 'break in upon them before they are formed or have a man to lead them' was James's advice, and he added, 'the only person capable (I think) of that employment (pardon me for naming him) is the Duke of Monmouth'.

The Princess's relations were behaving in a strange, and really rather ludicrous manner. Monmouth embarked on the royal barge which was to take him to Greenwich; hard on his tail was his uncle the Duke of York, who set off down the river on the first stage of his journey to Brussels. William, however, failed to see the funny side of his in-laws' odd behaviour. It would be hard to imagine a more embarrassing visitor than the Duke of Monmouth. The Prince had just returned from a pleasant shooting expedition at Moredyck when this new surprise was sprung on him. The Protestant Duke arrived in the Hague towards the end of September, and gave Sidney the pleasure of putting him up. He went to the Palace in the evening at the time when the Prince and Princess usually received their friends. Mary gave him a cold reception, in fact she hardly looked up from her cards when he kissed her hand. William appeared at eight o'clock and was equally frosty; he made stilted conversation which was limited to general subjects. When Monmouth said he intended to go away next day, William asked if he was leaving before he had been given a chance to dine at the Palace. Monmouth replied that he intended to have that honour. Accordingly he came the next day, and on leaving the table said in a low voice to the Prince that he would like to have the honour of a private audience. They went down into the garden and managed to rid themselves of Sidney who was following them. Monmouth showed William a letter from his father saying that he remained well disposed towards him, and assuring him that he would not be exiled for long. The Prince had recently received a letter from James denigrating Monmouth, but he was far too well versed in the art of diplomacy to mention it. He simply told the bastard Duke that he would support him, but that 'if he thought of the crown, he could not be his friend in that'.

The next day Sidney and Monmouth went out to walk on the dunes at Schevelingen. The Duke told Sidney just what he felt about his uncle of York, and said that many other people were angry with him; he waxed melancholy about his own prospects, for he knew that once his father was dead the outlook would be even bleaker than it was now. The only bright note, as far as he was concerned, was the letter he had received from his father, which he now showed to Sidney, who confirmed that it was very kind in tone.

Monmouth's legendary charm soon began to have its effect; even the stern-hearted William found himself unable to resist his blandishments, or to keep up the cold manner. Within a day or two, almost against his will, he was treating him as an honoured guest. One evening, after dining with Sidney, he went on to the Italian opera to meet the Princess, who found it equally difficult to resist her childhood idol, and that night he finished up at the Palace where was he 'mighty well received'. According to Sidney, the Prince offered him his house in town, invited him to go hunting, and dissuaded him from leaving at once for Hamburg.

William had been quite nonplussed by Monmouth's sudden arrival, and in the end he asked him bluntly why he had been sent out of England. Monmouth replied, equally bluntly, that it was because James had refused to go unless he went too. Although the Prince and Princess had no desire to be caught up in this sordid family quarrel, Monmouth had the ability to make them behave pleasantly towards him. This was in spite of the fact that he was indiscretion itself and undoubtedly talked openly about his interview with William in the garden, since a version certainly filtered through to d'Avaux. And because he could not resist the temptation of vexing York, he did not fail to tell his father how kind the Prince had been to him.

Sidney was acute enough to see that such behaviour was bound to alienate William in the long run. Monmouth, for all his charm, simply did not possess the delicate touch required in such complicated half political, half family relationships. There was no doubt that the Prince was finding it all very trying. Twice, in early October, Sidney dined with him and thought him out of humour. In August William's stock had been very high in his own country; he had been working on van Beunighen, leader of the difficult Arminian faction in Amsterdam, and had been meeting with considerable success; now the antics of his father-in-law and uncle were beginning to undo all his good work. Such perpetual difficulties were wearing him down and cancelling out the effects of his restful months in Gelderland. There was little time now for pleasurable distraction, though on October 1 he did manage to have a carefree evening dining at the Bentincks, where he was joined later by the Princess.

In spite of Monmouth's arrival, Mary still hoped to visit her sisters in Brussels, but on October 7 she received a letter from her father telling her not to come. His daughters were going back to England, and as he had seen so little of them owing to his precipitate journey into England, he had decided to accompany them for part of the way. In his most peremptory manner he asked if William would send his yachts to collect them as soon as possible so that they could board them 'and then make what haste we can to you'. A visit from James at this moment was the last thing that anybody wanted but at least Monmouth had left the Hague, bound for Utrecht, his original destination. Later he went on to Amsterdam. He was continually engaged in research on the subject of his mother and the circumstances of his birth, for he was always hoping that somebody might emerge from obscurity flourishing the marriage certificate which would make him heir to the throne.

James had expressed the desire that Mary should meet him at Delft, to avoid attracting a crowd at one of the larger cities. He and his party, which included the Churchills, arrived at about three in the afternoon, and James immediately collared the Prince and took him aside, talking to him for half an hour without stopping, so that William found it hard to hide his displeasure. The Duke was at the Hague just long enough to hold a levée, but the evening after his arrival an express came from the King telling him that he was to be recalled from banishment and sent to Scotland by way of England. William was relieved that his father-in-law's visit was to be curtailed. The Duke was not an easy guest, and as for his servants, William told Sidney he had never seen such people.

At about eight o'clock on October 8 Mary's father began his journey. The Princess, with her husband, accompanied the party as far as Maaslandsluys. It was the last time she was ever to see her father and stepmother, or the little stepsister she hardly knew.

CHAPTER 9

THE TWO DUKES

ON THEIR RETURN to the Hague after saying farewell to the Yorks, the Prince and Princess dined with the Bentincks. William had intended to go on to Soestdyck the next day, but he delayed his visit, perhaps out of deference to his wife's feelings.

The alterations and improvements at Soestdyck had been going on for several months now, and William wanted to keep an eye on the builders. This charming summer palace had only one drawback, common to many others in the Netherlands. It was set in a flat landscape and the lack of different levels ruled out the possibility of fountains or cascades. Old John Maurice of Nassau, who had settled in Cleves after a life of distinguished service in the army, wrote tantalizingly of the undulating situation he had found there for his house, which was surrounded by mountains and meadows, and where there was a brook which never ran dry. He had five or six cascades in his garden of which he was inordinately proud, and he offered to send his architect, Rust, to advise the Prince, as well as the Bentinck family, what to do at their houses at Soestdyck and Sorgvliet. Rust was an exponent of a casual and informal style of gardening which was not acceptable in the Dutch setting, and old Huygens wrote to the Prince expressing strong disapproval. He was shocked to hear that one of the walls being built around the new garden had been only half completed, and that William had been persuaded, against his better judgment, to leave it like that. Huygens was insistent that it should be made symmetrical; correctitude dictates, he said, that in order to embrace satisfactorily, you must have two arms. The whole plan, in his opinion, was illogical, because in any case a hedge of alder was to be planted as a wind-break, which would hide the view just as much as a wall.

Huygens offered further advice. He advocated figures painted on canvas which could be placed in niches on the exterior walls; this, he thought, would break up the stark whiteness of the front and cheer up the whole place considerably. He assured the Prince that he had installed similar canvases at his own cottage thirty-eight years before and had only just had to touch them up. On the other hand he disapproved of the paintings that were being carried out in the entrance hall for, as he put it, 'I would prefer that the hall was not painted at all but left quite white and empty, and as spacious as the room which it leads into. I have certainly seen some drawing-rooms and studies in Italy and France, decorated with painting, but not entrance halls for princes, which only serve for pages and lackeys. Here your Highness may with all justice rap my fingers for my temerity, but as the Latin tag has it, *he who builds on the high road exposes himself to criticism from all*'. Whether or not William accepted his old friend's advice about the entrance hall, he let several artists loose in the other rooms, which were decorated in a mood of pastoral fantasy by Lairesse.

The plans for Soestdyck included a thickly wooded avenue leading up to the long, low house, with an enclosed deer park. Large windows led out from the downstairs rooms on to a little lawn with shady trees. Beyond the enclosures the countryside stretched away towards the tower of Utrecht which could be seen on the skyline. Soestdyck was one of the first of the stately homes to boast a zoo, and before long an overseer for the menagerie was added to the establishment.

Throughout the United Provinces building was in progress. Moated castles were being pulled down or altered unrecognizably. Hedges were planted in place of battlemented walls; tanks and ponds were being dug out. The Prince followed the growing fashion for geometrical flower gardens, but he also ensured that his estates were productive. If there was any surplus it was ploughed back into the property. Amalia of Solms, for all her failings, had a good financial sense, which she had imparted to her grandson, explaining to him all the intricacies of the estates he was to inherit. Temple had written admiringly of her 'order and economy'. In spite of her relatively small income, which was never more than twelve thousand pounds a year, she had managed to live in great luxury. Her meals were served off gold plate, and everything she was likely to touch in the course of her everyday life was made of gold, from the 'great bottles for water' down to the key of her closet. 'I think 'tis what the greatest Kings of Christendom have not pretended to do, nor any I have heard of on this side Persia,' Temple wrote. Sophia of Hanover was impressed by the way Amalia had educated William in money matters, which was quite contrary to the English custom of bringing up princes in complete ignorance of such affairs. It was thanks to her tuition and his own careful nature that he was able to make his limited revenues stretch to maintain a staff augmented by Mary's forty or so attendants. The gardens and farms were run to ensure that the household was more or less self-supporting, and in the summer the Prince's trumpeters and drummers were sent out to help bring in the harvest, while in the spring they were put on to the planting of maize.

Towards the end of October, the Princess paid a visit to Amsterdam, where she spent over a thousand gelders. It is possible that William sent her on a kind of good-will mission, hoping that her charm would do something to repair the damage which King Charles's vacillating behaviour had wrought in that town. In November she went with the Prince to Soestdyck and Hooge Soeren. William was feeling perplexed. He simply could not understand the instability of English politics, and he was disgusted when he heard that there had been another prorogation. He had worked hard to persuade the States that it in was their best interests to side with England, but how could they be expected to come to any agreement when affairs were so unsettled on the other side of the water? That summer he had so nearly managed to wean van Beunighen from his dependence on the French, but he was at a loss to know what to say to him now. One evening in late November, he and Sidney talked far into the night trying to work out a policy. 'He is in pain to know what to do,' Sidney wrote.

D'Avaux revelled in this state of affairs. Trouble-making was his métier, and during his years in the States he made a study of the technique of fomenting trouble between William and the City of Amsterdam. He worked on the 'French' faction there, making capital out of William's apparent friendliness towards Monmouth. The Prince realized now that he had made a mistake in showing his cousin any favours at all. He had himself warned Sidney to be careful, reminding him that if James came to the throne, anyone who had in the past shown open friendliness for the hated bastard would certainly lack employment in the future. But, as they both found, to resist Monmouth's charms was not easy. He was, as the Prince put it, so 'pressing', that it was difficult not to be kind to him. The gossip that had resulted from his fairly harmless conversations with the exile was extremely provoking, especially as it had made the King indifferent towards him as a result. D'Avaux made out that William and the Duke had been closeted together for days, making plans to upset the English political scene.

In November, Monmouth made an unwelcome appearance at the Palace. He had been at Amsterdam, apparently conferring with his English friends there. All he was waiting for was a letter from his father giving him permission to go home. The letter came, but without the desired permission. Monmouth visited William and rumour had it that they were together for three hours, after which Monmouth had made up his mind to go to Cologne for a fortnight to three weeks. It was also given out that Monmouth had left orders that a house should be found for him at the Hague, where he intended to live during his absence from England. As it turned out, the quixotic charmer had taken it into his head to return to London without his father's permission. He crossed from Brill in a packet boat, accompanied by his barber, and was greeted enthusiastically by a number of supporters. This alarmed the King, who was coming round to the opinion that his natural son was after the crown.

When anyone really came to thinking about it carefully, it seemed unlikely that William would encourage Monmouth's pretensions. If the Duke were to prove his legitimacy, William's own claims, and his wife's, would be jeopardized. D'Avaux tried to explain this away by saying that the Prince was simply using Monmouth for his own purpose, which was to cut the Duke of York out of the succession. In any case it was easy enough to make out that Monmouth had gone over to England to put himself at the heads of those Lords who had been called to London for a meeting of Parliament, and to pave the way for William.

Ever since the autumn, the Prince's friends had been urging him to go to London for talks with his uncle. They felt that this was the only way of making his position clear. In September, Sidney, after dining at Honselaersdyck, had walked in the garden for over an hour with the Prince, telling him the reason why a visit to England was considered advisable. There was even talk of making him Duke of Gloucester, although it would have been difficult for him to take the oath of allegiance. In any case, Sidney found the Prince 'unapt'. James's sudden visit to England at the time of the King's illness had made it inadvisable for the Prince to go then, and now, if he had followed hard on the Duke of Monmouth's heels, this could only have been open to the worst interpretation. The Prince realized too well that many English politicians were trying to use him as a tool, even though they hid their motives under grandiose professions of concern for the Protestant succession.

There seemed to be no limit to the trouble-making of d'Avaux, and no area of the Prince's life which was sacred. His relationship with his father-in-law was, for example, a most tempting province. William and James had managed up to now to keep on friendly terms at least on the surface, but it was easy enough to sow suspicion, particularly by spreading it about that the Prince was maltreating his wife, refusing to let her keep her English retainers about her, and forcing her to live a life of solitude. Another ruse was to place an agent in a strategic position, and Colonel

Edward Fitzpatrick, who was taking messages from James to William, was apparently in the pay of the French.

William had to walk warily, but in discretion and cunning he was more than a match for his enemies. The Princess was less experienced in such matters, and d'Avaux did not scruple to make trouble for her. The French would have liked to break up a Protestant marriage and were awaiting their chance. They watched the Princess, as Burnet put it, 'with a sort of malicious criticalness', longing to find something to censure. They had a disappointing task, for she moved through the delicate situations of that autumn, with its family friction and political turbulence, with a kind of innocent charm which silenced any potential critic. She had all the high spirits and cheerfulness of youth tempered with a natural discretion. At a stretch her charming manner could be described as coquetry, and the d'Avaux element did not hesitate to do so; other people felt that she was too good to be true and would have believed in her virtue more readily if the reports of it could have been mixed with some more spicy information. There were complaints, it is true, of 'junketings' with her women, but these, too, could be explained away by the fact that she was very young and cheerful, that she enjoyed dancing and walking in the fresh air. She appeared to many observers to be more beautiful than ever at this time; she had lost weight during her illness, but still retained her fresh colour and her healthy appearance. She was well spoken of on every side, a great achievement for a Princess who was so much in the public eye, whose husband had so many enemies, and whom so many people would have liked to denigrate. At that same time, as Susanna Huygens put it, she was 'as beautiful as an angel', an even greater tribute when paid by one woman to another.

CHAPTER 10

FAMILY FRICTION

WHILE THE year of 1679 drew to its close the agitation aroused by the comings and goings of the two Dukes began to die down. As Temple pointed out, the best solution to the whole problem would have been for William to beget a son; he offered to send a recipe for it. There had been no further talk of children since the fiasco of the year before, but although the Prince often went his separate way, hunting or visiting his estates, even the most acute and inimical observer was unable to see any crack in the edifice of his marriage.

There was a great deal of gaiety that winter, to the disgust of the more Calvinistic type of Dutchman who jibbed at such unnecessary luxury and expense. The Prince set the tone with an enormous banquet to which all the great world of the Hague was invited, and the city was rapidly filling up with people. Each evening the Princess's court became more crowded, with the addition of German Duchesses and Princesses who were meeting Mary for the first time and looking at her with considerable approbation. On December 10 the Odycks gave one of their famous balls for the habitués of the Princess's court, and Mary danced the whole night through without growing at all tired, even though the proceedings did not finish until seven o'clock the next morning. It was said that nobody had ever seen anyone dance better than she did. It was a memorable occasion and the ladies were particularly delighted with the *confitures* with which they were presented, and with the refreshing lemonade which helped to quench their thirst. There were several more balls before Christmas, and at the new year the Prince and Odyck contrived to give the Princess a magnificent surprise. Odyck was a patron of Adam Loofs, a brilliant Dutch silversmith, who had been working in Paris making furniture in the ornate French fashion. William commissioned a set of wrought silver furniture and this caused such admiration, and was so appreciated by William himself that he offered Loofs a post as his official silversmith, to take charge of the silver, to maintain, repair and clean it, offering him a very good salary 'and I don't know what else' as one rather disapproving Dutch observer put it. Loofs, delighted by this unexpected turn of events, and by finding a Dutchman in his own country artistic enough to appreciate his work and generous enough to pay for it, went back at once to Paris to fetch 'his little wife and all his family', and thereafter remained at the Hague, resetting Mary's diamonds for her and in general tempting her to overspend her allowance.

In the midst of these and other excitements, the Princess was feeling very happy. A letter written to Frances in January 1680 was devoid of such phrases as 'pity me oh poor me' which had flowed freely from her pen the year before. She had been too busy to write at all over Christmas and now she only managed to dash off a quick letter, finishing up 'I must end, going to the play hinders me writing, but nothing shall ever hinder me loving'. William, though still busy, was much encouraged by the attitude of the States, who now said categorically that they were unanimously against making an alliance with France. He was finding Sidney a great stand-by. They went coursing, dined together and talked business when the meal was over. Whenever Sidney wrote a memorandum, the Prince went through it carefully, corrected it and gave it back to him in the evening. Both the Prince and Princess had reason to be grateful to him for his indefatigable efforts to outwit the French. D'Avaux came to dislike him more and more; Sidney told the Prince he cared as little about that as any man in England. The Prince said it was true that the French were enraged against him—'and with some cause,' he added.

The winter passed pleasantly enough with William in a more sociable mood than usual, dining at Madame Obdan's or with Sidney and some of the ladies. Now that plans had been set in motion for the improvement of the summer palaces, the gardens at Honselaersdyck were to have their turn. When Evelyn had visited the Palace in 1641, he had remarked on the 'fair garden and park, curiously planted with lime trees'. Now there was to be a new orangery by Van Swieten, costing 30,000 gelders, with improved parterres, new flower beds and trees, and a pheasantry as well. The Prince and Princess had also decided that they would keep their best pictures at Honselaersdyck, and they began to collect together the family and other portraits; by the time they left Holland there were a hundred and three in one room alone. For her own amusement the Princess was making a small collection of caged birds, which included a Virginia nightingale, a cockatoo and two little green birds with red heads. Making and mending the cockatoo's perch cost her thirty gelders, the bird cages only twenty-three apiece.

Since the Prince was so preoccupied with State affairs, the Princess began increasingly to take the initiative in matters concerning the houses, furniture and gardens. As her taste was very good, William encouraged this development. Interference from her English retainers, and particularly from her chaplains, he accepted less readily. The conscientious Dr Hooper, who discovered that at one of her houses the Princess lacked a regular chapel for divine service, persuaded her to convert her own dining room for the purpose, and from then on she meekly agreed to eat in a 'very small parlour'. When the new chapel was fitted out, the Prince came to inspect Hooper's handiwork, which he viewed without enthusiasm. He kicked the steps leading up to the communion table and asked what they were for. When told, he answered with a disapproving 'hum'. Although the Princess dutifully attended chapel twice a day, the Prince limited his appearances there to Sunday evenings, which was quite enough in his opinion.

At the end of 1679 William had the satisfaction of knowing that he was soon to see the last of Dr Hooper. His technique of studied rudeness had worked at last, but not on Hooper so much as on his wife, who was, it seems, rather less thick-skinned than her husband. Hooper had requested leave of absence to claim his bride the previous year; she was, in his opinion, a 'very fine woman', though she apparently failed to impress the Prince who consistently found himself unable to recognize her. William often talked about 'saluting' Mrs Hooper, and welcoming her to Holland, but somehow never did so. This, however, was typical of him; it was a great joke among the English ladies to hear him proposing a civility to someone in his wife's service, and never carrying it out.

The Princess, according to Hooper, had been reluctant even to let him go back to England for his marriage, and now, Mrs Hooper being 'great with child', she was insistent that a midwife should be sent for from England, to save her having to part with her chaplain. Fortunately Mrs Hooper determined to go to England for her lying-in and showed no inclination to return to Holland afterwards. This was not surprising in view of William's behaviour, and the fact that her husband, knowing the Prince's 'great economy' and his dislike of the English, had never allowed her to eat at court, where she only went twice a day for prayers. The Princess, having resigned herself to the fact that she would not see the Hoopers again, gave her chaplain as a parting present a cup, cover and salver 'of the weight of gold' with the Prince's and her own arms impaled on it. She said she was sorry she could not afford anything better, for she only had £4,000 a year for all her expenses and charities, in which, Hooper said, 'she was very liberal'. Hooper could not resist pointing out that she lost £200 every year as the Dutch always paid her in their own coinage. He also averred that during all the time he was in Holland he was never offered any money, which he looked upon as just another ruse for getting rid of him. Fortunately he was a man of some substance, and was not dependent on the Prince's bounty; on the contrary he took the opportunity while he was at the Hague of spending a thousand pounds on books in order to improve his education, to the amazement of the Dutch, who called him 'the rich Papa'. In Holland they were more used to the clergy being poor and dependent.

Just as Hooper was about to embark with Mrs Hooper, a servant came from Bentinck, carrying a bag containing seventy-six pounds, with an apology that it had not been sent sooner. Dr Hooper took out a crown piece with which he tipped the servant and the rest he sent back to Bentinck, saying that he had discharged all his debts and paid his passage. The sum was later paid to him in England, and it was, he said, all he was ever given for a year and a half's service—a typical 'specimen of Dutch generosity' in his opinion. He had his revenge in any case by recommending as his successor one of his friends from Oxford days, Dr Ken, a man of similar ideas and attitudes. Ken did not agree with the Prince any better than his predecessor—if anything rather worse. Like Hooper, however, he was a 'good pulpit man'; he preached at the Hague soon after his arrival in December, and dined with Sidney on Christmas day.

In February the court went into mourning for the Queen of Bohemia, who had spent so many exiled years at the Hague, and in March, the Princess, who had been much better since her visit to Aix, was once again taken seriously ill. William wrote to tell her father that she was in great pain, and the next letter was equally disturbing. It was a full week before he received any better news. Sidney, who was ill himself and taking physic, had no end of callers asking for news. On March 18 Colonel Fitzpatrick came to see him and stayed for most of the afternoon; their main topic of conversation was the Princess's illness and how it was not likely that she would live. The next night she was even worse. There was a theory abroad about her illness—which could have been a miscarriage, or a bad bout of 'flu, or a continuation of her old trouble—and some people made it their business to spread the opinion that it was caused by William's indifference. Dr Ken let it be known that he was 'horribly unsatisfied' with the Prince because he was not being kind to his wife. It was said that Ken had every intention of having it out with William 'though he kicks him out of doors', but one doubts if his bravery would have stretched as far as that.

On April 6 James wrote to the Prince expressing relief that Mary was so far recovered as to be able to take the air, but although she was over the worst, it was some time before she felt really well again. Temple, who had heard all kinds of conflicting reports, felt very concerned about the Princess's health, especially as the Prince also was none too well. Dr Ken continued to murmur about William's behaviour, and he found a willing listener in old Sylvius. Sidney reported that he had found them with their heads together:

Sylvius and Ken were both here, and both complain of the Prince, especially his usage of his wife; they think she is sensible of it, which doth contribute to her illness; they are mightily for her going into England, but they think he will never give his consent.

The news from England was still encouraging. Charles remained resolutely friendly, while his brother was meddling so little that it looked as if he had grown wise or subdued; 'I say 'tis the first,' Lady Sunderland told Sidney. The Duke himself was pleased with the course of events. 'Except the D. of Monmouth do some hot-headed thing, which I think him capable of, all things are likely to be very quiet here,' he wrote. In May the King caused some alarm when he fell ill with 'an aguish distemper', but he quickly recovered with the help of the inevitable Jesuit's powder, and was well enough to go to Newmarket earlier than usual to see a race in which the two best horses in England were running. Lady Sunderland was of the opinion that he was likely to remain in good health if he could be 'kept from fishing when a dog would not be abroad'.

On the continent the situation was less reassuring. It seemed certain that Louis would attack in Flanders in the spring, for he still had a large standing army which would need an occupation once it came out of winter quarters. There was nothing Louis appreciated more than to keep the whole of Europe in a state of nerves. Van Beunighen told Sidney that he did not like the way French troops were massing, and there was much speculation as to where the first blow would fall. The Prince was watching the situation closely, and he assured Sidney that the United Provinces would declare war at once if the French struck at any of the towns in Flanders.

Throughout the whole of May the situation continued to look serious, but as the month drew to its close and no blow fell, William decided that he would no longer postpone the visit to Dieren. The weather was cold and very wet, which was suitable for stag hunting, though it did not please the ladies. Mary's letters to Frances contained little except apologies for not writing more often, and gave no details of her life or feelings. In her position it would perhaps have been rash for her to do anything else. It was an uneasy summer, with William in indifferent health, and the news from England becoming increasingly worrying. The Duke, who had been allowed to come back to London that spring, spent most of the month of August hunting frenetically—which at least kept him out of mischief; now it was Monmouth's turn to behave with unbelievable folly. There were strong rumours that the legendary black box which was said to contain the longed-for marriage certificate had turned up somewhere in England. The King decided to put an end to the matter for good. Several witnesses were examined but they all tended to become vague when questioned. It was quite obvious that there never had been a certificate, just as the King had always maintained. But, in spite of the fact that he could no longer pretend to be the Prince of Wales, Monmouth set out on what amounted to a royal progress in the West country 'a long ramble' was how James described his nephew's journey. Although the justices of the peace, deputy lieutenants and 'all the people that mattered' kept well away, large crowds gathered wherever he went, attracted by his spectacular good looks and Protestant standpoint. Some said he would be 'King Jemmy the Second' within a few weeks. 'God bless the Protestant Duke and the Devil take the Pope' was a popular cry that summer.

With the situation abroad so gloomy and quarrels in the family mounting, the summer at Dieren was far less peaceful than usual. There was a feeling of uncertainty, prompted by the knowledge that at any moment William might have to go to England. Sidney had been back on his old theme as early as April, urging the Prince to go over, but found 'he had no mind to it'. In July, when William paid a visit to Honselaersdyck, Sidney dined with him and afterwards returned to the subject of the English visit. The Prince was still very unwilling, and said that in any case there was nothing that could be done until September. The situation might appear serious for his father-in-law, but what could he do to prevent James's ruin? Things had not been the same between the Prince and his father-in-law since Monmouth's visit. On the surface the Duke's letters were polite enough, but references to the weather had grown more frequent, and William must have known that the protestations of loyalty had a hollow ring. When Sidney brought up the subject of James yet again, on July 16, William said frankly that he thought it was 'not a very wise nor a pleasant thing to ruin oneself for one that does not love me'.

Ten days after this meeting with Sidney, the Prince rejoined his wife for a few days at Dieren, but he was soon off again, this time to Breda, where he fell so seriously ill that the doctors feared he could, at the most, have only a few years to live. He had barely recovered when tragic news came from England; Ossory, his intimate friend, and one of the few Englishmen he liked and trusted, was dead. He had fallen ill with a high fever, become delirious almost at once and died while the physicians stood impotently by. William, in a letter to Arlington, wrote simply that Ossory was one of the best friends he had in the world. Although he had never irritated the Prince by vaunting his beliefs, Ossory had been a good Church of England man—'an honour to the communion he was of' was how Sir Leoline Jenkins put it—and several eminent divines wrote eulogistically about him. Now, in the opinion of Dr Fell, Bishop of Oxford, he was 'above the malice and designs of naughty men', and the Dean of Bangor brought the news to Jenkins with tears in his eyes. Mary's father wrote a dutiful letter of condolence, slanted as usual, in his irritating way, to the Stuart interest: 'It had really been a very great loss to our family especially at this time, when we are like to have so much need of friends.'

In August the court spent a few days at Soestdyck, and then travelled on to Dieren for the rest of the month. Dr Ken accompanied the Princess to Dieren. Her chaplains were inclined to cling, even in the summer season. Dr Ken was preoccupied with the question of unity with the Dutch Church, for there had recently been some proposals suggesting a basis of agreement. Ken told Compton that he did not feel over-sanguine; Dutch divines, he said, were too inclined to look on Church of England clergy as 'at least half-papists'. They naturally revered the great doctors of the Reformed Church and had little respect for 'ecclesiastical antiquity'. Ken foresaw considerable difficulties over preferment arising in a united Church; he was also afraid the Princess would be expected to go to the Dutch sacrament, the thought of which filled him with foreboding. 'If ever she does do it, farewell all common prayer here for the future,' Ken wrote pessimistically. The best thing, he thought, was to lay the whole controversy to sleep, otherwise he could see himself having to desert his own Church, or leave the Hague altogether, a pity in view of the fact that he had overcome his first aversion to William. As he put it to Compton:

I am at present in as much favour with the Prince, and I am as obligingly treated by Mr Bentinck and all here, as I can desire, and therefore am a scrupulous *quieta movere*. I hope your Lordship will pardon me.

A little while later, Ken had more cheerful news to give the Bishop. Colonel Fitzpatrick, once the Duke of York's trouble-making go-between had failed to follow James to Scotland and had remained in the vicinity of the Dutch court, ingratiating himself with people of importance. Throughout the summer he had been dining frequently with Sidney who still did not altogether trust him, and found it hard to forget that there had once been rumours that he had been charged with forging bills of exchange. In any case, it seemed as if the Colonel, who was a man of substance and much courted by the Catholics, was undergoing a change of heart, and he often unburdened himself to Sidney, telling him of the struggles that had been going on in his soul.

One evening, when Dr Ken was also in Sidney's room, Fitzpatrick announced that he had decided to join the Anglican Church. He had, it seemed, been turning the matter over in his mind for the last six months, reading the most important books on the subject, taking instruction and coming to the conclusion that his best 'title to heaven' was to become a convert, though it is tempting to wonder whether there was not an element of social expediency in his decision. The Princess was delighted. 'I may tell you the good news,' she wrote to Frances, 'of Colonel Fitzpatrick being turned Protestant and that he is to receive the sacrament next Sunday with me . . . he has done it of his own accord which when he first spoke to the Prince of it he immediately sent Dr Ken to him who is very well satisfied with his reasons and will this post give a full account of it to the Bishop of London.' Ken was beside himself with delight. He told the bishop that the main considerations which had prevailed with the Colonel had been 'that peremptory sentence of damnation' which Catholics passed on all those who dissented from their communion, and the difficulty he had in 'digesting' the doctrine of transubstantiation. In his elation Ken allowed himself to imagine a stream of influential converts following the Colonel's example. He himself had undergone a startling change of heart regarding the Prince. The Princess, of course, had always given 'demonstrations of her great and zealous concern for the Protestant religion', and further acquaintance showed that her husband, far from being the uncourteous heathen of Hooper's description, was a man whose zeal for the Protestants should not go unacknowledged; Dr Ken, indeed, thanked God for raising up 'so powerful and resolute a patron of the Reformed Church'.

The following Sunday Colonel Fitzpatrick received the eucharist in the royal chapel in the presence of the Prince and Princess, Sidney, Bentinck and several other 'persons of quality'. The next day the Prince left for a visit to his German relations, ostensibly to have some hunting, but mainly to cement the alliance against France. He evidently felt that it would be more profitable and far less compromising than the journey to England which Sidney repeatedly urged him to undertake. It was also thought that William intended to discuss the question of his sister-in-law Anne who, at the age of fifteen, was ripe to be disposed of in a politic manner. The King of Sweden had been thought of as a possible suitor, but as this would have given Anne a higher rank than her sister, the Prince did not favour such an idea. Prince George of Hanover, son of the lively Sophia, seemed to him a far more suitable choice, and a visit to the German states would obviously provide an excellent opportunity to sound out the ground. A little judicious bribery among German ministers might also prove beneficial especially in the important matter of keeping some standing armies ready to oppose France if she should become more than normally aggressive.

The Prince decided that he would not take Mary with him. The trip was likely to be strenuous, and she herself chose to stay at Soestdyck. Walking, working and riding, she told Frances, were her only diversions there, but it was her own choice of milieu. 'I like it better than any other I could have,' she confessed. During this peaceful interlude she had more time than usual for letter writing, and she accused Frances of being too restrained, of sending grave, ceremonial letters, and becoming 'insupportably formal'.

When William returned he brought forty delicate-flavoured ortolans which he had been given as a present for the Princess's table. But he had no time for feasting. Sidney, who had been over in England, came to see him almost at once, confirming the news that had recently come through about the troubled situation there. In particular Sidney reported that James's prospects were deteriorating rapidly, and now there was even talk of excluding him from the succession. Sidney was more convinced than ever that the Prince would have to make a journey to England and many of the German relations had been of the same opinion. But William still refused to go himself though he had already decided to send a special envoy, van Leeuwen, and had in fact written several letters in his own hand from Germany to act as credentials. What most people feared was that unless the Prince bestirred himself, the Exclusion Bill would serve to ensure simply that Monmouth became the next in succession. Lady Sunderland wrote to say that the situation had worsened even in the short time that Sidney had taken to return to Holland. 'If the Prince thinks it not worth going over a threshold for a kingdom,' she wrote, 'I know not why he should expect anybody should for him . . . and fancy if you could but see all that is to be seen, the Prince would not be such an ass; and so farewell.'

Mary, afraid that her husband might at any time be forced into a dangerous journey to England, was feeling ill at ease. She knew that her father was behaving more foolishly than ever, and she had probably been told that the Duchess of York looked very melancholy when she stepped onto the barge which was to take her to Greenwich on the first stage of yet another journey to Scotland. Nobody quite knew whether her sad appearance was caused by her own bad health, the dread of a sea voyage, the fear that she was with child, her dislike of the political situation or her disgust that James had so openly owned his mistress, Catherine Sedley; it could have been a mixture of all these things.

Everything, Temple agreed with William, depended on the English Parliament, but he could hardly help feeling perplexed when he thought how much weight everyone put upon 'five hundred men being temperate and wise'. The news that Parliament was determined to bring in an Exclusion Bill, removing James from the succession, was causing consternation throughout Holland, and not only in the Prince's household. Sidney said that several of the States came to him, crying out that they were lost and ruined, that they had rejected all other alliances and thrown themselves entirely upon England 'and now there was like to be such a disunion that they did almost despair of any support or assistance from thence'. A copy of the Bill arrived one evening when the Prince and Princess were dining with Sidney. William was melancholy at the new turn of events, and in Edinburgh James was in a state of great agitation, fearing rebellion or worse; everything, he thought, was going in just the same way as it had in 1640. He kept warning his son-in-law that it was not only himself they were aiming at with the Exclusion Bill, but the whole family.

When the Bill was defeated in the Lords, the political temperature dropped, and for the time being it seemed less urgent for the Prince to go to England. All the same, the news from London was still unpleasant. James's warnings to William were reaching a new pitch. 'You see no way is left unpractised to ruin our family,' he pointed out; now, it seemed, a further Bill was to be brought in, this time with the object of limiting the royal prerogative, and once they began to tamper with the rights of the Crown, who knew where it would all end?

William charged his envoy van Leeuwen to tell the King that he disliked the idea of any restrictions on the royal prerogative, for these struck at the root of monarchy. The whole hereditary system was in danger, and largely because the Duke persisted with such zeal in 'une réligion perverse'; was there no chance that even at this late stage James could be persuaded to change his ideas? The answer was that he was as unbending as ever. He became quite indignant when people suggested he might alter his private beliefs for the good of the whole. 'Do but think what a base mean thing it would be in me besides the sin of it to dissemble and deny my religion,' he wrote to his friend Legge. He said he intended to be as careful of his conscience and his honour as the old Earl of Dorset who, when commanded by Charles I to carry the Princes away from the battle of Edgehill, had refused, saying 'he would not be thought a coward for never a King's son in christendom'. It would have been better for everybody if James could have put the old Earl of Dorset out of his head; a little moral cowardice might have done a lot of good at this juncture. All the same, James was probably right when he said that even if he did announce that he had turned Protestant, nobody would believe him. They would think that he was dissembling, and that he might as a result prove even more dangerous.

In December William was completely absorbed in English affairs. 'He is day and night studying how these great miseries may be prevented which are so evident to all the world,' Sidney reported, in a letter to Sunderland. He added that if the King thought the Prince's presence in England would be helpful, he only had to send the word and William would be ready to leave at once:

If his Majesty pleases to send a yacht for him, he will make all the haste to wait upon him that is possible. His Highness also desires to know your opinion whether it be best or not to bring the Princess; he will bring her or leave her, as he is advised by you.

The King did not send for him. He did not need his nephew's help in settling this difficult matter, for if there were two questions on which Charles never vacillated, they were exclusion and restriction. He said that to support either was like offering a man money to cut off his nose.

One evening Sidney showed William a stern letter which he had received from the King. The Prince treated it as a joke, but all the same, Sidney had made a serious error in allowing his name to be associated with the States in their recent plea that the King should support his Parliament. In doing so he not only brought disfavour on himself, but he also aroused the suspicion that William himself was ready to agree to a policy of exclusion. This was far from the truth; the Prince would have been a fool if he had not realised that it was totally against his wife's, or his own, interests, to support the Bill, and in any case he was convinced that it would be unjust to exclude James, however much he disliked his religious attitude. Weeks before, he had put the matter succinctly enough to Sidney himself:

He spoke admirably, and it would have charmed anyone to hear him; in fine, he is convinced he may be a great Prince if he does what he is advised to, and that he shall be undone if he does not; but that he will rather chose that than do a thing against his conscience.

In these troubled waters the French were dabbling happily. Louis had set up a new court at Metz whose task it was to unearth old deeds and titles which could be used to prove that more and more territories belonged to the new French conquests and should therefore be ceded to France. And all the time there were more stories of persecutions being perpetrated against the Huguenots. 'Whoever does not kneel, meeting the host, shall be whipped through the streets by the hangman,' Savile reported from Paris. Halifax supposed that all this tyranny gave satisfaction to the French King's 'heroic mind'; for his part he could think of a hundred things that would please him more 'than to keep Flanders and Germany from sleeping for fear of him'.

Mary's sympathies were all with the Huguenots and she made no secret of the fact. It may have been the desire to teach her a lesson which prompted the French Ambassador to deliver a deliberate personal insult. D'Avaux told Odyck, one morning in December, that he intended to wait on the Princess that evening. Odyck forgot to deliver the message, and so it came as a complete surprise when the Ambassador walked into her room about a quarter of an hour after she had sat down to play bassett with her ladies. She stood up, and asked him if he would like to join her at play, and sat down again. To everyone's amazement, instead of doing so, he looked all round the room and then took the trouble to walk to the far corner to fetch a chair with arms, which he promptly sat down in. The move was not difficult to interpret. An armchair was the symbol of diplomatic precedence; the Princess naturally sat in one, and to take the only other available was an unmistakable gesture of disrespect. Mary, however, said nothing, and went on playing her cards in a dignified manner. The Ambassador continued sitting in his armchair in not very splendid isolation. After a while, somewhat shamefaced, he capitulated and joined the company at the bassett table. By the time William arrived everything appeared to be more or less normal, and he sat down to play without comment. The next day the Ambassador told his friends that he had received positive orders from his master that whenever the Princess sat in a large armchair he must do the same, and if there was only one in the room, and she was sitting in it, he should snatch it from under her. Mary's dignity, and the fact that there had been two armchairs in the room, had prevented a flare-up, and the French Ambassaor did not risk using such tactics again. Far from achieving a triumph for his master, he had only succeeded in making himself look a fool.

A more welcome visitor to the court that Christmas was the Prince of Hanover, who stopped at the Hague for a few days on his way to England to bid for the hand of Mary's sister. The Prince and Princess gave him a friendly welcome, and there was more gaiety in one week than there had been all that autumn, for William had been too preoccupied with affairs of State to enjoy himself. On December 17 Sidney invited the two Princes and the Princess to his house. 'They shall have music and dancing, and the best entertainment I can give them,' he wrote. It was a good evening, and the assembled company danced until morning light; there was more gaiety and dancing throughout the week.

After a few days, Prince George left for England. On his arrival he was allowed to kiss his cousin Anne of York, but this apparently did not arouse any desire in him, for he went back to Hanover without making a serious overture, and as a result Anne nursed a life-long grudge against him. Some said he was unnerved by developments in England, for he had arrived at an unfortunate moment when the English were at their maddest. As he himself put it, 'they cut off the head of Lord Stafford yesterday, and made no more ado about it than if they had chopped off the head of a pullet'.

At the Hague, the Christmas festivities continued. Sometimes, in the evening, the guests at a ball would be called outside to gaze up at a great comet, shaped like a sword, that blazed in the clear frosty sky; Huygens, who was always interested in astronomical phenomena, reported that it was so clear and bright that it was almost frightening. The meteor lent an atmosphere of uneasiness to that Christmas season, for there were people who could remember a similar phenomenon appearing in the year 1640 before the outbreak of the Great Rebellion, when the English King and his Parliament had been at loggerheads, just as they were now.

CHAPTER 11

A DARK NEW YEAR

THE OUTLOOK in the new year of 1681 was unpromising, and John
Evelyn expressed a common belief when he said that the comet was one
of many 'forerunners of animadversions' and warnings from God.
Whenever Sidney saw the Prince he thought him troubled and out of
humour; at the back of his mind was the constant fear that war might
break out again before the end of the year. William was more perplexed
than ever by his uncle's behaviour. He still believed that the salvation of
Europe lay in the ability of the King of England, backed by his Lords
and Commons, to enter into an alliance with the Dutch, but such a
possibility was receding, for Charles had dissolved Parliament, and many
people suspected that he had 'taken measures' with France.

To add to their public worries, the Prince and Princess suffered a
personal loss that January. Mary's favourite dwarf, a '*petit indien*', was out
walking in the Hague when he saw a runaway coach without its coachman
hurtling towards him. He tried to get out of its way, but lost his balance
and fell into its path. He was badly injured and died two hours later, which
caused the Princess great distress, and there was general sorrow in the
court, for the dwarf had been universally popular. It was partly to help
the Princess recover from this shock, and partly for political reasons that
the Prince decided to pay a visit to Amsterdam early in February. A new
opera company had just begun its first season in the town and all the
monde distingué was flocking to see this novelty. The opera had been in
vogue in Paris for ten years now, and in Amsterdam farces had for a good
many years been sometimes sung to popular tunes. Among the many
foreign musicians who had been drawn to Nimeguen, hoping to earn a
living by soothing the jangled nerves of the peace delegates after a day's
negotiations, was a man of Amsterdam origin, Dirk Strijker, who had
been brought up in Venice where his father was the Consul for the United
Provinces. He wrote the music for the first Dutch opera, and made a
pioneer attempt to establish the opera on Dutch soil. After many heart-
breaking setbacks, this enterprising impressario was able to open early in

1681 with *Le Fatiche d'Ercole*. Another piece which was put on to charm the fashionable world was *Helen rapita da Paride*.

Old Huygens, despite his eighty-five years, went off gamely in mid-February with his family to view this novelty. They were all very impressed by the scenery—there were many scene changes—which struck them as being well painted and architecturally impressive. The dresses in general were rich and pleasing, although those of the ladies were cut rather low for Dutch taste; also, 'a certain horse called Pegasus' could have flown through the air with rather more grace. The *castrati* sang well, but it was felt that they were better heard and not seen, and were therefore more suitable for performances in church. The ballet, too, left something to be desired; it was the general opinion that the Italians were better at singing than dancing.

The Prince must have been impressed by the opera, in spite of these defects, for during the next two years, he made plans to form his own company at the Hague, where the Burgomasters gave permission for opera to be performed in the tennis court of Pierre van Gool. Politically as well as socially the visit to Amsterdam was worth while, for the Princess was greeted with the enthusiasm which she always inspired. She was one of the Prince's most valuable assets. Nobody had ever seen such a fuss made of any important personage. The people kissed her coach wheels and tried to tear off anything she was wearing, for a souvenir, or, as they called it in those days, a relique. The French were displeased when they heard about this outburst of public feeling. 'The great reception of the Prince of Orange was no welcome news here,' Savile reported from Paris.

The Prince and Princess returned, as so often happens after a pleasant break, to a crisis. Zuylestein, William's cousin, had been conducting a passionate affair with one of Mary's ladies, Jane Wroth. Persistent rumours that Jane was pregnant had now proved all too true, although Zuylestein did his best to put the blame on a Switzer or a lackey. Some reports said that Mistress Wroth had tried to hide her shame by taking obscure lodgings in the town as she neared her time, and that one of the troublemakers at court, probably Mrs Langford, had advised her to make her condition public, so that she could shame Zuylestein into marrying her. Another account says that the Princess, hearing the whispers that were going about, asked Jane kindly whether they were true and said that if they were she would do all she could to help. She was met with a blank denial. It was therefore a shock to return from Amsterdam to find that her maid of honour had been delivered of a child and that virtually as she was giving birth she had been married to Zuylestein according to the

Anglican rites. The Prince was extremely angry. Zuylestein's name had for some time been coupled with that of a rich heiress, Elizabeth Pompe, and William had believed that it was only a matter of working out the formalities before his cousin could conclude this very favourable match. Although Zuylestein was descended from Prince Frederick Henry through his natural son, he had been accorded considerable rank at the court, and if he had exerted himself fully, spent less time flirting with maids of honour and made the most of the favour extended to him by his cousin, he could have been one of the most influential people at the Hague. He was attractive and charming, with an aristocratic air, but he was a weak character, 'an enemy to all work and constraint'.

The Prince was naturally provoked when he found that his favourite had succumbed to Jane Wroth's charms, but such scandals were not uncommon in courts, and they could usually be resolved in a sensible manner. It was all very annoying in view of the fact that a far more advantageous marriage had been more than a possibility. Most of the Prince's rage was focused on Dr Ken, who had known about the affair and who, in William's opinion, was guilty of intolerable meddling and trouble-making. It mattered little to William that Ken felt a certain responsibility for the girl who was related to one of his early patrons.

The Prince dismissed Ken at once, but the Chaplain pointed out that in fact he had no power to do so, since he had not been responsible for the appointment in the first place. Ken told the Princess that he was quite ready to withdraw, but it seems that she managed to soothe her husband down. It may have been that Sidney was also instrumental in bringing the olive branch, for he was one of Ken's most intimate friends, and was also related to Jane Wroth. In any case, William, overcoming his pride, invited Ken to stay at the Hague for a further year, and Ken agreed to do so out of affection for the Princess. He looked back later on his last year in Holland as the happiest of his stay there, which seems to give the lie to reports that William nursed an implacable grudge against Ken and also took a long time to forgive the Princess—some said that he refused to sleep with her for months after the affair. Such reports probably emanated from the same people who had been eager to put it about that William had never shared a bed with his wife in the first place.

Jane Wroth was not the only English girl to find herself in trouble. One of Gibsone's beautiful and full-sized daughters had produced a child which she said was by a young gallant named Blondin who had since become involved with another young lady, a widow, who was said to be beautiful and *spirituelle*, though she was no better endowed with worldly goods than Miss Gibsone. The strain of so many troubles at court and such friction among her retainers, not to mention all the worry and uncertainty of the political situation, soon affected the Princess's health. She was at Dieren in April and, when William went on a hunting trip to Hummeling at the invitation of the Duke of Zell, she accompanied him, although she was suffering from sore eyes. They were away for six weeks. She had bought some gold thread for the bed hangings she was embroidering, probably knowing that she would have ample time for her own work while William was out on horseback. The hunting lodge was set in the wild marshy country which suited William so well, but Huygens, who went in William's train, found the place a desert, where nobody talked of anything except hounds and horses. James was envious when he heard that his son-in-law could hunt every day, for he was unable to enjoy the same facilities in Scotland; 'where the stags are, there are such hills and bogs as 'tis impossible to follow any hounds,' he complained.

It was just as well that the Prince and Princess were able to go right away from the Hague that spring, for the news from England was not encouraging, and Sidney reported that he had never seen William so perplexed; 'he confesses he does not know what to do, that he never was without some project till now.' Charles, afraid that if he called a Parliament in London there would be outbreaks of violence, had announced that the next one was to be held at Oxford. It met in March, but its existence was short-lived. Some Members had been planning to introduce a Regency Bill, which would stipulate that although the Crown would descend to the Duke of York, his daughter and her husband would act as Regents during his reign. This was an embarrassing and impractical idea, hardly calculated to improve family relations, but the King allowed it to go forward, knowing that the Whigs would reject it. They did so without hesitation, harping back to their now well-known theme of exclusion and nothing but exclusion. Charles used this episode as an excuse to prorogue Parliament more or less indefinitely; what other solution was there, when there was the same *impasse* every time it met?

The Yorks did not have a good winter. The Duchess had suffered a miserable pregnancy, followed by the death of her child. Her affliction affected the Duke as much as the loss of the infant. 'For myself,' he wrote, 'I have been so used to such and so many other troubles and mortifications that I can, thank God, bear them well enough.' The greatest blow of all was the news that little Isabella had died in London. She had been ill with convulsive fits the previous summer, but her death was quite unexpected. However, the Duke bore it all philosophically, and felt more hopeful when he heard that the Oxford Parliament had proved to be almost as short-lived as his own infant.

The Prince and Princess came back refreshed from their holiday, but once again they were greeted by bad news on their return. Sidney came to see the Prince at Honselaersdyck and announced that he had been recalled to England. At first William simply could not believe it, and Sidney himself was incredulous. But there was no doubt that James had for some time been pressing his brother to have Sidney recalled, for it made him uneasy to think that a man who had once befriended Monmouth should be wielding such influence in his daughter's household.

The Prince received an abrupt letter from Hyde saying that Sidney must return and that Bevil Skelton was to be sent in his place. He remonstrated strongly with Charles about the withdrawal of Sidney, who, in his view, had been one of the most popular, faithful and successful envoys ever accredited to the Hague. And he entreated his uncle not to appoint Skelton in his place; he had many reasons for objecting to the choice. The truth was that Skelton was not a very likeable man. He had visited the Prince when staying at the Hague on his way to Venice the previous year and had not created a good impression. According to Burnet, he was experienced in foreign affairs, but had no particular capacity for them. He adopted a priggish attitude towards Monmouth's association with his kinswoman Henrietta Wentworth, and this must have endeared him to the Duke of York. In any case, whether he approved of the choice or not, William had grounds for complaint, because the King had promised that he would never appoint a Minister at the Hague without consulting his nephew first. But Hyde begged the Prince not to be too 'choqued'; the affair had gone too far, he said, for the King to retract now, and besides, he added, 'Mr Skelton is a person particularly known to the King and hath served him a long time.' He was most anxious that William should not take offence. 'For God's sake, Sir, though you should be in the right in this particular, agree with the King in it,' he pleaded.

The Prince had no intention of capitulating. He realized that Charles was being influenced by trouble-makers. Disturbing rumours that his uncle was on good terms with the French continued to multiply. The King was suspiciously well-off financially these days, and although his supporters insisted that this was because he had now decided to live within his income, many people thought that the fiasco of the Oxford Parliament had driven him to accept another subsidy from Louis.

February had seen the fall of Sunderland, who had in recent months become one of the Prince's strongest allies. The recall of Sidney was just another stage in a long process of alienation, and it made William think seriously, at last, of going to England in person, to see whether he could counteract the insidious influence of the King's counsellors. Up to now it had been his policy to keep out of English politics, and to 'leave the event to God Almighty', as Temple put it. But the time had come to try a different approach. On June 11, as he was driving in the Voorhout with Sidney, he announced that he was planning a visit to England, for he had come to the conclusion that it might do good, and in any case it would do no harm. Sidney was delighted, and he suggested that the Princess should go too, in order to drink the waters at Tunbridge Wells.

Plans were quickly made, and James wrote a letter giving his blessing. 'I am confident you will be better informed of his Majesty's affairs than you have been of late, and that you will take such measures for the future as may be for the good of our family in general' was what he put, though secretly he believed that the motive of the visit was 'to blast the Duke's expectations of ever seeing the end of his miseries'.

It was decided that the Princess should not accompany her husband, and she left for Dieren at the end of July. It was a double parting, for not only did she have to say goodbye to William, but also, more permanently, to Sidney. It was perhaps almost a relief to the Princess that the visit was to take place at last. In any case, although he originally intended to go for a month, William was back after only a fortnight. On his return he went straight off to Dieren 'to divert yourself there', as his father-in-law accusingly put it, with the insinuation that he himself did not have time for such things. The journey to England had not been an unqualified success. It was rumoured that at play in London the Prince had lost a large sum of money, and that he had made a bad mistake by accepting an invitation to dine in the City, which was well known to be a hot-bed of Whigs. The King, it was said, had prevented him from attending by summoning him to Windsor, where he had been severely reprimanded for trying to supplant his father-in-law in the succession, a most unjust accusation.

During his talks with the King at Windsor, William won an important point, for it soon became clear that Charles had thought better of sending Skelton to Holland. A letter came after the Prince's return in which the King suggested Mr Hales, one of the Lords Commissioners of the Admiralty, and said he wished to consult William before pursuing the matter further, his original suggestion having, as he put it, 'rancountred with accidents'. If Bentinck is to be believed, Charles also confided in his nephew during the course of their conversation, that he was sure his brother, if he came to the throne, would be 'so restless and violent' that he would not stay there for more than four years. A rather unlikely story was that he showed William one of his seals, and said that only the letters stamped with this particular one would express his real wishes; anything else would be 'only drawn from him by importunity'.

In Scotland, James remained suspicious and peevish. He had written to Legge appealing to him to be 'very much with his Ma.' to observe what happened when he met the Prince. At first he was optimistic; 'I think,' he wrote, 'if the Prince be spoken homely to, if his head be not quite wrong turned his eyes will be opened and he will see how he has been abused by those who gave measure of affairs in England.' But he became increasingly uneasy as he pictured his brother and nephew with their heads together. His distrust of Sidney had become an obsession, and when he heard that the Prince was angling to keep his friend in Holland by appointing him as commander of the English regiments in the Netherlands he made no secret of his feelings. 'As to what you say of my having had ill impressions given me of you,' he told William, 'I assure you nobody durst say anything to me to your prejudice.' He went on to say that he, for his part, was sorry to see that William had been so badly informed about affairs in England, 'and by such misinformation to have countenanced some people that will never be true friends to you nor none of our family'. Rumours that Sidney's appointment to the regiments had already appeared in the Brussels *Gazette* brought another cross letter. 'I should be very sorry,' wrote Mary's father in his stiffest manner, 'to see Mr Sidney at the head of such a body of men of his Majesty's subjects, that is so influenced by some of the greatest enemies I have in the world.'

It was a long, hot summer in England and Holland. The corn and hay had been affected by the drought and the fields were parched and dry. By the autumn, what with the heat and the French King's war of nerves, tempers were severely strained. The Prince was disgusted by the English and made no secret of the fact; Hyde remonstrated with him, saying that he was acting a dangerous part. 'Your Highness is so discerning as to know all my meaning by this little hint,' he wrote. The rift between James and William had been split wide open by the events of the summer, and if there had ever been trust in James's mind it had now vanished. An unpleasant tone had crept into his letters. 'I see those that come to speak with you at London cannot be brought to reason, at which I do not at all wonder, seeing how barefaced and impudently they have gone about in several Parliaments to destroy monarchy and overturn the government.'

As the quarrel developed between her husband and father, so, as the new year of 1681 grew old, the Princess found herself in an increasingly difficult dilemma. Her father tried to show that his argument was not with her but with the man she had married, the man whom he had now recognized as a political enemy. But as he battered William with his sour comments, James was unknowingly preparing the ground for the great choice she would eventually have to make between loyalty to a husband and loyalty to a father. In this conflict her deeper feeling for her husband and her great love of the Protestant religion gradually alienated her from the father she had always loved, and led her towards that point where she could even agree to occupy the throne he had vacated. In the perspective of history, this might appear to be a sudden and unnatural act; unnatural it was, and indeed it seemed so to her; but the process leading up to it was long and gradual, and it was the natural outcome of her father's folly and obstinacy, which she had begun to see in their true colours during this dark and difficult year.

CHAPTER 12

THE ATTACK ON ORANGE

THE STRAIN of the summer of 1681, together with the hot and dusty weather, exacerbated the eye trouble with which the Princess had been afflicted in the spring. Soon after William arrived back from England, she began to talk of going to Aix, where she had found the waters so beneficial after her illness two years before. Both she and William could have done with some kind of treatment to help them through the difficult months that lay ahead, but Louis XIV was acting in such a way that it was essential for William to remain on hand in case of an emergency. In September he was 'allarumd'—James's spelling—when he heard that the French had occupied Strasbourg, and by early November it became clear that Louis had designs on Luxembourg. At this rate it seemed likely that once again the enemy would be at the frontiers of the United Provinces. Charles, having calmly pocketed a bribe from Louis, was prepared to sit back and watch the French blockade whichever town they chose. He had given a promise that he would call a Parliament, but obviously had no intention of doing so. With the English so effectively silenced, Louis felt no compunction about making further encroachments, and there were signs that Louis intended to make more trouble in William's inherited principality of Orange in the south of France. But at least for the Princess there was one piece of news interesting enough to distract her from the international situation, and uncontroversial enough for her to be able to discuss in a letter to Frances.

A few days after the Prince's thirty-first birthday, Lady Temple received an interesting visitor, Elizabeth, daughter and heiress of the Earl of Northumberland, who had been married at the age of twelve to Henry Cavendish, Lord Ogle. He died after a year of marriage, and Lady Ogle, who was still only fourteen, had recently re-married. Her new husband was Thomas Thynne of Longleat, a well-known Whig and supporter of Monmouth. Almost immediately after her marriage, she abandoned her husband and fled to the Hague; Sidney accompanied her, boarding the yacht and conducting her as far as Gravesend. Her arrival caused a sensation, and the Princess longed to know what everyone was saying about it in England:

You complain for want of news but I believe we have the most now to send from hence having my Lady Ogle here. I long to know what people say of it in England, sure nobody can blame her for getting from such a man as Mr Thynne was.

Was there any political significance behind this strange behaviour, everyone wondered, or was it simply that the girl disliked her new husband's face? The question was at the moment unanswerable, which allowed the ladies of the Hague to indulge in some pleasurable speculation.

In spite of the danger from the French, the Princess was still able to enjoy herself, and she often went several times a week to watch William's company of French comedians. But the enemy was watching even this apparently harmless compartment of the Stadholder's life. His leading actor, William Marcoureau, Sieur de Brécourt, had fallen into debt, and was therefore an obvious subject for bribery or blackmail. Louis had once said of him, years before when he was playing in Paris, that he could make the very stones laugh. While he amused audiences at the Hague, he also tried out his skill at playing a part in the grimmer farce of international espionage. He became involved in a plot, with other conspirators, to kidnap people of importance, including a leading French Huguenot named Sardan, and it was believed, the Prince himself. 'We were all extremely surprised yesterday with the news from the Hague of a design of seizing your Highness and carrying you away,' Hyde wrote in a letter to William on December 2. The plot was uncovered, Brécourt escaped and fled to Paris, and the other conspirators were arrested. One of these, La Garigue, was sentenced to death, but William pardoned him, thus for once calling forth expressions of approval from his father-in-law:

I see by your letter that a French officer of dragoons that commanded the party which were to have carried away the French man from Amsterdam, was condemmed to be beheaded, but that you had pardoned him. I do not find by your letter that you thought they had any other design than that for which they came, tho' 'twas reported here they had some more considerable design, but let it have been what it will, I am glad you were not aimed at by them.

William himself showed no sign of alarm. He wrote to thank Hyde for expressing concern about his safety and assured him that the conspirators had no more sinister plan than to carry Sardan back to France, though he had to admit there were many circumstances 'which would lead one to think otherwise'. He was indifferent about his own safety, an admirable attitude, but a worrying one for his wife.

The Prince and Princess spent a quiet Christmas at the Hague. In the new year of 1682 they had the pleasure of a private visit from Sidney, who crossed from Greenwich in one of the King's yachts. At about this time Mary received a long letter from her father giving details of Mary Beatrice's fall from a horse; she had been dragged and kicked, but had been fortunate enough to fall on to soft ground and had escaped with some bad bruises. The Duchess had promised her mother and husband after this that she would never ride again, a great deprivation for her, as she was a far keener, more accomplished and more courageous horsewoman than Mary, who preferred to keep her feet firmly on the ground.

The year began uneventfully enough; the Princess gave out her usual new year's gifts, amounting in all to over a thousand gelders. At church on January 1 and at communion on the same day, she put five gelders into the collection, and set eighteen more aside to be used for the offertory up to April. She paid back to Bentinck the sum of 104 gelders which he had lent her long ago in the summer when she was at Dieren, treated herself to three new Virginia nightingales, and paid a bill for chocolate, a delicacy which she was to find all too tempting. She was still working on the bed-hangings, for which she had ordered more silk and worsteds. It was not surprising that her allowance did not always stretch as far as she would have liked, with payments to poor women and to various ladies about the court ('To Lady Hamilton for this month 15—15'), the servant who looked after her birds, and a payment for twelve pairs of gloves for the chimney-sweeper.

In the new year, after weeks of rain, there were fierce storms followed by widespread flooding, which caused great damage to trade, as ships were unable to leave harbour. The inundations were said to be the greatest ever known; most of Zetland was under water, and in several towns there were horrifying stories of people being swept away and drowned. Damage was estimated at ten millions, and William himself lost property valued at £15,000. Such acts of God had to be accepted philosophically, but it was less easy to sit down under the inroads of a human invader. In February the expected blockade of Luxembourg began. The Spaniards appealed to William for help and to England as well.

Feeling more confident now that he was siding with France, Charles invited his brother to London. So, with the Duke of York at his side telling him that to call a Parliament or to go to war would cause the ruin of monarchy in general and the family in particular, there was little hope that the King would give his nephew any help or even any sympathy. In Holland, French propaganda was having its effect. Friesland, which was headed by a separate Stadholder, Henry Casimir, was beginning to veer, and Amsterdam, traditionally Gallic in its allegiance, needed even less persuasion. The Prince was working himself to the point of exhaustion trying to keep his country loyal to the cause, and he attended as many meetings of the Assembly as he could. He was sure that the treaty of Nimeguen should be honoured, which meant that the United Provinces were under an obligation to support Spain in the defence of Luxembourg, to which France had no right under the treaty. Amsterdam, as usual, led the resistance to any idea of going to war. Amsterdam's leader, van Beuninghen, had been over in England, having long conversations with everyone, sending lengthy despatches home, and holding daily meetings with those who were well known to be opposed to the court. He even went so far as to ask the King whether it would not be better if he persuaded his brother to be a Protestant, whereupon Charles raised his eyes to heaven and said it was not for lack of trying. Van Beuninghen was a loquacious man, far more ready to talk than to listen, and his efforts in England did William little good.

In March, the Prince achieved a treaty between his own country, the Emperor and Sweden. Some of the German relations with whom he had hunted so fast and furiously also looked like joining this alliance, but a Turkish offensive in Hungary took everyone's mind off the subject which to William was the only one that mattered. At the end of the month, the French suddenly withdrew from Luxembourg and suggested that the controversy should be solved by arbitration with England as the mediator. The Spanish rejected this idea; Charles's previous unreliable behaviour made them understandably chary, and they must have realized that in spite of all William's urging, it was unlikely that the English King had any intention of calling a Parliament. The end of the month also saw the finish of Sidney's visit, and the ex-envoy went away with a letter from William in which the Prince urged his father-in-law to look more favourably on his friend. The Duke replied that Sidney would have to justify himself by his own actions.

After spending most of April at Dieren, the Prince and Princess returned to the Hague for the May celebrations. 'I hope you will have fair weather for the Kermesse, for otherwise there will be very dirty doings,' Mary's father wrote. The festive season passed off uneventfully, with the usual pattern of entertainment and military show, the city militia parading in front of the Prince and Princess to the thunder of gun salutes, and their orange scarves making a splash of colour. In the evening William and Mary went out masked to visit booths at the fair with their friends, the Princess entering into the fun and changing her clothes several times to avoid being recognized. On one occasion, when visiting the opera, they witnessed an undignified scene. Three musicians in the orchestra, the brothers Charles and William Martinelli and Etienne Ramboire, attacked one of the theatre officials and started to pull out his hair, incapacitating him so badly that he was unable to collect the audience's money. All the same, although the Prince had hardly seen Charles Martinelli in a favourable light, he later negotiated with him and gave him permission to present opera in partnership with Augustin Fleury with whom he was to share the profits. Fleury retired after several months, but Martinelli persisted, running the company with thirty actors and as many musicians. He managed to establish a monopoly by extracting permission from the sheriffs to carry on for three years to the exclusion of any other director. The sheriffs, flattered at being asked to indulge in artistic patronage, gave their consent on condition that the director put at their disposal a row of seats or a box for at least four people. The enterprise probably did not last for as long as three years, for the overheads were extremely high, and support tended to fluctuate.

When the Kermesse was over, the Prince and Princess left the Binnenhof and went to Honselaersdyck. They were there when they heard the news that the usual rejoicing for Charles's birthday had been damped when he fell ill with a 'feverish distemper', though he had recovered in two days, 'to the joy of the nation'.

In June the Princess fulfilled a long-standing ambition to visit Brussels. Even a private tour was dependent on political conditions, and she had not been able to visit the Spanish Netherlands before because William and the Governor, the Duke of Parma, had not seen eye to eye. Parma's successor, the Marquis of Grana, was a more sympathetic character, and since William had in recent months been pressing his own country to support Spain against French aggression, his wife's appearance in Brussels helped to reinforce his own position. It was an enjoyable visit, and she was kept so busy while she was there that she did not have time to write to her father or her sister. Meanwhile, William took the opportunity of visiting the frontier towns, and on the way back from Flanders gave everyone a shock when he was nearly drowned in a boating accident.

When Mary returned to Honselaersdyck she learned that Frances Apsley had been married to Sir Benjamin Bathurst, an important man in the commercial world. The Princess wrote to her at once, expressing the hope, in her generous-minded way, that Frances would have the blessing which she herself was denied:

To begin my letter in the forms to a new married Lady it must be with wishing you much joy, and nine months hence two boys, for one is too common a wish.

She had to admit that she felt hurt because Frances had not seen fit to tell her the news before it was known to everyone else:

I know 'tis a hard thing to say 'I am to be married', yet one can always write more than one can say and to a friend one need semple [sic] nothing, especially so true a one as you have always found me, and indeed I won't forgive it till you write me all the particulars.

As the Princess had never heard of Sir Benjamin before and knew nothing about him, she was eager for details, which her friend seemed reluctant to give, so that she was forced to write again, this time in 'a chiding mood'. 'I find the changing of your condition has also changed your mind a great deal,' she complained. But a letter from Lady Bathurst soon put the matter right:

Since I writ my last I have received a letter from my dear Aurelia which had it come sooner would have prevented my last, for in it you give me a full account of all your business and by it I find you think yourself very happy and you are the best judge in that matter. I am glad with all my heart for your sake you are so well satisfied and I hope your happiness will increase every day as long as you live, such are my wishes for you.

She told Frances that her letters were always welcome; she only regretted that she herself could not write as often as her friend, for she so seldom had any news to send that would be of mutual interest.

The Princess left the Hague in mid-July and, as usual, after spending a few weeks at Soestdyck, she went on to Dieren. During the summer months she was constantly receiving letters from her father, who appeared to be in a far more exuberant mood that usual. From Newmarket in the spring he had written to say that things had so far improved for him that he was to be allowed to return to London. Well bolstered by French support, the King now thought that he could risk having his brother back permanently. But when James went to Scotland to collect his Duchess, he met with a disaster which nearly settled the succession question for good and all. His ship foundered on the Lemon and Ore sandbank and went down with great loss of life, but he himself was saved, as well as Mumper and other dogs, his priests and a box of valuables. Catholic sources gave it out that the pilot was a Presbyterian, which was enough to explain why the ship had wandered off its course; on the other hand, there were a good many Protestant murmurs about the fact that so many good sailors, including Hyde's brother, had lost their lives, while the Catholic element, not to mention a boatload of hounds, had escaped unscathed.

James's return journey was less eventful. He made sure that his wife travelled in a large steady boat, for she was four months gone with child. 'His Ma. is master,' the Duke wrote triumphantly, when he had been in London for a few days. The dirge about the Duke of Venice was silenced at last. He wrote frequently to tell his daughter or son-in-law that everything was, in his customary spelling, 'quiat'. The Duke of Monmouth was out of favour, which added to his high spirits, and furthermore there was the hope that, before long, Mary Beatrice would produce the much-awaited son.

The only slight cloud on the York horizon was the behaviour of Anne, who was in such uncharacteristically high spirits that people were beginning to believe that she must be in love. She was surprising even herself by arising at an unnaturally early hour. 'Since I came to town,' she told Frances, 'I am grown a very good housewife for I am constantly dressed by prayer time and I have been very often ready between nine and ten.' In August there was a good deal of scandal circulating on the subject, for it was known that Lord Mulgrave, later Duke of Buckingham, was making advances, writing love letters, and even proposing marriage. The Duke of York was naturally displeased, for he had far more ambitious plans for his daughter. Since it was even suspected that Mulgrave might be a member of Monmouth's faction, James did not waste any time in putting an end to the affair. Mary also felt vexed by what she heard, though for rather different reasons, and she expressed her anxiety in a letter to Frances:

If I could love you better than I did before, you last letter would make me do so, to see the concern you are in for my poor sister. I am sure all who are truly her friends must be so, for my part I never knew what it was to be so vexed and troubled as I am at it, not that I believe my sister very innocent; however I am so nice upon the point of reputation that it makes me mad she should be exposed to such reports, and now what will not this insolent man say being provoked. Oh my dear Aurelia 'tis not to be imagined in what I concern I am that I should ever live to see the only sister I have in the world, the sister I love like my own life, thus abused and wronged.

In mid-August, a letter arrived from James. 'The Duchess,' he announced, 'was this morning delivered of a girl.' The news came as a relief to William and Mary. King Louis, on the other hand, said flatly that he wished it had been a son, and hoped that such a *bénédiction* would not be long delayed.

More alarming news came a few days later when the court was at Hooge Soeren. The Prince appeared at the supper table with a serious face and at the beginning of the meal he said, '*Hébien, messieurs, les françois m'accom-*

modent bien.' He went on to tell the company that a regiment of dragoons had arrived at Orange under the command of Montanègre who announced that he had orders to break down the walls of the town, adding other boastful threats. The Prince was so angry that he could hardly contain himself. For months now the French had been humiliating him; in Burgundy a petty court was trying to prove that his estates there really belonged to the Countess d'Isenghien. D'Avaux had been behaving more rudely than ever, and now there was this direct attack on Orange. The Prince kept returning to the subject, saying how necessary it was to have patience until the time came when one was in a strong enough position to have one's due revenge. He added that he hoped he would not die before he found the means to achieve it.

William had been single-minded before, but the news of this latest act of aggression proved to a be turning point both for him and for his wife. His desire for vengeance became the driving power that was to rule his life and hers, cutting across family ties, allowing no distraction. William was now a dedicated man. His wife, sensitive, thoughtful and compassionate, could not remain unmoved by the reports she heard about French brutality in Orange. It might be her general aim to keep clear of the troubled world of politics, but her principles were too strong and her religion too sincere for her to remain impassive in the face of this new crop of refugees which came flooding into Holland. When it was a question of the victims of French aggression, the Princess could not be non-committal. D'Avaux noticed her partiality and commented on it with distaste.

CHAPTER 13

PROTESTANT CHAMPIONS

As soon as William heard about the attack on Orange he wrote to Charles protesting strongly, invoking the family link and demanding help in the name of the Stuarts. His uncle paid no attention to his appeal, and William then wrote to Hyde imploring him to use his powerful influence to support the supplication. 'It is a long time since I tormented you with my own particular interests,' he wrote, 'but now I find myself obliged, to my great regret, by the outrages of France against me.' James, in a letter, rather half-heartedly promised to speak to the French Ambassador, and he then went on hastily to other matters.

The attack on Orange cast a blight over the rest of the summer season. After a few days at Hooge Soeren, the Prince went to Dieren, and the Princess, who had been at Staveren, joined him 'with all her *volck*'. For once William abandoned his usual custom of dining at mid-day with his men friends, and he ate in mixed company with the Princess and her ladies. Everyone was taking it in turns to keep the Prince amused, but it was no easy task to entertain him and to take his mind off the perfidy of France. One evening, Lord Cornbury visited the court. He was Hyde's nephew, a thick-set youth, who lacked the intelligence to realize that William might not feel too friendly disposed in view of the fact that Hyde had not per-suaded Charles to intercede for him in the Orange affair. The Prince, who had suffered so much humiliation himself, took the unkind step of revenging himself on this rather harmless boy, and, for a start, refused to put him up. When Cornbury came to supper, the Prince sat next to him, but did not speak to him once. Sylvius, who never missed anything, was soon spreading it about that the young guest was so upset by this treatment that tears came into his eyes. He was not only the person to find William disagreeable at this time. Most of the courtiers were only too glad to escape from him and to be given a chance to wait on the Princess, who was much better at hiding her feelings, and continued to be charming to everybody. Huygens was delighted when the Princess sent for him to come to her antechamber, where she was doing her embroidery. Even more

delightful for him was the occasion when, after the court had moved to
Soestdyck in October, he walked to the mill with the Princess and let her
look at the clock-tower at Utrecht through his spy glass.

When the court was in the country there was little for anybody to do
except to gossip about William and Mary and the other courtiers—about
who had had a child by whom, and other interesting subjects. Bassett
was played, ducats were won and lost, and a great deal of delicious,
fattening chocolate was drunk. Among her possessions the Princess now
had a great silver chocolate-pot, which was undoubtedly in constant use,
to the detriment of many courtly figures. The appearance of Halley's
Comet, which came into view when all the constellations were in con-
junction, as well as the three superior planets, Saturn, Jupiter and Mars,
caused a welcome distraction. Huygens went to the trouble of getting up
at four o'clock in the morning for several days running to observe this
phenomenon. He was very irritated by the fact that he was away from the
Hague at this time, and therefore cut off from his mathematical instruments and his *machine planisphérique*. He wrote to his brother Christiaan
asking him to despatch his glass at once, advising him to wrap it in sable
rather than in a woollen cloth. To his disappointment the glass he had
ordered from England had proved too dark to be of use.

Van Citters, the Dutch Ambassador in England, reported that everyone
there was in a great state about the comet. It was being said that such an
astronomical event, when all the constellations found themselves together,
had only occurred four times since the creation—at the time of the Flood,
the birth of Christ, the ruin of the temple at Jerusalem, and at this present
moment. 'Here are things that you still know nothing about,' said Huygens.

For the Princess, at any rate, the comet did not presage any dramatic
incidents. It is true that her half-sister, Charlotte, was to die at six weeks
old, but otherwise the news from England was happy. Anne had extricated
herself from the unfortunate affair with Mulgrave, and Frances was
enjoying married bliss. On her return from Soestdyck the Princess concentrated on domestic affairs; she bought herself a new cockatoo, two
copper tea kettles, four porcelain basins, a chamber-pot, a tea-pot, a sugar
box and a little dish. Towards the end of the year she was pleasantly tantalized by a hint in one of Lady Bathurst's letters:

Your kind letter dear Aurelia puts [me] in a strange impatience to know what it is
you dare not writ . . . for God's sake put me out of my pain and let me know it,
if ever you have loved me . . . if ever you have loved or do either father mother
sister brother, and last of all if you love your dear husband I conjure you to let
me know and that quickly . . . put no name nor no superscription but put it for

me in what you writ to my Mam or let my sister herself send it these, or any other way you can think of so I do but know it.

It was a trying winter for the Prince, with d'Avaux more active than ever—he was continually urging the more peace-loving States to resist the Stadholder's proposal to raise an army of 16,000 men—and van Beunighen behaving more foolishly than ever in England. For years now, William had tried to humour this Amsterdamer, but his patience had evaporated at last, and when in January 1683 van Beunighen resigned his post and came home, the Prince made it clear that he would have no more to do with him. Van Beunighen was an unbalanced man whose loquaciousness turned him, for all his brilliance, into a bore. 'Out of the abundance of his imagination [he] is apt to reason a man to death' was how Temple described it, and Voltaire said he had 'the vivacity of a Frenchman and the pride of a Spaniard'. He reacted to events in 'the enthusiastical way' and was not to be trusted.

The Prince decided to go to Dieren early to escape from the frustrations of political life, but even when he was away he could not avoid hearing what was going on in the world outside. While he was still enjoying the hunting season, he learned that Louis had treated a delegation from the States with indifference. The deputation had been sent to remonstrate with the French King for razing the walls of Orange, but he used his most high-handed approach and refused to give the Dutchmen any satisfaction. Worse still, Charles simultaneously made it clear that William need not expect any support from him over the question of Orange. When he heard this the Prince became very angry indeed, in fact he was in such a bad temper for several days that everybody did their best to keep out of his way, and even the Princess did not dare go near him.

He soon recovered. At Dieren, his faithful friends—Zuylestein, Bentinck, Borselin and Fagel—suffered a long exile from the Hague in order to be with him, keeping boredom at bay by playing cards in Huygen's room until eleven o'clock at night. Sometimes William called Huygens in to play bassett with the Princess, which helped to pass the time a great deal quicker.

Frances Bathurst was expecting her first child shortly. 'As for your illness,' the Princess told her, "tis you know what nobody was ever pitied for and therefore you must not expect it from me, though I wish you might have a child with the least trouble that could be.' Strangely enough, when Frances gave birth in May, she brought into the world boy twins—exactly what the Princess had wished for her. One of them did not survive, and

Mary wrote to her in her usual sympathetic way: 'When I wish you joy of your son you may believe I do it from the bottom of my heart, and that you may have as many more as you can wish, to repair the loss of the dead one.'

The Princess returned to the Hague for the Kermesse according to her usual custom, but she was back at Dieren when she heard that Frances had lost the second twin. Her friend was suffering from severe toothache, but Mary hoped this might be a sign that she had become pregnant again. 'I fancy you would be very glad,' she wrote, 'as you have reason to have some children to live and be a comfort for those you have lost, but I need say no more of this for you know my heart, and therefore may believe I wish you all things that may conduce to your happiness.'

In June startling news came from England. A plot had been uncovered, and it was revealed that some conspirators had planned to seize the King and his brother at Rye House, on their return to London. By good fortune they had left earlier than expected owing to a bad fire which had broken out in Newmarket. For once the Princess heard the news first-hand, from her father, which pleased her, for, she complained, 'everybody puts me off to better hands as they call it and I hear nothing'. James was full of indignation. This, he told William, was 'not such a plot as that of Dr Oateses but a real one . . . the conspirators . . . are most of them phanaticks in principels [*sic*] or conversation'. He reported that arms had been found in one house, three-pounders, suitable for street fighting. 'The blunder-busses were prepared,' wrote one commentator. 'Those bloody villains who design my destruction' was how the King described the conspirators. The Duchess talked of '*L'orrenda cospirazione*', Louis of the '*détestable conspiration*', and Cordebò of the '*diabolico disegno*'. The Duchess was sure that the fire at Newmarket which had made her husband leave early was the miraculous effect of the divine providence.

Soon after the discovery of the Rye House plot, William sent Bentinck to England. Although he had written himself, before the discovery of the plot, assuring the King that he nursed '*une extrême aversion pour une rupture nouvelle*', as soon as he heard about the conspiracy he knew that he would have a hard task to persuade his uncles that he, as the great Protestant champion, had not had a hand in the plan. Bentinck was there-fore to carry a secret letter which he was to give the King at his own discretion, assuring him that none of the Rye House plotters would be harboured in Holland. In general Bentinck was charged with the task of re-gaining the King's confidence and of enlisting his help against the French.

Bentinck was delayed for several days by unfavourable weather, and while he was waiting to embark he received a letter from the Prince who was at Breda. William enclosed a lock of hair which he wanted set in a ring, and he added a postscript—'Do not tell the Princess that I have written to you nor about the ring.' The air of secrecy given by this has been used as a basis on which to build a theory that William was being unfaithful to his wife, but husbands have been known to make presents to their wives as well as to their mistresses, and it seems natural that William was planning to give the Princess a surprise. He had been visiting towns in the south and was hoping to join Mary at Dieren later in the month. Bentinck was to ask Loofs to send the ring, when he had set it with the Prince's lock of hair, to Dieren.

Mary had not been in Gelderland for long when the Prince arrived after a particularly tiring journey; it had taken him three days to come and he had travelled all night. He was greeted with the news that the Turks were besieging Vienna—'for my consolation', he put it, with weary sarcasm. Because of this new turn of events he had to change his plans and go off to the Hague after only a day's rest, leaving the Princess and all his suite at Dieren. 'On Saturday my wife arrived at Dieren,' he told Bentinck, 'and she was very upset that I had to leave on Sunday; I was no less so.' This hardly gives the impression of a man who is planning a clandestine present for his mistress. His one day at Dieren had been happy enough, and he noted to his satisfaction that everything there was growing exceedingly well in the garden and the plantations, though there was little fruit and the melons had been spoilt by the rain which had been heavier in Gelderland than in Holland.

William found that affairs in Hungary were not as serious as he had at first feared, and after staying at Zuylestein where he indulged in a *rude* chase lasting five and a quarter hours, during which time no fence was refused, he set off again for Dieren where he was soon enjoying more hunting. Meanwhile he waited impatiently for news from Bentinck. 'I don't know how I shall do without you for so long,' he had written. Bentinck was shown great friendliness in England, but his visit produced little result. He talked to the King 'at large' about the peace, and left Charles under no illusions about the Prince's attitude. The King said he was sorry that the Prince had made up his mind that a general peace could not be made on the conditions that France was offering. 'I cannot imagine,' he told his nephew, 'as matters stand now in Christendom, that the agreement can be made upon easier terms . . . You may be assured that, whatever happens, I will ever be as kind to you as if you were my own son, and I will not fail to do all that lies in my power for your satisfaction about the business of Orange, though I must tell you that I apprehend it depends very much upon general agreement'.

Hyde, now created Earl of Rochester, treated Bentinck with great civility. William thanked him for this, and also for his candour. 'I believe you are acquainted with my disposition sufficient to know that it is a thing I esteem above all others,' he wrote. He was pleased by Rochester's assurances that he would do all in his power to set William right in the minds of his uncles. At the same time he was grieved by the thought that the King and Duke were so opposed to him in public affairs. As far as the internal affairs of their respective kingdoms were concerned, it was obvious that they must go their own ways, but, he added, 'I hope that in future they will have a little more faith in me on the subject of foreign affairs, since assuredly, from being nearer the scene of action, we are better informed. . . .'

William asked Bentinck to look out in England for a quiet horse that would make a suitable mount for Mary. But the Prince was not allowed to enjoy a peaceful time in her company for long. Early in September the French began annexing territories in Flanders, and the terrified de Grana was appealing for support as tales of burning and plundering came through, and Brussels was flooded with refugees.

The Emperor was too busy with the Turks to give any help, and when William tried to persuade the States to sanction new levies he began to find out how busy d'Avaux had been that summer. Each day there were angry scenes in the Assembly, and William came home bitter and frustrated. On November 5, a date that tends to invite drama, d'Avaux went to the States-General and spoke to the Assembly reassuringly about his master's intentions. French encroachments in Flanders, he insisted, were caused by the unco-operative attitude of Spain in general and the Marquis de Grana in particular. He was followed by the Pensionary of Amsterdam who harangued the company for over an hour, telling them how harmful war must prove to the Dutch economy, and raking up the old argument that had so incensed William's father about Amsterdam having to pay more than its share of the cost of the levy. At this William could contain himself no longer. He took the oath and began to speak, pointing out that there were other cities which showed less interest in trade and more in the protection of their country. What right had Amsterdam to dictate to all the others? William grew so impassioned that he lost his temper completely; 'He who is usually master of himself left the Assembly brusquely before the session ended, so little was he in command of himself,' d'Avaux reported.

As soon as the Prince had gone, Pensionary Fagel rose to his feet and treated the Assembly to a heated harangue. Fagel was now one of William's most faithful supporters and friends, and he was rapidly filling the gaps left in William's life by the death of Ossory and the recall of Sidney. 'A very sincere and understanding man,' Arlington had called him, and his strong religion made him incline towards William and England rather than d'Avaux and France. The two men had a natural affinity, and Fagel, coming of a family that was greatly respected in Holland, proved a useful and influential friend.

The Prince had need of allies. All his patient work with the States seemed now to have been in vain. As usual, although he was the only man who was working realistically to save the peace, he was being branded as a war-monger, for men only become national heroes when they have saved their country from an almost fatal state of weakness brought about by the short-sightedness of their compatriots; and though he appeared to be hard and unfeeling, he was, as those who knew him intimately could testify, someone who cared deeply about his country, who was sensitive to slights, and who was also human enough to be as concerned about a scandal concerning one of his own Blue Guard as he was about the most vital affairs of state. Both he and the Princess had been chastened by experience, and in Mary's case the constant background of uncertainty against which her six years of married life had been played out, had already made her grow into a character more understanding and sympathetic than the self-pitying girl who had first come to Holland.

The Princess was now far more outward-looking and full of concern for other people, most particularly for Frances who had recently lost her father and also suffered a miscarriage. 'One can hardly go about to comfort you, and indeed upon such occasions 'tis only from God it can come whom I beseech to grant you may bear it like a Christian,' she wrote, and on December 10 she added:

I have had two dismal letters of late from my dear Aurelia and indeed I don't wonder at it for I fancy nothing can be more melancholy than after the loss you have had of such a father and of a son (it may be) and now to see your Mother in such a weak condition would make anybody so; but I hope in God Lady Apsley will quickly recover herself again and you get another great belly which are the two greatest comforts you can have.

The Princess was delighted to learn that her sister, who had married Prince George of Denmark in the summer, was finding him a congenial companion. 'You may believe it was no small joy to me to hear she liked him and I hope she will do so every day more and more,' Mary told

Frances, 'for else I am sure she can't love him and without that 'tis impossible to be happy which I wish her with all my heart as you may easily imagine knowing how much I love her.' The Prince of Denmark was fair-haired, tall, and good-looking, and he had created a far better impression than William had when he came to claim Mary. The marriage was not quite the one that William had planned, and some people said he had sent Bentinck over to prevent it. All the same it was a relatively harmless match, for an alliance with Denmark was not likely to alter the balance of power, nor would it give Anne precedence over her sister.

Mary hoped that Anne would trust her with some commissions, 'for', she confessed, 'there is nothing pleases me more than to be so employed'. Sadly she had to admit that most things were better in England. Each new chaplain came over with a load of tomes, and in the previous spring Aurelia had ordered for her a slim volume in blue Turkey leather with gilt leaves, probably for use as a diary or a commonplace book. 'The outside I leave to you,' she told Frances, 'because there may be some new way which I have not yet seen of ordering it. I only desire once more it may be fine; as for the bigness I would have it of the size of Salles' Introduction to a Devout Life, the paper also of that thickness but not above 120 leaves in it, this I would desire you, dear Aurelia, to send me as soon as is possible.'

At about this time the Princess began to be rather more extravagant in her spending. Perhaps this was due to the fact that Loofs was a good salesman, or his work so exquisite that she found it difficult to resist, but in any case, by 1683 she was owing him over two thousand gelders for diamonds. Later in the year she paid him a further fifteen hundred, and also spent four hundred on 'silver playthings'. Her book-keeping was becoming careless, and apart from the usual bills to the workwoman and the bookbinder, there were other sums which she was quite unable to account for:

Besides laid out for which I have no bills according to my account ... 4590
So that I have lost and given away which I have forgot   358–615

The Princess's shopping habits were influenced by the international situation. Earlier on she had ordered some of her more fashionable clothes from France; for example, in April 1680 there had been an entry in her account book which ran 'Things from France . . . 228–9', and in January 1682 'Combs from France'. Now she was no longer patronizing French merchants, though there are frequent references to small purchases from French Protestant refugees.

Both William and Mary found it impossible to ignore the plight of the French Protestants who were now arriving in the Netherlands in increasing numbers, bringing with them frightening stories of persecution and torture. Those who were caught trying to escape were condemned to the galleys, but many managed to reach freedom, and they regarded Holland as their haven. Between 1684 and 1685 the campaign reached its crescendo; hundreds of Protestants were herded into the Catholic churches, and unless they testified at once, they faced all kinds of tortures—in the case of one couple, the wife had a fleur de lys imprinted on her forehead with a hot iron and the husband had his ears cut off; both suffered gangrene and subsequently died. Others were kept from sleep for so long that their brains were turned. Even children and old people were put under pressure and the women were sent to the nunneries where they were almost starved to death. Those who refused to take the Catholic sacrament were denied burial and their corpses left for wolves and dogs to eat. Many of those who escaped were skilled workers who were able to find employment without great difficulty, but the particular plight of young girls and widows of good family was brought to the notice of the Prince and Princess. As the restrictions became increasingly severe, it was often impossible for these unfortunate ladies to carry anything with them; lonely and penniless, they soon became a prey to temptation. A French refugee from Poitou, the Marquis de Venours, accused of trying to prevent conversions to the Catholic faith—a hanging offence—had escaped to Holland with his two daughters, and in 1683 he had proposed to the Burgomasters of Haarlem a plan for setting up a society where French Protestant ladies could live in a community 'without taking any vow nor anything approaching or savouring of papist superstition'. He chose Haarlem for its good air, 'poetic tranquillity' and proximity to the sea; and similar establishments were set up later at Rotterdam and the Hague. The Princess took a great interest in the scheme and contributed a thousand gelders a year to help in its upkeep. This came at a time when the directrice, Mlle de Moulin, and her assistant, Charlotte de Venours, one of the daughters of the Marquis, were almost in despair, their coffers empty and no more than three or four ladies in the large house that had been taken for the purpose. However the numbers grew rapidly, and the community was established with a chapel of its own, its finances and administration carefully watched over by the burgomasters. The ladies admitted were of all ages, from those under twenty to at least one octogenarian, and a set of sixty-three rules was drawn up to ensure that the society was run in a disciplined manner. The atmosphere was Calvinistic and austere. Only modest dress was

allowed, and no books could be read without the permission of the directrice, who possessed a master-key to all the rooms. No member could
receive a male visitor except in the presence of the directrice or her
assistant, and only fathers, brothers or uncles were allowed in the ladies'
private rooms. On no account was any man allowed to sleep in the house,
or even to eat there, unless he happened to be one of the pastors who came
in to take prayers.

It was part of the original plan to link the society with the establishment
in Holland of a Poitou carpet factory, as well as a hose and bonnet industry. Venours hoped that the Burgomasters would lend some money to
launch the scheme, which would later be financed by the sale of its
products. This project was never realized, but the inmates of the Society
were encouraged to use their hands and the aim was to bring them up
virtuous and well-educated in the fear of God.

Every lady was allowed to stay in her room until eleven o'clock in the
morning, and it was hoped that she would attend to her private devotions
during this time. As soon as everyone was downstairs, there was a session
of bible-reading, psalm-singing and prayers. Following the pattern of the
Princess's court, the rules stipulated that after lunch all the members must
do some kind of work with their hands, while somebody read aloud from
an edifying book.

The Princess was naturally most closely associated with the house for
refugee ladies which was opened at the Hague a little after the Haarlem
Society. A property was acquired called the Huis ter Noot outside the
town on the edge of the wood. Another house just behind the Kloosterkerk
was used at a later date, and refugee ladies who come from a less distinguished background were lodged by the municipality in a house in the
Westeinde. The Princess took a personal interest in the running of the
House, and she contributed 500 gelders twice yearly towards its upkeep.
She saw to it that the ladies carried out work suitable for their sex, and
that they were taught Dutch and given the opportunity to worship in
'the true Christian reformed religion.'

The municipality gave additional financial help, as well as exemption
from the normal tax on wine and beer. Those who joined were expected
to give whatever sum they could afford, and, if they subsequently married,
they were required to leave some of their original contribution behind.
Further help was requested from various sources for members who were
particularly in need of assistance. Some who had been able to salvage more
of their property than others were allowed to have their own servants, and
to eat with their own silver knives and forks rather than the tin ones sup-

plied by the establishment. At Haarlem those who were unable to pay the three hundred francs *pension* sat at a communal table where they were only given meat once a day and had to be content in the evening with a diet of milk and vegetables.

Once they were well established the Societies at Haarlem and the Hague continued to flourish. At one time the house at the Hague became so full that M. Mesnard, the Protestant pastor, put up in his own home those who were unable to find accommodation in the main building. It seems that the Protestant ladies were prepared to endure the strict regimen which did not allow them to go out without permission, and certainly not except in the company of other ladies, for the sake of enjoying security and liberty of conscience. Only 'honest recreations' were permitted, and every form of gambling, however harmless, was forbidden.

It was not surprising that in this boarding-school atmosphere there were sometimes squabbles, and there was serious unrest in the Haarlem Society in 1692, caused, it was thought, by dislike of the directrice who was altogether too haughty and formal. The problem of finding a suitable intendant, who was virtuous, zealous in the Protestant religion, of noble birth and of a humane disposition, can be well imagined, and the Hague Society also had some difficulty in appointing the right person. Mary's advice was sought by Mlle Obdan, whom she had chosen to be her representative in matters concerning the Society, after her departure for England, but she expressed her inability to advise without personal knowledge of the candidates. She put her complete trust in Mlle Obdan, and said sagely that it was only to be expected that quarrels must arise from time to time in a community made up entirely of the female sex.

The Societies continued for many years, and the one at Haarlem did not finally close until 1743. It was certainly due to the Princess's influence that they were able to overcome their initial difficulties and become a refuge for the victims of the French King's cruel intolerance. In those dark days when it seemed sometimes as if the light of the reformed Church must be extinguished for ever by Catholic tyranny, the Prince and Princess of Orange stood out as the great Protestant champions, with the Prince prepared to give his life to countering the menace of French aggression, and the Princess actively helping those who left everything and fled to a foreign country rather than submit to religious pressures.

CHAPTER 14

MONMOUTH IN HOLLAND

EVER SINCE the discovery of the Rye House plot the Duke of Monmouth had been under suspicion, and James certainly believed that his nephew had condoned the plans even if he had not actually been involved. As Burnet put it, Monmouth had 'lurked in England all this summer', writing letters to his father which everyone knew to be penned by Halifax, since the style was far more vehement and accomplished than anything he could have produced himself. The King tried to make his son confess publicly that he had played a part in the conspiracy, and hoped that he might extract an apology from him, but he was still incapable of concealing the strong paternal affection he felt for Monmouth. Rumours that Monmouth had fled to Flanders were current towards the end of October, but then he turned up suddenly and 'surrendered himself to Mr Secretary Jenkins at Whitehall, where (the thing being concerted) the King and the Duke went to him and after an hour's discourse allowed him to go to his lodging in the Cockpit, attended by his own servants, and under no other constraint than that of one sergeant-at-arms'.

The new year of 1684 opened under the threat of war and with Europe in the grip of a bitter cold spell. The winter had begun to set in early in December. In Holland the Zuyder Zee was quite frozen up, and in London an ox was roasted on the ice in front of Whitehall Palace. Commerce came to a halt, the rivers were sealed and the sea frozen three miles out. By that time it was generally believed that Monmouth had left England. On January 4 James, in a letter to William, said that Anna of Buccleuch was telling people that her husband had gone abroad, and in Holland it was thought that one of two mysterious travellers who had landed at Zeeland would prove to be the Protestant Duke.

Monmouth must have left London sometime before the packet boats stopped running. He travelled to Brussels with only one friend and a servant, but the Spanish Governor, de Grana, gave him a noble welcome and called him 'Royal Highness'. King Charles's instructions to Bulstrode, the British Resident in Brussels, that no military honours should be shown to Monmouth, were probably York-inspired, and James also saw to it that when Henrietta Wentworth followed him to Brussels in April, her luggage was well searched. Once the cold weather had lifted, Monmouth gave himself up to the pleasures of the turf, which was no great hardship to himself, and an activity that presented little menace to the affairs of his country. He was as firm as it was in him to be with the exiles who came to him uninvited and offered to put him in touch with Argyll and the Scottish malcontents; he simply told them it would be unnatural for him to rise against his father.

The Princess found the cold weather very trying. 'I have such terrible sore eyes,' she told Frances on February 1. 'The weather is now so terrible cold that if you will believe me my fingers ache with cold as I write so that this time you must expect no more but the assurance that my heart can never change.' To make things worse, the Prince was facing trouble on all sides. In the Assembly he was being criticized for sending the fleet to fetch Swedish mercenaries, and for having troops ready under orders to go to the aid of the Spanish. The English court was scheming with van Beunighen and the government of Amsterdam, and in Whitehall, as Reresby put it,' the Duke of York did now chiefly manage affairs, but with great haughtiness'. The 'French party' was growing in strength, while the French lady, as they called Louise de Kéroualle, Duchess of Portsmouth, had more influence over the King than any of his mistresses had wielded before. This situation made Louis feel more confident than ever, and all he would promise the frightened nations of Europe was a truce on condition that he was allowed to retain everything he had gained in peace or war. When the Elector of Brandenburg advised him to accept these terms, William exploded. 'France will take more in peace than she did in war,' he wrote. 'If ruin shall come upon us it is more honourable to lose what is ours with arms in our hands, than through submission to the farce of the "Chambers of Reunion", and in the end an honourable death is better than a cowardly life . . . As for me I was born in misfortune and reared in misfortune, but by God's grace I am again restored to the Honours of my fathers. One thing only pains me deeply, that the Elector, who has loved me from the cradle like a father, whom I honour as a son, has ranged himself on the side of the City of Amsterdam, which prides itself on always opposing me.'

William had given up trying to pacify the pro-French element in the Assembly. When de Grana, by a stroke of luck, intercepted a letter from d'Avaux which showed that some of the Deputies were fraternizing with the French, the Prince told Fagel to read it out in an Assembly of the

States of Holland, and then, shedding his customary reticence, he openly called his enemies '*ces coquins d'Amsterdam*', adding that van Beunighen deserved to have his head cut off.

There was yet another cause of friction. Chudleigh, the new British Envoy, was blatantly encouraging the opposition in Amsterdam. William found him 'a very foolish and impertinent man', and he certainly behaved with unbelievable insolence. D'Avaux maintained that William offered personal insults to Chudleigh, even, on one occasion, thrusting his walking stick into the Envoy's face, but if he did so it was probably under provocation.

The cold weather seemed to be going on for ever. 'We have the coldest Easter I think that ever was for it freezes every night still which makes the spring very backward,' the Princess complained. But the nearer summer came, the greater was the threat from the French armies. On May 15 there was unusual activity in the Prince's stables; horses were saddled up and baggage loaded. Early in the morning William set off for an unknown destination. He could have been off to Dieren for all anybody knew, but before long it became clear that he had gone to take command of the army.

With the coming of spring, Monmouth found that he could travel about more easily and he did not hesitate to do so. In his tactless way he had taken for his companion Lord Brandon, who had been under suspicion for complicity in the Rye House plot. Brandon had been imprisoned in the Tower and had only escaped execution because of insufficient evidence against him. Monmouth's first act after coming out of hibernation was to meet William at Brabant, and rumour had it that the Prince had forced the English regiments to give Monmouth military honours.

If William was hoping to provoke his father-in-law, he succeeded, and on May 20 James penned an angry epistle from Windsor:

I find by your letter, that the Duke of Monmouth had been to see you: I do not at all wonder that he did not send to advertise you of his coming to you, but do think it odd enough for him to present himself to you, after his having been engaged in so horrid a conspiracy, for the alteration of the government, and ruin of the King and our family.

On June 6 James wrote Mary an equally stiff letter which was brought to her by Sylvius. Her father told her that all loyal, 'monarchical' people were scandalized to hear about the civility which the Prince had shown Monmouth, especially as he was accompanied by Lord Brandon. 'I easily believe,' he told her, 'that you might have forgotten for what he had been in the Tower, yet others could not be ignorant of it, nor have short memories.' The time had now come, her father considered, for her to use her influence; 'in this affair methinks you might talk with the Prince (though you meddle in no others),' he wrote. He then went on, in the same scholarly vein:

And let the Prince flatter himself as he pleases, the Duke of Monmouth will do his part, to have a push with him for the crown, if he, the Duke of Monmouth, outlive the King and me. Some posts since I wrote pretty freely to the Prince upon this subject in general, to which I have yet had no answer: however, it will become you very well to speak to him of it.

As soon as she had finished reading this letter, Mary burst into tears. She told Sylvius that she was not her own master; it was the Prince who wished her to be civil to her cousin, and as a good wife she must obey him.

William returned from the front at the end of May on a short visit, but only a few days later he heard that Luxembourg had fallen and he wasted no time in going back to the army. He knew that the fall of this town opened the way into the Netherlands. Mary was left desolate, and she wrote to Frances from Honselaersdyck on June 9: 'The Prince is gone into Brabant so that I am now alone here; when he comes back is uncertain for which I am sure you will pity me.'

In the Prince's absence Fagel did his best to stand out against the majority which was clamouring to agree to a twenty-year truce with France, but there was little he could do, and William soon received a message telling him that he must not allow any hostile acts in the Netherlands. 'The very thought of it drives one mad,' William wrote to Waldeck '. . . but if such is the will of God we can only submit to it, having this consolation, that we have done our best for the public good.'

William left the army as soon as he heard that a treaty had been concluded in which France was to retain all her conquests—and these included Luxembourg. The situation could not have been more disheartening. A cold, anxious winter had been followed by the threat of imminent war and the ignominy of a great political defeat. His enemies at Amsterdam knew, and revelled in the fact, that they had triumphed over him. The United Provinces had once again deserted their allies, and the Prince doubted whether the Dutch would ever again find friends willing to help them if France should strike again.

June was a depressing month altogether, with days of ceaseless rain. The Princess was concerned about William's safety, and she was also worried about her sister, who had given birth to a stillborn child in May; it had been dead for some days, and as their father observed, ''tis a great mercy it came as it did and that she is so well after it'. This was the first of the many children, conceived at the rate of about one a year, who all died, 'so that,' as Burnet put it, 'the fruitfullest marriage that has been known in our age, had been fatally blasted as to the effect of it'. Mary wrote to Frances expressing her anxiety. 'You know how dear she is to me, and therefore will not doubt how much I was troubled for her. I am sure if it had bin myself I could not have been very much more, but I think we have all reason to thank God she is come off as she is, which methinks is almost a miracle to be so well of a dead child.' The only good news was that Frances was with child again. 'I wish you better luck than either the Duchess or my dear sister have had,' the Princess wrote.

The Duke of York had been so much in favour lately that he had grown insufferably haughty. His brother had made him Lord High Admiral, giving him the power, without the name and the patent, for, as a Catholic, he was not allowed to take the oaths and the sacrament and was officially barred from office. In his new exalted position, he felt he could dictate to everybody, not least his son-in-law. He kept harping on the subject of Monmouth; 'I can never trust to what he says or believe in him', he wrote, 'and I think you will be to blame if you do.' But William was not prone to following his father-in-law's advice at the best of times, and it seems that at present he had nothing to lose, even something to gain, by open defiance. Charles, like his brother, had been writing unpleasant letters, warning the Prince against his bastard son, and nobody can say exactly what William's motives were in ignoring his uncles' wishes so flagrantly. It is possible that the King's letters were not sealed with the special seal he had shown to William during his visit to Windsor, and it was for this reason that the Prince took no notice of their contents. It is more probable that he wanted to show the King and the Duke that if they wished to let themselves fall under the influence of France, they could not expect any further co-operation from him; if he felt like entertaining his wife's cousin, he would do so.

It is not clear whether William actually invited Monmouth to join a hunting party at Dieren in July, but it seems unlikely that the Duke would have hazarded the three-day journey from Brussels to Dieren if he had anticipated a snub. On the last lap of his journey from Nimeguen onwards, he was given an almost royal reception, and he was generously entertained at the hunting lodge. One day William received a message from van Beunighen who was trying out some conciliatory tactics. The *inflexibilité républicaine* for which this loquacious man was famous, was softening a little, but too late, for William felt he could not trust him—he had developed an air of eccentricity which was bordering on madness. Next came an urgent summons from Fagel who was laid up with gout and thought that William should come to keep watch in the Assembly as he was unable to do so himself.

Everyone waited to see whether the Prince would decide to return to the Hague, but on July 31 Huygens heard that he had made up his mind to go to Hooge Soeren, where the hunting was even better than at Dieren. In mid-July an eclipse of the sun had taken everybody's minds off the international situation; at Dieren there was great excitement among the ladies and gentlemen of the court, from the greatest to the least important, and Huygens manufactured a little *oculaire* of smoked glass for the Princess, who looked at the sun through it, and took great pleasure in doing so. The court remained at Dieren throughout September; a magnificent grotto was being built there with stones from a Lingen quarry, of a delicate pink, the colour of sugar candy, and glittering with crystals. Work began that autumn on a new hunting lodge at Hooge Soeren.

Monmouth remained with the court throughout the rest of the summer, and William even allowed him to introduce Henrietta Wentworth to the company there. The Princess had known Henrietta as a girl—she had been one of the cast of *Calisto*—but d'Avaux thought it very odd that she should be expected to show *honneurs extraordinaires* to Monmouth's mistress, however well-born she might be. When he heard this latest development Charles was so angry that he sent a complaint by Chudleigh who delivered it with even more than his customary insolence. William lodged a counter-protest, but the King did not reprimand his Envoy. On the contrary, he encouraged him.

Rumours had been reaching Charles that William was appointing officers recommended by Monmouth to the English regiments in Holland, and this did not please him either, for if the regiments came under the command of disaffected persons, they might be used against him at a later date. The Prince assured his uncle that he had not, in fact, made any such appointments, but the King remained unconvinced. The Duke of York, in October, heard that Monmouth intended to stay at the Hague for the winter. 'I could say more to you upon this subject,' he told his son-in-law. When van Citters visited the King, he found him enraged against his nephew. 'Without communicating with me, yes, ignoring my ban, he has acted entirely as he fancies,' the King declared, adding that he was as unmoved by William's excuses as he would be if a man went into a brothel and tried to justify himself by saying he had gone in only to convert people. Van Citters said, agreed, but if the man in question were known to live an irregular life and to be habitually debauched that would be one thing; if he were of known probity then at least that should be taken into account and his excuses given some consideration.

Owing to the threat of war, the Dutch court had been forced to spend more of the summer than usual at the Hague, and now, to compensate, William prolonged his stay in the country, giving it out that he would only go back in time for the opening of the Assembly at the Hague in mid-November. In October everyone went to Hooge Soeren, spending a few nights at Dieren before finally returning to the Hague. On November 13 the Princess wrote to Frances from Dieren:

I long very much to hear you are brought to bed, and hope in God you will have better luck than the last time. I have heard nothing of the 3 books you spake of, but believe I may find them at the Hague whither I am going tomorrow if it please God.

Monmouth tactfully absented himself once the court returned to the Hague. He went from Rotterdam to Delft by boat, and turned up in England with Henrietta and her mother in attendance. He behaved so discreetly that nobody really knew what had happened to him; at one time he seemed to have vanished altogether. There was a great deal of talk, and James told William that it was generally believed he had come to England for one reason or another. Eventually he returned to Brussels with Henrietta who had by now, according to her disapproving relation Skelton, 'bid farewell to all modesty'.

The Prince's health was very bad that autumn and he had several acute attacks of asthma. His battle with Amsterdam continued unabated, for that forceful city was more jealous than ever of his power; it even went so far as to pass a motion setting up Henry Casimir, Prince of Nassau, William's cousin, as its own Stadholder. In November, to prevent family misunderstandings, William arranged a meeting between himself, the Princess, Henry Casimir, his wife, and her mother, the Princess of Anhalt. A rendezvous had been arranged at Naarden, but Henry Casimir, a faint-hearted individual, sent his mother-in-law to conduct the interview. The Princess of Anhalt had been told what to say, but she had not progressed very far when the Prince interrupted her. 'I know what my cousin can do, I know what he would like to do, and I have seen what he has done,' he said impatiently, and went on to accuse the *Messieurs d'Amsterdam* of prostituting him in the eyes of all Europe, and of sacrificing him to France. 'As for me,' he added, 'I know what I have to do; if they have anything to say to me, they can talk to me in the Assembly of Holland.' When the Amsterdamers heard about this conversation, they became more convinced than ever of the *obstination insurmontable* of the Prince of Orange.

The Prince took his wife on a visit to Amsterdam, hoping that she would help to revive his flagging popularity. She was expected to be polite and gracious to the people of Amsterdam in order to help him win his political battles. She had to sit by and hear her husband being firm to the point of rudeness with his cousin's mother-in-law (she was also William's aunt). The backwash of his quarrels was continually threatening her. There were probably spies in her own household; d'Avaux was certainly bribing William's valet to bring him information. After the row in the summer, King Charles had recalled Chudleigh for consultations, and had sent him back to Holland with instructions to refuse to speak to the Prince or to pay him any respect. William in any case would not have let him set foot in his house, and Chudleigh asserted that he actually locked the gates of Honselaersdyck against him. One evening, early in January 1685, there was an incident at the Hague which could have been the prelude to a general eruption.

Snow had fallen at the new year, and it was now deep and crisp, giving those in the great world a chance to go out and show off their swift, ornate sledges. The Prince took Mary out for a ride in the Voorhout. Like everyone else at that carnival season, both the Prince and Princess were masked, though presumably their royal sledge was easily recognizable in the throng. Suddenly everybody's attention was attracted by a sledge which was being driven furiously, pushing through the traffic and finally cutting in in front of the Prince and refusing to give way, a blatant case of dangerous driving. William got out of his sledge and found himself standing whip in hand, in front of a gathering crowd, face to face with Chudleigh. The two men glared at each other; for a moment it looked as if William might use his whip, but he just managed to restrain himself.

On Saturday, January 9 the Princess spent a quiet evening and retired early. None of the ladies of the Hague visited her, knowing that she intended to go to Communion the next morning and would therefore prefer to be alone for rest and meditation. She was already half undressed when a message came from the Prince asking her to dress again and to come down to the audience chamber. This she did unwillingly, according to d'Avaux, but we have only his word for it. She descended to find her husband chatting amicably to the Duke of Monmouth. It was d'Avaux, of course, who said that William had sent for him; others maintained that the Duke had arrived unexpectedly at the Hague and that Bentinck had sought him out at the hostelry and brought him to the Palace. To have offered him hospitality at Honselaersdyck would have been pursuing trouble, but the Prince invited Monmouth to stay at the Mauritshuis in the Hague and sent servants to look after him. D'Avaux was justified when he said that people could only be astonished at this latest *démarche* on the part of the Prince, who in one breath announced that he had abandoned the Duke of Monmouth altogether, and in the next made him welcome at the Hague and loaded him with favours.

Monmouth's arrival was the signal for an outbreak of gaiety more brilliant than anything the Hague had seen for years. Asthmatic though he was and no lover of the dance floor, William went to several evening parties with his wife and her ladies, who included Elizabeth Villiers, Anne Bentinck's sister. In those first weeks in January, the Princess was often seen in public with her handsome cousin, leaning on his arm as they walked along the tree-lined Mall, or, most delightful and most shocking of all, learning to skate under his tuition. It was not surprising that there were some people, d'Avaux among them, who raised their eyebrows when they saw a royal princess with her skirts half tucked up—*à demi-retroussées*—clinging on to her uncle's bastard as she slid first on one foot and then on the other. The sober Dutch seemed to come alive in the cold weather, gliding on the ice, tearing across the snow on their sledges, and Mary, it seems, was infected with the general gaiety. She was past caring about the raised eyebrows; she was young and she was happy and there was a bond of natural affection between herself and her cousin. She blossomed in his presence and people commented on the laughter and the pleasantries that passed between them. One evening, with a large party, they drove over on sledges to the House in the Wood, up the great driveway and across the stable court. They went up the steps into the entrance hall, past the life-size marble statues of the Princes William I, Maurice, Frederick Henry and William II, and then up into the magnificent Orang-Zaal, the painted room decorated with allegorical pictures of the achievements of Prince Frederick Henry and the House of Orange. There, under the domed ceiling with its voluptuous ladies emerging from clouds, its swans, angels, peacocks and *putti*, the Duke of Monmouth led out his cousin, Mary of Orange, in the dance.

William's acquiescence in all this caused universal amazement. He was known to be the most jealous of men, and yet he was pressing the Duke to come over in the evenings to teach the Princess how to do country dances, allowing him to dine with her every day and walk with her in public, when as a rule she was never seen on foot outside her own garden. Normally he discouraged his wife from becoming too familiar with

anyone, man or woman, and some people thought that he welcomed the
Duke because most eyes were riveted upon the handsome visitor, which
gave him a chance to enjoy, unobserved, the witty conversation of Elizabeth Villiers. It is more probable that William's welcoming attitude was
due to reassurances from the Duke himself; before leaving England on his
most recent visit, the latter had been granted an interview with the King,
who, he maintained, had told him that York's period of favour was almost
over. Another stretch of exile in Edinburgh was inevitable and even
imminent. Ever since the summer, the King had been showing his
independence of the Catholics, and Monmouth probably advised William
that it was in his interest at this time to flout his father-in-law. It was said
—by d'Avaux of course—that the Prince forced his wife to go to the Hague
with Monmouth to hear the preacher Jurieu, who had published a book
casting aspersions on her father.

The Princess had been brought up to wear black and to fast all day on
January 30 in memory of her grandfather's execution, and this year, as she
sat all alone in the evening deprived of her supper, her husband appeared,
ordered her to take off her black dress and put on something gay, and then
swept her off to the comedy. This was all the more strange as William so
seldom patronized the theatre and had only been to the comedy three
times since All Saints' Day, although there were always four performances
a week. Furthermore, he made Mary dine in public; it was a large dinner,
with course following course, and the Princess did not appear to be hungry,
in fact she hardly touched anything. This was d'Avaux's story, and he was
the only person to tell it.

After this flaunting of the Stuart ethos, the round of gaiety continued
unabated, with balls, skating, theatre visits and sledge rides, until, quite
abruptly, on February 20, it all came to an end.

CHAPTER 15

A QUARREL FOR THE CROWN

ON FEBRUARY 20, 1685, in the evening, the Princess was entertaining some ladies of the Hague when she received a message asking her to go to William's room. Monmouth had also been sent for, and the Prince told them that a letter had just arrived bringing news of the death of Charles II. The Princess showed great emotion, and Monmouth was so overcome with grief that he had to go back to his house. He returned later in the evening and was closeted with the Prince until midnight sounded. The Prince lent him some money, and he left the Hague that night. It was given out next morning that he was still asleep, and he was well away before anyone realized he had gone. Some said they had been able to hear his cries of mourning outside in the street. His father's death had come just at the time when he had believed himself to be returning to favour, and had allowed himself to hope that he would be permitted to go back to England and the court life he loved. Now even his source of money was cut off, and there was nothing for him except the fortune of the wife he had left or the money of the well-bred English girl who had abandoned her reputation to become his mistress. His enmity with James went too deep for him to be able to grovel before the new monarch, and he found it hard to say amen when others cried 'God Save the King.'

It was easier, and altogether necessary, for William and Mary to send messages of entire submission. The new King announced his accession in a warm letter to Mary and a dry one to William:

I have only time to tell you, that it had pleased God Almighty to take out of this world the King my brother. You will have from others an account of what distemper he died of.

The news came as a shock to everybody, especially as the King had been looking better that winter than he had done for years. Having been cupped, let blood in both jugulars, 'and other sharp operations about the head', the King, not surprisingly, succumbed to a succession of apoplectic fits. On this occasion Jesuit's powder made him worse rather than better, and even Lady Portsmouth, sitting in the bed 'taking care of him as a wife a husband', and his brother, kneeling by the bedside in tears, were unable between them to bring him back to health. Knowing that he was nearing his end, and being able to indulge his own conscience at last without fear of political repercussions, the King allowed his old friend Huddlestone to administer the last rites behind locked doors; meanwhile, the Anglican Bishop, Sancroft, added his contribution by making 'a very weighty exhortation', and Bishop Ken began a discourse which went on until the King breathed his last, 'the other Bishops giving their assistance both by prayers and otherwise . . . with very good ejaculations and short speeches'.

James II immediately took steps to ensure his own security. He kept a close watch on the ports in case Monmouth should try to enter the country. In general, however, his accession was unexpectedly peaceful. Some people, like Evelyn, were relieved that Charles's reign, with all its vice and profanity, had come to an end. Reresby noticed wryly that those who had been so anxious to exclude the Duke from the crown of his ancestors 'should submit to his now coming to it with so great deference'. James was wise enough to assure the Privy Council that he would defend the Government of England, both in Church and State, and would follow in the steps of the late King in kindness and lenity to his people in order to take care 'that no uproars or disorders should arise'. The Queen Dowager retired to her room which was hung, ceiling, walls and floor, with black. Nothing, as Evelyn remarked, could have been 'more lugubrious and solemn'. The new Queen, who was still only twenty-seven, looked very thin and ill, and many people—including herself—did not think she would last long. Terriesi informed the Grand Duke of Tuscany that she had 'una colica nello stomaco'.

Many people's first reaction was one of fear for the Protestant religion, but James's declaration of good intent, which was printed and distributed, was reassuring. He promised solemnly to maintain the Church as by law established. William wrote, humbly, to his father-in-law, 'I shall be, to the last breath of my life, yours, with zeal and fidelity.' He had dismissed Monmouth with promptitude, advising him to go as far away as possible, Hungary for preference, and to lie low. To the States he chose to read the warm letter which James had written to Mary, rather than his own somewhat cold one. Overkirk was sent to London to present his congratulations. Rochester wrote to William discussing openly the problems that would have to be solved. William thanked him for his frankness. 'You know there is nothing I love more,' he wrote.

Overkirk met with kindness, but the King made it clear to him that he expected his son-in-law to take a more friendly attitude towards France. He

James II when Duke of York with Anne Hyde
and their two daughters Mary and Anne

Photo: A. C. Cooper

The Honeymoon Voyage – William of Orange returning to
Holland with Princess Mary in 1677, the *Mary* and
other yachts becalmed in the Thames

Frances Apsley,
later Lady Bathurst

Mary II when Princess
of Orange, probably painted
in 1677 soon after her
arrival in Holland

Photo: H. C. Coates, Alnwick

Charles II

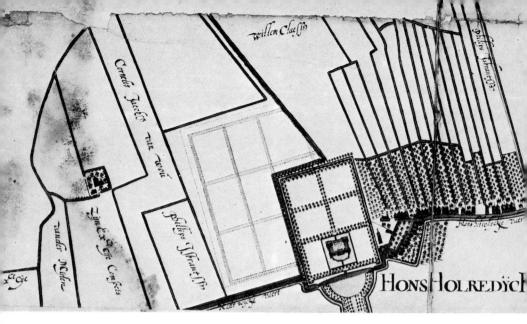

Plan of the palace and grounds of Honselaersdyck

The Voorhout in 1668

Photo: Dutch State Institute for Art History

The Menagerie at Het Loo

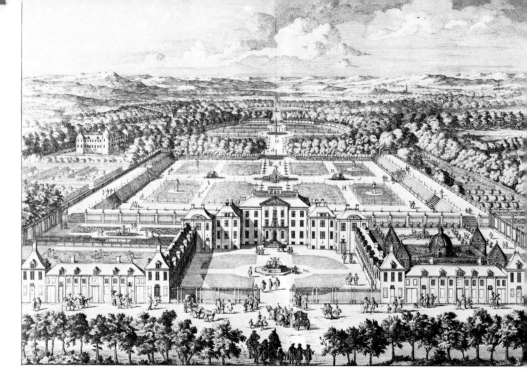

The palace and gardens at Het Loo

Detail of the garden

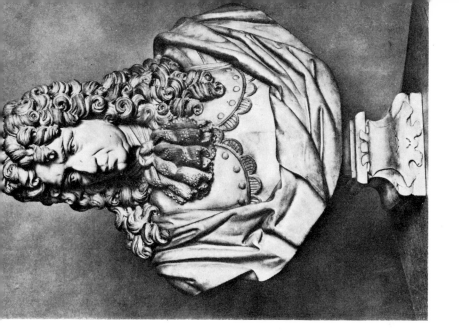

Marble busts of
William and Mary

*Photos: Iconographisch Bureau,
the Hague*

William and Mary with attendants at Helvoetsluys
prior to his departure in 1688

The Coronation

Mary II

Photo: A. C. Cooper

William III

Photo: Annan, Glasgow

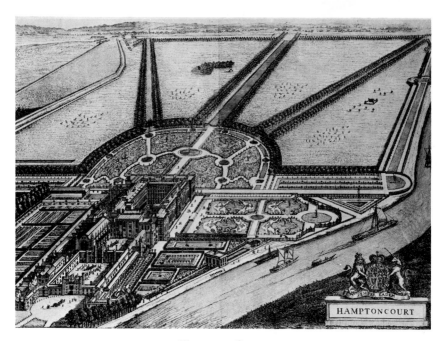

Hampton Court

Kensington Palace

Bishop Gilbert Burnet

Archbishop John Tillotson

Charles Talbot,
Duke of Shrewsbury

Daniel Finch,
Earl of Nottingham

A miniature of William and Mary

Designs for chimney-pieces at Hampton Court by Grinling Gibbons

Photo: Oxford University Press

Facsimile of a letter from Mary to William, July 5/15, 1690

La Maison Royalle d'Angleterre

Guillaume 3.me Roy d'Angleterre d'Ecosse et Irlande né le 4. Novembre 1050. 2 Marie Reine d'Angleterre son epouse est née le 30 Auril 1662 et mourut le 20 Decembre 1694. 3. Georges Prince de Danemarq né le en 16 a epousé en 4. Anne Princesse d'Angleterre 5. Gu.llaume c de Glocester leur fils Unique est né le 24. Iuillet 1689.

William III with Prince George of Denmark,
Princess Anne and their son William, Duke of Gloucester,
with a portrait of Mary

Photo: A. C. Cooper

With mourning pen, and melting eyes,
with bleeding heart, and sobbing Cries.
here lament the loss of one,
who was the brightness of the throne.
Printed and sould by Ioh: overton att the White horse without newgate

Our loss is her eternal gain,
and yet we cannt but Complain,
as having lost the sweetest Queen,
as ever in the Realm was seen

Mary II lying in state

also demanded bluntly that all Monmouth's suspected adherents should be dismissed from the English regiments in the Dutch service. James of course insisted that Monmouth should be sent out of Holland, but this was easier said than done, and there were persistent rumours that the Duke was wandering about somewhere between Rotterdam and Amsterdam. Monmouth was in fact living at Gouda with Henrietta, and it is probable that Bentinck paid him a visit and implored him to go further away. Rochester told the Prince that it was not the King's intention to drive Monmouth from country to country, but he certainly did not want him in Holland, for it was not, in his opinion, 'decent that he should be hovering just over against England, and as it were always in a readiness to transport himself'.

The coronation took place at Westminster Abbey in April 'with all the pomp and splendour imaginable'. The King did not risk the usual cavalcade through the City, but he walked in procession through the Palace Yard with the Queen, and returned afterwards to a sumptuous dinner at Westminster Hall. The Dutch delegation, which was lodged in a vacant house in St James's Square, was not accorded a public entry. It included six pages and ten footmen, and it came up the river, refusing to lower the flag until its leader had come ashore.

James won approval at the outset by making economies in the royal household, cutting salaries and doing away with unnecessary offices. But by the end of April there were murmurs when it was realized that he was having Mass said openly at Whitehall. The French were already tempting him with the promise of subsidies, in the hope of persuading him to dispense with Parliament and detach himself from Holland.

Monmouth's behaviour was also giving cause for concern. There had perhaps been method in William's madness when he had invited the Duke to Dieren or the Hague, allowing him to amuse himself hunting, dancing, charming the ladies, teaching his cousin to skate, playing the role that suited him best—the delightful companion, the graceful repository of courtly virtues. Under William's watchful eye he was isolated from those harmful influences to which he was so unfortunately susceptible, but as soon as he left the court, he became a magnet drawing the malcontents, the disaffected, the exiles, and anybody else who stood to lose under a Catholic monarch. They flattered him into believing that he was their chosen leader and the great Protestant saviour. He knew, in his heart, that he was miscast in this role. Much as he disliked his uncle, he had no desire to act speedily in the Protestant cause. There was an innate idleness and irresolution in his nature which incensed his more active supporters. He

kept reminding his friends about the imponderables, and the obstacles
that lay in the way of a successful rebellion. 'Pray do not think it an effect
of melancholy,' he wrote, 'for that was never my greatest fault . . . I have
not only looked back, but forward; and the more I consider our present
circumstances, I think them still the more desperate, unless some unfore-
seen accident fall out.' Unfortunately he was beset by persistent people
who told him that a rebellion was more likely to succeed if it took place
before the new King had been given a chance to consolidate his position.
Argyll, the banished champion of the Scottish Covenanters, reminded
Monmouth that as long as James was on the throne he had nothing to lose,
therefore the sooner he struck his blow the better. There was another
reason for urgency. Such ships as were available were waiting at Amsterdam, and at any moment the English might prevail on the Lords of the
Admiralty there to detain them. So Argyll went off precipitately with the
first favourable wind, and Monmouth promised to follow in two days.
Argyll wished him to cause a distraction in England to give the Scottish
expedition more chance of success. Having promised, against his better
judgment, to give Argyll his support, Monmouth felt obliged to carry out
the plan.

Chudleigh had been recalled to England after the sledge incident in the
Voorhout, and James had sent Skelton in his place, although he must have
known how William had fought this appointment in his brothers' reign.
Skelton was as yet unused to the intricacies of Dutch government; he
did not realize that Amsterdam would have to refer any decision to the
higher authority of the States. Had he applied direct to the States for an
order preventing the vessels from leaving, Argyll would have been unable
to set out. Even then, obtusely, Skelton failed for a second time to apply
to the right authorities, and this blunder gave Monmouth a chance to
slip out to sea with his tiny expeditionary force.

Monmouth had managed to collect a few officers, a rabble of bored
exiles, a frigate which had proved very expensive to hire, and a pitifully
inadequate collection of arms. He had little money, and what he had
included the sum he had raised by pawning his own jewels as well as
Henrietta's and her mother's. His information was inaccurate; for example, one of his supporters had told him that he would be able to march to
Whitehall 'with no more than a switch in his hand'. While Skelton awaited
the necessary written orders from the States preventing his departure,
Monmouth boarded a lighter which took him out to his hired ship waiting
in the Texel. Disguised somewhat melodramatically with great bushy
whiskers, he set off with eighty-two men at the end of May.

Monmouth's departure put William in an equivocal position. Why, James was bound to ask himself, had the Prince failed to warn him? Surely he could have stopped the expedition altogether? He must have known that arms were being bought and the warship made ready; it had been common knowledge for some time that banners were being made bearing the motto *Pro Religione et Libertate*, and it seemed unlikely that the Prince was the one person not to hear about them. James could never rid himself of the fear that his nephews were in collusion, and William's protestations of innocence sounded, to him, a trifle disingenuous.

The Prince's strong dislike of Skelton made liaison difficult. Towards the end of May, Bentinck did warn Skelton that the rising in Scotland would probably be followed by another in the west country; and whether the Prince was powerless, or tactfully neutral, he made out that Monmouth's folly and double dealing had come as a shock. 'I never believed the Duke of Monmouth capable of such an action after the assurances that he gave me to the contrary when he took leave of me,' he told Rochester.

William did his best to placate his father-in-law by sending the three English regiments to help defend England against the invader. They were encamped at Blackheath, where Evelyn saw them and thought them 'excellently clad and well-disciplined'. The Prince offered to come over to England himself, but the King told him he would be better employed looking after the family interests in Europe. Instead Bentinck was sent over to explain the Prince's position and to help clear up any misunderstandings.

First reports of Monmouth's landing and initial success alarmed the Prince and Princess. Much as they liked Monmouth as a man, it was no part of their plan to see the bastard usurping the throne which in all likelihood would be Mary's at some future time. They were afraid that the English might underrate Monmouth and fail to appreciate the power of his personal magnetism. But anxiety about the outcome of the rising did not last long. The battle of Sedgemoor was fought on July 6, and the exquisite dancer on whose arm the Princess had leaned in the heady weeks of that bitter new year was found, dirty and bedraggled, in a ditch. He had on him a small pocket book written in his own hand, a mixture of charms and spells, songs and prayers, routes of journeys he had taken in Holland in happier times, a cure for sore gums, a recipe 'for to make Bouts and Choos hold out water', music for a drinking song, and a love song:

> Accept, sweet Phyllis of that little part,
> I can present, of my unruly heart.

When Monmouth lay in the Tower, the Princess's former chaplain, Dr Hooper was sent to prepare him for death. Hooper would have liked to administer the sacrament, but this was impossible, as the Duke insisted that Henrietta was his wife before God. His Duchess, Anna, whose virtue he commended, was, he said, 'a wife the King gave him, but not the lawful one before God'. This casuistry conveys the adolescent quality of Monmouth's character and his inability to face reality. Hooper, for all his persuasive manner, found it impossible to make Monmouth admit that that he was in the wrong, though he sat up with him all night and accompanied him to the scaffold, where they prayed for him, and finished with a short prayer for the King, 'at which he paused, but at last said, Amen'. Hooper turned his face away, to avoid the sight of the fatal blow, which was as well, for the executioner was none too adept; 'the wretch made four chops before he had his head off,' Evelyn reported, adding 'thus ended this quondam Duke, darling of his father and the ladies, being extremely handsome and adroit'.

Henrietta Wentworth returned to England a few months after Monmouth's death. She was in a bad state of health and died less than a year later. A poem in Monmouth's pocket book forms a fit epitaph for them both:

> With joy we leave thee
> False world and do forgive
> All thy false treachery
> For now we'll happy live . . .
> No quarrelling for crowns
> No slavery of State
> No changes in our fate.
> From plots this place is free
> There we'll ever be . . .

Monmouth's death removed one contestant for the English throne to which, since the death of her uncle, the Princess had moved a step nearer. The King, a distant but very real father-figure, a writer of letters that were sometimes affectionate and sometimes stern, was at the moment the only person to stand between her and the crown that would bring to her and, indirectly, to her husband, all the power of England, a power strong enough to quell the recalcitrant city of Amsterdam and the truculent King of France. She had no desire, as yet, to change her fate, to quarrel over the crown, or to accelerate the process of gaining it. All the same, her new importance was reflected in greater ceremony at court, for now she was served by kneeling pages, as befitted the next in line to the English throne.

CHAPTER 16

THE PALACE AT LOO

I T W A S Walter Harris, William's doctor, who recommended a garden for its therapeutic value, especially for those who were 'cloy'd with the pleasures and vanities of the world' and who had suffered their fill of crosses and disappointments. A complete and spacious garden, furnished with a variety of interesting walks and groves, was the nearest thing, in Harris's opinion, to a paradise on Earth. The Prince and Princess, harassed as they were by political difficulties and family troubles, had particular need of such a retreat, and the planning of houses and gardens helped to take their minds off the insecurity of their situation, and to forget the grand designs of France.

When William bought an old and dilapidated castle at Het Loo in Gelderland, not far from Dieren, he had in mind a plan to build himself a large country palace where he could live in style and entertain important guests while still enjoying a season's hunting. The old turreted castle was situated on the edge of a large heath which extended southwards in the direction of the Rhine, and north to the Zuyder Zee. The surrounding countryside was ideal for hunting, with an abundance of stags, roebuck, wild boar, foxes and even wolves, not to mention woodcock and pheasants, It was probably sometime during the summer of 1685, when Monmouth had already set out for England, that the Princess laid the foundation stone of the Palace that was to take nine years to build.

Daniel Marot was the architect. A Huguenot artist and craftsman, Marot had brought from his native Paris all the magnificence and grandeur associated with the name of Le Nôtre, but he had toned down the style to accord with the more domesticated Dutch way of life. The building work was put in charge of de Marais, 'a gentleman of great endowments and capacity', and Bentinck also took a lively interest and supervised the work when he had time. Marot's artistic and mathematical brilliance combined with the practical skill of de Marais was reflected in the spectacular waterworks which were fed by a natural flow of water. At Versailles, by contrast, the water had to be pumped up by engines into vast cisterns, so that the fountains had to be turned on a day or two before the arrival of any important visitor to work off the stench of stagnant water. At Het Loo there was a multitude of fountains of every size and description; there were tritons spewing water, gilded swans, a marble Hercules rising from his cradle with serpents in his hand, Arion playing on a lute and riding on a golden dolphin with two spouts six foot high rising from its nostrils. There were canals and basins paved with coloured pebbles and mosaic figures in black and white, with fountains throwing water forty-five feet in the air, or others spraying out in the pattern of a peacock's tail. Here the water always smelt sweet and the green slopes between the different levels of the gardens were kept fresh by little pipes set a foot apart which were made to 'rain a small shower' on a summer evening, without offending the noses of the courtiers who strolled along the gravelled walks or rested on marble seats in the shelter of high hedges.

The architect's aim was not to blend the garden with the surrounding countryside but to fence it firmly in, keeping wild nature at a distance. There was only one carefully planned prospect which led the eye away to a high pyramid placed half a mile away across the heath. This could be viewed from semi-circular galleries at the end of the Great Garden, which were paved with red and white brick and had thirteen gods and goddesses in fresco on the walls. Tree-lined rides were envisaged to lead in from the heath to the gilded gates of the front courtyard. The garden was an extension of the Palace, a suggestion of open-air rooms designed for a Princess whose chief delight was to take a walk every day so that she could, if she pleased, stroll for several miles through labyrinth and wilderness. At every step she was to find something to admire—elaborate parterres bordered with flowers and box hedges, orange and lemon trees in pots, juniper trees, urns full of flowers, a life-size statue of Venus, innumerable Cupids—one drinking from a stone cup, another reading a book through a pair of glasses. She would be able to visit the aviaries and admire the exotic birds or the domestic fowl, and rest for a while in a summer-house with a cupola, or sit in a grotto and watch the fountains play. Though she would not realize it, her garden was to be a crystallization of the world of Locke and Newton and the mathematically minded Huygens brothers, a world where everything was measured and exact, and no effect unrehearsed. The romantic, the careless, the untamed was shut away beyond the hedges, and even the flowers were regimented and made to conform to the rules of geometry, being grouped in circles, diamonds, quadrangles and squares. Balance and proportion were the gods worshipped here; grove answered grove in the interests of symmetry, and the gardener's skill was matched by the geometrician's virtuosity. One of the sights of the Princess's garden was an arbour where thanks to the artistry of mathematician and topiarist, it was possible to look diagonally through the windows cut in parallel hedges and glimpse carefully-placed fountains playing in the distance.

All this was still on the drawing board, but that summer, as Monmouth sailed to his doom, the Prince and Princess stayed in the old crumbling castle. The Princess and her ladies could walk out over the wooden bridge across the moat, they could play hide-and-seek in the untamed woods, leap over ditches and run through the rough meadows which were to be transformed into the chess-board perfection of a formal garden—bowling green and lawn, 'green room', grove and grotto. The Prince and his wife could view the bare site, and picture the unpretentious palace that was to rise there, with its quadrangle flanked by stables, its nine steps leading up to the front door, its sash windows, its hall paved in black and white marble, its dining room, gloriously gilded, its chapel and state apartments. In April Rochester had sent William the present of a fine new horse, a most acceptable kind of peace offering, and the Prince made good use of it, taking every opportunity to have a day's hunting, as the army of workmen was gradually assembled and the building began to rise from its foundations. They were staying at the old castle on October 6 when William, in his enthusiasm, chased a stag into a little ditch by the moat; about a hundred hounds savaged it under the very eyes of the Princess and all the court until one of the hunstmen killed it with a blow of his sword.

It was as well that the Princess could occupy her mind with plans for the new palace, for she needed some distraction. Every letter from her father was calculated to upset her. He told her that he was shocked by the friendliness the Prince had shown Monmouth, even though the Duke had continually asserted in his letters appealing for mercy, that the Prince and Princess had never given him the slightest encouragement and, on the contrary, had made him promise that he would never take up arms against the lawful King.

After the death of Monmouth, James busied himself with the renovations he had planned at Whitehall, and these were known to include a new Catholic chapel for the Queen. The rebellion had given him an excellent excuse to keep a large force under arms to discourage others who might be tempted to follow the bastard's example. In his speech to Parliament he pointed out that the militia was inadequate and that nothing 'but a good force of well-disciplined troops, in constant pay' would meet the demand. For most Englishmen this sounded an ominous note; a permanent encampment on Hounslow Heath such as the King envisaged, would undoubtedly be staffed by Catholic officers all ready to enforce their religion at the point of the sword. He had not wasted much time in removing from the English regiments in Holland anyone who could have been infected by Monmouth, and soon he was proposing Carlingford, a Catholic, to take command. Such a suggestion was unacceptable to William who did not hesitate to say so. It seemed that the King was bent on bringing matters to a head. He was grieved to think that his daughter was drifting away from him into the hands of the Calvinists, and he thought it was time she realized her filial obligations. Unrealistic as ever, the King even believed it might be possible to win her back from her Dutch husband. There were no children of her marriage, and besides, there were interesting rumours that William's eye was roving a little these days. Some judicious trouble-making could produce a happy result. There was nothing the King would have liked so well as to have Mary available for remarriage, this time to a Catholic of the French royal family.

CHAPTER 17

A MALICIOUS SPY

IF the Princess realized that domestic trouble was brewing during the autumn of 1685, she gave no sign that she was apprehensive. Her letters to Frances dealt with unexciting matters, small commissions and debts, and payment to a Mr Knot for 'a romance which I thank him he took pains to bind so finely'. She had plenty of time to meditate, for the King had sent over William Wissing to paint her portrait and the Prince's, but there is no indication that as she sat for her portrait she brooded over her husband's attachment for Elizabeth Villiers; in fact it is possible that she might have remained unaware of the situation, had her father not made it his business to see that she was told.

Wissing had started life at the Hague, where he was born in 1656, and he had worked in London under Lely, though in Huygens's opinion he had not yet reached the perfection of the master. He had brought with him his portrait of the Princess of Denmark, but Huygens did not think much of it; '*ce n'est pas grande chose*' was his frank comment. The Prince was painted wearing his own hair for he still refused to have a wig.

The King's intention was to hang the portraits of his daughter and son-in-law side by side on one of the walls of his renovated Palace, but in real life he was doing his best to separate them. Whispers that William was seeing more than he should have done of one of the maids of honour had been current for some time, and there had also been complaints about the Villiers family, which, as a whole, was thought to be wielding too much influence at William's court. Anne, who had married Bentinck, was one of the Princess's closest friends; Catherine had become the wife of the Marquis de Puissars, an exiled Huguenot, and was established in a suite of rooms at the Binnenhof; and there was also their brother Edward. Elizabeth was less inclined towards matrimony than the other sisters; she was graceful, but rather plain. 'I always forget myself and talk of squinting people before her, and the good lady squints like a dragon,' Swift wrote, years later, in his *Journal to Stella*. Swift found her conversation dazzling, and even in her young days she had achieved a reputation as a witty talker. William was unlikely to appreciate the fact that Elizabeth was a good dancer, but he may have found her sophisticated conversation a welcome contrast to his wife's more artless chatter. Alternatively his interest could have been mainly of a business nature. If he relied on them for nothing else, the Prince expected the maids of honour to act as unofficial intelligence agents. Elizabeth's wit was an asset at any party, and she was considerably in demand among the diplomats. It was possible for her to pick up such secret information as dropped from the mouths of inebriated Envoys at the Hague's more glittering soirées. It could have been to discover what she had heard that William visited her apartments, or the reason why Elizabeth was seen by one gossip 'enveloped in a scarf in the Flemish fashion, passing through Bentinck's apartments into those of the Prince'.

It seems probable that the Princess had guessed something was wrong, though, as she told the Prince later, 'she had kept her sorrow locked in her heart'. Anne Trelawney and Mrs Langford—'my mam'—made it their business to open her eyes and to nourish her jealousy. It was certainly true that the Prince had often been staying up very late in recent months, giving as his excuse the pressure of business, and saying that he had to write despatches. If the story told by several doubtful witnesses is true, the Princess, stirred up by her retainers, was determined to try out the truth of the Prince's assertions. One evening, after pretending to go to bed as usual, she crept along at a late hour and waited on the back stairs that led to the apartments of the maids of honour. Sure enough, at two o'clock in the morning, William emerged from the ladies' quarters to find a reproachful wife waiting for him on the stairs in her dressing-gown.

William was very angry. He did not think it fitting that he should be discovered in such an undignified position, and he showed his displeasure without giving her time to vent hers. She resorted to tears and retired to her bed, where the Prince, for several nights afterwards, failed to join her—or so said those gossips who spread it about that he never slept with her at the best of times. A few days later, when they were both feeling calmer, the Prince broached the subject, telling his wife that he believed some of her English retainers were trying to stir up trouble. 'What has given you so much pain is merely an amusement, there is no crime in it,' he assured her. 'Hé bien,' he added, 'if you believe the oath that I now make to you before God, not to violate the faith I have given you, you will abandon your servants to my just resentment.' The Princess accepted his explanation, and the quarrel was made up. But the Prince was determined to ensure that there would be no further trouble.

The whole affair had become quite out of hand; it was almost approaching a public scandal. Somebody was 'injuriously reporting many concocted stories', and the Prince would not rest until he had discovered the culprit. Mrs Langford and Anne Trelawney were obviously suspect, since they had incited the Princess to wait on the stairs, and it was noticed that Ken's successor, Dr Covell, appeared to be in league with them. Covell was an elderly, prattling man who preferred spreading gossip to preaching the gospel. The Prince suspected that he was making use of his privileged position at the Princess's court to observe the comings and goings of Elizabeth Villiers and to give a full record of them to Bevil Skelton.

In October the court was at Dieren, but the usual pleasures of country life were being ruined by the atmosphere of strain and suspicion. At last the Prince could stand it no longer, and before he went out hunting one day, he left instructions for the Princess's secretary, d'Alonne, to intercept any letters that Dr Covell might have written to Skelton. A footman, who had been used as a go-between, was caught with a letter on him, and the next stage was to find the key to the cupboard in which the reverend gentleman kept his cypher. 'Your honour may be astonished at the news,' William read when the letter to Skelton had been deciphered, 'but it is too true the Princess's heart is ready to break: and yet she, every day, with Mrs Jesson and Mad. Zuylestein, counterfeits the greatest joy, and looks upon us as dogged as may be.' Covell said that he and his cronies did not dare speak to the Princess any more because the Prince had 'infallibly made her his absolute slave'. It would be as well, Covell thought, if King James were to grant Skelton a good pension for life, because he certainly could not expect anything from the Prince, and as for Chudleigh if he was not fixed up with something before the King should die, he was likely to be in a very bad position. 'But I wonder what the devil makes the Prince so cold to you,' wrote Covell, adding, by way of an explanation, 'none but pimps and bawds must expect any tolerable usage here.'

The Princess, to be on the safe side, had despatched Mistress Villiers to England after the midnight scene; one story said that she had been sent with a letter for the King which she had opened at Harwich. She disliked the contents so much that she had destroyed it before returning to Holland on her own initiative. Another probably more authentic version said that her father had told her to go back and beg William and Mary to take her into their service again. This they refused to do, and she took refuge with her sister, Catherine de Puissars, for the Bentincks would have nothing to do with her. 'I do not wonder at the new Marchioness's behaviour,' wrote Covell, 'it is so like the breed. We shall see fine doings if we once come to town. What would you say if the Princess should take her [the Marquise de Puissars] into the Chapel, or in time into the bed-chamber? I cannot fancy the sisters will long agree.' Covell then added his most revolting innuendo: 'You guess right about Mr d'Alonne, for he is secretary in that, as well as in other private affairs.'

Life at Dieren could become tedious for those who were not enamoured of outdoor pursuits, and it was not surprising, perhaps, that Covell resorted to some spying, as he had little else to do except read through the sermons which the Bishop of London sent over for the Princess. 'I shall not be wanting', he had assured the Bishop the previous August, 'to the utmost of my power to keep her steady and the work will be much easier, it being (as I ever could see) her own proper inclination and opinion.' Such good works soon palled, and Covell longed to escape from rusticity. 'I fear I shall not get loose to meet you at Utrecht,' he told Skelton; 'it will not be a month before we meet at the Hague. The widow and maid and I, do often remember your Honour and your most excellent Lady . . . I never so heartily longed for to come to the Hague: God send us a happy meeting. The Princess is just now junketing with Madame Bentinck and Mrs Jesson, in Madam Zuylestein's chamber.'

Covell was given no chance to return to the Hague, for the widow, the maid and the ecclesiastic were all sent back to England forthwith. The story told was that the Prince called his wife into his room, shut the door and showed her this letter. He assured her once again that his crime was '*pur amusement*', at which she flung herself on his neck, in tears, assuring him that she herself had played no part in the correspondence. The letter proved that she was harbouring members of the household who were intent on breaking their union. The Princess dismissed Dr Covell at once, and William sent a strong note to Rochester, enclosing a copy of Covell's letter. 'The Princess and myself,' he wrote, 'have done nothing further than to turn him out of the house, leaving his punishment to the Bishop who has authority over him.' Miss Trelawney and Mrs Langford were given a few hours to pack, as well as Mrs Langford's son who was the second chaplain, and another maid of honour, both of whom were also implicated. In a letter to Frances, the Princess revealed that she was completely resigned to parting with her nurse:

My Mam having put herself out of a condition of ever doing anything more for me of which I have not spoke it being a thing for which I was good-natured enough remembering what she had bin to me to be sorry for at first, but her behaviour has been such as has given me but just cause to forget that. I will say no more upon this subject because I think that when what is past can't be recalled the less one thinks of it the better.

Skelton was understandably alarmed when he heard that d'Alonne had intercepted one of Covell's letters. He wrote to William in a self-righteous manner, saying that he would have thought he should be exempt from such treatment. He protested that his correspondence with Covell was altogether innocent, and that if he looked into it more carefully, the Prince would find it far less criminal than it appeared at first sight. William, however, made it clear that he was extremely displeased, and he wrote to James demanding Skelton's recall. 'You can well judge,' he pointed out, 'that after this I can no longer live with him as formerly.' Skelton eventually composed a grovelling letter, full of apologies and a plea that the Prince would pardon a fault caused by a pen that had been indiscreet rather than malicious.

In Holland, most people who were in the secret, approved of the Prince's action in dismissing the servants. 'They have a little merited it, particularly Covell,' Huygens wrote. Bentinck told Sidney that he thought it was 'a horrible thing people can be wicked enough to injure those to whom they owe their bread, but much worse that ministers should be capable of it'. Bentinck was very displeased by the part played by his brother-in-law, Edward Villiers. It seems that he had been trouble-making with the rest, and there was a story that Edward's wife Barbara—she was a daughter of the notorious Chiffinch—had written a letter which Bentinck had intercepted and found to be full of abuse of himself. He asked Sidney whether he had heard the tale which had been 'charitably made at our expense', and which accused him and his wife of failing to pay their respects correctly to the Princess on their arrival at Honselaersdyck. 'I cannot tell you anything about our affair except that it is not ended,' he said wearily.

At Dieren there was considerable relief, and indeed it was as if a cloud had lifted. The Prince and all the Dutch retainers were delighted to know that Mary was now free to enjoy her friendship with Dutch ladies without any malicious spy in the household to send exaggerated accounts back to England. As a result of the crises, the Princess had won through to a deeper understanding of her husband, and if he continued to see Elizabeth Villiers it was always with complete discretion and out of range of prying eyes. Knowing how openly and distressingly her father and uncle and most other monarchs carried on their *amours*, the Princess could afford to be appreciative about her husband's lack of ostentation. There is no proof that Mistress Villers continued to be anything more than a shadow in the past. In any case she never again constituted a serious threat to Mary's happiness.

The letters the Princess wrote soon after the grand revelation and the departure of Covell and his cronies were cheerful enough. She was occupying her mind with a length of 'black raised satin' which she hoped Frances would buy for her since she did not think it would be available at the Hague. The border was to be embroidered in Holland, and the 'shapes of the body' were also to be carried out there. 'I am in great haste for it', she confessed. To Lady Mary Forester she wrote happily on October 29 from Loo. Lady Mary, like Mrs Langford and Anne Trelawney, was leaving Holland, but for a far better reason, and the Princess was much less resigned to losing her than she was to parting with the others:

I had been very glad your concerns and your condition would have permitted you to stay longer since I have learnt to know you too well to be willing to loose you quite, and I could now chide you for being so good humoured while you were here, but that your grave letter makes me think that I am writing to that sober Lady Mary Forester I once knew at the Hague. If you had always been seen at the bassett table making al pios and wanting an interpreter to ask for what you won you might have gone away almost without being missed, but since you have been at Loo working, walking and romping, you must not wonder if I should have been very glad to have found you still at the Hague for all you deceived me so much as you really did when we played at hide-and-seek in the little wood; if I had then known your condition you would have never got the reputation of as good a walker as myself, at least we had never passed ditches as we did together, but I am very glad it has succeeded so well and hope you will get into England and have a good deliverance which I think is the best wish can be made you now . . . I hope you have learnt to know me enough to believe though I can make no compliments that nobody can wish you better . . . than I, Marie.

The Prince and Princess went back to the Hague towards the end of November. After such a long absence there was a great deal of business to be done, and many visitors to receive. John Horne brought a letter and books from Bishop Compton for the Princess who, he said, received them and the messenger very graciously, which made him feel quite refreshed after a tedious five-day journey from England. Mary was so occupied that she found it hard to find time to write to Frances, but when she did so, on December 11, she asked for two cotton petticoats, 'a pair of sleeves such as may be worn now, and a roll or what else you may call it I know not, but I mean such a thing as is worn upon the head with a black gown'. Through the Princess, the influence of English fashion was being felt at the Hague, but she herself, copying the Dutch, wore a great deal of black, and she was careful not to set a trend that might prove too extravagant.

'As for what I did not send for,' she explained to Frances, 'it was not because I had not heard of them but because I would not bring up such a fashion here which purses could not bear.'

Mary's health was poor in the new year of 1686, perhaps as a result of the stresses of the previous year. She had a recurrence of her eye trouble, which curtailed her letter-writing, and she had begun to put on weight, not, as some people hoped, because she was expecting an heir. When on February 13 she wrote to congratulate Lady Mary Forester on the birth of her child, she said she felt overjoyed 'to find the same Lady Mary Forester I knew at Loo' and she told her friend that she welcomed her letters as much as ever, for, as she put it, 'I am not changed in my humour though I am in my shape, but that not by so good reason as you had when I saw you last, but mere fat. I like this subject so little I shall say no more upon it'. Always at the back of her mind was the spectre of her enormous mother.

In the new year the Princess had a fall when she was out riding, and she was treated by Dr John Hutton, a graduate of the University of Parma who was near by when the accident happened. Her injuries were not serious, but they helped to make the beginning of 1686 a trying time. Although she was as generous as ever with her congratulations, the fact that both her friends, Frances and Lady Mary, were happily delivered that spring may have aroused latent sorrow at her own childlessness. She was deeply affected, too, by the regular reports of torture and persecution borne by Protestants in France, and in particular she was horrified by a story of two Protestant girls who were made to suffer dreadful torment at the stake. D'Avaux complained that she had been relating this tale at court, without sparing anybody the details about how the fire was lit and the girls made to undergo anguish for two hours. He was very annoyed to hear that she was giving credence to such rumours; naturally many others followed her example, and a large number of Amsterdamers whom he had so patiently wooed were now being alienated because they were foolish enough to believe these exaggerated stories.

The attitude her father was adopting was enough to upset anybody's equilibrium. His letters to Holland were either cross or querulous. He complained that rebels were being harboured in the United Provinces, where he was sure they were stirring up sedition. One day in January it was reported that the Prince had bestowed *caresses* on an Englishman who had been Monmouth's friend and confidant. It was said that the Princess had received the same man courteously and had even allowed him to kiss her hand. Skelton immediately rushed to lodge a complaint to the Prince, who answered coldly, 'one cannot prevent things like that'.

William would have liked his father-in-law to intervene on his behalf to save the Principality of Orange from the French but James refused to do anything except register faint disapproval, which was quite useless in the Prince's opinion. 'What will the world say,' William asked Rochester, 'if it sees that his Majesty suffers one who has the honour to be his son-in-law and his nephew to be ill-used without any just reason and does not resent it? . . . I confess that this matter affects me very deeply, and if I do not see myself protected now, I have nothing to expect in future.'

In the early summer of 1686 Skelton was recalled, and replaced by Ignatius White, an impoverished Irish adventurer who was no great improvement on his predecessor; in fact, of all the dislikable diplomats who had been sent to Holland, this one was probably the worst. He masqueraded under the title of the Marquis d'Albeville, which had been conferred on him by the Emperor. Even d'Avaux distrusted him, though he was not past paying him *'une espèce de pension'* to secure his help. He had a reputation in Holland for double espionage, and for serving those who would pay him the most.

In July 1686 the League of Augsburg came into existence. The Empire, Spain, Sweden, Brandenburg, Bavaria and several minor principalities all bound themselves to act together if faced with aggression. James, however, remained firmly neutral and refused to enter into any alliances. He was sure the Protestant States were about to embark on a religious war, and he had no desire to be distracted from his in-grown aim of turning his own country Catholic. When, in August, William invited the Elector of Brandenburg to review troops encamped at Nimeguen, and the Princess was asked to go too to meet the Electress, James wrote a letter disapproving so strongly of the ceremonies that she decided to stay away.

Such interference removed any vestige of affection which the Princess still felt for her father. His unsavoury private life did not endear him to her any more than his political behaviour. The Papists wished he would conduct himself in a manner that would prove a better advertisement for their faith. The Countess of Dorchester, having been banished to Ireland, had now returned, and was wielding as much influence over the King as ever, which was all the more shocking when one considered that the Queen was such a good Catholic and a faithful wife who continued to love her husband in spite of everything. 'She is Italian and very *glorieuse*,' Barillon told Louis. Evelyn noticed that for two days running she hardly ate a morsel of food and refused to speak to the King, or to anybody else, though as a rule she was very pleasant, 'full of discourse and good humour'. Like Elizabeth Villiers, Catherine Sedley, Countess of Dorchester, was less remarkable for her beauty than her wit. She had been James's mistress for about six years now, but she always said she could not understand why the King found her so fascinating. 'It cannot be my beauty because I haven't any,' she is reputed to have said, 'and it cannot be my wit because he hasn't enough of it himself to know that I have any.'

In August disturbing news was received from England. Compton, the most outspoken of the English Bishops, was to come before an ecclesiastical court set up by the King and presided over by none other than the notorious Judge Jeffreys, his main crime being failure to reprove one of his clergy, Dr Sharp, for preaching against the Papists. Covell's successor, Dr Stanley, reported from Dieren that everyone was in a state of great concern on the day that Compton was due to come before the commission. The Bishop had little hope of a fair hearing, for Jeffreys was no friend of his, in fact they had exchanged angry words in the Lords; and Nathaniel Crewe, another of the Commissioners, was James's favourite Bishop, who owed his position in the see of Durham to the fact that he had been courageous enough to perform James's marriage ceremony. Sancroft, the Archbishop of Canterbury, was far too timorous to make a stand.

Stanley told Compton that the Princess had written to the King on his behalf: 'She discoursed with me about it, arguing thus, that things being gone so far, by such an address she could do your Lordship no harm, but it was possible she might do some good.' All she gained, however, for asking her father 'to be gentle with the Bishop', was an unpleasant letter reproving her for meddling with affairs which were none of her business. Because of his so-called 'disobedience and contempt', Compton was suspended until further notice.

Meanwhile the King was building up his permanent establishment of 12,000 men on Hounslow Heath, in order to 'overawe the nation and make slavery familiar', to use Welwood's words. Van Citters, the Dutch Envoy in England, could not speak or understand English very well, but he saw enough to feel certain that James intended to alter the succession so as to ensure that the crown would rest on a Catholic head. His partiality for Jesuit advisers was causing general alarm, even among more moderate Catholics, and these included the Pope. Father Petre, the most favoured of all the Papists, was now lodged in the apartments at Whitehall which James himself had occupied before becoming King. Everyone predicted that before long he would be a cardinal, and as the year went on it became increasingly evident that he was dominating the King's actions. Influenced as he was by a Jesuit priest and a woman not noted for her virtue, it seemed to those who observed him that the King was no longer capable of impartial judgments.

As James went along the downward path of obstinacy and bigotry, his daughter Mary continued to grow in maturity. She did not owe her now famous charm either to her father or to her mother; perhaps this came to her from her uncle, the late King, though the moral fibre she possessed most certainly did not. In Holland she wielded considerable influence simply by setting a good example, and her industry and her simple way of life appealed to the frugal Dutch. Her ladies, although they played bassett in the evenings, were prompted by her example to sew and do embroidery and read pious books at other times of the day. 'I come as a schoolmaster among my people,' she told Huygens. Not that she was anaemic or prim in her outlook. The letters which she wrote to Lady Mary Forester in 1686 prove that she had advanced beyond the pale unrealities of her schooldays and they also show that her style was beginning to develop a cutting edge:

'Twas well 'twas a cold season, and the lady's blood not very warm at this age . . . My Lord Clifford and his Lady are of an age that I believe may be left abed together . . . if the Lady be as fruitfull as her sister, 'tis likely Mr Boyle who had been here lately won't be long the youngest brother . . . Lord M was put to the necessity of endeavouring a rape to satisfy his heroic passion. I believed his pride to have bin too great to stoop to such beast-like inclinations; I thought his love had been more refined and would not have gone beyond ogling, though now I think on't his great eyes may gogle about for fashion's sake, but he is too purblind to see at a distance or else his friends bely him.

The poet Wharton had been fatally wounded in a duel, and the Princess said she wished poets had more wit than to fight. ''Tis a cruel thing to hazard both body and soul for a jest' she reflected. 'I find we women have the better of the men for that, since raillery does not cost us so dear.'

Mary's married life with William, having survived a crisis deliberately engineered by trouble-makers, had reached the stage of a more mature understanding which became for both of them a bulwark against the constant pressure of outside anxiety. However insecure the political situation might be, however menacing the appearance of France, the Princess went on living quietly and without ostentation, furnishing the houses and growing increasingly fond of the countryside and of the people who had adopted her. Living in an atmosphere of liking and admiration, she naturally blossomed and grew more gracious with the years. She had made many friends among both the men and the women who came to her court. When Odyck arrived at Dieren that summer, the Princess made him go with her to Loo, where they looked over the new building and talked to each other as man to man '*en qualité d'Architecte*'. Old Huygens loved her so much that he dedicated poetry to her, and continued to advise her about the furnishing of her houses. On one occasion he gently reproved her for planning to cut up a gilt and lacquer screen, one of her few lapses in taste:

... the whole and universal nation, both male and female, of the most famous and mighty Empire of China, to the number of a great many more millions of people than your skilfullest arithmetician were able to sum up in a summerday ... to their inconsolable grief and mortification, ... have lately been told, how some most ignorant, barbarous and malicious people, moved only by mere envy and jealousy of our ancient original China honour, should have so far prevailed with your Highness's renowned sweet, mild, and gracious disposition, as to let the same illustrious monument [be] sawed, divided, cut, cleft and slit asunder and reduced to a heap of monstrous shivers and splinters, and all this desolation to no higher purpose than to see the walls of some miserable cabinet decked and adorned forsooth with our unhappy ruins ... We return humbly and most fervently to beg, it may please your Royal Highness, if so inhuman a resolution may have been conceived, that it may be, as a monstrous embryo, smothered in its birth and destroyed before. And shall this be an action perfectly worthy of your great and generous genius, and most properly becoming your clear and perspicacious wit and judgment, of both which a constant fame hath blown over the noise and notice even to these remote parts.

The Huygens family was always deeply interested in the Prince's collections, and it was old Constantine who told William of the whereabouts of an original portrait of Charles V by Titian, of which the Orange family already had a copy. Huygens doubted whether the Prince, however great his 'Italian enthusiasm', would be justified in spending a further £3,000 on the original.

The Princess found her new chaplain, Dr Stanley, a sympathetic character. He arrived at the Hague towards the end of 1685 and was delighted to see a large congregation at the sacrament on Christmas Day. This he attributed to the good influence of the Princess. He arrived bringing with him *The Answer to a Papist Misrepresented* as well as his own book *Devotions of the Church of Rome* and he told Compton that he had received a far better reception than he had ever expected. 'Her Highness,' he added, 'is doubtless one of the best-tempered persons in the world and everyone must needs be happy in serving her.' He recorded, approvingly, that the Princess was 'extremely constant and regular in her public devotions' and, he told Compton, 'I think we are all bound in an especial manner to pray and give thanks for her'. After celebrating her birthday at the end of April he was moved to exclaim, 'God send us a joyful keeping of very many of them, and make her every day more and more a blessing to our Church and nation.'

The Princess made an equally good impression on Dr Gilbert Burnet, who came down the Rhine in the summer of 1686, having been advised by his friends to station himself as near his home country as possible in order to hear what was going on. This Scottish divine had fallen into disfavour after preaching a sermon in which he had inadvisedly referred to James I's imprecation against any of his descendants who might revert to Rome. He had spent some time in France but now he had the intention of settling in Groningen or Friesland. His fame had gone before him, and when he arrived at Utrecht he found letters from the court with an invitation to wait on the Prince and Princess. William and Mary seemed ready to confide in him almost as soon as he arrived, and in September he was at Dieren with the court. He promised to show Huygens his microscope, and the two men compared notes about glasses. 'It seems to me that he is a bit of a boaster,' Huygens commented.

Burnet was captivated by the Princess from the start. She was certainly irresistible to most ecclesiastical gentlemen. 'Her person was majestic and commanded respect,' he enthused, and 'there was a sweetness in her deportment that charmed, and an exactness of piety and virtue that made her a pattern to all that saw her'. He was impressed by her wide reading in history and divinity, and noticed that although she was not able to read as much now as formerly, on account of her eyes, she had taken to doing needlework 'with such a constant diligence, that she made the ladies about her ashamed to be idle'. On the other hand Burnet thought that she knew too little about the real state of affairs at her father's court. He therefore took it upon himself to tell her, and to explain all the intricacies and intrigues. She showed, he said, a 'true judgment and a good mind, in all the reflections that she made'. She wanted to know why the King had been so 'sharpened' against Jurieu, the Protestant preacher she had gone to hear in the days when Monmouth was at the Hague, and Burnet told her that it was because of the preacher's virulent acrimony of style and the fact that he had written 'with great indecency' about Mary Queen of Scots, thus indirectly casting aspersions on her descendants. The Princess did not think much of these reasons:

She said, Jurieu was to support the cause that he defended, and to expose those that persecuted it, in the best way he could. And, if what he said of Mary Queen of Scots was true, he was not to be blamed, who made that use of it: and, she added, that if princes would do ill things, they must expect that the world will take revenges on their memory, since they cannot reach their persons: that was but a small suffering, far short of what others suffered at their hands.

All this Burnet reverentially wrote down for posterity. He was completely struck down by Mary's modesty, her humility, her sweetness of temper and knowledge of the Christian religion. 'She is the most wonderful person that I ever knew,' he told Dr Fell after only a few weeks' acquaintance.

None of the clergy found William as amenable as his wife. Burnet at first thought him a trifle taciturn, and realized that 'the depression of France' was his ruling passion. Stanley was disappointed that he could not interest the Prince in establishing a Protestant library at the Hague, but all the same he found him good tempered and well disposed towards the Church of England. Stanley told Compton that the Prince joined the Anglican community for prayers on Sunday afternoons and was always 'very grave and regular' at Church services. At Dieren William attended prayers on Sunday and 'sermons' on other days of the week but he was often otherwise engaged, 'for indeed' Stanley wrote, 'he hunts and is abroad all day besides. But he professes an admiration v. often for our church'.

Burnet observed that the Prince was one of those people who do not impress at first sight, but who grow in a person's estimation on further acquaintance. Burnet soon discovered that he showed a total disregard for his own safety. He often went off quite alone to drive along the shore at Schevelingen, or to race over the sands in his yacht. A bold plot had been laid to seize the Prince on one of these solitary expeditions, to take him out to a small ship lying out at sea and to convey him to France. Fortunately, the main conspirator's contact in Paris proved to be 'a talking man', who gave the secret away to Mr Fatio, a celebrated mathematician, and the plot came to the ears of Burnet who warned the Prince. William refused to take any notice, but the Princess was very alarmed; she asked Fagel to approach the Prince with a petition asking him to take a guard when he went out. He agreed, but not with any willingness. Burnet guessed that his belief in predestination made him more adventurous than was necessary. 'But as to that, he firmly believed [in] a providence,' Burnet wrote, 'for if he should let that go, all his religion would be much shaken; and he did not see, how providence could be certain, if all things did not arise out of the absolute will of God.' The Prince assured Burnet that he liked the Church of England, and he added that if he ever succeeded to the English throne the only thing he would try to enforce would be toleration. He himself did not care for bowing to the altar, or making the cross at baptism, or seeing the clergy in surplices, but he would not prevent anyone else doing these things if they felt in all conscience that they were right.

James tried to warn his daughter against Burnet. He told her that the Scotsman was 'an ill, dangerous, ingenious man' though he appeared to be an angel of light. He might be a good conversationalist and an artful flatterer but he was not to be trusted. The Princess wrote back coldly, saying that she had received quite a different impression.

Not everybody at the Hague shared William and Mary's confidence in Burnet. Dr Stanley felt some pangs of jealousy when he observed the interloper taking the sacrament in the early morning with the Prince, and at noon with the Princess and everybody else. He noted disapprovingly that Burnet was perpetually asking to talk to the Princess in private, and too often having his request granted. 'I am verily persuaded,' Stanley told Bishop Compton 'it is only Dr B's intolerable impudence and pressing importunity (observed and laughed at by all the Court) rather than her kindness for him, that procures him so frequent access. But Dr B is everything here. He goes in a cloak like one of their ministers.' Stanley was sure that such intimacy would do the Princess no good, 'for men will be apt to think or suspect that she is as deceitful and full of tricks as Dr Burnet'. The Chaplain said he was very glad that he had kept aloof from this man 'who so constantly and imprudently haunts everybody here'.

In spite of Stanley's disapproval, Burnet continued to talk to the Prince for hours at a time and more often than not in the Princess's presence. It was therefore easy enough for him to ask her the question which must have been in many people's minds. What part did she intend the Prince to play, he asked her, if she herself should come to the throne? She replied that she imagined anything that accrued to her would also come to him in the right of marriage. Burnet then explained Henry VIII's title and told her that 'a titular kingship was no acceptable thing to a man . . . and [that] such a nominal dignity might endanger the real one that the Prince had in Holland'. The Princess wanted to know if there was a remedy, and Burnet told her that there was, if she was contented to be the Prince's wife, and to hand all authority to him as soon as it came into her hands. This he told her, would help to lay the foundation of 'a perfect union between them which had been of late a little embroiled'. Burnet assured her that nobody had prompted him to broach this subject, and he asked her to forgive him 'for the presumption of moving her in such a tender point'. He told her to think it over, and, having once made up her mind, never to go back or retract. 'She presently answered me,' he went on, 'she would take no time to consider of anything by which she could express her regard and affection to the Prince'.

The Princess asked Burnet to give an account of this conversation to her husband. William was out hunting that day, but the next morning Burnet told him what had happened, after which they went to the Princess together. Then, 'in a very frank manner', she told him that she had not realized the laws of England were so contrary to the laws of God. She had not imagined there could ever be an occasion when the husband had to be obedient to the wife. She promised William that he would always be the one to rule; all she asked was that he should remember the commandment 'husbands love your wives', whilst she would abide by the one which said 'wives be obedient to your husbands in all things'. In saying this the Princess cleared the air so thoroughly that they went on to have a frank discourse about English affairs in general.

William, undemonstrative as ever, showed no gratitude or emotion at the time, and did not even thank Burnet for the part he had played in extracting this pronouncement from the Princess. So reserved was the Prince, it seemed, that in the nine years of their marriage he had never found the strength to bring up the subject which Burnet 'had now brought about easily in a day', as he himself noted with pride. To other people in his confidence, William spoke in warm terms of what had happened.

In England, people were beginning to look around to see whether there could be some alternative to James's unpopular rule. The king was now packing the judicial benches with his supporters and he had nominated four Catholics to the Privy Council. All the time he was attempting to convert influential people—there were really far too few Catholics of merit to fill all the necessary places—and keeping Catholics in the army although they were not supposed to hold commissions. More and more people were being exempted from the Test Act to suit the King's purposes. The universities were beginning to brace themselves to resist Catholic infiltration. The Catholic Tyrconnel was to be appointed Lord-Lieutenant of Ireland 'to the astonishment of all sober men', Evelyn commented. Papists were being appointed to posts in Scotland which, in Reresby's words, 'gave great disgust in that kingdom'. All good Protestants viewed with mistrust the opening of the new chapel at Whitehall. Evelyn, who witnessed the first public service there, said the Bishop was 'sumptuously habited'; in front of the altar he did 'diverse cringes', which caused the diarist to exclaim, 'I could not have believed I should ever have seen such things in the King of England's Palace, after it had pleased God to enlighten our nation.'

As a result of James's machinations and the work of the clergyman spy, the Prince and Princess had, for a while, become a little 'embroiled'. But the difficulties they had been through had strengthened their union, giving them confidence to face the formidable future that was now opening up before them.

CHAPTER 18

IMPORTANT VISITORS

As soon as James realized that he had failed to break up his daughter's marriage, he changed his tactics and sent an envoy, William Penn, in an attempt to heal the widening breach between himself and his son-in-law. Penn, a worthy but sombre Quaker, had been James's friend for many years. He was extremely confident of success, and immediately begged the honour of an interview which was the first in a series of somewhat unrewarding confrontations. In his loquacious way he set out to persuade William and Mary that his master intended to help non-conformists just as much as Catholics. The Prince agreed with the principle of toleration, but he remained firmly of the opinion that the official Church must still retain its status. Nobody, he thought, must be allowed to hold office unless he could conform to the requirements laid down in the Test Act— in other words, that he could prove he was a communicating member of the Church of England. Penn told William that many people, including some of the Bishops, believed that most of the penal laws in the Test Acts were cruel and should be abolished. But the Prince refused to discuss such matters and said he would rather lose 'all the revenues and the reversion of the kingdom of Great Britain to which his wife was heiress before one should be abolished'. The Princess was even less impressed by Penn's arguments than her husband, and indeed she seems to have taken a great dislike to the famous philanthropist. She spoke so sharply to him that the Marquis d'Albeville was astonished by her tone and manner. She said, among other things, that if ever she became Queen of England, 'she should do more for the Protestants than even Queen Elizabeth'.

William told Penn that he would be more ready to come to terms with his father-in-law if Mary were granted a pension of £48,000 a year. James could have afforded this; he was better off than his brother had ever been and was free of debt. Anne had been well endowed on her marriage, but James was always afraid that any sum sent out of the country would be used against himself. He was a bad psychologist, for it would have been more difficult for Mary to occupy her father's throne if she had been indebted to him financially. As it was, his failure to give her anything aroused adverse comment in many circles, and helped to alienate Mary herself, who had fallen into debt this year, having inadvisedly spent her meagre allowance on four large diamonds. She had been forced to borrow ten thousand gelders, which she was to pay back with interest in four instalments.

Penn returned having achieved little in his discussions. William Wissing, 'the picture drawer' as Mary called him, also went back to England in the autumn, to finish his portraits there. The Princess told Frances that if she wanted a copy she must ask Wissing direct. The Bathursts had just lost their infant, Mary's godchild, and she wrote to Frances sympathetically, although she admitted that, having no children of her own, she found it hard to imagine the grief that such a death must cause:

I pity you for it very much, but submitting to the will of God as I see you do is the only remedy in such cases, and when one considers all one has is but lent from God one can look upon the loss as a payment which must be made one time or other; and children who die before they are capable of sinning are I think very happy being only taken out of a troublesome world which few who know it perfectly, if they had nothing they loved in it, would be sorry to leave; and if one could hinder oneself setting one's heart too much upon those we love we should be the readier to die.

A far more welcome visitor to the Hague than William Penn was Philip of Brandenburg, better known as Flips. His mother was thought to be pushing him forward as William's heir, and d'Avaux told Louis that the Prince might well ask if he could be brought up at the Hague so that the Dutch could learn to know and love him. The Prince was not above making capital out of his own childlessness, and one way of keeping his relations in the right camp was to hint that the succession might go to their hopeful progeny if they behaved properly. Henry Casimir of Friesland was probably the most favoured runner, but the fact that he had flirted with the opposition in Amsterdam put others in the field. Flips, whatever his pretensions, was a personable young man, and during his stay he called on the Princess several times a week and they danced English dances together.

This year, William's birthday ball was a magnificent affair, held in the painted room at the House in the Wood. The company was as brilliant as the surroundings. This was no black-and-white Calvinistic occasion and the ladies wore dresses in multi-coloured brocade, blue, gold, orange and red. The Moroccan Ambassador was one of the guests, a striking figure among the Gentlemen of State. The dome, the crown and cypher over the door and the walls of the room were illuminated with hundreds of candles. As the visitors drove up to the main door they saw every window lighted up. Supper was served at a round table and the food was brought in to the court ladies held aloft by an army of servants. The Princess herself wore a glittering dress, cut low on the shoulders and edged with lace, and her husband was dressed in blue and gold. In the well-known engraving by Daniel Marot he is seen standing incognito in the crowd with Flips. Dancing went on all night to the sound of violins, 'cellos and oboes. In the succeeding weeks there were more revels, as well as reviews of the army and the fleet. Flips stayed in Holland over the new year, and he was still there at the end of April 1687; he gave Mary an amber cabinet for her birthday and the next day was with her when she watched the military parade which marked the opening of the Kermesse.

Throughout Philip's visit, the situation in England continued to deteriorate. At the beginning of the year the Hyde brothers had fallen— Rochester was relieved of the Treasury and Clarendon was forced to make way for Tyrconnel in Ireland. William found that a valuable link had gone with Rochester's retirement from the scene. In the new year bad weather made communications doubly difficult; first of all the Maas was frozen over, then, as soon as this gave, the frost set in over London, where the King noticed with disgust that the lake in the park was covered with ice. In January the Prince, Dyckvelt, Bentinck, Fagel, Burnet and various intelligence agents were frequently closeted together. In February Dyckvelt was sent to England, and the family caucus waited impatiently to hear how he would be received. The King saw him briefly on his arrival, and he then retired to bed for a week or two with a bad foot. He spent his convalescence talking to all the right people, who made a point of coming to his house to commiserate with him. His bad foot also gave him an excuse to keep out of James's way, for it seemed that the King was not in a benign mood.

The Prince still refused to countenance any suggestion that the Test Act should be altered, but when James finally saw Dyckvelt he handed him a draft of the Edict of Toleration which he intended to publish some weeks later, and which was to give dissenters immunity from the Test Act. Towards the end of March, James told William that he had decided to prorogue Parliament until the following November, so that all his subjects might be 'at ease and quiet, and mind their trades and private concerns'. He was quite incapable of gauging the effect of his actions, and, like many tactless people, he was hurt and surprised when he encountered criticism. Now, when he asked the Prince for his opinion, he was greatly offended by the frankness of the reply.

After the Edict of Toleration there was a marked increase in the number of visitors who came over to complain about James's behaviour. In the weeks before the Kermesse, the Prince and Princess were at Dieren, and afterwards they went to Loo, which was habitable now though far from finished. The gardens were already a mass of spring flowers, but the peace and beauty of the scene was spoilt by the stream of glum-faced visitors who were all saying that the next thing James would try to do would be to alter the succession. It was an accepted fact that he was hoping to convert Anne to Catholicism. Having done so, it was certain he would see to it that she came to the throne to the exclusion of Mary. Dyckvelt, however, sent reassuring messages on this score. Anne was never easy to move on any subject once she had made up her mind. John Churchill said that she was resolved 'by the assistance of God, to suffer all extremities, even to death itself, rather than be brought to change her religion'. Barillon told Louis that she had been giving public testimony of her zeal for the Protestant faith, and had even been visiting, incognito, churches where the preachers were '*le plus de vogue*'. Zealous Protestants, he said, were sure that nothing would shake her, but James remained hopeful, remembering how his first wife had seen the error of her ways and had become a firm and good Catholic. Inept as ever, he refused to let Anne visit her sister in Holland when her husband went to Denmark. She was forced to stay at home in a fury, attracting a good deal of sympathy.

James had also angered Mary by sending a message through d'Albeville requesting her to forbid Burnet her presence. Dr Stanley felt smug; how right he had been, he now thought, to shun the doctor. 'I dare say if anybody had been here and seen his busy flattering and insinuating carriage, he would have been as strange to him as I was,' Stanley wrote. He maintained that Burnet had courted the ladies to gain influence, and suspected that it was due to his intervention that one or two promising young men had not been taken on to the paid staff but had been given unsatisfactory posts as 'honorary gentlemen' to the Princess, without any salary.

There was now an uneasy atmosphere at court. Stanley felt discomfited when d'Albeville and some of his Catholic friends came to the Protestant services—'as spies to hear what I preach'—but he consoled himself with the thought that both on the anniversary of Charles I's death and on the present King's birthday, he had said nothing 'but what the King himself might have heard'. In general, Stanley felt that he had done nothing wrong, unless his loyalty to the Church of England could be considered a fault. He had heard that the King considered him too zealous in the

Anglican faith, and he had a hard task convincing d'Albeville that Compton had advised him not to favour Burnet.

By now everyone at court was convinced that the mail from England was being intercepted, and it was thought inadvisable to send anything important unless it could go by private hands. Several of Compton's letters were thought to have been lost, and when the Princess received some auricula plants at Christmas time, there was no letter with them, which seemed strange. Lady Sunderland, who wished to warn William not to listen to any of James's ambassadors enclosed her letter in one to Bentinck about her garden. Lord Sunderland was beginning to veer in the Catholic direction, obeying the dictates of expediency rather than his conscience, and his wife disapproved strongly of this vacillation. She was a firm Protestant and felt that the time had come to meddle a little although she had never had any commerce with the Princess before, except about 'treacle water, or work; or some such slight thing'.

During the summer of 1687 James busied himself trying to gather up a new Parliament which was to meet in November, consisting of Catholics, other dissenters and malleable Anglicans. He was incredibly self-deluded; in fact there is a touch of madness in the complacency with which he wrote to Sophia of Hanover on May 23:

I easily believe you are well pleased to hear my affairs go so well as they do, and am confident you will have approved of my having given liberty of conscience to all my subjects, of what persuasion so ever, and be pleased, with it having so good an effect, for the much greater part of the nation are very thankful to me for it.

Dyckvelt returned in June telling a different story. He brought with him letters which showed there would be plenty of support for William and Mary in England if it should ever be needed. He had dined with many important Protestants who assured him that the tide was running against the King.

D'Albeville visited the Prince and Princess before they went away to Loo and made another attempt to persuade them that the Test Act should be abolished. Once again they refused. They had always avoided making any public declaration of their feelings in the matter, knowing that it was unwise to intervene in such a troubled situation. But after rumours began to circulate that they had agreed to the repeal of the penal laws, they instructed Fagel to write a letter to James Stewart, a former Scottish Covenanter who had offered his services as a go-between. The letter confirmed that they felt it right for everyone to practice their own religion, but this did not mean that they would ever agree to the repeal of laws which kept Catholics out of Parliament and all public employments, ecclesiastical, civil and military. 'More than this,' Fagel wrote, 'their Highnesses do think ought not to be asked or expected.' It would never be possible for them to consent to things which they believed to be 'not only dangerous, but mischievous to the Protestant religion'.

For the Princess, life went on as usual. She did her shopping, read her pious books, worried herself about some pincushions (spelt 'pinschens') which were being sent from England, agreed to be a godmother to Aurelia's expected child, listened to Stanley when he lectured her about the state of affairs in England. Always there was an undercurrent of anxiety. In August, Mary Beatrice's mother died, and Zuylestein was sent over to England, officially to condole with the Queen, but in reality to take a closer look at the country, and to find out whether James's confident belief that he would be able to summon a favourable Parliament was justi- fied or not. Mary Beatrice, like many other people, was quite taken in by Zuylestein's artless, pleasure-loving exterior, which hid a great talent for diplomacy, and she sent a warm letter to William thanking him for his concern. Carrying on where Dyckvelt had left off Zuylestein did some good work, and brought back encouraging reports of the King's lack of support amongst the English nobility. Among the disaffected who visited the Prince and Princess at Loo that summer was Shrewsbury, young, handsome and charming. Rochester visited Spa, but thought it too dan- gerous to call in at Loo; in any case there were enough ambassadors of the growing opposition without him.

The King still appeared to be magnificently unaware of the troubles that lay in store for him. He went off gaily on a meet-the-people tour of the West country, returning to London via the Midlands. He breakfasted in Coventry, at St Mary's Hall, off venison pasties, Westphalia hams and neats tongues. In the crush a table was overturned 'which created a scramble, whereby many dresses were greatly disordered, and clothes spoiled with sweetmeats, fish, custard and other liquids very divertising [sic] to his Majesty; some commodities were tossed about, and some bare bums appeared, as some say, and were clapt by persons of honour'. He had gone north as far as Chester, and at Holywell, where there was a miraculous shrine now in the keeping of a Jesuit, he knelt in prayer, as Catherine of Aragon was reputed to have done on the same spot; and, attended by much publicity, asked God to grant him a son and heir.

At Oxford the King had a sticky interview with the Fellows of Magdalen. He wished them to elect a new Bishop in place of the recalcitrant Dr Parker, but they refused, saying that they were not empowered to elect another head when they had a perfectly good one already. 'You have been a stubborn, turbulent college these five or six and twenty years,' he told them in his tactful way. '. . . Get you gone home! I say again, get you gone, and immediately repair to your chapel and elect the Bishop of Oxford, or else expect to feel the heavy hand of an angry King.' The Fellows were, in the fulness of time, removed, and when the Princess heard about this, she contributed a sum to the fund which was opened to benefit those who had lost their livelihood as a result of her father's obstinacy.

After this unfortunate incident, the King made another detour to join his wife who had been spending several weeks at Bath where the waters were renowned for promoting fertility. Mary Beatrice's health had improved considerably since the coronation and instead of dying, as everyone had prophesied she would, she had gradually regained her strength. The improvement had been going on for at least a year, but there was no sign that she would have any more children; she had not conceived for several years now and everyone believed that she had finished with child-bearing. It appeared, however, that the King was still prepared to see what prayer and the waters of Bath could do. His optimism at this time seemed to know no bounds; when Shrewsbury visited Loo in September, he brought a letter from Fitzpatrick who said that the King still believed he would get a House of Commons 'to his licking', as Fitzpatrick put it with typically bad spelling.

Stanley went over to England for at least a month in September, carrying with him a letter from the Princess to Archbishop Sancroft. Courageously she set out the position, and made it quite clear where her loyalties lay:

Though I have not the advantage to know you, my Lord of Canterbury, yet the reputation you have, makes me resolve not to lose this opportunity of making myself more known to you than I have been yet. Dr Stanley can assure you, that I take more interest in what concerns the Church of England than myself, and that one of the greatest satisfactions I can have, is to hear how all the clergy show themselves as firm to their religion as they have always been to their king, which makes me hope God will preserve his church, since he has so well provided it with able men. I have nothing more to say, but beg your prayers, and desire you will do me the justice to believe I shall be very glad of any occasion to show the esteem and veneration I have for you.

Marie.

Sancroft was not brave enough to answer, though he drafted a reply which was never sent, in which he wrote, 'Blessed be God who hath caused some dawn of light to break from the eastern shore, in the constancy of your Royal Highness and the excellent Prince towards us.'

When Stanley returned to the court he brought supplies of all the remedies which the Princess did not like to be long without—plague water, treacle water and surfeit water. He was also loaded with *livres curieux* for the Huygens brothers, with whom he had struck up quite a friendship, discussing such matters as refraction and the *globosité* of the earth. Most important of all, he was able to report that James's position was deteriorating fast. The King had sent out a questionnaire to the Lord-Lieutenants of the counties asking them to test the reactions of important people to his projected abolition of the Test Act and penal laws. Many people thought that an opinion-poll of this kind was unconstitutional, and believed that such matters should be discussed in Parliament rather than at local meetings. All kinds of excuses and quaint reasons were given by those gentlemen who preferred not to commit themselves until Parliament met—if it ever was to meet. There were sudden outbreaks of mysterious illness all over the country, and a surprising number of people suddenly felt the onset of age.

The Prince's growing confidence was reflected in the manifesto which was published under the title *Their Highness the Prince and Princess of Orange's Opinion about a General Liberty of Conscience*. This was a joint declaration of their position with regard to tolerance and Catholicism, and their belief that though there should be no persecution of any sect, monopoly of office must remain for members of the official Church.

The King, having failed to win over his daughter Anne—she had now become more defiant than ever in her attachment to the Anglican Church—decided to see whether he could be more successful in capturing Mary's soul for the Catholics. On November 4, 1687, he wrote reminding her that he himself had been brought up strictly in the Anglican Church according to his father's instructions, but as he went into it further he discovered that the Catholics had been much maligned by the Protestants; looking into their reasons for the infallibility of their Church, he found that to deny this was to destroy the foundations of Christianity. He quoted chapter and verse to prove his point. As for such Protestants as Luther and Calvin and the English reformers, they had their heads full of temporal rather than spiritual considerations, and had let everyone feel capable of judging for themselves according to their own whims, rather than trusting to the authority of the scriptures.

Mary parried her father with quiet logic. She wanted to show him that she did not cling to the Anglican faith with a blind devotion, but with a mature belief reinforced by wide reading and deep contemplation. Glad though she was to know his reasons for changing his religion, she did not feel that she should be deprived of his affection because she was not of the same persuasion. Naturally she felt indebted to those who had instructed her in the Anglican faith during her childhood, but she had not clung to her belief simply out of gratitude. God gave man reason and meant it to be used, so she had read books about the Reformation weighing up the advantages and merits of the two Churches. It was hardly fair, she thought, to judge a form of religion by the life and behaviour of those who professed it—she could have added that James himself was no great advertisement for Catholicism. She said it would be presumptuous on her part to defend the reformed religion, and added (with a sting)—'if your Majesty wishes to give yourself the trouble to listen to them, there are plenty of subjects in your kingdom quite ready and capable of doing so. I only say this, that the Anglican Church has the advantage that it has never done anything in a hurry, but it has always proceeded according to the law, and has been established in this way.' As for the infallibility of the Catholic Church, she believed that this had never been proved, for the Catholics themselves were still uncertain whether the infallibility rested with the Pope himself, or with a general council, or with the two together. And had there not been occasions, she dared to ask, when there had been more than one Pope at the same time, each one with his own council and all fulminating against one another? 'One does not need to read much history,' she observed, 'to find out that not all the Popes have been guided by the Holy Spirit; must they still be considered successors of St Peter, when their lives contrasted so blatantly with his doctrine?' The Princess ended by telling her father that she felt the truth propounded by the Anglican Church was so convincing that she was sure it would last her well enough until the end of her days, and so she leaned with confidence on the words of the Saviour. The gates of hell could not prevail so long as He was with His Church until the end of time.

It looked as if James had lost another round. His elder daughter was likely to remain as firm in the Anglican faith as the younger. But towards the end of 1687 disturbing rumours began to emanate from England, and when the Princess returned to the Hague after a spell in the country she found a letter awaiting her from the Queen. Mary Beatrice, whose fruitful days everybody had believed to be over, was pregnant again. The Catholic cause, it seemed, might not be lost after all.

CHAPTER 19

THE BIRTH OF THE PRINCE

THE PRINCESS was able to say that she felt no twinge of jealousy when she heard about her step-mother's good fortune, for God had given her a contented spirit and enabled her to accept her own deprivation. All the same she knew that the Queen's pregnancy could prove a great blow to the Protestant religion. In England, indeed, there was considerable despondency when it was known that the Queen could present the country with a Catholic successor the following year.

On the first day of the new year prayers were offered up at Whitehall, thanking God for this latest benediction. James, convinced more than ever now that he had the Almighty on his side, renewed his onslaught on Mary's soul. She, for her part, began the new year by thanking God that she felt strong enough to withstand her father's attacks. She gave out her new year's gifts, bought three suits of nightclothes, paid the chimney-sweep, the English clockmaker and the French embroidery woman, bought two pounds of hair powder, green cloth for card carpets at the House in the Wood, a point handkerchief and stockings of white thread. Out of her pittance she gave fifty gelders to the master of a packet boat which had been stranded. Thinking that it was time to let her friends know where she stood, she drafted letters to her sister, to the Bishop of London and Dr Stanley, which she read out to the Prince. He was full of approval and praise; he had not realized that she was capable of writing so succinctly. She was so pleased with his reaction that she hastily had to pull herself up before she fell into the sins of pride and vanity, and she began to pray fervently; when the first Sunday in February approached, she prepared herself for the Sacrament, reminding herself of her own lack of merit.

James had now resorted to new tactics, and he began sending books to d'Albeville for her to read. He also suggested that she should have religious discussions with an English Jesuit, Father Morgan. She made her way dutifully through one of the tomes provided by d'Albeville—*Réflexions sur les Différents de la Religion*; she tackled her mother's papers and those of

the late King, and remarked that she felt 'sensibly afflicted' to see how far
God had abandoned her mother to such blindness, for she had always
imagined her to be gifted with great wit and intelligence.

January 30 was celebrated, not it is true with the old mockery of fasting
and donning a black outfit, but in prayer and confession of her own sins
and those of her country which 'Hélas! has drawn down on us all that we
most fear at present'. With Dr Stanley at her elbow she persisted with the
Réflexions. Stanley, who had taken the trouble to study the original work,
pointed out that in the version they had lent her, the Papists had extracted
a few phrases that suited their purpose, and had mixed them up with
their own inventions, thinking to pass off the result as the real thing. He
illustrated his point by reading passages aloud, and this was enough to
convince her—if she was not convinced already—of 'the typical impudence
and partiality that one finds nowhere else except among the priests'.

The King was now demanding the return of the six regiments in Holland.
There was a coolness in Mary Beatrice's letters, and the Princess
now found her a model of all that was indifferent, unconcerned and detached. The behaviour of her father and stepmother was making her
feel increasingly that it was her duty to aspire to the throne, both for the
sake of the Church and of the Prince; her love for William made her
wish for anything that could benefit him. 'And although I regret,' she
wrote, 'that I have only three crowns to bring him, it is not my love that
blinds me; so, I can see his faults, but I say this because I also know his
merits.'

In March, Verace, the Princess's Hofmeister, suddenly handed in his
notice, without any very good reason. He was an austere, brusque,
domineering man who justified his rudeness by pretending that it was a
kind of honesty. The Princess believed that this was due to the fact that
he had too much philosophy and too little religion. In her opinion,
charity should always be the predominant virtue, and Verace had little
enough of that. The Prince was puzzled by the Hofmeister's sudden
resignation, and as there were rumours that Verace had been seen recently
with the valet of a cousin who was said to be in the pay of the King of
France, he asked the Pensionary to make an investigation. Nothing
suspicious was found among Verace's papers except a seal which had been
given him with the instructions that he was to use it if need be as a pass
to the favour of any of the Kings and Princes of Europe. The Princess,
who by now had had ample experience of the wickedness of the world,
was inclined to fear the worst; reluctant though she was to condemn a man
without good evidence, she was ready to believe that Verace had been

motivated by evil intentions, and she was for a while very apprehensive about the Prince's safety and her own. Verace held that he had been underpaid, and had only been able to stay on as long as he had because his friends had subsidized him. The Princess did not think much of this excuse, and her friends agreed that if his reasons were genuine he should have given in his notice months before. When Verace sent her a letter presumably justifying his behaviour, she threw it on to the fire without reading it.

The fact that there were no sinister happenings after Verace's departure gave the Princess new confidence. It had pleased God to preserve them, and she found it easier to believe than ever that she and William were being used as instruments of God's will. She was now in a mood of resignation, for it seemed that she had learnt to look at life with something of William's fatalism. She hoped that she had learnt 'never to murmur again' and felt better prepared for death; she also hoped that when this came it would be for both of them the gate to heaven.

Verace was replaced by Lord Coote, son of the Earl of Mountrath. The new Hofmeister kissed her hand on the morning of March 29 and the same day she and the Prince left the Hague, arriving at Loo the next evening. Soon afterwards she had a letter from her father who expressed disapproval of the new appointment; he complained that Lord Coote was a man who on every occasion had spoken of him without respect. The breach with her father was now complete. She had given back all the books to d'Albeville and had made it clear that the Prince did not wish her to be troubled further with Papist propaganda.

'I am certain that it was the title of *Lord* that carried it for him,' wrote Stanley, who disapproved of Coote's appointment. He had been putting in a word for Compton's nephew, Mr Nicholas. Another reason was that Coote was notoriously impoverished, in spite of his noble birth, and the Princess had taken pity on him as a result; she had told Stanley that she thought Nicholas was too young for the post.

James was becoming increasingly sensitive about appointments in her household, and was naturally uneasy when he observed that so many of the English nobility had suddenly contracted a desire to spend their holidays in Holland.

With the current situation it was considered more prudent by some to seek places for themselves or their children at the Princess's rather than at the King's court. Danby, for example, wrote requesting Mary to take his daughter, the Countess of Plymouth, into her service. He had originally intended that his son Peregrine, Viscount Osborne of Dumblane, should bring the letter, but in the end decided that it would be more discreet to ask Dr Stanley to deliver it. 'I am confident,' he wrote, 'that my son's motions will be observed.' In a second letter, he told William that when Dumblane asked permission to go abroad, the King replied with some heat, that he could, 'provided it be not into Holland for I will suffer nobody to go thither'. Dumblane said mildly that his only reason for going abroad was to see a country he had not visited before, to which the King replied, 'perhaps so, but he had relations who had other designs there, and he knew there were those in Holland who gave themselves hopes of seeing some English Lords at the head of some of their squadrons, but he would take care to prevent it'. The next day, when Dumblane went to collect his pass from one of the Secretaries of State, he met the King accidentally. James drew him aside and said, 'My lord, I had newly received some news last night when you spoke to me, which had disturbed me, and made me speak to you in some disorder, therefore I would not have you take notice of anything I then said to you, for I dare trust you to go where you will but . . . if you go only for curiosity, you might as well satisfy that elsewhere as in Holland.' In any case, for the time being, Danby decided that his son was too young to be trusted with delicate and important commissions, so he despatched him to Flanders, with instructions to find a trustworthy messenger there who would carry the letters to Stanley. He also thought that it would be wiser not to pursue the matter of his daughter's entering the Princess's service until a more seasonable time. She wrote to him a month later, thanking him for suggesting his daughter to her:

The Bishop of London gives her an extreme good character and all I have ever heard agrees so well with what he says, that I believe I should like her extremely, but by your second letter I see, you think this an unfit time to make any such propositions to the King and I believe you are in the right; I am sure I should be very sorry you should expose yourself to any inconvenience upon my account or meet with any unpleasing answer, which makes me think we must refer this business to another opportunity, that may prove better; but by this occasion, my Lord, I must let you know that you have laid an obligation upon me, I can never forget; I need not tell you it is my being here I mean, where I find myself so well, that I shall have cause to thank you for it as long as I live, and you may be sure, it shall be returned you whenever there is any opportunity in the power of

MARIE

At Loo the Princess felt tranquil and resigned. Her eyes were better than they had been for some time; this she looked upon as a renewed opportunity to serve her God, which, to use her own word, she felt 'ravished' to do. She wrote to Lady Mary Forester, harking back to old times:

I have bin but once in the little wood where we played at hide-and-seek; since I came hither, the ill weather will not suffer much walking, but I never go there without remembering how you ventured your great belly, big enough for you to brag about as long as you live—I believe there's another coming by this time. I expect it in your next letter for I never knew anybody ashamed after one child.

There were no current romances among her own ladies, but if any of them married, 'I warrant,' she said, 'they shall know the matrimony by heart and answer to all with an audible voice.' Although she had written so respectfully to Danby, she was not above making some facetious remarks at the expense of his wife, for she suggested that Lady Mary should put on a forehead cloth 'to which if you will add a good large muffler so as to hide your face, you might pass for an old lady such as she [Lady Danby] and then you may give instructions with authority'.

The Princess made the most of her improved eyesight and read as many books as possible, but even so she was unable to study all the literature sent over by English divines. She told Stanley, as her chaplain, to select the most important, and so she dedicated herself more and more each day to the Anglican cause. It was a little disconcerting, however, to find that she was not quite so detached from worldly matters as she had hoped. When the Elector of Saxony came to pay his compliments to the Prince, he visited Loo on April 22, the Thursday before Easter. The Prince celebrated this according to the new style, but the Princess insisted on treating the date according to the old style as part of Holy Week. The Prince, perhaps fearing that his wife was becoming rather too pious, encouraged her to neglect her duty in favour of enjoying the novelty of such an important visitor. He took it upon himself to dress her up in all her jewellery, and went to a good deal of trouble to distract her from her devotions. She comforted herself with the thought that her heart was really averse to such temptations, but the Devil was bound to amuse himself by inventing ways of turning her away from God, though two more unlikely instruments for the devil to toy with than William of Orange and the Elector of Saxony it would have been hard to imagine.

While she was still at Loo, the Princess received a letter from Anne warning her against Sunderland. The Princess's reply was cautious. She did not refer to Sunderland, or to the Queen, which Anne found provoking. 'Though we agree in matters of religion,' she complained, 'yet I can't help fearing that you are not of my opinion in other matters, because you have never answered me to anything that I have said of Roger [Lord

Sunderland] nor of Mansell [the king].' Mary later tried to placate the Churchills with a letter entrusted to Stanley, in which she thanked them for their friendship to her sister.

Princess Anne suffered yet another miscarriage that spring. There was no apparent reason why she should have lost her child; she had not undergone any accident or suffered a shock of any kind; people were beginning to fear that the good God, having denied Mary the gift of progeny, was now seeing to it that her sister would never give birth to a live child. The Catholics, too, were alarmed in April when there were fears that the Queen was going to miscarry. There were even rumours that she had already done so. Lloyd, a biased reporter if ever there was one, had heard that Lady Clarendon had seen the Queen sitting up in bed beating herself in a fearful manner and crying 'I am undone, I am undone'.

The Queen had written to Mary confessing that she had grown unusually large, far more so than she would have expected at twenty weeks. Anne also wrote to say that she thought the Queen's 'great belly' was rather suspicious. Wasn't it strange that the Bath waters, which the best doctors had said would do her nothing but harm, 'should have had so very good effect so soon, as that she should prove with child from the first minute she and Mansell [the King] should meet?' Another odd aspect of the affair was that the Queen seemed so convinced that she was going to bear a son. The Catholics, Anne was sure, would 'stick at nothing, be it never so wicked, if it will promote their interest'. Like many other good Protestants, she was beginning to wonder whether there was some foul play intended.

In May, Mary left Loo and went to the Hague for the Kermesse. The Prince's health was giving cause for concern; he arrived at the Hague the day after she did, and to her relief agreed to try various remedies for his cough, which proved effective. On the last day of the month they went to Honselaersdyck, and they were still there when the news came from England that James had committed six Bishops to the Tower. Incorrigible as ever, he had ordered the Edict of Toleration to be read in all churches throughout England on May 5. This had brought the Bishops hurrying up to Lambeth. Ely and St Asaph dined with Clarendon on May 16 and then went on to the Bishop's Palace for consultations. Two days later the six Bishops and Archbishop Sancroft presented a petition to the King begging him to recall the order. James took them into his bedchamber and when he had read the petition he became very angry; he had not expected such a thing of them, he said. The Declaration was proclaimed in only four churches in the City.

It was a singularly bad move on James's part to send the Bishops to the Tower since they were not likely to suffer any hardship as a result of their incarceration, and at the same time their plight was bound to arouse a great deal of sympathy. Reresby watched them embark at Whitehall steps in the boats that were to take them to the Tower, and he said they all looked very cheerful; the Bishop of Chichester called out to him, asking him how he did. They went by barge to avoid disturbances, but the banks of the river were lined with people and there were shouts of acclamation from windows overlooking the Thames. Even the soldiers guarding them knelt down in prayer, and a multitude followed them to the gates. Reresby was of the opinion that if the King had really known the excitement his action was going to cause, he would never have ordered the Declaration to be read; Clarendon thought that at one time he had been on the verge of letting the whole matter drop, but his own pride and the influence of those men who were bent on hurrying him to his destruction prevented him from taking a conciliatory step.

The Prince and Princess, like all true lovers of the Reformation, were full of approval when they heard how the Bishops had behaved. They told Stanley to write to Sancroft on their behalf:

Our excellent Prince and Princess [he wrote] were well pleased with it, (notwithstanding all that the Marquis of Albeville, the King's envoy here, could say against it) that they have both vindicated it before him, and given me a command, in their names, to return your grace their hearty thanks for it, and at the same time to express their real concern for your grace and all your brethren, and for the good cause in which your grace is engaged; and your refusing to comply with the King is by no means looked upon by them as tending to disparage the monarchy, for they reckon the monarchy to be really undervalued by illegal actions. Indeed, we have great reason to bless and thank God for their Highnesses steadiness in so good a cause.

On June 10 Mary Beatrice gave birth to a son. 'A young Prince born which will cause disputes,' Evelyn noted in his diary. According to her own calculations, the child was a month early, and nobody had thought, by the look of the Queen, that it was due for several weeks yet. Princess Anne had been warned by the Protestants to stay close to the Queen, but she had gone off to Bath for a cure and was caught unawares by the early arrival.

Clarendon saw a great deal of whispering going on during the service at St James's Church and when he came out his page told him that the Queen was brought to bed of a son. As soon as he had dined he went to court and found the king shaving. James told his brother-in-law that the

Queen had been so quick in her labour that he had not been able to dress until then. He invited Clarendon to inspect the child who was asleep in his cradle; the little Prince, Clarendon observed, was 'a very fine child to look upon.' Barillon heard with delight that the child had cried with *'beaucoup de force'*, and the Venetian envoy spoke of his robustness. When the King wrote to William telling him the news, he did not omit to add that the Prince was 'a very strong boy'. This was not the usual puny Stuart offspring; all the same, to ensure that he did not die of convulsive fits like so many of Mary Beatrice's other children, he was given solid food at an early age, as well as a variety of remedies that might well have killed a less healthy infant.

Whatever their private feelings on the subject, the Prince and Princess had to walk warily. They were immediately faced with the problem of whether they should offer up prayers for the child. The Princess did not wish anyone to think that she had taken an aversion to the poor inno-cent infant, and felt that it was only human to say prayers on his behalf. William took her side; he did not want an open quarrel with his father-in-law at this moment. He ordered Stanley, who did not agree with him, to pray for the Prince, and he sent Zuylestein to offer congratulations. Chosen for his 'careless, unsuspected air', Zuylestein was a useful man to have in England, and before he came back he managed to gain an impression of the real state of public opinion there. He reported that many people were sceptical about the Prince of Wales and that there was a growing conviction in Protestant circles that the Jesuits had carried out a hoax.

The King was doing his best to convince everyone that there was great cause for rejoicing. On the day of the Queen's 'up-sitting' the finest fireworks that had ever been seen in England were let off at his expense. But in spite of his efforts, popular reaction was cool. Services of thanks-giving were sparsely attended; only three or four people went to St James's Church and it was much the same elsewhere.

Princess Anne was now convinced that the whole pregnancy had been an invention of the Catholic imagination, and she would not concede victory to the Bath waters and the Papists. Perhaps it was natural that out of pride the Queen had not allowed her stepdaughter to touch the famous belly and to feel the child move, but why should she not have let one of her ladies do so if they had chanced to be near her when she was undressing?

To be faced with the prospect of an endless Catholic dynasty just when Mary seemed to be established as the Protestant heir was a cruel blow.

Fear of the Papists ran deep, not so much for religious reasons, but because in the last resort the Catholics owed their allegiance to a foreign power, that of Rome; a Papist country ran the risk too, of falling under the domination of France. If James had been a quiet Catholic, content to rule with the help of Parliament, nobody would have questioned the reality of his son's conception and birth; it was his tendency towards authoritarianism that frightened the democratic Englishman. It was a strange mixture of fear and political expediency that made responsible people give credence to the theory that Prince James Edward had been smuggled into his mother's bed in a warming-pan. In moments of desperation even intelligent people believe what they want to believe. More and more politicians, especially those of the Whig persuasion, were coming round to the view that their only salvation lay in William's intervention. The birth of a Prince, supposed or not, had precipitated a crisis, and at the end of June, Admiral Herbert, disguised as an ordinary seaman, left for Holland carrying an important document.

Herbert's arrival came as the climax of weeks of visits from representatives of the opposition. Edward Russell, cousin of the Lord William Russell who had been executed for his supposed complicity in the Rye House plot, had been over several times. The Earl of Manchester had paid a short visit before returning to England to make preparations for William's arrival. Lord Mordaunt had been one of the first to come, and one of the first, also, to tell the Prince that he could come to England any time he liked and meet with little opposition. He was a facile talker, not the kind of man to persuade the Prince, and William said Mordaunt's idea was 'too romantical to build upon it'.

The momentous paper delivered by Herbert was signed by 'the immortal seven'—Devonshire, Danby, Shrewsbury, Lumley, Russell, Compton and Sidney. They thanked William for being so ready to give assistance, as Zuylestein had assured them he was. 'We have great reason to believe,' they wrote 'we shall be every day in a worse condition than we are, and less able to defend ourselves, and therefore we do earnestly wish we might be so happy as to find a remedy before it be too late for us to contribute to our own deliverance.' The situation, they said, was likely to deteriorate before the end of the year, with a 'packed' Parliament and Catholic officers being appointed to the army in large numbers, and they advised William to lose no time in making his preparations.

The seven took up a definite stand in relation to the new Prince; 'your compliment upon the birth of the child (which not one in a thousand here believes to be the Queen's) hath done you some injury,' they told William, and they added, 'the false imposing of that upon the Princess and the nation, being not only an infinite exasperation of people's minds here, but being certainly one of the chief causes upon which the declaration of your entering the kingdom in a hostile manner, must be founded on your part, although many other reasons are to be given on ours.'

The Princess was now in a dilemma. She was not a woman to thirst after a throne, and if she were to go to England it was to be only in the interests of furthering the Protestant cause, and not with the object of obtaining glory for herself. The arrival of the stepbrother was an unnecessary complication; if James Edward were acknowledged to be a genuine heir, the moderate Catholics, who had been standing back from the King's extremist policies, might be encouraged to lend him their support. There could also be a crop of conversions amongst those who had hesitated to go over to Rome fearing that the King would not live for long and remembering that on his death the Protestant Mary would have little use for apostates. The most convenient action was to accept the warming-pan theory and to ignore the claims of the new-born child. It was easy for William to do so in the interests of expediency, far less so for his wife. A letter from the Queen, written on July 13, only made matters worse. 'The first time that I have taken a pen in my hand since I was brought to bed, is this, to write to my dear Lemon,' Mary Beatrice wrote, adding that she could hardly have hoped that everything would be over by now, for 'I came a month sooner than I reckoned, which mistake I thought I could not make, counting as I used to do . . . If my child had not been bigger and stronger than any I ever had, I should have thought I had come before my time.' This sounded genuine enough, and it was not without heart-searching that the Princess agreed that in view of all the strange rumours, prayers for the Prince should be discontinued. When d'Albeville wrote inviting her to attend the party he was giving to celebrate the birth, she sent an ambiguous reply and neither she nor the Prince, nor any of their court, went near it. D'Albeville had arranged a magnificent fête, and he was understandably put out when hardly anybody came.

The simplest solution would have been for the child to die, like so many of the King's other offspring. Soon after his birth Evelyn reported that he was 'somewhat ill of the wind and some gripes' and on July 9 Anne wrote to tell Mary that she thought it would not be long before he was an angel in heaven. At the beginning of August he was extremely ill, but a nurse was provided for him 'and upon sucking he visibly mended'. Lloyd, Mary's ex-chaplain, was sure that he had actually died a day or two after his birth, and that the Catholics had hastily found a substitute, then the substitute had died in its turn and another one produced, in fact 'divers children were laid out about this time to be in readiness'.

The Prince did not die, and the only other solution, which was the one William still continued to hope for, was that the King would see the folly of his ways before it was too late. But James was in an unbalanced state; he either would not or could not see that the Protestant tide was running against him, that he would face disaster unless he could moderate his policies and placate the Anglican Church. On the day that Herbert had sailed for Holland, the Bishops had been brought to trial and acquitted. Westminster Hall, the Palace Yard and the streets round about had been so full of people, and their huzzas and shouts of joy so loud, that Reresby said it sounded like 'a little rebellion in noise'. There were bonfires in the City and in all the important towns in England, even though the magistrates had been told to prevent any celebrations. But the King still clung to his Jesuits and refused to admit that his intended repeal of the Test and penal laws had not won over the Dissenters as he had hoped. All he could see was that God had granted him an heir, which in his view gave divine sanction to his policies.

So the necessity for immediate intervention on the part of William and Mary became increasingly obvious, and with it the urgent need for the Princess to make up her mind on the troubled question of her step-mother's child. Unless she could salve her conscience on this point, she might find it morally impossible to answer the summons of the seven brave men who had risked their lives writing the letter of invitation. Painstakingly she wrote out a questionnaire for Anne to answer, touching in detail on all aspects of the confinement. Anne, who had not found such satisfaction from the Bath waters as her step-mother, had now gone to Tunbridge Wells, since the doctors had told her this might help to prevent another miscarriage if she should become with child again. She told her sister that she was looking forward to escaping from all the people who now forced her to dissemble, and to 'put on a face of joy, when one's heart had more cause to ache'. Frankly, she found the questionnaire an effort. 'I am generally lazy,' she admitted, as she tried to apply her mind to Mary's searching enquiries. At what time had the Queen fallen into labour? When was the King told? Had the news been given to him secretly? Was there a screen at the foot of the bed between it and the rest of the room, or not? There was no screen, Anne said, taking her evidence from Mrs Dawson, who had been present at the time. The curtains at the sides of the bed were drawn back, but nobody could see whether the Queen had the face of a woman in great pain, for she had asked the King to hide it with his periwig since 'she could not be brought to bed and have so many men look on her'. Anne replied with some technical details about the after-birth and the cutting of the cord, and then described how the King had intercepted the nurse as she carried the infant into the little bedchamber, and had told the councillors to follow him into the next room to witness whether it was a girl or a boy. Anne gave a long list of the many lords and ladies who had been present at the birth, who all, she said, 'stood as near as they could'. Mrs Dawson had stationed herself behind the Dutch chair on which the midwife sat, but at the critical time nobody had held the Queen except the King himself. Mary had heard it said that some people had noticed that at first the child had seemed to be of the slender type, and later appeared to be 'round and full', but Anne admitted that she had not heard about this, though she said that hardly anybody had been allowed to see the child whether it was dressed or undressed. As for the question of whether the Queen appeared to be fond of the child, Anne had observed that even when it had been 'very ill of a looseness', her stepmother had come up from prayers and gone straight into dinner without looking at it, 'and after that played at comet, and did not go to it till she was put out of the pool'. There were further questions about the Queen's milk, and the astringents she had taken, to all of which the Princess gave somewhat guarded replies. But it seems that Mary was satisfied by the results of her enquiry, for her attitude towards the Prince became cooler, a fact that was immediately noted by James and Mary Beatrice.

The Queen wrote on July 31 saying that she suspected Mary of being less kind than she used to be:

The reason I have to think so is (for since I have begun I must tell you all the truth) that since I have been brought to bed, you have never in your letters to me taken the least notice of my son no more than if he had never been born, only in what Mr Zuylestein has brought, that I look upon as compliment that you could not avoid, though I should not have taken it so, if ever you had named it afterwards.

On August 17 she complained further that when Mary did write, she spoke of the new Prince so formally that she obviously thought of him with great indifference. The king said that whenever he mentioned the Prince in letters, Mary made no attempt to answer 'anything concerning him'.

The whole situation was very distressing. 'One cannot help having a thousand fears and melancholy thoughts,' Anne had written, and Mary did not succeed in living through those dark weeks without considerable mental torment. When the Prince found her in tears on one occasion, he was full of pity, and indeed there was great sympathy between them. They talked openly about present events and future plans. It was not easy for her to accept the belief that her father had tried to deceive the nation, but once she had done so, it was simpler for her to convince herself that there was no other way of saving Church and State except for her husband to go over to England to dethrone her father.

The Princess wrote to James on August 17, and on the 19th, with this unpleasant task off her mind, she left Honselaersdyck with the Prince. They arrived at Loo on the 20th and, released from the embarrassment of social calls and official visitors, she was able to pray and work—for her eyes were better than they had been for years. In a sense her position was more difficult than William's; all that she could do was to think and to brood, while he could occupy his mind with practical preparations for the descent on England. Ships had to be hired and troops assembled; a vast camp was being built up at Nimeguen.

James was beginning to feel suspicious. 'I do my part to preserve the peace of Christendom,' he wrote self-righteously to Sophia of Hanover; 'but have reason to believe that some in Holland have a mind to war by the preparation there.' William and the Dutch Envoy tried to reassure the King, telling him that the massing of troops was caused by French movements, for Louis's army was on the march, its destination unknown. It was more difficult to explain away the growing activity in the ports of Holland. At the end of September the master of a ship that had come from Rotterdam reported that he had been forced away from the quay to make way for several large vessels which were loading horses, hay and oats, working every day of the week. By the middle of the month the English court had become in such a state of nerves that Evelyn was astonished at the change that had taken place while he was away in the country. The King told Clarendon at his levée that the Dutch were now coming to invade England in good earnest. Clarendon presumed to ask whether the King really believed this, to which he replied with some warmth, 'Do I see you, my Lord?' He went on to add that an express had arrived the previous evening with a report that 2,000 men had already been shipped while 7,000 more were marching 'to the seaside'. 'And now, my Lord,' said the King, 'I shall see what the Church of England will do.' Clarendon answered: 'Your Majesty will see they will behave themselves like honest men, though they have been somewhat severely used of late.'

As the first Sunday in September approached, Stanley asked the Princess whether she wished to postpone the Sacrament, but thinking that it was more important than ever to offer up all possible prayers, she told

Stanley not to delay it. Who knew whether the Prince would still be with them in a month's time, or whether she herself would be in a suitable place to attend the Communion service? Soon after she had partaken of the Sacrament, William left for an eight-day visit to the Elector of Brandenburg. She found this separation difficult to bear, especially as she had some very trying letters from the King and Queen while he was away. The Queen told Mary that people were saying the Prince was planning an expedition, but she herself refused to believe it, and certainly would not credit the rumour that Mary would come with him: 'I don't believe you could have such a thought against the worst of fathers, much less against the best, that has always been kind to you and loved you better than all the rest of his children.'

The fear that France might attack at any moment was worse when the Prince was away, but, when he had visited the Elector, as well as the Duke of Zell and the Landgrave of Hesse, he returned to Loo in good health, and stayed with Mary for three precious days before returning to the Hague. On September 23 she left Loo and went to Dieren to wait for the Prince who had gone to review the army. D'Albeville came to visit her there bringing letters from the King and Queen which were very different from the ones she had been receiving recently. They were full of compliments, and she could tell from their tone that her father and stepmother were growing alarmed about the preparations being made in Holland.

For a few days the Princess remained by herself, enjoying the peace of Dieren, and preparing for the ordeal that lay ahead. Without her religious faith, she would have been unable to stand the strain of knowing that the Prince, whose life was 'a million times more dear to her than her own', was soon to be exposed to danger in a war against her own father. At the end of the month, the Prince sent for her, and she left the tranquillity of Dieren for all the activity and excitement of the Hague. She arrived there on October 6 to find that William's cough was troubling him, though not enough to prevent him attending to all the preparations for the expedition 'which seemed directed by Providence and God himself'.

At the Hague Mary found a letter awaiting her from her father. He had heard that the Prince had sent for her. 'I suppose it is to inform you of his design of coming to England which he has been so long contriving,' he wrote. In a subsequent letter he complained that he had not heard from her for several posts: 'I easily believe you may be embarrassed how to write to me now that the unjust design of the Prince of Orange's invading me is so public.' He was putting on the emotional thumbscrew now. 'And though I know you are a good wife,' he went on, 'and ought to be so, yet for the same reason, I must believe you will be still as good a daughter to a father that has always loved you so tenderly, and that has never done the least thing to make you doubt it. I shall say no more, and believe you very uneasy all this time, for the concern you must have for a husband and a father. You shall still find me kind to you if you desire it.'

Far too late James was realizing the error of his ways. As rumours came in about the Prince's growing forces, and the fleet all ready to sail, he began to panic, and started restoring some of the Protestant Justices he had previously removed in favour of Catholics. The Queen was begging him to make concessions. At court there was an atmosphere of perpetual hurry and everyone was being rude to everybody else; continual false alarms were being received about landings on the coast and the numbers of casualties that had occurred. The King was now thoroughly alerted, and became so busy making preparations that he hardly slept at night. Realizing at last that the stories about the new Prince of Wales must be taken seriously—'they that believe such falsity must think me the worst man in the world,' he told Sophia of Hanover—he instituted an enquiry, again far too late. He summoned all the lords and ladies who had been present at the birth and ordered them to declare what they had seen and done, so that everybody might be convinced of the authenticity of the Prince of Wales; 'there was such a long discourse of bawdry [spelt "badery"] held up,' wrote one observer:

that put all the Ladies to the blush. The King made a long speech to them and told them he was not ignorant of the troubles that were coming upon England and that God knew what would become of him, and that when he was dead he should be glad to leave everything in peace and quietness and that the Prince of Wales must enjoy the Crown peasable [sic] after him.

William was now in no mood for delay. The security covering his preparations had been inadequate and he was afraid that James was being given too much chance to prepare himself and to weaken the resolution of the Protestants by empty promises of better behaviour in the future. D'Avaux warned Louis that William's intentions were real and the French King was evidently making up his mind whether to go to James's rescue in England, or to cause a distraction on the continent. Louis did in fact put his navy at James's disposition, but with Stuart stubbornness the King replied that he did not need any assistance. Louis, piqued, removed the troops which had been menacing the Netherlands, and marched them away into the Palatinate, which at least removed the fear that the Prince, in going to England, would leave his own country open to attack. One of the greatest anxieties had thus for the time being been laid at rest, but the imponderables and uncertainties remained. Most worrying of all was the attitude of the English people themselves; how many, when it came to the point, would rise against the lawful King? Faced with so many anxieties, William was struck down by illness, and for a week he was unable to take an active part in affairs, but his own determination and belief in God dragged him back to the point where he was strong enough to take his leave of the States. He went to the Assembly on October 26 and an emotional scene took place. He thanked the Deputies for their loyal support, and finished by saying: 'What God intends for me I do not know, but if I should fail, take care of my adored wife who has always loved this country as if it were her own.' Many Deputies were in tears, and William, though as dignified as ever, also wept.

The Prince told Mary that if she were in any difficulty she must ask advice from Waldeck, who had been left in charge of the forces at home, or from Dyckvelt, or from Fagel who was, however, mortally ill. He told her that she could trust these men in anything. Then, with tears in his eyes, he said that if it pleased God that she should never see him again (words that stabbed her to the heart, so that when she wrote them down in her diary she could still feel the pain they caused), 'if such a thing should happen,' he told her, 'it would be necessary for you to marry again'. The thought of never seeing him again had struck a cruel blow, but the sug- gestion that she should remarry surprised and shocked her so much that she felt, in her own words, as if her heart had melted. 'There is no need for me to say,' he went on, 'that this must not be to a Papist.' As he said this, the Prince was so overcome that he could not control his tears, and he showed her such tenderness throughout the scene that Mary never forgot it as long as she lived.

The Princess was so astonished by what her husband had said that she was unable to reply at once, and he reassured her, saying that it was only his concern for their religion which made him talk in such a way. She was unable to remember afterwards what she finally replied, but she knew that she made her answer confusedly, assuring him that she had never loved anyone but him, and would never be able to love anyone else. Besides, since she had been married for so many years now without God blessing her with a child, she believed that this was enough to prevent her from ever contemplating what he had proposed. She told him that all she asked of God was that she should not survive her husband; if this had to be, since God had not granted her a child by him, she would not wish to have one by an angel. 'Oh my God!' she burst out in her diary, 'if I have sinned in this passion, as I fear I have, forgive me I beseech thee. But

praised be thy name that I have not murmured against thee.' She admitted
that she had thought too much about herself, and it was this selfishness
which made her wish not to survive her husband who was so good and so
dear to her, nor ever marry another. 'For assuredly,' she wrote, 'I should
never be able to find his equal.'

When the emotion had died down, the Prince and Princess talked
quietly of other matters and she asked him to forgive her for all her faults.
He replied with such tenderness that if it could have been possible this
increased her love for him. On October 26 he took her out to Honselaersdyck for dinner, and afterwards she accompanied him to the river's edge
where she saw him take a boat for Helvoetsluys. God alone knew when
they would meet again, or whether it was the last time they would ever see
each other. This thought almost deprived her of her reason. She sat in her
coach without moving and could not find the strength to order the coachman to drive away as long as she could still glimpse the Prince. That
evening she went back to the Hague, struck down with an indescribable
grief, unable even to feel the comfort that God could give her, but never
once questioning what she described as '*l'œconomie de ta Providence*'.

CHAPTER 20

GOD'S WEATHER

ALL POSSIBLE PREPARATIONS had been made to ensure that the expedition would be a success, and now all that was required was some co-operation from the Almighty. October 27 was set aside as a day of general fasting in all the States, and the Jews joined in as well as the Spanish Envoy, who allowed masses to be said for the success of the enterprise. Only the French Ambassador and d'Albeville refrained. In spite of all the prayers, it looked as though God was on the side of the Catholics, for the wind blew hard from the west for days on end, making it out of the question for the fleet to set sail. As Lady Sunderland put it to Evelyn, 'the wind being west you can expect no news, and I truly think that is the strongest thing we can rely on, being infatuated as to doing anything reasonable'. On October 20 James wrote to Dartmouth confidently: 'I see God Almighty continued his protection to me by bringing the wind westerly again.' At about the same time William told Herbert that he was in pain on account of this continued gale from the wrong quarter.

In London the Protestants watched the weathercocks, and prayed for the wind to veer. There was an atmosphere of tension. On October 14, the King's birthday, the sun was eclipsed at its rising and no guns sounded from the Tower. In Holland, William's preparations were complete; all he needed now was a sign of the divine approval. On October 29 the wind shifted, only slightly, but enough to make William feel that his opportunity had come. He embarked on his flagship, and the fleet then set sail from the mouth of the Maas into the open sea where the wind was already freshening. It was blowing from the south-west and a landing was planned on the Yorkshire coast, but by October 30 it had changed back to the west, reaching gale force. By nightfall the fleet was scattered, and during the hours of darkness 'when most men's hearts were as stones, dead with fear', the Prince remained calm and 'his countenance was observed not to alter . . . but like a true Paul . . . he encouraged all in the ship where he was'. Next day the ships came struggling back to Helvoetsluys; the set-back was great and the loss of time serious, but the damage was less than might have been expected. Only one ship had been lost, and the worst casualties had been among the horses, many of which had been suffocated when the hatches were battened down in the storm.

In England James and his supporters looked on the storm as a kind of victory, and they thanked God for saving them from their enemies. William, however, refused to be downcast, and Mary said that in the letters he wrote after he had been driven back into port, he still showed great calmness and resignation to the will of God. She herself had been through a traumatic experience during the storm, when she had been unable to hear any news of him. 'All I can say about it here,' she wrote in her diary, 'is, that I proved how hard and disagreeable it can be, to love so much, when the person loved is absent.' Someone who saw her at the Hague found her 'turmoiled with many prayers and deep cognitions'. And while the Prince waited patiently for *le temps du Seigneur*, God's weather, the Princess continued to pray for him celebrating every Wednesday as if it were a *fête*, with a service and sermon, and holding a service each morning with prayers suitable for the times. Chambrun, or Chafubum as she called him, the Protestant refugee Minister who the year before had dedicated to her his book *Larmes*, said prayers with the household in French, and further prayers were offered up in all churches during the afternoons. At the same time the Prince took care that wherever he found himself, prayers were read twice a day in three languages.

Although the Prince had promised that he would not sail without seeing her again, Mary was sure that he would have to set off now that the wind had become favourable. She knew that he could not neglect a good opportunity simply for love of her. On November 7 she took the Sacrament, but she believed that the devil had been doing all he could to prevent her receiving this comfort, for he filled her mind with such strange thoughts that she felt incapable of prayer. The amiable and kindly Dr Drelincourt told her that this disturbance of the mind was caused by the fact that her blood was heated and disordered. She was in great discomfort from kidney pains and gravel and was finding it hard to sleep at night. She was given remedies, and they also took away eight ounces of blood, but she remained in very low spirits.

Then on the evening of November 9 a letter came from William asking her to meet him at Brill the following day. The fleet had reassembled at Helvoetsluys and the Prince could not easily be spared, but he was fond enough to put aside a few hours for a last glimpse of his wife. The road to Brill was very bad and he had a difficult journey. Meanwhile, the thought of seeing him had filled the Princess with such ecstasy that she had been unable to think of anything else or to listen to the sermon that was preached on the evening before she left. But the second parting proved to be even worse than the first, and she felt as if someone had torn out her heart. Unable, this time, to find relief in tears, she sat quite still in the room where he had left her, and all she was able to do was to commend him to God. She sat alone in the room for an hour and a half, after which she opened the door and went out. She was told that there was a service being held in the town, so she went there, feeling that this was the only possible place for her to be.

The following morning she was forced to stay indoors longer than she had expected because of a recurrence of the flux. Public prayers had been ordered for ten o'clock, the Prince being due to set sail that day. She attended prayers, and when they were over, she went up into a high tower to watch the fleet. In every direction as far as the eye could reach there was nothing to be seen except the masts of ships. The wind was now as favourable as any Protestant could wish. At one o'clock the Prince embarked. Fifty warships and over two hundred transports sailed slowly off in fine weather before the north-easterly breeze with banners streaming out from the masthead bearing the motto *For religion and liberty—I will maintain.* The banners, like those manufactured for Monmouth's expedition, had given the secret away to the King's agents sooner than anything else.

The Princess went back sadly to the Hague; the journey took her three hours by water. On the way she encountered a vast crowd at Maaslandsluys where the Prince was particularly popular, and she found its enthusiasm almost frightening, especially as she herself felt in no mood for rejoicing. With the Prince had gone so many of their friends—Bentinck whose wife lay dying, Huygens, Schomberg, Burnet. The fate of the expedition now lay in the balance; vast though the invading fleet had seemed as it passed out of the Maas, how small the force really was when there was no sure guarantee that the English would not decide after all to put national pride before religious considerations. Messages had been coming through from various agents who had been sent ahead to distribute propaganda leaflets, and these, on the whole, brought encouraging reports, but a packet boat from England had carried the message that the King was preparing for the invasion. Lights were out along the coast, and the marker buoys taken down from the beaches. James had also called the Bishops together and told them to condemn the invasion, but Sancroft hedged, saying that not enough Bishops were in town for any declaration to carry weight.

The expedition headed out to sea and then turned south into the

Channel. For those who waited in Holland the anxiety intensified as the armada sailed away and all contact was lost for days on end. There were unofficial reports that the fleet had passed between Dover and Calais by break of day, with the English in pursuit. At any moment news could come through of a naval battle or an unsuccessful landing. These days of waiting were the worst of all; there was nothing to do except to pray and submit to God's will 'who orders all things for the best tho' we don't know it', as Mary herself had put it to Lady Mary Forester that September when condoling with her on the death of her sister.

The anniversary of her wedding and William's birthday passed, and there was still no news. To add to her troubles, she received a message from d'Albeville who said that he had something to communicate from King James. Remembering William's advice, she asked Dyckvelt what she should do. He advised her not to become embroiled, so she sent d'Alonne to d'Albeville with the excuse that she did not want to see anybody because of the Prince's departure, and asking him to send a message by word of mouth or in a letter. He chose the latter course, and delivered the paper which the King had printed concerning the Prince of Wales. When she had read this she instructed d'Alonne to write to the envoy, which he did on November 9:

Sir, the Princess has both received and read the Paper you desired me yesterday to deliver to her; and have Her Royal Highness's commands to tell you: that she does not wonder at all that after what has been publicly talked, and generally believed of the matter contained in the said paper, the King should think of means to convince the world of the contrary, but as for Her Royal Highness, she thinks she neither can at this distance, nor ought in other respects to judge of it, seeing 'tis of that nature, that nothing but a Parliament can satisfy therein the minds of everybody, as I was persuaded that yourself are fully enough convinced of this.

D'Albeville seemed 'not much to give his assent' to this reply, but at least he was silenced for the time being.

Everyone else showed the Princess extraordinary kindness and understanding. The States-General begged her to take care of herself, for fear of what the Papist party might do to her. She was spending all her time now in public and private prayer. In the mornings she went to those which were being said in French in her own house, at mid-day to Common Prayer, and at five o'clock to hear a sermon, finishing up with Common Prayer again in the evening. Fortunately her health was good enough to enable her to do all this, but, she admitted, 'my enemy the devil found the means to revive the scruples and fears of my spirit in making me understand by all these public devotions, that I attracted admiration, and this reawakened my vanity'. At the same time she knew that if she stayed at home she would be setting a bad example, so she found a way out of the dilemma by telling herself that a good example was more important than her own vanity.

At last, on November 19 letters came through from London giving the news of William's landing at Torbay. There was nothing from the Prince himself as the ship he had sent off with despatches for Holland had been intercepted on the way. It was a relief to know that the landing had been achieved without naval intervention, the English fleet, as Evelyn put it, having done 'nothing to the purpose'. But there were still many unknown hazards ahead, and it was not yet known how much support the expedition would gain as it penetrated farther into the country.

Rejoicings at the Prince's success were tempered by the death, on November 20, of Anne Bentinck. She had suffered a great deal physically, but though she did not have her husband with her during her last hours, her faith enabled her to bear her pain with patience. She had plenty of time, the Princess observed, to prepare herself for another world, and to resign herself to the thought of leaving her husband and her five children, of whom the oldest was only nine years old. On the day before she died, she recommended her family to the Princess, who promised to do what she could. She died so peacefully that she could have been simply falling asleep, and the Princess hoped that her serenity and courage would influence all those who were present and teach them 'to number their days and apply their hearts to wisdom'.

When William had been still at sea, Mary had refused to see anyone, but once the news of his landing came through, she relaxed a little and gave up four days a week to entertaining ladies, though she still avoided playing cards. The days went by and still she did not have a letter from William, though she had the consolation now of receiving news from London which spoke of her husband's continuing success. She knew that she ought to have been in a state of great inquietude, but was amazed to find herself 'in a kind of tranquillity'. The kindness of everyone around her enabled her to carry a burden which might otherwise have been too heavy to bear. She was haunted by the Prince's words about his death and her remarriage, and she could not help wondering whether these had been uttered as a kind of prophecy. When at last a letter came from William himself, confirming all that she had heard from other sources, she allowed herself to believe that God had ordained a happy ending to the perilous crusade on which her husband had embarked.

Gradually, as letters and despatches came through, people in Holland were able to piece together the story of William's first weeks in England—his march to Exeter and then to Salisbury, the rising in the north, James's irresolution, Churchill's desertion and Anne's flight. In a letter to his brother Constantine, who was still with the Prince, Christiaan Huygens expressed the feelings shared by many people in Holland, including the Princess:

You can imagine with what joy we have learnt of the great and happy success of affairs from there after all the inquietude and apprehensions since the beginning of this expedition, either from the dangers of the sea or for the uncertain outcome of the war, for although from your disembarking the news has always been very good . . . one could not have imagined such a sudden reversal . . . Now we wait with impatience the news of your arrival in London, and of the reception they will have made, which without a doubt would have been an admirable thing to see. What joy for the nation, and what glory for him to have come to the end of this noble and hardy enterprise.

Londoners would have liked to give William a stirring welcome, and although it was raining ceaselessly on the day he was due to arrive, a large crowd turned out to see him, 'so powerful,' as one commentator put it, 'is the concupiscence of satisfying one's curiosity'. All the ladies were out on the balconies holding oranges in their hands, and had ribbons in their hair of the Prince's colours; the bourgeoisie was also provided with a quantity of oranges. It was unfortunate, therefore, that the Prince had chosen to enter the capital by a quiet route and that many people, as a result, were disappointed, and began at once to think less well of their liberator.

King James, seeing his world crumbling, had sent his wife and child away to safety; at midnight they had departed secretly on a barge down the river and, 'the wind being fair, wafted over to Dunkirk'. He had then taken flight himself, but his boat had been boarded by a party which was priest-codding, or searching for escaping Catholics. Having discovered the most important fugitive of all, the party treated the King very uncivilly and brought him back to Whitehall. It would have been better if he had escaped successfully, for his presence in London was nothing but an embarrassment to the Prince, and as long as he remained there he continued to arouse sympathy. It was William who provided the guards that carried the King away down river on the morning that he himself was due to enter London, and he had given orders that this time James should be allowed to make his escape. They saw to it that he was not intercepted. He had been unable to make any courageous attempt to save the kingdom for himself, and now he felt there was nothing for him to do except to place himself under the protection of Louis XIV.

The Princess heard the news of her father's flight on December 30. At the same time she had a letter from the Prince telling her to prepare for her journey to England. 'I could not think without chagrin,' she wrote in her diary, 'of leaving this dear country, where I had had such happiness, both spiritual and temporal. I fear that I sin in attaching my heart to it too much . . . fearing to be sent out of this country for ever and (much as I longed to see the Prince) I finished the year of 1688 in these various hopes and expectations, a year that had seen some of the strangest events the world has ever known, as well as a particular bounty and spiritual benediction which God had shown towards my soul, and for which I will glorify his name as long as I live.'

CHAPTER 21

THE RETURN TO ENGLAND

THE KING'S FLIGHT was a shock to everybody. 'It is like an earthquake,' Clarendon complained. The Princess was glad to feel that her father was safe, but she could not help brooding over his plight, even though his conduct during the last weeks had not been any too admirable. Her elation on hearing of the Prince's success gradually began to fade in the first days of the year. Although William had now decided not to send for her until his own position was clarified, she knew that it was only a matter of time before the break with her beloved Holland would have to come. The prospect did not please her. 'Self-love made me shed a flood of tears,' she wrote, 'at the thought of leaving a country where I had the esteem of the inhabitants, where I had led a life so suitable to my humour, and as I think not unacceptable to my God, where in a word I had all earthly content.'

In the first cold weeks in January the Princess spent her time putting her own affairs in order; she distributed the new year's gifts, settled various outstanding debts and tried to sort out her accounts which had become increasingly muddled over the last year. On March 23, 1688, she had written:

Too much here, if I have not reckoned wrong, must be some of the money of the half year before. I hope the Prince will pardon all the faults in these accounts and forgive the debts I have made. If God give me life I shall pay them as fast as I can, if not I hope the Prince will let none be wronged by my folly.

By November 8 she was even more confused. 'I can't tell how the rest has bin laid out,' she wrote, 'but I know 'tis all gone.'

There was a pleasant distraction in January when the Elector and Electress of Brandenburg visited the Hague. Frederick III had succeeded his aged father the previous year, and it was important to keep him friendly. Mary found him a strange man to look at, 'but they say,' she added charitably, 'he has many good qualities which I could not judge of in so short a time'. The Electress was not only pretty but also agreeable and not without wit, but the Princess noted with disapproval that her religious education had been badly neglected. When the Electress took to the dance

floor, Mary desisted, some said because she was too cast down by her
father's misfortunes. With affairs in such an uncertain state it was impossible to mount any public entertainments or parades, but the Princess
amused them at her various houses and, out of politeness, sat up playing
cards with them until two o'clock in the morning. She was gratified to
notice that she had overcome the desire to dance, which had once been
one of her 'prettiest pleasures', but she still found that she was not quite
immune to worldly distractions and that she even enjoyed having company.
To salve her conscience she rose early even after her late nights, and attended prayers in French as well as in English, which had to make up for
the fact that she was too busy entertaining her guests to go to church in
the afternoons. Like most other people, the Elector and Electress found
their hostess charming; 'her beauty equalled her mental gifts,' the Electress told her mother.

From England came the news that William had agreed to fill the gap
left by James's precipitate flight and was willing to accept the responsibility
of government until the Convention Parliament could be called. The
Princess composed a prayer asking God to give the Prince the grace and
strength necessary for his task, and added a similar plea for the Convention. They had need of her prayers, for already the unanimity which
had flourished among Protestants in adversity was beginning to give way
to faction and friction. Now that James was a penurious exile, it was all
too easy to forget his stubbornness, his fanaticism, his despotic tendencies,
and to see him as a tragic figure, a Lear whose daughters had driven him
out into the storm. Suddenly it became convenient for those who realized
they had little to hope for under the new régime to develop a strong loyalty
to the monarch who had fled to France, and to feel repelled by the thought
of paying homage to the usurper. The Earl of Arran put it neatly when he
said of James, 'I must distinguish between his popery and his person;
I dislike the one, but I have sworn and do owe allegiance to the other'.
Some people were all for establishing a Regency; the throne, they said,
could not be considered vacant as long as James was alive; they thought the
present position could be treated as if the King were 'in a state of lunacy
or non-age'. Another group, headed by Danby, intended to make Mary a
Queen in her own right. Danby wrote her a letter suggesting that she
should accept his plan. She answered at once, though her reply was delayed by contrary winds, assuring him that she would never accept such a
scheme. Meanwhile Bentinck made it clear to one of Danby's followers
that William had no intention of becoming his wife's 'gentleman usher'.
No man, the Prince said, could think more of the Princess than he did,

but his nature was such that he could not contemplate being tied to his wife's apron-strings. He must be given a reasonable share in the government or he would go home at once. So the debate went on, between those who wanted a Regency, and those who either wished William to reign unconditionally, or who stipulated that he could only be King during his wife's lifetime. At last he decided to make his position clear. He had been invited to head an expensive and precarious expedition with the object of freeing the English from their Catholic oppressor. This he had already achieved. If they wished him to stay and be their Protestant King, he would do so, but only on his own terms. He would accept the Crown if it was offered to him for life, and his one concession was that Anne's children should have precedence over any heirs he might produce by a second wife. He agreed that Mary should receive the title of Queen and that they should reign jointly, provided he was to be the administrative head. He knew his wife well enough to realize that thanks to her unselfish character this would be as practicable as it would have been impracticable for him to reign as Regent with the revengeful James at liberty and backed by all the power of France. Members of the Convention, realizing that they could not do without William, agreed to these terms, grudgingly in many cases, and on February 1 Admiral Herbert crossed to Holland carrying a letter in which the Prince told his wife to come to England as quickly as she could.

Only a few days before, the Admiral had been confined to bed with a bad attack of gout, though he had risen indignantly from his pillow when Bentinck, who was visiting the sick-room, had suggested that the Prince intended to make Mary his Queen Consort rather than a Queen in her own right. 'I would never have drawn my sword in the Prince's favour, if I could have suspected him of acting in such a way towards his wife,' he had exclaimed. The prospect of fetching the new Queen was enough to make him forget his indisposition, and his open and official trip to Holland was a strange contrast to the clandestine expedition he had carried out in the guise of a common seaman not seven months before.

The Prince's letter, though it was expected, came as a shock to the Princess. That night she was unable to sleep; she turned over and over in her mind the difficulty of taking her father's place and the uncertainty about her reception in England, where she would be looked on as a total stranger. Worst of all was her strong premonition that she would never see Holland again. It was many hours before she could control her thoughts or look into the future with the necessary resignation—'with much ado I calmed myself and brought myself as I thought to an entire submission'

was how she described it. Having achieved this state of mind, she got
up and began to make preparations for the journey; everyone came to see
her to proffer help and advice, and from six in the morning until late at
night she was not alone for a moment. "'Twas I think a great mercy of
God my brains were not turned by the quantity of persons and difference
of subjects they talked to me of,' she wrote.

The Sunday after the Admiral's arrival was the first of the month, and
in her hurry to be off she decided to forego the Sacrament; she intended to
sail on the Saturday if the weather should prove fair. Dr Stanley disapproved of the omission, and he observed that 'in matters of such consequence devotion was not to be neglected'. She was duly punished, for
contrary winds in the end kept her in Holland for another week, and she
redeemed herself by taking the Sacrament for the last time at the Hague the
following Sunday:

The day before, I writ down my mind upon that matter, being sensible of my
fault and truly sorry for it, and thankful for the great mercy of my God in
suffering me so well to prepare for such a journey, after my wilful neglect of so
necessary a preparative.

When the wind finally changed, enabling her to embark, large crowds
gathered to see her go, and both she and many of those who watched her
were in tears. Already at the Hague there was a desolate atmosphere;
outside many of the large houses there were To Let notices and the price
of property was falling. Constantine Huygens said it was only the English
who were likely to benefit from the revolution, and as far as Holland was
concerned the only thing that could be said was that William's expedition
might have saved the country from worse misfortunes.

On the Saturday evening the Princess went aboard a yacht that was
lying in the Maas ready to sail, but that night the wind freshened and
veered, which she took as a sign that God disapproved of her grief at
leaving the Hague. The punishment was not so prolonged this time, for
by noon on Sunday the wind had dropped and the sea was like glass, with
a breeze strong enough to carry her across to Margate by twelve the next
day. Her sensations as she neared the shores of England were strange and
confused:

It would be hard for me to express the different motions I felt in my heart at the
sight of my own native country. I looked behind and saw vast seas between me
and Holland that had been my country for more than eleven years. I saw with
regret that I had left it and I believed it was for ever; that was a hard thought, and
I had need of much more constancy than I can brag of, to bear it with patience.
Yet when I saw England, my native country, which long absence had made me

a stranger to, I felt a secret joy, which doubtless proceeded from a natural sympathy, but that was soon checked with the consideration of my father's misfortunes which came immediately into my mind. The joy of seeing the Prince again, strove against that melancholy, and the thoughts that I should my husband see owned as the deliverer of my country, made me vain; but alas, poor mortal! thought I then, from who has he delivered it but from my father. Thus were my thoughts taken up, and while I put the best face on, my heart suffered a great deal, but at last I came.

William, accompanied by Anne, was waiting for her at Greenwich, The sisters greeted each other affectionately, and Mary was glad to find that Anne looked in good health, though she was now several months pregnant. William, on the other hand, had grown very thin and was coughing ceaselessly; she was quite shocked by his appearance. They went straight to Whitehall, where apartments had been made ready, and as soon as they were alone together, William and Mary shed tears, partly for joy at meeting again, partly out of sorrow that the meeting had to be in England—'both wishing it might have been in Holland, both bewailing the loss of the liberty we had left behind and were sensible we should never enjoy here'. Then they had to compose themselves, and William told his wife that whatever her private feelings were, she must try to appear as happy as possible in public.

Obedient as ever, the Princess did her best to follow William's instructions and she evidently overplayed the part. Her forced gaiety seemed discordant to those who expected a grave expression as befitted a woman who had usurped her father's throne. Others compared her to Tullia, who had made her husband kill her father to gain a throne. Lady Churchill, Anne's constant attendant, who waited on Mary during her first day at Whitehall, considered that this superficial cheerfulness was just one of many instances which proved that Mary was heartless by nature, or, as this formidable woman expressed it, that *she wanted bowels*. It was natural that the Princess, who had never nursed any ambition greater than that of being a good Dutch housewife, should take a homely interest in her surroundings, but Sarah Churchill noted her naive curiosity with disapproval:

She ran about, looking into every closet and conveniency, and turning up the quilts upon the bed, as people do when they come into an inn, and with no other sort of concern in her appearance, but such as they express; a behaviour, which, though at that time I was extremely caressed by her, I thought very strange and unbecoming. For, whatever necessity there was of deposing King James, he was still her father, who had been so lately driven from that chamber, and that bed; and, if she felt no tenderness, I thought she should at least have looked grave, or even pensively sad, at so melancholy a reverse of his fortune.

After a busy afternoon receiving crowds of visitors, the Princess retired, but she was up early next morning, and Evelyn was shocked to hear that 'in her undress, before her women were up [she] went from room to room to see the convenience of Whitehall; lay in the same bed and apartment where the late Queen lay, and within a night or two sat down to play at basset, as the Queen her predecessor used to do. She smiled upon and talked to everybody, so that no change seemed to have taken place at Court since her last going away, save that infinite crowds of people thronged to see her, and that she went to our prayers. This carriage was censured by many. She seems to be of a good nature, and that she takes nothing to heart'. Her reputation for piety had gone ahead of her, which made her levity all the more surprising. 'She came into Whitehall laughing and jolly,' Evelyn complained, 'as to a wedding, so as to seem quite transported.' By contrast, the Prince seemed dour and unapproachable. Evelyn found him 'wonderful serious and silent', and he was obviously quite wrapped up in affairs of State.

Having explored the Palace at such an early hour, the Princess went with her husband to the Banqueting Hall, which was so gruesomely associated with her grandfather's execution. There they received the two Houses of Parliament, who arrived in state to make them both jointly a free gift of the Crown. The conditions on which this gift was given were read aloud, and the Declaration of Right which had been drawn up with such heart-searching was also presented. Both Houses then went out to lend some splendour to the public proclamation, which was received with great enthusiasm. It was noticed that when her father's name was mentioned, Mary 'looked down as if she was troubled'.

That evening there were candles in every window and a great many bonfires. The Court was crowded with people who had come to pay homage to the new sovereigns. Most of the ladies were as astonished by Mary's beauty and charm as they were disappointed by William's sombre appearance. The general opinion was that there had never been such a beautiful Queen or such an ugly King. Lady Cavendish, daughter of the Lord William Russell who had been executed for his supposed part in the Rye House Plot, went to see the man and woman who had saved the country from her father's murderer. William, she thought, was a man 'of no presence' and very homely, though she noticed that a more searching look revealed something 'both wise and good'. As for the Queen, Lady Cavendish continued, 'she is really altogether very handsome. Her face is very agreeable and her shape and motions extremely graceful and fine. She is tall but not so tall as the last Queen'.

William's health continued to cause concern. The strain of preparing and carrying out the expedition and, worse still, the frustrating weeks of political discussion in the damp, ill-ventilated rooms at Whitehall had caused several acute attacks of asthma. In Holland the fresh air and exercise he had found in the hunting field had helped to keep him in good health, but so far he had had no opportunity to get away from the London mists, apart from one Saturday spent hunting on Banstead Downs. Since he was feeling ill he naturally shunned company and refused to see anybody except on essential business. During his first weeks in England his public relations had been abysmal and he had already offended a number of people. Ambitious statesmen were beginning to complain that he was inaccessible; his wife's uncle, Clarendon, who was eager to give him advice about the solution of Irish problems, had tried to gain his ear for days and had been rebuffed with a variety of excuses. 'You will find him a worse man than Cromwell,' James had warned them all, and now they were beginning to wonder if he was right. The fact that William was moderate, tolerant, lacking in vanity and totally unvindictive could be easily overlooked; it was all too noticeable that he lacked the graces.

The new Queen faced a difficult task and one that afforded her little pleasure. The glitter of court life and the glamour of a Crown meant nothing to her. She would have found it easier to be reduced to 'the lowest condition in the world':

My heart is not made for a kingdom and my inclination leads me to a retired life, so that I have need of the resignation and self denial in the world, to bear with such a condition as I am now in. Indeed the Prince's being made King has lessened the pain, but none of the trouble of what I am like to endure.

In Holland she had been at ease in the unsophisticated milieu where her simple charm and piety had been appreciated. Here, at Whitehall, there was a stench of uncleanliness and corruption. Catherine Sedley soon gave the Queen a taste of her now famous wit, if it is really true that she said, 'Remember Ma'am, if I broke one of the commandments *with* your father, you have broken another *against* him.' Sir Charles Sedley, Catherine's father, looked upon the honour King James had conferred on his daughter as a 'splendid indignity' and remarked epigramatically that 'he wished to make the King's daughter a Queen in return for his Majesty's having made his daughter a Countess'. Mary found such flippancy distasteful and she was generally shocked by the worldly attitude of those around her. 'The first thing that surprised me at my coming over,' she confessed, 'was to see so little devotion in a people so lately in such imminent danger. I found a great change in my life, from a strict retirement where I led the life of a nun, I was come into a noisy world full vanity; from having public prayers four times a day, to have hardly leisure to go twice, and that in such a crowd, with so much formality and little devotion, that I was surprised.'

The attitude of the Church was most disillusioning. A majority of the Bishops felt embarrassed by James's flight; badly though he had treated them, they remembered, now, that they had vowed their allegiance to him, and that there was such a doctrine as the divine right of Kings. How could they in all conscience take the new oaths to William and Mary? Dyckvelt told Clarendon that 'he wondered to find several of the clergy in different sentiments from what he expected.' Sancroft, in his timid way, had refrained from attending the debates concerning a Regency, and only Compton and Trelawney had voted against it. Crewe, 'the obnoxious Bishop of Durham,' who had spent most of his career toadying to James, and had recently passed several weeks lurking on the coast ready to take the first vessel to France if it seemed expedient, now returned to London and changed sides rapidly, while the Archbishop sat on the fence and refused either to support or condemn the new régime. The established Bishops were suspicious of Burnet, who had kept close to William from Torbay onwards, and whom they regarded as an interloper and 'a complete creature' of the Prince. Clarendon thought Dr Lloyd was lukewarm about the Regency idea because he was too much 'wheedled' by Burnet. The Bishop of London was fervent in his support of William's cause, but both he and Burnet were inclined to let their enthusiasm run away with them; they had done their best to persuade the Prince to alter the prayers in the liturgy concerning the King and the Prince of Wales, but he had refused to do so, for he was reluctant to meddle in Church affairs. Burnet ran the risk of becoming a bore with his constant conversation about deposing the King. A week after Mary's arrival, Compton visited her with some of his clergy and made a short speech of welcome, to which she replied simply 'that she desired nothing more than the prayers of the clergy for her'. His loyalty was at least some consolation, especially since so many Churchmen seemed to have forgotten already that the Prince had saved them from Popery. William was 'a usurper, but the best of usurpers' —this was how Sancroft grudgingly put it.

Men with a thirst for power were disappointed to observe that the new King did not intend to put his faith in any particular adviser. He told Halifax that 'Lord Churchill could not govern him, nor my Lady, the Princess his wife, as they did the Prince and Princess of Denmark'.

Halifax saw that this showed William's dislike of Churchill's 'assuming too much'; it also proved that he did not intend that anyone should rise to power through his wife. Halifax sagely concluded: 'Note, a great jealousy of being thought to be governed. That apprehension will give uneasiness to men in great places.' As he felt his way, William tended to put his trust in people he already knew, such as Bentinck and Huygens. William's predilection for Dutch advisers was causing much disapproval, as did the presence of Dutch troops in the town; the streets of London, Reresby complained 'were filled with ill-looking and ill-habited Dutch and other strangers'. Nor were the Dutch themselves particularly pleased with the situation in which they found themselves. Huygens was already talking of resigning. Both his wife, who had remained in Holland, and his brother, approved of the idea, but Christiaan warned him to make sure that the Prince granted him a suitable pension, for there was no guarantee that he would be able to find employment in Holland.

Once William had been officially offered the Crown he was no longer able to postpone the delicate task of settling his Household and other appointments. For the time being he made Bentinck Groom of the Stole with the title of Earl of Portland. Zuylestein became Master of the Robes, and Overkirk Master of the Horse. The Council appointments were less predictable and were awaited with some trepidation by both parties. The Whigs, who had been in the forefront of those who had encouraged William to come over, were confidently expecting the best jobs as a reward for their pains. To their surprise they found that they were not to be given a monopoly. The King's policy was to make all parties happy by choosing representatives from each. Nottingham, who had opposed the Settlement 'with great earnestness, in his copious way of speaking', as Burnet put it, agreed now to serve the King even more loyally than those who had been anxious to hand him the Crown. It was thought wise to bring him in to placate the High Church party which was already talking about bringing James back. With Shrewsbury he was appointed one of the two Secretaries of State. Shrewsbury, though considered very able for his years, was hesitant of accepting the post; he was always tempted to remain in the less exacting role of a charming courtier rather than wearing himself out with high responsibilities. Halifax, 'the Trimmer', a moderate man after William's heart, became Lord Privy Seal. The danger of such a mixture was soon apparent. Nottingham, dismal-looking and serious-minded, made no attempt to agree with the Whigs who were to be his colleagues on the Council, while such Whigs as the wild Lord Mordaunt, whose enthusiasm for the expedition was now rewarded with a lucrative post as First Commissioner of the Treasury, had no intention of coming to terms with the Tories. Godolphin also became a member of the Treasury Board; he had a flair for finance and was likely to prove an asset in that position—as the King said to Halifax 'if he had a mind to keep Lord Godolphin in, who should hinder him?' Danby was rewarded for his helpfulness in the past with the rather less important office of Lord President. Mary's uncles, Rochester and Clarendon, were not included.

It was essential that some form of effective government should be put into operation without delay. There were rumours that James intended to land in Ireland; Scotland was in a turmoil and there was little doubt that before long France would be making trouble on the continent. The Council having been formed, the next step was to regularize the Convention Parliament. The Tories were of the opinion that it should be dissolved and a new Parliament summoned, but this would have caused delay, and the damp, as Burnet called it, that had spread through the nation since the Revolution, might have brought back a majority unfavourable to William. To plunge the nation into a debate about the rights or wrongs of William's presence in England was hardly wise at this juncture, nor was it politic to subject it to the ferment of an election just when it was threatened by so many immediate dangers. So, when the Convention reassembled on February 18, William went to address it from the throne. Eight Bishops failed to take the oaths, including Sancroft, Lake and Lloyd.

For Mary the most pressing problem was her husband's health. There was little doubt that life at Whitehall was rapidly killing him. She knew him well enough to understand that if she wished to save him she must remove him at once to an atmosphere and a way of life that suited him better. For this reason, towards the end of February, they moved to Hampton Court. The Palace there was old, ramshackle and inconvenient, but at least it was well away from the worst of the London fogs and for the time being there was no other solution. The move was not at all popular in court circles. As the King only came to town on Council days, the whole pattern of life was disrupted, and the rooms at Whitehall, where everyone had foregathered to gossip, flirt or work their way into the King's favour, were now deserted. The King himself was far too silent and unassuming to be a great social attraction, and although the Queen was charming and vivacious, it soon became clear to everybody that she was determined not to meddle in State affairs and that therefore it served no practical purpose to visit her. In general she made herself pleasant to anyone who did take the trouble to approach her, but she was uncertain what attitude to adopt towards her uncles, who had behaved disagreeably to the Prince. She refused to give Clarendon an appointment, and she told him that although she could not prevent anyone coming to the withdrawing-room, she would not see him anywhere else or speak with him in private. She also declined to receive Rochester's children.

It was natural that the King and Queen should wish to reward those who had assisted them prior to and during the Revolution, but they tended to make themselves unpopular when they did so. There was a great deal of murmuring among the clergy when Burnet was appointed to the see of Salisbury, for the Scotsman was looked upon as an outsider who was far too partial to the dissenters. The King sent for Burnet himself and told him of the appointment 'in terms more obliging than usually fell from him', or so it seemed to Burnet. The Queen said she hoped he would now put into practice all those notions which he had been pleased to entertain her with in the past. Secretly the King and Queen treated him as a joke; he was far less bigoted than many of his fellow Bishops, but he was ludicrously vain and talkative.

The Coronation was to take place on April 11. When the previous King had been crowned, he had told Sancroft to leave out the Communion and to cut down the length of the service as much as possible. This, in the minds of most observers, had caused 'impoverishment and complete dislocation'. It was felt that a new form of service must be devised and, since Sancroft was not feeling co-operative, Compton was chosen for the task. The Bishop of London would have been more at home heading a troop of horse than he was in working out liturgical details—he had ridden into Oxford with Anne the previous year in a purple cloak and a martial habit 'with pistols before him and his sword drawn'. Now he faced a month in the study, but he emerged at the end of it with a form of service which has stood the test of time and has undergone little change. He went back to the oldest precedent, found in the version of Archbishop Egbert, in which the coronation itself was placed in the middle of the service. The crowning ceremony came at the end to form a climax rather than the less meaningful investiture of the sceptre. The sovereign was then presented with the bible—'the most valuable thing that the world affords'.

The King, who in any case had little sympathy for such ceremonies which to him smacked of Rome, was so ill at the beginning of the month that it was questionable whether he would be able to go through with it. His cough had been growing steadily worse and he had been spitting blood. His doctors thought that he had not long to live, and he was inclined to agree with them. Compton was determined that the occasion should not be attenuated, or less magnificent than usual, although in view of the King's health it would have been wise to cut out the elaborations. The procession to the Abbey was very splendid, although it was noticed that some of the nobles were absent. Clarendon, for one, stayed in the country; he found the bells which rang all day very irritating, as well as the bonfires which were lit in the parish that evening. Several Bishops failed to appear, for eight of them altogether had refused to take the oaths of allegiance to the new King, and many of the rank and file of the clergy were following suit. A familiar figure from Dutch days, Dr Lloyd, now Bishop of St Asaph, walked beside the King and Queen carrying the paten, and he also presented them to the people. Burnet preached one of his best sermons, and, according to Evelyn, received great applause. He chose his text carefully: *the God of Israel said, he that ruleth over men must be just, ruling in the fear of God. And he shall be as the light of the morning when the sun riseth, even a morning without clouds: as the tender grass springing out of the earth, by clear shining after rain.*

In the absence of Sancroft, Compton crowned the sovereign, but the ceremony was not without its hitches. The King, who was feeling too ill to concentrate, failed to respond when he was due to offer up a roll of silk and thirty pieces of gold. There was an embarrassing silence as William, who lacked the histrionic instinct, did nothing to help tide over the awkward moment. Fortunately Danby had the presence of mind to lend him the necessary money. The diamond and ruby ring which William had given Mary, and which had been specially enlarged for the occasion, was placed in error on William's finger, and indeed, for the Queen, the whole day was most unenjoyable. Eleven years in Holland had put her out of sympathy with the English love of ceremony. 'The Coronation came on; that was to be all vanity,' she wrote wearily. Compton gave her a discourse on the subject, trying to persuade her that his version of the service could be looked on as an act of devotion. She agreed that his alterations were very good, but was troubled by his insistence that she and her husband should receive the sacrament during the service. She was sure that in all the pomp and vanity of the occasion she would hardly be in the right mood, and as it turned out, she approached the Lord's table with such a lack of devotion that she never ceased to reproach herself.

In the Abbey the Commons were seated behind the altar, above the Confessor's chapel, and that evening they sat on scaffolds erected along one side of Westminster Hall. The King and Queen dined there, and the Parliament men, who had their meal in the Exchequer chamber, were each presented with a gold coronation medal. On one side of the medal were effigies of the King and Queen 'inclining to one another', and on the other Jupiter throwing a bolt at Phaeton, and the words *ne totus absumatur*.

To make up for her lack of devotion at the Coronation, the Queen worked herself into a state of contrition when she next received the Sacrament, which was on Easter day at Hampton Court. But one of her grievances was that whenever she and William attended the Communion, there was a great deal of pomp and excitement. 'There was an old custom,' she complained, 'left since the time of Popery, that the Kings should receive almost alone; this had been always observed, this I could not resolve to do.' She tackled Compton on the subject, but found him unreasonable, and insistent that she should keep up the 'foolery'. On Easter Day Burnet was consecrated, the ceremony being performed by Compton and four other Bishops, as Sancroft still found himself unable to take the oaths of allegiance. The Queen had given a few words of advice to the young heiress who was to assume the responsibilities of a Bishop's wife. She expressed the hope that Mrs Burnet would 'by simplicity of attire and deportment' set a good example, which 'was woefully to seek among the parsons' wives of the day'.

The Queen was not happy. For the Protestant cause she had given up a quiet life, had left the country she loved, and all her friends. In England she found herself 'very much neglected, little respected, censured of all, commended by none'. Everybody around her seemed to be discontented, the Dutch were homesick, the English suspicious of the Dutch. Scotland and Ireland were in confusion, the Highlands about to rise against the Lowlands, and the Irish Catholics mounting a brutal campaign against the Protestant settlers. Her father had landed at Kinsale, supported by French arms, and accompanied by French officers; he had quickly thrown in his lot with Tyrconnel. He could equally well have made trouble in Scotland, and indeed, at one time, there had been rumours that he had landed in the north. John Temple advised William to send an envoy to find out if it was possible to come to terms with Tyrconnel, and recommended as a messenger Richard Hamilton, brother of the author of the Gramont memoirs. Hamilton, finding Tyrconnel intransigent, had immediately turned his coat and joined the Jacobites. Temple, believing himself to be responsible for this disaster threw himself in the Thames from a boat in which he left a letter written in black lead. 'My folly in undertaking what I was not able to execute,' ran the sad message, 'hath done the King great prejudice; may his undertakings prosper, and may he have an abler servant than I.' His suicide was a sad shock to William and Mary in the midst of so many other difficulties. Only a short time before they had been talking to his father, Sir William, who was one of their oldest friends, and John himself had been among the Prince's closest advisers before and during the expedition. The Queen found such a tragedy almost unbearable, coming as it did on top of the anxiety caused by her father's appearance in Ireland. There were critics who thought her reaction to the news of James's landing had been callous, but it is probable that she would have broken down if she had not kept a firm hold on herself. Stanley reproved her at this time for showing signs of peevishness, and she knew that he was justified.

William, too, was very irritable, which did not make matters any easier. He was as disappointed by the behaviour of the English as she was, and he was amazed to see how Members of Parliament set out to promote, rather than to resolve, their differences. It appeared that they were determined to prevent him from ruling effectively; his father-in-law's old cry, that he had no more power than the Duke of Venice, was already on his lips. He told Halifax that 'The Commons used him like a dog, their coarse usage boiled so upon his stomach, that he could not hinder himself from breaking out sometimes, against them'. Halifax told him he must practise the art of flattery and dissimulation, even though such qualities were alien to his character, for, as he put it, 'the world is a beast that must be cozened before it be tamed'. William's knowledge of the everyday workings of English government was elementary and these were puzzling enough even to politicians who had been brought up in England. Worse still, he spoke English haltingly, could hardly understand it when it was talked, and found writing it a penance. It was difficult, with his ungregarious nature, to be convivial at the best of times, all the more so when he was in a low state of health and wrestling with a foreign language.

No wonder that he and his Queen and his Dutch advisers all felt nostalgic. When Huygens went in to him on May 10, William gave him some work to do and then broke out, 'The weather is warm; now, at the Hague, the Kermesse is on. Oh, if only one could fly over there now, just once, like a bird through the air! I would give a hundred thousand gelders, yes, two hundred thousand, just to be there.' Huygens and all the Dutch retainers felt the same; the secretary had been persuaded to stay in England at least for a while, and he consoled himself by drinking chocolate and gossiping with Burnet, Hutton and Stanley, just as he had done with Sylvius in the old days in Holland.

The Queen, like William, could let her thoughts run over to the Hague at this festive time, to the Voorhout where the trees would be coming into leaf, to the shuttered Palaces and the meticulously tended gardens. This summer, so different from the last, there was to be no escaping to Loo to see how the work was progressing, to measure the growth of the newly planted trees and hedges, or to stroll along the sheltered walks. But it was useless to brood over the unobtainable. Life had to go on, and it had to be lived in England. The English being 'naturally lazy' as Mary put it, she was determined to find some half-way house which would not put the politicians and courtiers to the expense and trouble of a long journey to Hampton Court. Lord Nottingham was offering Kensington House for sale, and at an interview on May 22 William told Halifax that 'the Queen was extremely for Kensington, but he was against'. The female will, however, prevailed, and a week later the house had been bought. They would both have preferred to be at the Hague, or at Dieren, or at Het Loo or the House in the Wood, but since they must remain in England to suit the whims of this strange island people, it was sensible to put down roots, to occupy the troubled mind with bricks and mortar, to engage architects and to plan an ordered garden which would serve as a retreat from the turmoil of public affairs.

CHAPTER 22

THE NEW HOUSEHOLD

WILLIAM'S FIRST PRIORITY had been to set the machinery of government in motion after the upheaval caused by his peaceful Revolution, but once the ceremonies of the Coronation were over, both he and the Queen began in earnest to regularize the makeshift household arrangements inherited from the previous King. To ensure the efficient running of the establishment, a comprehensive set of rules was drawn up cancelling all previous ordinances. All accounts were carefully kept and checked, and there was to be as little buying and selling of places as possible. For security reasons, no servants were allowed to import assistants without the approval of the officers of the Green Cloth. Detailed menus were drawn up for the meals to be served to the King and Queen, to the Maids of Honour, the chaplains, the pages of the Back Stairs and the Yeomen of the Guard, also 'to the 5 officers attending at the Cupboard when from Whitehall', and to Dr Hutton, who had come over with William and was now his chief medical adviser. Mutton roasted, beef boiled, turkey or goose large, capons fat, pigeons tame, cocks or quails, buck baked quarter or hen pie, and tarts of sorts were on the dinner menu, with 'morelles or trouffles, jelly or asparagus' to follow. For supper the diet was sometimes varied by the inclusion of larks ('ii doz') or plovers or 'snites' with 'ragou of Sweet bread, Pistachio Cream, Hartichokes or Pease' for pudding. On Sundays, instead of boiled beef, a chine was served, or on Thursdays a sirloin. Rabbits were reserved for the King's and Queen's waiters, and the chaplains were allowed one turkey between them or a goose or ten field pigeons or four chicks, with a 'tarte' to follow.

The Household below Stairs, under the supervision of the Lord Steward and the Board of the Green Cloth, was a vast department, which dealt with the kitchens and store-cupboards. The ingredients required were budgeted for down to the last rope of onions, the last ounce of saffron or the last pound of 'sugar refined' or 'sugar double-refined'. On meat days, eighteen pounds of butter were required in the King's kitchen, and on fish days twenty-four. Three hundred lemons a month were ordered for the King's kitchen, sixty for the household kitchen, with six yards of 'strainers coarse' and ten yards of 'strainers fine' for both kitchens. Hartshorn, orange-flower water, rose-water, broombuds and samphire were always in stock. Bread, beer, Lambeth ale and mead were available at all times and six bottles of claret, three of champagne, two of Rhenish and three of Spanish were set aside for the King and Queen's dinner and supper. A bottle of claret and one of Spanish went down to the tennis court when the King was playing, and the Spanish was considered good enough for 'washing the King's feet weekly'. Eight bottles of claret were allocated for the players on play nights, and two for the trumpets and kettle drums on Sundays. Dr Hutton was allowed to consume one bottle of claret with his veal, though the chaplains were only granted the Spanish variety on Sermon day.

Heating and lighting the Palaces in winter was another problem, and thousands of wax lights, yellow lights, tallow lights, torches and candles, faggots and billets had to be ordered, as well as pit-coal and charcoal. Fortunately the 'fewell' bill was less alarming in the hot months, but the board wages to staff in the counting house, the bake-house, pantry, cellar, buttery, spicery, chaundry, confectionary, ewry, pastry and laundry, continued all the year round. The 'necessary women', the grooms and yeomen, the bread bearers, wine porters, 'tail caretakers', the porters at the gate, the harbingers, and the 'painfull old servant in the scullery' all had to be paid, their board wages ranging from £1,360 for the Lord Steward, down to £205 for the chief clerk of the King's Privy Kitchen, £108 for a master cook, £45 for the Yeoman of the Mouth, £37 for the grooms, £28 for the daily waiter, and £10 for the organ blower in the Chapel.

The Master of the Horse also controlled a large staff of grooms, saddlers, farriers, sixteen footmen, six coachmen and a Master of the Stud. The thirty-six hunters, coursers and pads, and the forty-two coach horses, were given a generous allowance of hay, oats and beans, and a further charge on this department was the upkeep of the King's private roads.

To ensure an efficient system, the Counting House was re-equipped, with standishes, counters, pens, ink, sand, wax and wafers, paper, parchments and books for the accounts and green cloth, carpets, chairs and cushions. Even though such careful checks and records were kept and although William and Mary were not extravagant according to the standards of their predecessors, the expenses of such a household were great, as well as all the sundry items, such as the cost of running the Ice House; 'sweets for their Majesties' linen, and orange-flower water, and rose water for their hands', came to £50 a year. The estimated outlay on run-of-the-mill expenditure came to £76,000, and there was no guarantee as yet that an ungrateful Parliament was ready to fill the royal purse with any degree of generosity.

Sir Christopher Wren had been engaged to make plans for the extension of Kensington and the renovation of Hampton Court. For the latter he produced an imposing plan which involved the complete demolition of the old Palace, but he soon had to tone this down as it was clear that the English could not understand why the old building was not good enough for the imported King. In any case a new wing was to be added and in a remarkably short time the operation was under way. The first task was to make the existing apartments habitable for the household, and in May many of the mullion windows were removed and new casements provided. Battlements were taken down to make the outside look less formidable. The plumbing needed attention and pipes had to be renewed; a gutter over the meat larder was repaired, cisterns were installed and a length of piping laid in the fish larder. Thirty-two foot of shelving was installed for the Necessary Women in Pheasant Court. Most of the apartments were given new hearths in Reigate stone; Dr Stanley had some new flooring and an architrave, as well as a 'carriage over the door for the hangings'. Wall hooks, cloak pins, chest hinges and bell ropes were being fitted all over the place. A new window was made for the ground-floor room in the department of Sir Edward Villiers who had been appointed Knight Marshall, alterations were being made to Bentinck's confectionary, and Overkirk's kitchen was fitted with a new range. Apartments were prepared for Zuylestein's wife, the notorious Jane—'Madame Goulstein' was how she appeared in the accounts—as well as for Mrs Jesson, the lively widow who had made a sober Englishman wade shoulder-high into the Vyver for love of her while the court looked on with amusement from the windows of the Binnenhof.

Realizing that it would be a long time before the new apartments would be fit for habitation, Mary decided to convert a small pavilion that had been built at the water's edge to shelter those who had disembarked from the river. A modern bathing room was to be added on, as well as a dairy, and the existing rooms to be renovated and decorated with moulding and carving. Work began on this charming *pied-à-terre* in the early summer of 1689, with the re-laying of old slabs, the removing of battlements, and the installing of chimney pieces in veined or dove-coloured marble. That summer a great company of workmen moved in with spades and shovels, and the dirt and rubble was carried away in innumerable wheelbarrows, some of it going to fill in the old moat. The river was scoured and the mud thrown out onto the banks to enable the barges to come in with their loads of planks and stone. A new lock was fixed to the tennis court, which was to be used as a temporary store for the deal boarding. Plans for the garden were also being drawn up, and Bentinck, now Lord Portland, was appointed superintendent. Some pedestals were made for the Queen's flower pots, and in the Gallery, the old mats were taken up, the floor was swept and the dirt carried away, in deference, perhaps to the Queen's acquired fastidiousness.

William and Mary spent most of the summer at Hampton Court; the Queen kept a close watch on building operations, and was subsequently in consultation with Wren who visited the site as often as three times a week. All the same, it was not possible to escape the pressure of outside events. Whatever William had or had not achieved by coming to England, he had, after all these years, succeeded in making his wife's country declare war against France. The declaration, which took place on May 7, was precipitated by Louis himself. Deciding that the time had come to strike in the Netherlands, the French King withdrew from the Palatinate, and the devastation and atrocities carried out by his troops as they went, aroused indignation even among the insular English. They were made to see that tenderness in the French never lasted long, as William put it to Halifax, and the wavering states of Europe were furnished with the proof that France was the enemy against whom they must all unite. Less than a week after England's declaration of war, the Grand Alliance was signed, and the Emperor Leopold announced his acknowledgment of William as the rightful king of England.

Urged on by Burnet, Mary persuaded William to declare a day of public fasting. To her it seemed no coincidence that for a while the outlook was brighter for the Protestant cause. One summer evening a fisherman, drawing a net in the Thames between Lambeth and Vauxhall, became aware that he had landed an unusual and very heavy catch, which turned out to be nothing less than the Great Seal of England. James had intended to take it with him when he escaped, but finding it heavy and inconvenient to carry, he had thrown it into the river. Its recovery was regarded by the Queen as a mark of God's favour, and the birth of a live child to Princess Anne at Hampton Court she saw likewise as a sign that the Stuart family was winning divine approval. The Queen stayed with Anne all through her labour and William arrived at the Princess's apartments shortly before the baby was born. The child was called William after the King, who agreed to be his godfather. The Queen prayed for him continually, for he was not strong, and at the age of five weeks he had such violent convulsive fits that nobody thought he would live. 'It pleased God to hear the prayer made him,' the Queen recorded. 'In this, blessed be God, I saw the grace of God in my heart, for tho' I can truly say I was as heartily sorry for the child as I could be, yet I looked further; I considered it as a continuance of the righteous judgment upon our unhappy family and these sinful nations.'

The relief of Londonderry which took place at the end of July, a week after the birth of the Prince, was another hopeful sign. After the Protestants had been beaten back into the north of Ireland the town had been besieged for two months, and already thousands of the inhabitants, and in some cases whole families, had perished from hunger. At last a convoy, sailing up river with the wind and tide in its favour, was able to break through the boom, and the city was saved. All that summer troops were being raised, and in August a large force under Schomberg set off for Ireland, while a contingent of Englishmen—a token force of eight thousand—had been despatched to Flanders under the command of John Churchill, now Earl of Marlborough. In Scotland, Viscount Dundee had called the Highlanders to arms in support of James, and in July he inflicted a defeat on English troops in the pass of Killiecrankie. But he himself was killed during the battle and, leaderless, the clans returned to the hills.

The King's health improved a little at Hampton Court, but he was still anxious and depressed. In June he told Halifax that 'he was so tired he thought he must leave us', and added that if he did, he thought the Queen would probably govern better without him. Halifax said he could hardly do such a thing now, and accused him of wanting to go back to Holland so that he could command the army against France. Halifax had guessed right. 'He said nothing but did not deny it,' the Marquis noted. He was still trying to tutor William in the art of diplomacy. 'Personal compliments must prevail, if they are dextrously applied and not daubed,' he told William. The King was finding his Council unsatisfactory. Blathwayt was dull, though he had a good method, Boscawen was a blockhead, young Hampden was mad and would have to be sent to Spain. Mordaunt (newly created Earl of Monmouth) was the worst of all; he was governed by his wife, never did what he was told, he 'had a mind to be King, and my Lady to be Queen'. When Halifax suggested Lord Tweeddale as a possible Secretary for Scotland, the King cried out, 'Pish, he cannot be', and in fact he had very little good to say about anyone.

William confided in Halifax that he thought Shrewsbury was in the wrong job. The young mother-ridden Earl was of the same opinion, and on August 27 he wrote tendering his resignation. 'My incapacity to go through with a place of so much toil and trust, does every day grow more apparent, as my health and strength decay,' wrote the weary twenty-nine-year-old. Nevertheless, William at last persuaded him to continue.

The behaviour of the English continued to perplex the King; at the Coronation there had been pro-Jacobite demonstrations in some provincial towns, and there were said to be many disaffected people in the Midlands and the north. The irony of it was that the Anglican clergy were in many cases promoting the unrest. There were still men in high places who felt unable to take the oaths, and although they had been given six months' grace to wrestle with their consciences, the time would come when vacancies would have to be filled. The King, who was all for tolerance in Church affairs, told Halifax that he would dispose of the Bishoprics as they fell vacant naturally, but would demur for the time being where it was a case of the Bishop refusing to take the oaths. Sancroft still continued in what Burnet described as 'his inactive state', refusing to take the oaths himself, but refraining from any attempt to influence other people's decisions. The King was in no hurry to dislodge him; he believed him to be sincere, and he thought that in the end he might decide to change his mind. It was also difficult to think of a substitute; mild and moderate men were not easy to find, and William was afraid that Compton would expect the post in recognition of his services during the Revolution. The King did not relish the thought of an aggressive and forceful Archbishop.

A Toleration Act, which exempted dissenters from penalties imposed for going to their own churches, passed easily enough, but when the King went on to encourage a Comprehension Bill, which aimed at bringing the Churches closer together, he began to find the Churchmen uniting against him. Now that the danger of Catholicism had been removed, the will to make any concessions in favour of the dissenters quickly dissolved. The King took no interest in heated debates about small liturgical points, and it mattered little to him whether or not people knelt at the sacrament, or made the sign of the cross at a baptism. He was prepared to forgive his political enemies and to take up a tolerant attitude towards the Catholics. He believed that in this way he could avoid schism, promote national unity, and utilize the power of England in the struggle against France.

The Queen was naturally more concerned about the welfare of the Anglican Church than her husband was, but as yet the King refused to let her meddle in the troubled sphere of ecclesiastical appointments. Although he acknowledged that he owed his position to his wife, he made it clear

to everyone from the start that he would not brook any female interference. In the main she was prepared to accept this situation, and to feel
a vicarious pleasure in his success. She told Sophia of Hanover that she
was able to rejoice in the satisfaction of having a husband who had done
his duty. She agreed that it was not her place to dabble in public affairs,
although from the start she did what she could to bring about the reform
of manners and to ensure that the underprivileged were cared for. In the
household accounts £30 was set aside for 'Relief to be given in case of
sickness and poverty to the under sort of servants', and on a wider scale
she did what she could. Refugee Protestants were still very much to the
forefront of her mind; she promised Mlle Obdam, whom she had asked
to keep an eye on the French Society at the Hague, that she would speak
to William at the first opportunity about its affairs, though, as she wrote
on March 5, 'the multitude of affairs that the King has on his hands,
prevents me at present'. The plight of French refugees in England was
recognized by the King and Queen, when the Commissioners of the
Great Seal were authorized to organize relief for French Protestants, and
in July a Proclamation was issued, in the name of the King and Queen, for
their 'Encouragement'. The Queen announced, in the same month, that
she intended to make an annual grant to the refugees of £15,000 out of her
Privy Purse. The Irish Protestants were not forgotten, and similar measures were taken to support those who had fled from Tyrconnel's persecutions.

All through the summer the Queen remained miserably homesick for
Holland. Her greatest pleasure was to talk for hours together with her
chief lady in waiting, the Countess of Derby, who was a daughter of one
of the Nassaus and the widow of the Earl of Ossory, and who spoke
Flemish well. When the Queen went out of London into a neglected part
of the country, where the air was fresh and clean, she still compared it
unfavourably with the landscape and amenities at Dieren; any place or
any Palace in England had one great drawback—the lack of Dutch neigh-
bours. She still could not think of the Hague without the tears coming
into her eyes; this, she told Mlle Obdam, was not only because of the
beautiful buildings and trees that she had left behind, but also because of
the friends she might never see again. In England she found herself
overwhelmed by the world around her, which made her regret even more
the peace and tranquillity she had lost. Often her thoughts wandered
back to happier times at Loo or Dieren, with the ladies all busy at their
embroidery, while Mlle Obdam read aloud to them, or to the walks in the
country which she had enjoyed so much and which she still missed more

than she could say. 'I lose myself in such thoughts,' she wrote, 'which obliges me to change the subject.'

As the summer lengthened out into autumn, the grim prospect of returning to London loomed ahead. Kensington was unlikely to be ready in time, and the thought of subjecting William to the November fogs at Whitehall was unthinkable. The King therefore borrowed Holland House, and they moved in on October 16. There, the Queen found herself 'very ill-accommodated all manner of ways' and she felt very unhappy. With her father in Ireland and so many nations at war, gaiety seemed unseemly, but the King and Queen were persuaded to give a ball on William's birthday. The English nobility, now starved of royal occasions, came in large numbers, jostling and pushing for a sight of the King and Queen. They refrained from dancing themselves—this was certainly no deprivation for William—and when they came into the room there was such a crush that Portland was pushed from side to side by the ill-mannered English, and the Marquis de Muse might have been knocked over and trampled on but for the Queen's presence of mind. The doors into the room were open and people were still pushing in; only just in time she gave an order that the doors should be closed, and a disaster was avoided. The King and Queen also agreed at this time to dine in public, and the Queen promised to worship at Whitehall where she instituted a programme of afternoon sermons which she knew would be approved of by sober people.

Mary felt most unsettled at Holland House and she found that 'the devil was very bussie'. Any woman impatient to instal herself in a new house in the process of construction is a fruitful subject for Satan's machinations, and perhaps it was he who drove her to spend a great deal of time harrying the workmen, who may or may not have exerted themselves more industriously as a result of this female intervention. She felt sure that once she was installed at Kensington she would be more at peace, and she could not wait to be settled there. She often reproved herself for her impatience, and she was sure that God had seen fit to punish her when in November 'part of the house which was new fell down'. She had just left the apartments herself when the accident happened. A month later there was a similar incident at Hampton Court, in which two workmen were killed. It is probable that Wren, being driven on by the King and Queen, allowed the timber trusses of the roof to be put in position before all the brick-work had dried out thoroughly. One of the trusses in the south wing crashed through the floor of the State Apartments, causing the two casualties; two skeletons found during the nineteenth century under the Foundation Court may have been those of the two workmen,

buried hurriedly to avoid a public scandal. The Queen took the accident
very much to heart, for although the architect was more directly at fault,
yet she herself felt to blame; she said it 'shewed me the hand of God
plainly in it, and I was truly humbled'.

To complete the unhappy picture, an unpleasant quarrel arose that
autumn. William had not taken to his sister-in-law; he found her heavy
and dull, a great contrast to his graceful and vivacious wife, and he told
his friends frankly that if it had been his fate to marry the younger sister,
he would have been the most miserable of men. Her greed disgusted the
abstemious Dutchman. At first, however, the two sisters were the best of
friends. They had been united in their dislike of James and Mary Beatrice,
but now that the object of hatred was removed, friendship all too easily
dissolved. After the birth of Anne's child, the Queen had been as attentive
as everyone would have expected her to be both in her private and her
official capacity. The first fortnight had been very busy; she had been
continually in and out of her sister's room, surrounded by all the people
who had come to call on the mother and child. It had been a time of great
rejoicing, for no one had expected the pregnancy to end happily.

The Princess gained considerably in importance once she had produced
a Protestant heir, and her advisers felt that she need no longer play the
part of the younger sister dependent on William's bounty. The King had
observed, at an early stage, the influence which the flamboyant Sarah
Marlborough exerted over the more pedestrian Princess. When he heard
rumours that the question of Anne's revenue was to be raised in Parliament, he did not have far to look to find out who was making trouble.
There was little doubt that it was through Lady Marlborough that Parliament had come to take notice of the Princess's finances, and all this without a word either to the King or the Queen. William discouraged Mary
from tackling her sister on the subject; he had a horror of quarrels at the
best of times, and a squabble between female relations on the question of
money was sure to be distasteful. But Lady Marlborough has it that one
day she found the Princess in a more resentful mood than ever before.
She had just seen the Queen, who had asked her what was the meaning
of the rumours about her revenue. The Princess replied nonchalantly that
she believed some of her friends had a mind to make her a settlement.
'Pray, what friends have you but the King and me?' demanded the Queen,
with, according to Lady Marlborough, 'a very imperious air'. Both ladies
were far too proud to apologize. Anne smarted under the Queen's rebuke,
and William and Mary were humiliated when they heard that the Commons had agreed to vote the Princess a life grant of £50,000. William

would have much preferred the next in line to be dependent on himself, and in any case he thought the sum was excessive.

There was a further dispute about the question of lodgings. The Princess had her eye on those which had been vacated by the Duchess of Portsmouth and which she maintained the King had promised her, provided she would let him have the whole of the Cockpit in exchange. But it seemed that the Earl of Devonshire had taken a liking to the lodgings, where there was a fine big room suitable for parties. This led to another sisterly exchange, when the Queen told the Princess that she could not have the rooms she wanted until the Earl had made up his mind whether he required them. At this the Princess said 'she would then stay where she was, for she would not have my Lord Devonshire's leavings', a reply that was hardly calculated to cement the relationship.

The Princess would also have liked to rear her family at Richmond, the house with so many childhood memories. But the Queen refused this request as well, though for many years afterwards the Palace remained tenantless. The Queen now felt that the time had come to speak. When Mary went to see her, Anne would not admit that she had behaved, at best, tactlessly, in allowing her friends to bring up the subject of her revenue in Parliament. Mary taxed her with a lack of respect both to the King and to herself, and they parted on bad terms.

Two days before Christmas the King and Queen moved to Kensington, and on Christmas Day they went to Whitehall where they received the Sacrament, in the company of any of the nobility who cared to join them. This constituted, for the Queen, one of her few victories. 'I had with much ado,' she wrote, 'gained that point to have others receive with us at all times, and not make it no communion by the foolish formality that had been observed before.'

The new year, as usual, was the time of spiritual reckoning. What had been the effect on this introspective woman of being raised to the state which many people believed to be the highest condition of human life? A more reluctant Queen it would be hard to imagine, and the only way she could resign herself to her peculiar fate was to see herself as an instrument for good in God's hand. She had to admit that her first year as a monarch had been nothing but a penance:

It had pleased God to make this a year of trial in every way. I was used to find but little difficulty in the performance of my duty, and much applause for what I did, which together puffed me up with so high a conceit of myself. This whole year from the beginning till now I have found several hindrances and difficulties, no doubt for trials as well as all the strong endeavours of the devil. In all these

I have found my own weakness and seen how little reason people had to commend or I to value myself. I have been often ready to fall, and ill custom has been near seducing me, but my God has then still upheld me by his grace; . . . my condition is much better for these trials, and I hope that the Lord in his mercy will either keep me from the like temptations hereafter, or continue his grace which I know is sufficient for me; and in this hope I end the year 1689.

CHAPTER 23

MARIE R

IN THE SUMMER TIME it was poignant to think of Holland with the
flowers in bloom and the trees in leaf and old friends enjoying themselves
in the clean pure country air. And in winter the Queen pined for the
frozen dykes and the skaters, the sledge rides in the Voorhout, the round
of parties, the evenings at the opera or with the Odycks. Winter in
England was dreary by comparison, and this year, after a damp warm
autumn, bitter weather was ushered in by a hurricane and a snowstorm
which raged through the night of January 11 causing much damage and
loss of life. The King and Queen did their best to win back some of the
popularity they had lost when William's health forced them to withdraw
from the public eye; they continued their formal dinners, and at the
beginning of 1689 they came into London and celebrated the end of their
first unhappy year in England with a musical entertainment.

There was still a depressing amount of work to be done at Kensington;
it was, as Evelyn put it, as yet 'a patched building', though he admitted
that all the same it was 'a very sweet villa'. A new straight road was being
cut through the park to make it more accessible, and plans for the garden
were under way. It was some consolation to be creating an oasis of Dutch
life in this English desert but the English were already groaning at the
expense, for it would have seemed more natural to them for the Queen
to cover herself in diamonds and other personal adornments, rather than
invest in bricks and mortar and in general improve the value of her
property.

The new apartments were airy and comfortable, and far more to the
taste of the Dutch retainers than the old ones. Huygens had grumblingly
overcome his homesickness and had weighed up the financial advantages
of being private secretary to the King. D'Alonne was also remaining
to help the Queen in the same capacity; he was an old friend of the family,
and some people believed that he was the natural son of William II by a
certain Mlle Brunier. Portland had acclimatized himself more easily than
some, for he had no wife now to lure him back to Holland. The King

sent him over as an ambassador to the States, and as a delegate to a conference of the allies; he left early in the year and had only just reached the
shelter of the Maas before the great hurricane struck. When he returned
in April, his sister, Madame Nyenhuys, came over with him, bringing
his children, who were probably housed in the apartments which he had
been allocated at Kensington. There was no rush among the Dutch
ladies to cross to England; those who had already arrived sent back reports
which were far from encouraging. They wrote saying that it was 'a devilish
country, so dirty and wicked'.

Stanley was still Mary's Chaplain, and Dr Lloyd had been appointed
to the Household as her Almoner. Burnet, in spite of the King's belief
that he was over-talkative, still frequented the Palace, and it was he who
first came to the Queen in great concern warning her that the King
intended to go to Ireland. The Queen had probably heard rumours that
William had such designs but she was content to wait if he saw fit not
to mention the matter to her for the time being. Burnet, however, was in
a great state of agitation. What would happen, he wanted to know, if
William went off to Ireland, leaving the country without a King—would
the reins of government be put into the Queen's hands?

Lloyd was her next visitor. Another aspect of the problem had occurred
to him:

[He] told me all that I but too well knew before, of the sadness of such a business,
to see my husband and my father personally engaged against each other. Of
these two discourses the last only made impression upon me. I knew very well
the King would do in government what was best, and as I trusted him, so I did
not think it kind in me to concern myself in it.

All the same, Lloyd's words chimed with her own thoughts; a confron-
tation in the battlefield between her father and her husband was what she
had always dreaded most. So she summoned up the courage to mention
the matter to William, who answered 'that he should go, if he saw the
necessities of affairs required it'. The Queen accepted this; other people
might have been offended by his unemotional, short reply, but she had
learnt to appreciate his straight-dealing as she trusted his judgment.

If the decision had rested with him alone the King would not have
hesitated. He was sure that there would be no conclusive victory in
Ireland until he could go there in person to supervise operations. Schomberg, old and weary, bewildered by the behaviour of English and Irish
alike, needed the support and authority of the master. Such troops as he
had were badly equipped and depleted by illness, and they had been
retreating steadily into Ulster. The King knew that if he could go to

Ireland with a well-organized force, he might succeed in removing the Jacobite menace from England's western horizon. But as the English began to guess his intention, so he faced the barrage of criticism which greeted most of his actions. He told Halifax on January 23 that he was afraid Parliament would make an address condemning his journey to Ireland. He was more tired than ever of the quarrels and intrigues which surrounded him. Like the Queen he felt unable to please anybody. The Whigs were disappointed in him; they had expected him to be vindictive where the Tories were concerned, and pliable when it came to their own demands. The Tories, for their part, were disgruntled because they had expected more support for the Church as by law established, and less tolerance towards the dissenters. The King was so weary of political faction and pettiness that he said once again, and this time more firmly, that he had decided to go back to Holland. At this, his Councillors grew alarmed, for he seemed to be in earnest and he told them that he had a convoy all ready to take him back to the country where he belonged. He did not know how to extricate himself from the difficulties into which the animosities of parties had brought him. There was a heated and passionate scene, several of the Council were in tears, and finally the King was persuaded to change his mind—but only on condition that he was not prevented from going to Ireland.

It was comparatively easy to be firm with a group of Council members, less so when it came to dealing with the corporate intransigence of Parliament. The King did not announce his plan until preparations were already under way, but on January 27 he told the Lords that he had made up his mind to go to Ireland and furthermore, to forestall trouble, he had decided to dissolve the present Parliament and call another one in March. As he spoke he could see from the expressions on the faces of his listeners to which side they belonged; the Tories were flushed with joy, for they believed that an election would increase their numbers in the House, whilst the Whigs looked morose, knowing that their party would certainly come back depleted.

The Queen was distressed when she knew that her husband had announced his resolution publicly, for she knew there was now no turning back. When he came to her, she broke down, telling him all her apprehensions and fears, but he tried to soothe her in his usual calm way, telling her that all this was only a continuation of the great work they had undertaken, which must now be finished. He said a great deal more, which helped her to resign herself to the situation, and finally he told her that he would rather not talk any more about so sad a subject. Calm though he was, he too felt upset; 'I pity the poor Queen who is in terrible distress,' he wrote.

Affairs in Scotland were also in a chaotic state, and it had been suggested that the King should go there before departing for Ireland, taking the Queen with him. The last thing she wanted was to be uprooted just when she was, at last, beginning to feel more settled in England, but she tried to make the most of it by having 'several good reflections upon the uncertainty of all things in this world'. While she made preparations for the journey and struggled to achieve a philosophical attitude, her husband weighed up the merits of such a visit, and at the beginning of February he was still trying to make up his mind whether to go. As for the journey to Ireland, Huygens wrote sourly in February, 'it is only too certain'; he had started thinking about the ten or twelve horses he would have to take with him. He had been fortunate enough to come upon a book of Leonardo drawings which he had bought for three and a half guineas. 'But what good are such things for somebody who is about to go to the barbaric country of Ireland?' he sadly inquired.

The winter was coming to an end, and still the English refused to back the expedition whole-heartedly, and delays multiplied. William soon realized that there would be no time to fit in a visit to Scotland. As the election madness intensified, so his irritation mounted. He was working himself almost to death trying to hurry on preparations for the campaign, while the English, apparently oblivious of the danger that threatened them from the west, expended endless energy vilifying each other. The King's patience was almost at an end, and his health was breaking up under the strain of overwork and anxiety. His friends implored him to take some rest, but their pleas had little effect.

William still pressed on with his meticulous preparations. He had no intention of landing in Ireland with unseasoned or ill-equipped troops, and his attention to detail was impressive. This was the kind of work that suited him, and it was often noticed that though he was cold and unresponsive to his courtiers, he became a different man, warm-natured and cordial, when he was dealing with soldiers. Politicians and counsellors he found a far more difficult problem, and he had been troubled all the year by the question of how the country should be run during his absence. He told Halifax first of all that there should be a Council which would report on its proceedings to the Queen, though she herself would not be allowed to 'meddle'. After the dissolution he asked her what her feelings were in the matter; would she prefer to leave everything in the hands of the Privy Council or govern herself? She told him at once that she would like the former; it had always been her opinion that women should not interfere in government, and in any case she was 'wholly a stranger to all business', being fortunate enough to have a husband who was so capable. The King gave her 'a very kind answer', and told her he would always take care of her.

This, for the time being, was how the matter was left, but when the new Parliament assembled, he announced that the government was to be left in her hands, with the help of an advisory Council of nine men. True to prophecy the new Commons had come back with the High Church Tories slightly in the ascendant, for they had benefited from the King's favour which had swung in their direction during the first year of his reign. For the moment they felt grateful and well disposed towards the Irish plan. The King made a firm speech, mentioning the delicate question of the revenue and reminding members that previous Kings had been granted settlements for life, and not for a grudging term of only four years, as so many people were anxious to do in his case. He finished by saying that 'as he was going immediately to Ireland, their session would be short, and therefore that they ought not to spend that time in debates, which the enemy would spend in the field'. The Commons responded; supplies were granted for that year, and the excise and hereditary revenue was settled on the King and Queen for life.

Thus affairs began to look more favourable for the King, and although he was irked by delays, he could at least immerse himself in military preparations. Sir Christopher Wren, who had been severely reprimanded by the King for his carelessness in allowing buildings to collapse at Kensington and Hampton Court, was now back in favour; he designed a hut that was (this time intentionally) collapsible, which was a far more practical dwelling than a tent for the asthmatical monarch to live in on his campaigns. Spring, and the thought of military operations, brought about a gradual improvement in the King's health, which was matched by a deterioration in the Queen's.

The thought of being left in charge of the country during William's absence naturally weighed on her mind, all the more so as her sister, urged on by Lady Marlborough, was continuing to defy William and herself. On the first Sunday in March, Anne pointedly absented herself from the Communion service at Whitehall and took the Sacrament at her own chapel, a fact which the town gossips were not slow to observe. Her excuse was that she had not felt well in the morning, but she was certainly not ill enough to deprive herself of a good meal when she dined in public with the King and Queen later the same day. She was a magnet

now for the more fanatical High Churchmen who still felt they owed
allegiance to the former King, and who were always ready to criticize
Mary if they detected any sign that William's Calvinism had rubbed off
on her. Most hurtful of all, they now began to ridicule her religious
practices, particularly the afternoon sermons, which were her particular
institution.

During Lent the Queen read all the way through the New Testament,
as well as several chapters of the Old. She prayed, meditated, and never
missed a sermon, but she simply succeeded in deepening her melancholy
until it reached the point of morbidity. When she fell ill with a bad sore
throat on April 7, she was quite ready to believe that she was going to
die. Over the week-end she felt so bad that she began to set her affairs
in order, and on the Monday was so much worse that she was convinced
the end had almost come. 'I was really rather glad than sorry' was her
pathetic admission.

The same day, Princess Anne, perhaps alarmed by her sister's illness,
appeared to have a fit of remorse; she came to ask forgiveness, which the
Queen very readily granted. The effect was spoilt, however, when the
Princess immediately started asking for an increased allowance.

For several days the sore throat failed to improve. Mary was beginning
to think that this was one of the best ways of dying, better even than a
consumption, for she had every chance of being in full command of her
senses, and at the moment she felt herself to be in a good frame of mind.
Perhaps she was not really as ill as she thought; in any case, after being
bled and taking physic, she suddenly recovered. The King did not take
her ailment too seriously; she had been wise enough to keep her premonition of an early death to herself and she even played cards a little to
prevent causing him undue alarm. She was rather disappointed to be
restored to health again so soon and to have to face her problems. The
only thing that had worried her seriously when she was ill was the fact
that some of her debts remained unpaid.

Thanks to Parliament, where many Members were still critical of the
scheme, the date of William's departure was continually postponed. In
the original settlement, the administrative power had been vested in the
King, and an Act of Parliament was required in order that some of this
power could for the time being be transferred to his wife. A Regency Bill
was prepared and passed, but some Members were as obstructive as they
could be. Although the new House was comparatively friendly, the King
found that he was still in no position to dictate. On one point, however,
he asserted his authority. He had tried, in the previous year, to put

through an Indemnity Bill, but his policy of mercy towards the supporters of the previous régime did not meet with general approval; it was too much a part of the established pattern of political life that any party coming into power should be able to enjoy revenging themselves on their predecessors. The King wished to put an end to such a tradition, for he could see that the thought of possible reprisals after every change of government must surely inhibit all political action. He therefore presented Parliament with an Act of Grace, which exempted all but thirty-five political offenders from further punishment. Thus the King, before departing for Ireland, took the terror out of English politics. In this use of an Act of Grace, he by-passed Parliamentary procedure, but in doing so made Parliament itself more civilized and secure. When the Act was read in the Lords, it was said that there was not one contradictory voice, and the peers all stood uncovered.

We do not know what persuaded the King to leave his wife in control rather than delegating the power to a Council, but it is probable that he knew she would be hesitant of taking any decisions on her own initiative, and that she would in every case, except the most urgent, be prepared to procrastinate until there had been time for her to consult with him by letter. The Regency Bill granted her the exercise of the administration during his absence, but she was only to deal with matters that called for immediate attention; anything that could be postponed must be left until his return. She was given the power to call a Parliament in an emergency, but she was not allowed to give Commissions or appoint Bishops. The Council, as finally named, consisted of Carmarthen as Lord President, Lord Stewart as Lord Chamberlain, Lord Nottingham as sole Secretary of State, Lord Marlborough as first Commissioner of the Treasury, Devonshire as Lord Steward, as well as Monmouth, Dorset, Russell and Pembroke. The King could not recommend any of them. He had always told the Queen that Shrewsbury was the one man she could trust, and it came as a great shock when he finally carried out his desire to resign just at this moment, and for no better reason, as far as she could see, than a quarrel with Carmarthen. Shrewsbury was himself so agitated by the situation that he fell into a fever that nearly cost him his life. 'He had a very good understanding,' the King told Halifax, 'but he was young and new in his place.'

If the one man William felt he could really trust decided to leave him on an impulse at such a critical time, the Queen wondered what she would be able to expect from the others. William told her to trust Carmarthen, but he was the kind of man she felt she could never come to like. Marlborough she had every reason to distrust, and Nottingham, a High Tory, was suspect. Although he had worked himself into the King's favour, he had been among those who in the early stages advocated James's recall. 'The King will return to his people,' he had written in a list of recommendations. Russell was renowned for his sincerity, but she did not know if he had any other desirable qualities, and as for Monmouth, she thought he was mad.

On June 2 William called this doubtful crowd of men together, and it was not surprising that he felt depressed after the meeting. Burnet found him in very low spirits; he told the Bishop that 'for his own part, he trusted in God, and would either go through with his business, or perish in it; he only pities the poor Queen, repeating that twice with great tenderness, and wished that those who loved him would wait much on her and assist her'. After deploring all the divisions in the State, particularly those fomented by the clergy, he admitted that 'it was no unpleasant thing' for him to be setting out on a campaign, but the fact that he was going to fight his father-in-law was a cause of uneasiness; he told Burnet that 'it would be a vast trouble both to himself and to the Queen if he should be either killed or taken prisoner; he desired my prayers, and dismissed me, very deeply affected with all he had said'.

On June 4 William went away from London at dawn. He was cheered all the way to the north; the send-off given to him by the English people, coupled with the knowledge that he was going to Ireland with a large and well-organized body of troops, over 40,000 in all, was enough to put him in good spirits. But for the Queen it was 'the terriblest journey he ever took'. When he had left Holland in 1688 there had at least been a hope that the controversy could be settled by Parliament without bloodshed; but she knew that only a battle could decide the outcome in Ireland:

Then the concern for his dear person who was ill in health when he went from hence, the toil and fatigue he was like to endure, the ill air of the country he was going [to] his humour when I knew he would expose himself to all dangers, then again the cruel thought that my husband and my father would fight in person against each other, and if either should have perished in the action, how terrible it must have been to me: these were the cruel thoughts I had upon his going, which none can judge of, that have not felt the like. When I looked on my self, I had no better; for I found myself now at Whitehall as in a new world, deprived of all that was dear to me in the person of my husband, left among those that were perfect strangers to me; my sister of a humour so reserved, I could have little comfort from her; the great Council of a strange composition, the Cabinet Council not much better.

The Queen had already resigned herself to the thought that she might never see William again. She put her trust in God, as she had done when they were parted before, but this time there was no opportunity to withdraw from the world and give vent to tears. Goodwin Wharton, who was given to receiving visions, felt that God had ordered him to visit the Queen on the day after her husband's departure, and he saw her as she passed, going to prayers. She turned her head away, he thought out of pride, perhaps, at her new importance, but more probably because she did not trust herself to speak to anybody.

For the first time in her life, after acting so long in the role of a background figure, she had to step into the centre of the stage and play a part for which she had received no training, and in which, as far as she could see, she was quite wrongly cast. To add to her troubles, her face had begun to swell, the result, she believed, of standing too near a window after taking the waters. It was with this embarrassing complaint that she had to face her nine advisers. These men, for their part, believed that they could treat the Queen as a characterless puppet, a pretty woman whose only talent was for frivolous conversation.

On June 11 William embarked at Hoylake in the yacht *Mary*. The crossing to Ireland took three days, and on June 20 the Queen wrote a letter to her husband expressing her relief at his safe arrival. To be able to express her feelings on paper—her grief at William's absence, her loneliness and fear—this was her only outlet. Nearly every day she sat down to write to the King. He kept and treasured her letters. They express the affection of a devoted wife, whose love for her husband and whose faith in God enabled her to remain calm and composed even though she knew that her country was exposed to as great a danger as any it had ever known.

CHAPTER 24

THE NINE

THE NINE MEMBERS of the Council looked upon the King's absence as an excellent chance to further their own interests. The fact that their country might at any time be threatened from France seemed hardly to occur to them, and they could see little beyond their own personal struggles for supremacy. They did not expect the Queen to play any part in this drama except as a pawn in their game, and it came as a shock to them to find that she was a woman of spirit.

William hoped that his wife would not be called upon to make any urgent decisions, but the advisers he had left her with were not slow to make use of the fact that it could take a week or more to receive a reply from the King on any disputed point. It was not long before they were testing the Queen with a small but crucial decision.

On the last day of June she found herself in good spirits. William had written with the welcome news that the Irish air, despite all prophecies to the contrary, agreed with him, and as a result he was feeling exceptionally fit. Ireland was enjoying one of its rare heat-waves, and the dry weather coupled with the satisfaction he always found when engaged in military operations, made him feel better than he had done for years. But just as she was feeling cheered by this news, the Queen's spirits suffered a drop, and she found herself facing her first trial of strength with members of the Cabinet Council.

Before leaving for Ireland, William, with his customary care for detail, had gone over with her a list of men who were under sentence of death, giving her his opinion as to whether or not they would be eligible for a reprieve. Soon after his departure, however, the Council met and recommended that some should have their sentence commuted to transportation. Lord Stewart came to her to plead specifically for one M'Guire. She answered that the King had said he must be hanged, having deserved such a punishment, but Stewart assured her that William had since received further information which would certainly have made him grant a pardon had he been in England. This put her in a difficult position.

She had no chance of finding out whether the King had in fact received the information; it was probable that he had not, but if by any chance he had, then she would always have on her conscience the knowledge that she had let a man go to his death needlessly. After careful thought she decided to go against William's original advice and let the man be transported with the others. 'In any other case than that of a man's life,' she explained to the King, 'you may be sure I would not have been persuaded so far after what you had said, but I thought there was too much cruelty in refusing that for the first time.' No sooner had she made this decision than the lugubrious Lord Nottingham appeared and reminded her that the King's policy was never to pardon burglary; he would have to make an announcement to this effect, so that she should not be 'importuned' any further.

Now that the King was away there was a grave danger that the French would strike, as they had struck in the Netherlands when William had gone over to England to fetch his bride. This meant that a special watch must be kept on all Catholics. The Queen Dowager, Charles II's unfruitful Catherine, was still living at Somerset House, and she had recently been foolish enough to omit the prayer for William's success in Ireland. It was reported that the clergyman involved had made the omission, after receiving an explicit order from Lord Feversham, one of James's 'creatures', who was still in charge of the Dowager's affairs.

The Queen decided that the time had come to act. She believed that Feversham was being foolish rather than seditious, but she expressed displeasure to the Council; 'I was extreme angry, which those Lords saw,' she reported to William. She ordered Lord Nottingham to go to Feversham and 'speak as angrily as possible'. The next day, just before lunch, Feversham appeared among the crowds of people who were always about at that time. She was struck immediately by his looks; he was 'as pale as death and spoke in great disorder', and he did his best to exonerate himself in a flow of words delivered with a strong French accent: ''twas a fault, and a folly, an indiscretion,' he declared. The Queen, by contrast, was calm and regal, and she answered him coolly that if he had been guilty of a fault, it was better not to try to make excuses. At this the ex-Frenchman became so exicted that he waxed incomprehensible; she simply had to wait until he calmed down. 'God pardoned sinners when they repented,' he reminded her, adding that he hoped she would do the same. She was ready with a quick response; 'God saw the hearts,' she told him, 'whether the repentance was sincere, which since I could not do, he must not find it strange if I would trust only to actions,' and with this she walked off. As she told her husband afterwards, anything that concerned his safety she could not, would not pardon.

The Queen Dowager hastened to make amends herself, she sent to enquire about the Queen's swollen face and the next evening arrived in person. She did not stay long, and after she had gone, Mary went out into the garden, hoping that a few minutes in the fresh air would make her face feel better. Dr Hutton had gone to Ireland with William, but another physician was treating her with leeches behind the ears, which had done her little good, and now one of her eyes was sore. That evening she wrote to William by candlelight:

I have still the same complaint to make, that I have not time to cry, which would a little ease my heart; but I hope in God I shall have some news from you as will give me no reason; yet your absence is enough, but since it pleases God, I must have patience; do but continue to love me, and I can bear all things else with ease.

The next day seventy-eight large ships of the French fleet sailed into the Channel in the brilliant summer weather. Nobody knew where they were heading, though it was thought they might be on their way to Ireland. Lord Torrington, who was in command of the English navy, had no more than forty ships at his disposal, since only part of the Mediterranean fleet had returned from Spain; to make matters worse the promised Dutch reinforcements had not yet arrived, and the ships which had escorted William to Ireland had not had time to sail back. In any case Torrington seemed to be in no hurry to engage the enemy; he was said to be ill, or waiting for Pembroke's regiment to arrive, and he was known to be a man of pleasure, who preferred entertaining his friends to fighting naval battles.

The rumour persisted all day that Torrington refused to move until Pembroke came, but when Pembroke received a letter from the Admiral summoning him, he proved to be equally dilatory. The letter was delivered at eight in the evening and he took no action for two hours, when he sent the opened letter to Nottingham who appeared in the Queen's room just when she was ready for bed. She liked Pembroke and thought him good-natured, but she found his procrastination hard to understand. 'Lord Pembroke is as mad as most of his family,' she wrote in her memoirs. That evening she felt unmoved, almost in a state of shock. 'Love me whatever happens,' she wrote at the end of her letter to William.

Before leaving England, William had asked her what she would do if there was a rising or civil disturbance in the City. Recently Carmarthen had asked her the same question. To both she had answered that although she knew she would be very frightened, she would not give way to panic, but would listen to the advice of those she believed to possess the most courage and good judgment. On the morning after the appearance of the French fleet, when her numbness had worn off, she realized fully the danger she and her country were in, menaced both from without and from within; for from the time that James had been brought back to London after his first abortive attempt to escape, a party had grown up which was dedicated to re-establishing him as King. The French fleet might give the Jacobites just the chance they had been waiting for. A list of the most dangerous men had been drawn up, and it was proposed that this should be read to the Privy Council in the morning, so that those named could be seized as soon as possible. The Queen knew that her uncle, Clarendon, would be on the list, for she had already been shocked to learn that he was in contact with the exiles at Saint-Germain, and when she arrived at the Privy Council, she witnessed a strange scene. Sir Henry Capel, whose sister had been Clarendon's first wife, did his best to defend his brother-in-law. Everybody stared at him, and there was silence. The Queen, believing that the other Privy Councillors were afraid to speak their mind in front of her, took it upon herself to answer him. She had seen one of Clarendon's intercepted letters, and she knew what William's feelings were on the subject. She therefore said, simply, that she thought everybody knew, what she was aware of herself, that too much was known about Clarendon for him to be left off the list.

'I believe it as necessary he should be clapped up as any,' she told William in a letter written on July 4. All the same, after the meeting, she suffered some qualms. 'I do not know when I ought to speak and when not,' she confessed. 'I am as silent as can be, and if I have done it now mal à propos, I am sorry but I could not help it.' She felt depressed and worried. There had been no news from William for several days; all she knew was that he was marching south, and that he might by this time be in great peril. It was impossible not to feel apprehensive, both about William's safety, and about the possibility of a naval defeat. A letter from Torrington, written at three o'clock in the afternoon hinted that momentous decisions were being made, but the delay was disconcerting. In the evening, for the first time since William had left England, the Queen drove out into Hyde Park, but she was not much comforted by the people she saw parading themselves there, for, as she told William, 'it swarmed with those who are now ordered to be clapped up'.

The appearance of the French fleet put the Lords of the Council into a state of agitation, but there was little that they or anybody else could do.

Nottingham earned the Queen's gratitude when he brought up, late in the evening after she had come back from the Park, William's 'dear letter' of the 8th. It was, she told William, 'so welcome that I cannot express it, especially because you pity me, which I like and desire from you, and you only'. The King was wondering about the progress of the building at Hampton Court, but she was unable to give any very favourable report; now that the situation was so serious there was not likely to be any money to spare, and with the French fleet in the Channel 'between Portland [off the Dorset coast] and us' the supply of stone was bound to be interrupted.

When the Queen wrote to William on June 20 there was still no definite news from Portsmouth. In London everyone seemed aware of the danger and yet paralysed when it came to positive action.

The fear at the back of most people's minds was that Torrington could have turned traitor. Although he was the man who had carried to Holland the manifesto of the Immortal Seven and who had fetched the Queen in person, his subsequent behaviour had not been impeccable, and he was known to have consorted with the Jacobites. Lord Stewart was angry and said that somebody should be sent to keep an eye on him. Carmarthen repeatedly suggested Russell as the second-in-command—because he wished to be rid of him, the Queen suspected. Monmouth was preparing to rush off to Portsmouth at any minute, taking his candidate with him. But the Queen was perceptive enough to see that the appointment of a deputy could lead to terrible quarrels, especially as Torrington had the reputation of being touchy and cantankerous. She could have spared Monmouth or Marlborough, neither of whom she liked, but she realized that if she once admitted in principle that an appointment should be made, Carmarthen would start pressing for Russell to go. She did not wish to part with one of the few men she felt she could trust. In any case, the King had left no instructions about such an appointment, so she called Nottingham and told him that she had no intention of making one; he was to thank Monmouth for his offer, and to tell him that it would not be proper for one of the Nine to abandon the position of trust to which he had been appointed in London. This made the habitually melancholy Nottingham break into a laugh; 'that was the greatest compliment she could make him,' he told her, 'to say that she could not use his arms, having need of his counsel'.

The nine men were turning out to be even worse than she had expected, and instead of working together, they were indulging in all their private feuds and dislikes. Nobody attempted to give her any balanced or disinterested advice. Meetings of the Council were being held at the Secretary's office to which she was not invited and of which she received no account. Marlborough told her that she should be present as often as possible, 'out of what intention I cannot judge,' she wrote. Carmarthen, ostensibly to save her worry, was grasping more and more into his own hands without consulting her, and she was afraid that they were all taking advantage of her inexperience and making this an excuse for leaving her out of their deliberations. As always, the most balanced and reliable man was hesitant to push himself forward, and indeed, to date, Russell had not been to see her once. The Queen sent him a message asking him to come. When he arrived, she said 'she desired to see him sometimes, for being a stranger to business I was afraid of being too much led or persuaded by one party'. He replied that he was glad to know this, and promised he would come to see her as the opportunity arose; he had only kept away so far for fear of being thought 'troublesome'. The King had recommended Lord Stewart, but he was proving to be weak and obstinate, while Monmouth was thought to be dabbling in dangerous waters in Scotland. Nottingham was very attentive, but this could have been because he did not wish the Whig members of the Council to have her ear, and there was a lurking fear that he could turn out to be a hidden Jacobite. As for Marlborough, she did not trust herself to say what she really thought about him. 'This,' she complained, 'was the Council I was to follow in all things,' The situation was enough to make anyone despair, let alone an inexperienced woman who lacked reliable advisers:

The Treasury was in a bad condition, there was no money, the fleet under the command of Lord Torrington, who lay drinking and treating his friends, till the French came upon the coast and had like to have surprised him. In this condition I was left with this powerful fleet on the coast, many enemies and discontented persons in the kingdom, and not above 5 or 6000 men to defend it; not secure of these at home, great reasons to apprehend dangers from abroad; so I believe never any person was left in greater straits of all kinds.

There was a further cause for disquiet. A series of letters, written in lemon juice and directed to France, had recently been intercepted; they revealed confidential information, and some of the details included could only have been known to one of the members of the inner Council. One of the Nine, it seemed, was indulging in treachery of the most blatant kind, which was hardly encouraging, especially with the French fleet in the Channel and the English Admiral also thought to be of doubtful loyalty. The Queen was being forced to rely more and more on her own judgment. Troubles threatened in Scotland; no answer had been received

to a letter written by Nottingham three weeks before, demanding an
immediate reply about the situation there. Further letters were now sent,
together with directives from the Queen to the Governors of Berwick and
Carlisle requesting them to search the mails and to stop anyone without a
pass. The Queen Dowager, that ancient focus of discontent, was removed
from London. She wanted to go to Bath, but it was thought too difficult
to put a watch on her there, so she was despatched by water from Hammer-
smith to Windsor, with all her 'closest things' and 'backstairs things', and
she spent the month of August harmlessly fishing from a four-oar barge,
which she hired for ten shillings a day.

'I ever fear not doing well,' the Queen told her husband, 'and trust to
what nobody says but you.' Thus, when she rose early on the morning
of June 28 to write to William, she was able to tell him that she had
remained firm in her resolution that none of the Lords should be sent
down to the fleet. When the Council met, most of the members agreed
that she was right. Russell, however, had drafted what seemed to her 'a
pretty sharp letter', which she and the others proceeded to soften down.
The main cause of dispute was the question of whether definite orders
should be issued to Torrington, telling him to fight. Terms were finally
agreed by everyone except Monmouth who had not appeared at the
meeting, and Lord Stewart who said frankly that he believed it was very
dangerous to trust Torrington with the fate of the three kingdoms, and
insisted that somebody should be asked to join in commission with
him. 'You must send for him prisoner then,' Russell said, and the others
agreed that such a policy 'would breed too much disturbance', especially
with the enemy so near.

The Queen signed the letter and left the meeting, which did not break
up at once. Most of the Lords, who had been joined there by Monmouth,
were still at the Secretary's office when Nottingham came up to find the
Queen who had by that time gone to bed. It seemed that Monmouth had
worked himself into one of his passions. He demanded that the Admiralty
should give him a commission as a captain; he had decided, he said, to fit
out a ship for himself at Portsmouth, to sail alongside Torrington,
swearing that he would never come back if the fleet could not be persuaded
to fight. Nottingham was sent up by the others to gain the Queen's
consent.

It was late by now and the Queen had had a long day; nevertheless she
was still clear-headed and calm. She thought to herself that as there had
been six men present, this constituted two-thirds of the committee, so
that the proposal in any case would have passed if put to a full Council.

It occurred to her that it might be wise to have Monmouth out of the way, for she had been wondering—and had recently discovered that others were of the same opinion—whether it was he who was responsible for the lemon letters. Wildman, the Postmaster-General, was one of his creatures, and it seemed possible that he was composing the letters, which were directed to Saint-Germain, and arranging for them to be intercepted. The object of this complicated operation was apparently to throw suspicion on Carmarthen. One would have thought that as one of the Queen's special advisers, he could have been spending his time in a more constructive manner.

The most recent lemon letter had given so accurate an account of recent debates in the Council that it could only have been written by one of the Nine. It was interesting to speculate whether the letters would cease as soon as Monmouth departed for Portsmouth. So, mainly for this reason, the Queen decided to agree. 'I think it a little irregularity,' she confessed to the King, 'yet I hope you will excuse it, and nobody else can find fault.' She was less pleased when the Lords went further and demanded that Russell should go to the fleet. She was still convinced that he was the one man she could trust. In the end she agreed to let him go. Monmouth came to take his leave next morning; he was full of protestations of loyalty and grandiose schemes, but it was difficult to take these seriously. Only that morning yet another lemon letter had been intercepted, containing minute details of the late-night meeting of the cabinet—but only that part of it which Monmouth had attended.

When Monmouth was still in the room, a letter from William was handed to the Queen. It told her that by this time the King would be ready to do battle, indeed he might by this time have already engaged the enemy. In the afternoon she had another letter, this time from Waldeck who, at Fleurus, had suffered a defeat at the hands of the French under Luxembourg. That night the Queen sat up by candlelight until her eyes ached, faithfully reporting to her husband all that had passed. She knew that sleep would be impossible, for she would be sure to lie awake wondering if he was safe. 'My heart is ready to burst,' she told him. 'I can say nothing but pray to God for you.'

Neither Monmouth nor Russell reached the fleet before it sailed. Torrington, stung into action by the 'softened' letter with its order to engage the enemy at all costs, had put out to sea in a disgruntled frame of mind; he did not appreciate being told by a collection of inexperienced non-seafaring men that he should seek a battle with a force which outnumbered his own. At a Council of War held on board ship it had been

decided that it would be unwise to engage the enemy who in fact had
far more ships than the number reported to the Queen and her Council,
but finally the Admiral had no alternative but to obey the orders from
London. He had by now been reinforced by the Dutch, and he allowed his
allies to bear the brunt of the action which was fought off Beachy Head.
After a somewhat half-hearted engagement, the fleet returned ignomi-
niously to the Nore, leaving the French in complete control of the Channel.
Torrington was universally condemned; in the Princess's drawing room
it was said he was 'an undone man'. Nobody was prepared to give him
any credit for the fact that he had kept the English fleet, such as it was,
intact. 'He will never be forgiven here,' the Queen told William.

Mary's chagrin was great. She was doubly sensitive, fearing that people
would attribute the defeat to the fact that the nation was in the hands of a
woman. Torrington was already saying that he held off because he was
ordered to do so by the Queen. The English did not appreciate being
defeated at sea, and public anger mounted as full details of the battle came
through. The Dutch were disgusted by the behaviour of the English, and
meanwhile the nine Lords fell into an undignified panic and sent William a
message demanding his immediate return. Alarm was general; 'as to your
fear of the French you are not singular, abundance are so,' wrote one
correspondent. The Queen understood the full implications of Beachy
Head as well as anybody, and was quite aware of the danger to which she
personally, and her country as a whole, were now exposed. She knew
too that the defeat could only encourage the disaffected. 'But God can
disappoint them all and I hope will take care of his own cause,' she wrote.
Her imperturbability at this time could only arouse admiration. 'Her
behaviour,' Burnet wrote, 'was in all respects heroical; she apprehended
the greatness of our danger, but she committed herself to God.' Her calm
bearing created confidence; she dined in public as usual a few days after
Beachy Head, visited a parade of the city trained bands in the park, and
gave no sign of anxiety or strain. On July 5 she managed to snatch three
hours of quiet and solitude at Kensington, the first respite she had had for
days—she had been so busy that she had not even found time to say her
prayers. 'That place made me think how happy I was there when I had
your dear company,' she confided in William, 'but now—I will say no
more, for I shall hurt my own eyes, which I want more now than ever.'

After the fiasco of the naval battle, one of her tasks was to write a letter
of apology to Evertzen, the Dutch Admiral. She had no sooner composed
a missive laboriously in Dutch than she was told that she had been wasting
her time as the Admiral spoke excellent English. At meetings of the inner

Council and the Privy Council most of the debates began to centre round
Torrington's successor—for the disgraced Admiral had resigned his post
and was now residing in the Tower. Monmouth was trying to 'fright' the
Queen, telling her daily of the great dangers that threatened, but she
refused to be intimidated, and, inspired by her calm determination, the
country began to prepare for a French invasion. Across the unguarded
Straits of Dover, France had twenty thousand trained men in readiness,
while England had no more than six thousand troops in the country.
It was harvest time, not the best moment to issue a call to arms, but it
was better to let the harvest rot than to succumb to an invader, and in
many areas the militia had already assembled. Attempts were made to
reinforce the fleet, but there was a dearth of seamen and the bad conditions endured by sailors at the time made recruitment difficult. There
was an urgent need for money and an attempt was made to raise a loan
of £100,000 in the City; meanwhile known Jacobites were watched and
guarded. Beyond this there was little to be done except to wait for the
French to take the initiative at any moment which happened to suit
them.

Under all this anxiety lay the deeper, personal worry about William's
safety. The Queen knew that at any moment she could hear that he had
been killed in battle. On July 6, the first Sunday of the month, when she
heard that an express had come from Ireland, she felt herself beginning to
tremble. Although she was on the edge of breakdown, wondering what
the news would be, she dressed ready for chapel, and was just leaving her
room when Nottingham came up with a letter. She searched his face;
he looked grave as usual, but immediately told her that the King was well.
The strain had proved too much at last. 'I could not hold so he saw me
cry, which I have hindered myself from before everybody until then,' she
confessed afterwards to William. It seemed that the King, always so
careless about his own safety, had ridden down from Drogheda, where the
army was encamped, to inspect the river Boyne. He was accompanied by a
large group of aides and courtiers and, since he was in full view of the
enemy camp on the opposite bank, it was not long before the party became
the target for two large cannon balls, one of which took away part of the
King's waistcoat, shirt and coat, and badly bruised his shoulder. Coningsby
staunched the blood with a coarse pocket handkerchief and it was then
seen that the wound was only superficial. It was a miraculous escape.
William himself made light of it, and insisted on remounting and continuing his inspection as soon as the wound had been dressed, but his wife
told him severely to take more care of himself in the future:

I hope it may be a warning to you, to let you see you are exposed to as many accidents as others; and though it has pleased God to keep you once in so visible a manner, yet you must forgive me if I tell you that I should think it a tempting God to venture again without a great necessity.

She returned to the same theme at the end of her letter. 'You will forgive me if I forget half what I have to say,' she added, 'for really my concern for you has got the mastery, and I am not able to think of anything else, but that I love you in more abundance than my own life.'

The next day the news was received of William's victory over the French and the Irish at the Boyne. It was brought to her first by Mr Butler—'whose face I shall love to see hereafter'—followed by Nottingham, whom she felt she knew well enough now to ask whether her father was safe. Nottingham replied that he was, and afterwards he told Burnet that she had not been able to express her complete satisfaction until he had reassured her about James's fate. William, in spite of the pain in his shoulder, had been present at the height of the battle, but James had kept well away and had fled to Dublin with all speed, taking ship for France from Kinsale at the first possible moment.

There was great rejoicing when the news of the victory was generally known. The Nine hoped that William would now be free to return and reinforce the troops encamped at Blackheath in readiness for the French; and meanwhile they continued to take panic measures. It was rumoured that the Queen intended to alter the Lieutenancy in the City by choosing from a list of names submitted by every member of the Privy Council. The argument concerning the naval command went on unabated. Russell firmly refused to accept the honour of commanding the fleet, saying that he lacked experience, although he was probably the most suitable successor for Torrington. Monmouth was far less diffident about his own qualifications, and he lost no time in suggesting himself. But the Queen told the Council that she did not intend to pitch on anybody until she had heard from the King. She herself favoured the idea that the fleet should be looked after by a commission of three—two experienced seamen, Sir Richard Haddock and Sir John Ashby, who were not forceful enough to command on their own, with a gentleman of quality as well. Pembroke, however, disapproved of this principle of a third person; he said it was 'only to send him to be knocked of the head, without the hopes of having any credit of what was well done'. Carmarthen offered to go; 'I put that off with compliments,' the Queen told her husband. Russell agreed with Pembroke that whoever went would be blamed for everything. The Queen half hoped that William would name Shrewsbury, for that delicate Lord had shown some willingness to return to the scene. To her delight he had appeared on the day that she dined in public, and she thought he looked in much better health; he had been at Epsom for the air and at Tunbridge Wells for the waters, and when a few nights later he came to supper, he went out of his way to make pleasant conversation. The Queen reciprocated, believing that the King would approve. But she was hesitant of appointing him as the third commissioner, for she feared that William would think he should not be forgiven so easily for resigning when he did. Besides, it seemed that even he had his antipathies, for he made it clear that he had a poor opinion of Sir Richard Haddock. In fact, all the Lords were far more ready to sink the fleet than their differences.

The only man she had really come to trust was Nottingham. 'It may be,' she admitted to William, 'that his formal, grave look deceives me,' but she felt that he had been 'hearty' throughout, and far more considerate and sympathetic than any of the others. She knew that if anybody else had brought her the news of the victory at the Boyne, she would never have dared mention the subject of her father. She believed that he was sincere, if only because he was not always taking pains to tell her so. Lord Pembroke kept away from her and only appeared at meetings, and Stewart was the same; she believed that his only ambition was to be 'a courtier among ladies', and that it was because of such interests that he frequently absented himself from the Council. Carmarthen could be difficult when crossed, and Monmouth was impossible. At times he was silent and sulky, at others he seemed quite unbalanced and his rages were alarming. At one moment he offered to take command of the fleet, at the next he announced he was going to Holland. In conversations with the Queen he said some 'extraordinary things' which she saved up to tell William on his return. It was noticeable that when Monmouth had gone off to Portsmouth the lemon letters had ceased, but had begun again as soon as he returned.

The Queen was still waiting for William's decision about the third man for the Commission when she returned to Whitehall on July 22, after a visit to Kensington. She was astonished to find Pembroke waiting for her with the entire Admiralty, whose members had come to tell her that they found the Commission an 'inconveniency'. When she told them that the King approved the plan, they still would not be satisfied, and so she procrastinated, saying she would like some time to think it over. It was quite late by the time they left.

On July 24, the Queen called the Council members together and told them what had passed. They agreed with her that as Russell still refused to take the command on his own, a Commission was the only solution.

Carmarthen informed members of the Admiralty of this conclusion when they arrived later in the morning. Sir Thomas Lee, who was their spokesman, went 'as pale as death' and told the Queen 'that the custom was that they used to recommend'. Carmarthen argued with him, and he confessed at last that Haddock was the stumbling block as nobody liked him. He went on at length, talking pompously about their privileges, until finally Mary's patience was at an end:

I said, that I perceived then the King had given away his own power, and could not make an admiral which the admiralty did not like; he answered 'No, no more he can't'. I was ready to say that then the King should give the commission to such as would not dispute with him, but I did not, though I must confess I was heartily angry, it may be I am in the wrong, but as yet I cannot think so. Lord President after some discourse desired them to retire.

The Council was now unanimously behind her, and it was agreed that the Commission should be prepared. Lee, and two others, sent to excuse themselves from signing, which stirred up the wrath of Carmarthen. 'He talked at a great rate,' the Queen reported, 'but I stopped him and told him I was angry enough, and desired he would not be too much so, for I did not believe it a proper time; he said, the best answer he could give from me was, that they would do well to consider of it. I desired he would add that I could not change my mind, if it were proper to say so much; he said it was rather too little.' The next morning Russell approached her when she was surrounded by people; he tried to excuse Lee, and said he could not believe he had really said the words attributed to him. The Queen had never seen Russell out of humour before, but he was really angry now, and he told her that the Commission could not be signed without a complete Admiralty Board. As there was so much company that morning, it was impossible to have a satisfactory conversation, but he pressed her to consider Shrewsbury, and in the afternoon Marlborough came to see her on the same topic. Devonshire, the Lord Steward, also brought her Lee's apologies. The trouble had arisen, he said, because the Admiralty Board was afraid that Haddock had been 'imposed' on the King—the implication was that he had been recommended by Nottingham. 'Indeed, my Lord,' the Queen broke out, 'if they only dislike Sir R. Haddock, because he is recommended by such as they don't approve, it will confirm me in the belief he is a fit man, since they can make no other objection against him. I confess, my Lord,' she continued, 'I was very angry at what Sir T. Lee said yesterday; but this is to make me more so, since I see 'tis not reason, but passion, makes Sir T. Lee speak thus.' Both she and Devonshire were angry, 'though not at one another'.

Devonshire, one of the Seven, had been among the most loyal supporters of the Revolution. He had sent his son, Lord Cavendish, abroad in the summer of 1688 to ensure the continuity of his line, and he had made him go on a protracted tour, looking at Palaces and antiquities, until he was certain there was no danger that King James would be brought back. At Chatsworth, 'seeing public affairs in a happier settlement, for a testimony of ease and joy, he undertook the East side of the quadrangle, and raised it entirely new'. He was saddened by the quarrels that had arisen. 'We fell into discourse of the divisions which we both lamented,' the Queen told William, and she begged her husband to return quickly, for she saw everything 'breaking out into flames'.

She was soon having misgivings about her own behaviour. 'If I have been too angry I am sorry for it,' she wrote apologetically. 'I don't believe I am easily provoked, but I think I had reason now.' In fact, William was delighted that she had taken a strong line and had shown such spirit— this was more than he had hoped for. 'Your approving my anger is a great ease to me,' she wrote, after receiving a letter from William on August 4.

At first the Queen thought that William would respond immediately to the summons from the Nine. On July 22 she received definite news that he was coming. 'It was seen in my face by those who knew the secret of it,' she told him. But the days passed, and by July 30 she saw the chances receding, though she still allowed herself to hope. 'When you do come,' she wrote, '. . . . I have one thing to beg, which is, that if it be possible, I may come and meet you upon the road, either where you dine, or anywhere else, for I do so long to see you, that I am sure had you as much mind to see your poor wife again, you would propose it but do as you please; I will say no more, but that I love you so much it cannot increase, else I am sure it would.' By August 2 she knew for certain that William intended to stay in Ireland until the end of the campaign. Her disappointment was acute, but she knew that if he were forced to return before the completion of his task in Ireland, he would be restless and dissatisfied.

The King, and even more important his troops, were less urgently required now in England. The tension had eased since the first anxious days after Beachy Head, for the French had quite failed to follow up the advantage they had gained during that encounter .The French fleet could have caused immense damage harrying the south-coast ports, but contented itself with a futile raid on Teignmouth which aroused the fighting spirit of the west. There was much sickness aboard the French ships, stores were running low and they had not enough troops to contemplate a large-scale landing. Louis did not love James enough to venture an army in England on his behalf, especially as there was no sign that the Jacobites would rise in any numbers.

The emergency was over, but the Council continued to argue and bicker about the naval appointments.

Monmouth was all the time keeping up what the Queen described as his 'bout' at Lord Nottingham. The Queen had made it just as clear to him as she had to Lee that she thought it was the King's responsibility to choose his Ministers. But Monmouth and his Whig colleagues were still smarting under the losses their party had received at the polls, which were due, they thought, to the favour the King had shown towards the Tories before the election. Might it not be possible, therefore, to reverse the process by holding an election whilst the King was still out of the country? With Machiavellian ingenuity they did what they could to sabotage the raising of the loan in the City, and Monmouth told the Queen that he could raise £200,000 on more favourable terms if she was prepared to call a new Parliament. Monmouth, in his unsubtle way, thought that the Queen, being a woman, would feel unable to resist such a bribe. But the Queen used the procrastinating technique, and said she would put the case to William on his return. Carmarthen warned her that such men would use any means to achieve their end, but he was confident that even if there were another election, the Whigs still had no guarantee that they would be any more successful in this one than they were in the last. Nottingham too was reassuring; he thought that if the City Whigs refused to raise any money, there were others, more patriotic in outlook, who would.

The Queen was too doubtful about Monmouth's loyalty to be taken in by his schemes. It seemed more than possible that he was involved in a Scottish plot to support a French landing, and the Queen, when she interviewed one of the conspirators, invited him to name English Lords who might be implicated. He replied that he knew nothing about England. 'I do,' she said, but what she knew was nothing more than a suspicion, and there was never any concrete evidence against the Lords whose loyalty was in doubt.

The Queen's elation on hearing the news of William's victory soon faded when she heard that he was returning to the army after a victorious visit to Dublin. People who had seen him there reported that he looked sunburnt and in good health, and Zuylestein, who came over from Ireland in August, looked so tanned that he 'frighted' her. Now she felt that William was in constant danger. 'A battle, I fancy, is soon over; but the perpetual shooting you are now in, is an intolerable thing to think on; for

God's sake take care of yourself.' His march to Limerick at the beginning of August was hazardous, for the country was full of enemy stragglers and snipers. But the King pressed on; he seemed tireless, riding all day, dealing with correspondence at night, writing to the Queen, reading her letters wherever they were delivered to him, sometimes sitting down on the nearest pile of army baggage to do so. After his victory, she begged him to take care of the Church in Ireland, which was said to be in a bad condition, with several Bishoprics vacant. She also told him that he must not be in too much of a hurry to dispose of confiscated lands, for some of the estates could be used to establish public schools, which were scarce in that land of bogs.

One thing the King could be sure of, in all the treachery and faction of the English scene, was his wife's absolute loyalty. Criticism of herself she took meekly enough, being certain that it was deserved; but she was sickened when people complained about her husband, saying first that he should not abandon the campaign in Ireland and then censuring him for staying on. Although she had grown to like Nottingham, she still felt that there was nobody in whom she could confide. When she wrote to William on August 26, she was unable to control her feelings any longer and she broke out:

I never do anything without thinking now, it may be, you are in the greatest dangers, and yet I must see company upon my set days: I must play twice a week; nay, I must laugh and talk, though never so much against my will. I believe I dissemble very ill to those who know me, at least 'tis a great constraint to myself, yet I must endure it. All my motions are so watched, and all I do so observed, that if I eat less, or speak less, or look more grave, all is lost in the opinion of the world; so that I have this misery added to that of your absence and my fears for your dear person, that I must grin when my heart is ready to break, and talk when my heart is so oppressed I can scarce breathe. In this I don't know what I should do, were it not for the grace of God which supports me. I am sure I have great reason to praise the Lord while I live for this great mercy, that I don't sink under this affliction; nay that I keep my health; for I can neither sleep nor eat. I go to Kensington as often as I can for air, but then I can never be quite alone; neither can I complain, that would be some ease; but I have nobody whose humour and circumstances agrees with mine enough to speak my mind freely to. Besides, I must hear of business, which being a thing I am so new in, and so unfit for, does but break my brains the more, and not ease my heart.

The weather, after a long and glorious summer, had broken at last, and in Ireland, too, the rainy season had begun. The King, fearing that sickness would soon spread among his troops with the wet weather, intensified his attempts to raise the siege of Limerick. Some heavy cannon had been brought up and the city was taken by storm on August 30. The campaign was almost over, though Marlborough, with the King's permission, had left for Ireland in charge of a small body of troops with the object of capturing Kinsale, the port which the French had found so useful as a base. 'As little reason as I have to care for his wife,' the Queen told her husband, 'yet I must pity her condition, having lain in but eight days: and I have great compassion for wives when their husbands go to fight.'

William landed at Bristol on September 6. After spending the night at Badminton, he returned to London, being fêted all the way. On September 9 the Queen went to Kensington to be in readiness, and on the 10th proceeded to Hampton Court where they were reunited. Her delight at finding him in such good health seemed to cancel out all the dismal events of the previous months, and best of all was his assurance that he admired the way she had managed affairs during his absence. Now she could retire from the work which she disliked and felt unqualified to do, and take time to say prayers again, both for herself and for William, for she felt that this was one small task she could shoulder for him. Her great fear was that people would think she would be reluctant to relinquish her power, having developed a taste for it, and so as soon as William returned she was careful to avoid seeing any of the men of her Council, particularly Carmarthen and Nottingham. She knew now, from experience, how tiresome it was when curious people questioned her about state affairs, and with this greater understanding, she more than ever avoided asking William questions about business, while he, for his part, confided in her more readily than before, for her letters had given him a high opinion of her intelligence and tenacity.

CHAPTER 25

RETURN OF THE HERO

THROUGHOUT THE SUMMER the Queen had been pressing the workmen hard at Kensington, for she was anxious that she and the King would be able to move into their own apartments on his return. She was afraid that she had started harrying the builders too late, for in July the scaffolds were still in position and all the windows boarded up. It was difficult not to be impatient with all the 'fideling' work on the outside of the house, which was taking longer to complete than she would have thought possible. Whitehall, she told William, was not unpleasant during the summer months, but he would obviously prefer to be at Kensington. 'We may liè in your chamber,' she told him, adding that they would probably have to dress in the Council room. She was experienced enough to comment, 'our being there will certainly forward the work.'

The delay in William's return ensured that Kensington was habitable by the time he came back, and it was also too late for him to go straight off to Flanders as he had intended, to be present at the end of the campaign there. He had not dared to tell the Queen about his plans, but she had read about them in a copy of the *Utrecht Courant* which somebody showed her, and which reported that William had written to the States promising he would be with them soon. She admitted that it had given her many 'ill hours' thinking that if she should see him again it would be only the prelude to another parting. But she knew now that he would not be going to Holland until after Christmas and then only to attend a conference of allied powers, and not to enter all the dangers of the battlefield. So she could look forward to several months of his company, with time to attend to her houses, to pray and meditate and to enjoy company. She was surprised and slightly apprehensive to find herself in a state of great spiritual equilibrium of a kind that she had only experienced twice before. Such 'heavenly mindedness', she told herself uneasily, was only granted to her when the Lord had some great trial in store for her, such as the onslaught on her religious beliefs by her father, or William's departure in 1688. But in any case those few months after William's return

were among the happiest in her life. It was almost worth having lived
through the dismal events of the spring and summer in order to experience
the exquisite relief of having William back, safe and in good health and
covered in glory, and of being able to rid herself of the work and responsibility which she so disliked. No longer was she forced to deal with
'the personal animosities which men have one against the other'. Now she
could leave all such hated tasks to the King. She reacted violently against
the nightmare loneliness and constriction of the last months. Kensington
was crowded every day with those who had come to offer their congratulations, and also, no doubt, to inspect the new royal quarters. Never,
before or after, was William so popular. He was the subject of adulatory
poems, prints and orations. At a banquet at the Guildhall he was elected
Grand Master by the Grocer's Company. There was a command performance of Congreve's *The Double Dealer*, to which the Queen went
alone, for the hot atmosphere of the English theatre was more than the
King could stand.

Congreve wrote a new prologue for his play which was recited by Mrs
Barry. He acknowledged the honour the Queen was paying to the stage
in general and his play in particular. It was a glittering occasion:

> But never were in Rome, nor Athens seen,
> So fair a circle or so bright a Queen.

Kynaston, who normally played the part of Lord Touchwood, was taken
ill at the last moment and Colley Cibber was called upon to deputize
with only a day's notice; 'the honour to act before the Queen, you may be
sure, made me blind to whatever difficulties might attend it,' he wrote.
He had learned his lines by the time he went to bed that evening, and
Congreve was delighted with his performance. His salary was raised from
fifteen to twenty shillings a week, but he did not become a star overnight
as he had hoped he would.

During the last months of 1690 the Queen visited her friends more
than at any other time. She went out of town one evening and dined with
the Duchess of Monmouth where she was very splendidly entertained.
One day Lord Wharton arrived at Windsor to find the Queen's coaches
waiting outside the door. He was told that her Majesty had taken it into
her head to visit his wife at Woburn. Lady Wharton had already had
numerous visitors that week-end and her larder was bare, in fact she 'had
great difficulty to contrive enuff [sic] for her family on the Sabbath day'
let alone for a Queen. Worse still, their only cook had taken the day off
and, being a man, her Lord 'had . . . so little presence of mind that he did

not think of sending one'. The unfortunate Lady Wharton had just sat down to her own dinner, but she left the table and tried to make some preparations. She told Lady Russell she would have given five pounds for a partridge, if only one had been available.

The Queen, who often complained that in England nobody appreciated her, was the subject of several eulogies. Tillotson preached a sermon in September in which he pointed out how the court had benefited from the example set by the Queen, who was the pattern of 'a decent and unaffected devotion, of a most serious and steady attention, without wandering, without diversion, and without *drowsiness*; such an example as I cannot but hope will in a short time gain upon us all, and by a more gentle and silent reproof win us to the imitation of it'. At the service held on October 19, the day of thanksgiving for William's preservation and success in Ireland, Burnet, avoiding 'a dry recital of too much history,' pointed out that the English had a Prince 'born an orphan and an abortive both . . . a plant that seemed to rise out of a dry ground, to be a great tree, under whose shade all the beasts of the field come for shelter, and in whose boughs all the fowls of the air now come to lodge'. His life, Burnet said was 'a sequel of wonders'; he was the David of the modern age. Turning to the King and Queen he said: 'You do both shine with the lustre becoming each sex, the one with the glory of conqueror of enemies, and the other with the softer rays of a preserver of your people.'

The Queen was not prepared to sit back and accept such compliments nor was she content simply to influence those around her at court by her own good example, and she was already urging William to take positive action to ensure an improvement in the moral standards of the country as a whole. Burnet confirms that the reformation of manners was one of her chief concerns, and that this 'was no sooner moved to her than she set it going'. The clergy had been instructed earlier in the year to preach more frequently against vice and debauchery, and at the end of October a proclamation was issued stating that William offered a reward for anyone apprehending robbers and highwaymen. In this way the Queen could do something to expiate the sin of deposing her father. James was now back in France; 'his sighs,' reported Elizabeth Charlotte, William's old flame Liselotte, 'are quite heart-rending. He took me on one side and cross-examined me about his daughter. Was it really true that she had been so grieved by his misfortune that she refused to dance at the Hague when the Electress of Brandenburg was there? Had she truly written to you she was glad he had not lost his life in Ireland? I assured him that it was all very true, and this assurance seemed to give the unhappy King a little comfort.' Liselotte still had a soft spot for William. 'Perhaps you will think that "old love never grows stale", but I certainly prefer an intelligence such as his to the other's handsome face.'

The Queen did not allow concern for her father to cloud her short interlude of happiness. She busied herself choosing the interior furnishings for Kensington House—she never called it a Palace, for it was essentially a home, a convenient and comfortable place to live in, away from the murk of Westminster but within commuting distance, unpretentious, but beautifully designed. She was now choosing damasks and velvets for the curtains and upholstery, and helping to plan the gardens with box hedges, yew trees and parterres, set out with Dutch precision in geometrical patterns. For the inside of the house she began to make a collection of porcelain, and in her gallery 154 pieces were to be housed in handsome marquetry cabinets. William too, when he had a moment to spare, began to delve into the storehouse of treasures accumulated by earlier monarchs. The Raphael cartoons which had been hidden away in store, were taken out and dusted, ready to be housed in their own room at Hampton Court.

At Kensington the Clock Court, its gateway surmounted by a little cupola, was now complete, and the main rooms were fit for habitation. Kitchens were built along one side of the Clock Court and beyond was another court, surrounded by the offices of the Board of the Green Cloth. Courtiers were accommodated in rooms along the Stone Gallery, and the Queen's maids of honour were allotted panelled rooms beyond the west staircase. Work was still continuing in the Queen's Gallery and elsewhere. The rooms where William and Mary lived were comfortable and homely, and great care had been taken with the plumbing. Isaac Thompson, an engine maker, had been employed to make a 'forcing engine', an ingenious machine that was to be used 'to force the water into the cisterns by the King's kitchen and into the Q's stool'. Thompson himself constructed the stool and made a seat for it, which was covered with velvet.

To make Kensington habitable had been the first priority, but work had been going on all through the summer at Hampton Court in spite of the national emergency. Now that she was free of State affairs, the Queen could take a more personal interest in the progress of the building. We have it on the authority of Wren's son that she 'pleased herself from time to time, in examining and surveying the drawings, contrivances, and whole progress of the works, and to give thereon her own judgement, which was exquisite'. In his opinion there were few arts or sciences in which the Queen had not acquired a knowledge far superior to other members of her sex in her own, or even any former, age. 'This is not said as a panegyric,' he wrote, 'but a plain and well-known truth, which the surveyor had frequent experience of, when . . . he had many opportunities of a free conversation with her Majesty, not only on the subject of architecture, but other branches of mathematics and useful learning.'

Christopher Wren's original scheme for Hampton Court, which was the Het Loo of the building programme, contained a vast central block complete with a large dome, architecturally all of a piece. At a meeting of the Board of Works, held on May 4, 1689, and attended by the King, Wren had presented his ambitious estimates for the cost of rebuilding the Palace with a fine garden and a network of canals and basins. But the Treasury considered the cost of an edifice large enough to rival Versailles an unnecessary expense, and the old Palace, with all its ghosts, was destined to remain. The Queen had to content herself with a smaller block, severe in outline, but softened by the pleasing use of mellow brick and Portland stone. The design of the interior was regulated by the demands of the contemporary court, to cater for the growing number of people who wished to live on the fringe of royal society as well as for the monarch's resultant need to guard his privacy more closely than ever before. The King's and Queen's public rooms were ranged along the south and east fronts, the King's looking out over the privy garden and the Queen's over the 'frontispiece to the park'. At the junction of the two fronts, in the angle, the King's writing room and the Queen's closet were situated, with easy access to the backstairs, but inaccessible otherwise except through the closely guarded Bedchamber. The King increasingly conducted all essential business in his study, the most important Ministers being given the password for the backstairs, which gave rise to a new pattern of 'closet' government, and the need, in a subsequent reign, to keep on good terms with Anne's Lady Masham. The Bedchamber, in William's reign, was always watched over by Dutch officials, and so the disgruntled English were kept at bay. Since the average courtier had little chance of seeing the King or Queen except when they passed through the public rooms on their way to chapel, the popularity of court life naturally declined. All the same Mary never developed the lofty aloof manners of her predecessor Elizabeth, and anyone who met her always found her polite and unassuming.

The main structure of the new wing had been completed by the time William returned from Ireland. Scaffolds were being constructed for the painters who were to put a coat of distemper on the walls of the two 'great rooms', and on the outside more scaffolding and tackle were being fixed to carry up the chimney heads. In October the accounts include an item 'for removing the stone that was misplaced being altered by the Queen's order in her own apartment', which indicates that she was keeping a close watch on the work. A shed for the masons had been set up in the garden, and they were busy now with the architraves, plinth and fascia, festoons and shields. The old Banqueting House had been pulled down, and the workmen were sorting out the good bricks which could be used again; meanwhile stone and timber were being delivered all the time to the new wharf by the timber yard. One Jasper English was receiving a fee for opening the gates in the King's meads 'for the horses to pass that draw the barges with timber, boards, stone and other materials'. Yards of 'woven sash lines' had been ordered for the new windows, and each month the Clerk of the Works put in his bill for candles at 6d a dozen, oil for the crane at 2s od, dog's meat at 4s 6d, and sometimes boat hire and a sum for 'the office dinner'.

The Queen's interest at this time was focused on the Water Gallery, or the Thames Gallery as it was frequently referred to in the accounts. It was perhaps extravagant to spend so much on a folly that would have to be pulled down as soon as the main building was completed as it obstructed the view to the river, but Defoe thought it was as if the Queen was conscious that she had only a few years to enjoy it and so ordered 'all the little neat curious things to be done, which suited her own conveniences, and made it the pleasantest little thing within doors that could possibly be made'. The original boat-house had three or four rooms downstairs and a long room upstairs overlooking the water which the Queen converted into a gallery. Garden doors downstairs gave out onto the Privy Garden, and the Gallery opened onto a balcony with a gilded railing. The towers and turrets of the original building were preserved, with spiral stairs leading up to the main towers, but most of the battlements were removed and iron railings put in their place. The dairy, like Marie Antoinette's, was to be a complete replica of a real one, neat and clean with blue and white tiles which William was to order specially from Holland for Mary's birthday. The new sash windows measured 9 ft 8 in by 8 ft 5 in and the stairs were made of elm and walnut. The plumbing was not neglected. The bricklayer took twelve days to make a drain in the Queen's garden by the Gallery, and in the bathroom all the fittings were in marble with brass hinges; the bath, copied from a Dutch original, 'was made very fine, suited either to hot or cold bathing as the season should invite'. The plumbers laid 235 yards of piping to carry the water to the Queen's stool, and their account included 'making 27 joynts and sodering on 3 stopcocks there, and making three cestrons and putting them up there'.

While the work at the Gallery was still in progress, the building, which presumably was out of range of the guard-dog, had to be guarded against vandals, and there were special payments to night-watchmen for 'watching and warding'. Once the shutters were up and fitted with large bolts, security became less of a problem, although the Gallery was in an exposed position, and in the winter-time there were bills for windows broken in the gales. For a temporary building, the Gallery was finished and fitted with great care, and the Queen made it a storehouse for her most precious treasures. Grinling Gibbons designed elaborate mantelpieces with shelves of diminishing sizes, so that she could show off all her vases; and the choicest pieces were to be displayed in cabinets specially designed by Gerrard Johnson. There was china all over the place, blue and white Oriental ware as well as Delft, arranged on ledges, shelves and carved wall-brackets. The Looking Glass closet was decorated by James Bogdane, the fashionable painter of animals, and the Queen commissioned Kneller to paint a number of court ladies for her Beauty Room. The long upstairs gallery had a fine lantern hanging from the 'compass roof'; there was a coved ceiling, and William Emmett carved out mouldings over the doors— 'half boys with foliage'—as well as a large Italian picture-frame with three 'enrichments'. All the rooms were exquisitely furnished, and people were fascinated by the chintz bed which the Queen had worked herself while in Holland. Such a curiosity had scarcely been seen in England before. Two exquisite wrought-iron weather vanes were designed by Tijou. Each one cost £80, and the sergeant-painter, Robert Streeter, who painted them for a pound, did not much enjoy going up on to the roof to put the finishing touches.

The charming Water Gallery was to serve the Queen as a private retreat, where she could be on her own, away from everybody, even the builders. Below the balcony, the Thames ran deep and clear, 'always cheerful, not slow and sleeping, like a pond', and in the summer-time the Queen could sit outside watching the fish swimming below in the translucent water, or embroidering the birds, animals and fruit for the hangings in her closet at the Palace, or reading aloud a book or poem to her ladies with comments—'the gloss,' Burnet said 'was often better liked than the text.'

William was content to leave the details to his wife. The main attraction of Hampton Court as far as he was concerned was that Bushey Park was close at hand; there he could forget the English and all their troubles in the excitement of the chase. He did occasionally 'deliver his opinion', and declared in public that Kensington and Hampton Court were not equalled by any palace in Europe 'for good proportion, State and convenience'.

Throughout the last months of 1690 the Queen lived entirely in the present, but in the new year she had to face another parting. It was very bitter for her to have to stay behind while William went to Holland, for, as she told Mlle Obdam, 'I am still as good a Hollandoise as ever and always will be, and I love all the friends I have left there as much or more than ever'. She could hardly bear to think of the King returning to Holland without her. Some day, perhaps, when affairs were more settled, and there was no longer a chance that her father would steal the opportunity to return if once she left the country, she would be allowed to visit Holland herself: 'What satisfaction that will be for me, what joy, to see again a country which is so dear to me, and people with whom I have lived so long, so happily and with such contentment.'

The King was looking forward to his journey with a mixture of pleasure and apprehension. He reminded Huygens that they must expect many changes; it was probable that their friends would hardly recognize them, or they their friends. His wife was disconsolate and full of fears for his safety. To risk the crossing at this time of year was madness, and she was afraid that she might never see him again. Even if he survived the journey she knew that he would be tempted to stay in Holland until the opening of the spring campaign, when he would be exposed all over again to the dangers of war. But the King was in no mood to take her feelings into consideration. He had been growing increasingly restless, eager to go and unable to settle to anything. So on January 26 he set sail from Gravesend with a large suite and a special baggage ship. His entourage included the best part of the King's musicians, his aim to waft tired diplomats into the alliance to the strains of Purcell. The *Mary* sailed slowly away in convoy into a thick mist. It was as well that the Queen did not know until afterwards that he had defied the English captains, who strongly advised him to put back, and insisted on pressing forward through the drifting ice floes. He arrived off the Dutch coast to be told that the Maas was full of ice, so he decided to put ashore in a small boat, believing that he would reach land in a couple of hours that way. Instead he and his courtiers spent the entire night in an open boat, sixteen hours in all, in freezing fog.

William entered the Hague at nightfall and the cannon announcing his arrival brought the populace out into the streets; bells were ringing, everyone was cheering and there were lights in every window. Rather reluctantly, for he was anxious to begin work, he agreed to a public entry.

It was a cold day, but fine, with ice on the Vyver, and the city was packed with people who had come in from the surrounding countryside. The triumphal arches, the cheering crowds, the bells and bonfires, were reminiscent of the day, thirteen years before, when he had introduced his young bride to the Dutch. 'Ah! if the Queen were here,' he said, 'you would see the difference. Where they give one shout for me they give ten for her.'

The King was kept busy with constant meetings; there were many Dutch matters, too, to attend to, for it was over two years now since he had left the States. Even so, he found time for some gaiety; he gave dinner parties to a background of the King's music, and he even visited the theatre. At home the Queen, encouraged by the good news from Holland, decided to show the world that she was not so selfish that she would fret at her husband's absence; so long as he was not in danger she decided to live a normal life. She went once or twice to see a play, passed the time every evening at cards—either comet or bassett—and on February 6, Anne's birthday, had dancing in her drawing-room. She dined with Lord Newport and Sir Edward Villiers in Carmarthen's rooms at St James's Palace where she was 'spendidly entertained' with peas and cauliflowers on the menu—the first of the season.

She did not, however, live a completely frivolous life. She continued her visits to Hampton Court, where the walks and the two staircases in the new building had to be cleared for her to walk on—a job that took three men six days. De Marot had been summoned from Holland to lend his skill to the interior decorations, and a shed had been made 'for the Frenchman to burn his plaster in'. The Queen was pressing on with her campaign to improve the morality of the country, and at a Privy Council meeting which she attended on February 19 it was proposed that a committee should be formed to help make the streets safe from robbers and disorderly persons. She had been distressed to hear of abuses and irregularities committed in the majority of hospitals and houses throughout the kingdom, and she now appointed a commission to look into the allegations. A warrant was issued to allow for the inspection of hospitals in London.

The Queen, unlike her sister, was an early riser; she usually woke at six and spent some time meditating or reading, having drunk a dish of tea and partaken of a very frugal breakfast. During the official dressing ceremony, she heard petitions and dealt with business. She went to prayers, walked in the garden and gave the gardeners their instructions, and then, if time allowed, sat down to her embroidery. The fact that the Queen was so often working with her hands rapidly set a fashion, and soon 'the whole town' was copying her. The knotting of fringe also became very popular through her example, and it was thought that thanks to her influence English ladies as a whole learnt to occupy themselves far more usefully than they had done in the previous reign.

In spite of all this virtue, however, the Queen could not altogether escape the calumniators, who were always watching her to see whether they could find any salacious rumours to spread. They had a difficult task, but soon after William's departure, a court trouble-maker took it upon himself to write to Dyckvelt, knowing that the Dutchman was close enough to the King to pass on the information. Jean Blancard, the informant, had probably once been secretary to Ruvigny, the Huguenot Marquis who had recently been created Earl of Galway. Blancard, if that was his true name, felt that it was his duty to tell the King any information that came his way, but in this case he was dealing with *une petite affaire mais délicate* concerning a certain lady and gentleman whose names would be put into cypher to foil the curious. The letter in fact concerned the relationship of the King and Queen, and raised all the old doubts that had once enlivened the letters of Covell and his cronies. The King's love, it seemed, was palpably cooling, and, more surprising, still, it was even said that the Queen herself was less of a mind to show the *grande inclination* which everyone had believed she had always felt for her husband. 'When one married so young, at fifteen years old,' she was reputed to have said, 'one does not know what one is doing.' From this and other conversations, people had learnt that the Queen was not happy. Her love was lessening, for a variety of reasons; for example, she was annoyed because the King was chaffing her about her *embonpoint*—she had put on weight recently and was sensitive on the subject. Worse still was her fear that William was being unfaithful to her, that he was in fact sleeping from time to time with a certain lady. Blancard was undoubtedly referring to the old enemy, Elizabeth Villiers, who had come over to England with everyone else after the Revolution, and moved on the edge of court society, arranging among other things to buy Huygens the drinking chocolate for which he had such a great weakness. Blancard now came to the most interesting aspect of all. Whispers, he said, had been going around concerning the charming Shrewsbury who, that autumn, before the King's departure had been seeing a great deal of the Queen: '*on dit a l'oreille parmi quelque spéculatifs curieux et envieux que 36* [Shrewsbury] *est amoureux de 5* [the Queen].'

And if it were really true that Shrewsbury was in love with Mary, the strange thing was that she, in her innocence, seemed to be quite unaware of the fact. Ignorant of all gossip and not knowing, as everyone else seemed to, that Shrewsbury's favourite fortune-teller had hinted that he might benefit in some way from the death of the King, she kept sending for him and inviting him to play cards with her. The gossip mongers were convinced that Shrewsbury was smitten, for it seemed that he had stopped taking out, or even looking at, young ladies who previously had interested him, and had become a dreamer, absent-minded, obviously in love. What with this and William's *fragilité*, the royal marriage did not look like lasting very much longer. What would happen, Blancard wondered, if 'my Lord 4', as William was romantically styled, should die? 'God preserve us from it!' Blancard sanctimoniously exclaimed, going on to expatiate on the Queen's virtue and piety, which proved nothing, since, as his lady informants told him, husbands seldom love their wives, however charming and beautiful they might be.

The rumours do not ring true, coming as they did after one of the most contented stretches in the Queen's married life. It is probable that she enjoyed Shrewsbury's companionship and that he, like so many others, was enamoured of her charm and vivacity. Even if Dyckvelt were indiscreet enough to pass on the contents of Blancard's letter, William took little notice of it, for he continued to court Shrewsbury and never ceased to tempt him back into public life. It was a strange coincidence that very soon after this letter was written, William's eye was attracted, not by another woman, but by a young man, one of his courtiers, who suffered a bad fall in the hunting field and broke his leg. Arnout Joost van Keppel, youthful and strikingly handsome in a somewhat effeminate way, bore his excruciating pain with great courage. 'He is such a good boy,' William told Huygens. The King visited Keppel several times during his convalescence, and so began a friendship which was to give the gossip mongers something far more spicy to spread about than a moribund affair with Squinting Betty.

The Queen admitted to William that she had been spoilt in Holland, where she had enjoyed so much friendship. She still found all those she was supposed to trust 'together by the ears, and a general peevishness and sylleness [sic] in them all'. Sidney was the exception to the rule, for he remained as sympathetic and friendly as he had always been in the Dutch days, but he was a trifle ineffective, and preferred pleasure to work. Although the situation had looked healthier during the autumn, and the King had found Parliament prepared to grant supplies for his campaign in Flanders, the Queen began to feel uneasy as soon as he went away. 'I heard daily, things which discouraged me extremely,' she recorded. People were telling her that she and the King were less popular than before, that they both had many enemies and no friends, on the contrary everyone was discontented and 'each seeking only their own advantage'.

The King had displayed a merciful attitude towards the Jacobites who had been under suspicion during his absence in Ireland. Most of them were now at large. Some showed great gratitude for the forgiveness he had shown, and Ailesbury never forgot, to the end of his life, how the Queen, when he was released on bail, had invited him to play bassett with her on one of the long hot evenings, and after greeting him 'with a most smiling countenance', had sat him next to Lady Derby and asked him questions about himself and his family. There were many Jacobites, however, who were now determined to take advantage of the King's absence in Holland, and one of these was Lord Preston who, though a Protestant, had played an important part in the pre-Revolution Parliament. He was called down from Scotland to take a message to James, for having served some time as Ambassador in Paris, he was considered particularly suitable for the task. He set off for France in a hired boat, but the owner of the craft, who was a government man, discovered all he knew; the boat was boarded and Preston's letters, which included one from the Bishop of Ely, were found in the hands of John Ashton, a servant of the Queen's, to whom Preston had handed them just before he was seized. The men were taken to Whitehall and quickly brought to trial, in the hope that the fear of death would make them reveal a great many Jacobite plans and secrets. Ashton refused to give away any secrets, but Preston, who tended to face the idea of death bravely when heated with wine and in the company of friends, was less courageous in the cold light of morning. He made a few confessions, but both he and Ashton were condemned to death.

Ashton's friends made ceaseless attempts to persuade the Queen to show him some mercy. She had signed the warrant for his death in great distress, for she had known him since he was a child. The grave responsibility of holding a man's life in her hands was the one test which she feared more than any other. To salve her conscience she went into the circumstances with great care. Her inclination was to grant him a reprieve, but she felt that he had been justly condemned, and knew that in the dangerous situation her country was in, it was in the interest of the nation that the law should take its course. 'So I forced my own inclinations,' she wrote, 'and refused all the instances [that] were used, so that at the time appointed he was executed.' He suffered 'with great decency and seriousness' as Burnet put it, and went proudly and silently to the scaffold. The paper which he left behind showed that he was ready to admit his dependence on King James, although he was genuinely ignorant of the contents of the letters which were found on him.

Preston was made of softer metal; he continued to vacillate, veering between the desire to die heroically and the wish to live longer. Letters and petitions asking for his reprieve appeared every day on the Queen's desk. His daughter was stationed in front of a portrait of James II; the Queen saw her there and asked her what she was doing. 'I am reflecting how hard it is,' replied the girl, 'that my father should be put to death for loving your father.' The Queen managed to resist such ruses, but a reprieve was granted when Preston promised to give the names of his fellow conspirators provided his own life was spared. He named the Earl of Clarendon, the Bishop of Ely, William Penn, Carmarthen, Devonshire and Dorset.

The necessity of facing such decisions wore the Queen down. Naturally compassionate, she found it a heart-rending experience to sentence to death any mother's son. The question of a young apprentice who had murdered his master troubled her just as much as the cases of men who were condemned for high treason. The victims and their relations played on her known soft-heartedness. Twenty-four young girls, all dressed in white, came to plead for the apprentice. His mother, who allowed herself to hope for mercy, because the Queen had already reprieved two other murderers, one of whom had a wife and five children, also came herself. She was almost distracted. 'I never saw so moving a sight in my life as she was,' wrote the Queen, 'yet the fears I had of the threats in scripture against a hand defiled with blood, and the theme from thence, one's eye must not pity a murderer, this made me stop my ears to all that could be said on his behalf.'

Meanwhile, the Hague Congress was going so well that the allies had agreed to put a vast army of over 200,000 men into the field. But the sight of the triumphant William sitting at the head of the delegates and moulding them to his will was too much for Louis. To cut short the Congress, he decided to open the winter campaign far earlier than usual and before the allied plans had time to mature. On March 15 he appeared in front of the barrier town of Mons with an army of a hundred thousand men under the command of Luxembourg. Gastanaga, the Governor of the town, called on William for help, and the King, who was snatching a few days hunting at Loo, was forced to go to his aid. By then there was little that the King could do except to watch the town fall. At this stage he had no more than fifty thousand men at his disposal, and the Spanish failed to provide more than a fraction of the baggage waggons they had promised. Had William been able to arrive earlier than he did, he might have saved the town or encouraged it to hold out a little longer, counteracting the propaganda of the priests within the walls who were advising the townspeople to surrender.

The fall of Mons was a blow to the allied cause and to William's prestige. Louis, who, it was said, never attended any campaign personally unless he was sure of its success, emerged from the siege with his image unimpaired. Mary, as she admitted herself, was almost out of her wits with fear when she heard that William was going to Mons. The news of the attack had been so startling and unexpected, for 'it was scarcely etiquette,' as Winston Churchill has put it, 'to begin operations before April or May'.

For the time being there was nothing to be done except to wait for warmer weather and the green grass which would feed the horses and make the army independent of the broken or non-existent forage wagons. William decided to fill in the time with a quick visit to England. The Queen was overjoyed when she heard the news, but her sense of pleasurable anticipation was destroyed when, on April 9, a few days before William set sail, a disastrous fire broke out at Whitehall in the long stone gallery, consuming the lodgings which had been pulled down and rebuilt three times to please the Duchess of Portsmouth 'and other lodgings of such lewd creatures, who debauched both King Charles 2 and others, and were his destruction,' as Evelyn described it. Although some, including Evelyn, saw the hand of God in this occurrence, the fire was probably caused by the carelessness of a maid who left a bunch of candles burning in the store-room. The Queen and her ladies, roused from sleep, could not find a single man to help them, but they ran out into the Privy Garden, where the Queen, her hair hanging loose on her shoulders, stood calmly watching the flames until her Guards arrived and she was led off to take refuge at Arlington House. It was noticed that she kept very calm in this emergency and was even able to laugh at the clumsy messenger who was sent to fetch her Guards and who in his hurry stumbled into a bed of nettles.

The Queen had already been troubled by a Jacobite, Sir John Fenwick, who had insulted her by putting his hat on instead of removing it when she had passed by in her coach. She had forbidden him to enter the Park again, but as she crossed it to go to Arlington House on the night of the fire, he and a fellow Jacobite, Colonel Ogelthorpe, called out to her through the darkness that this was but a foretaste of punishments she must come to expect.

The arrival of William, who landed at Gravesend late in the evening of April 22, took her mind off these troubles. Almost as soon as he was home he broke it to her that he would not be able to stay longer than a fortnight, and if she had looked forward to some quiet hours with her husband, she was to be disappointed. 'Ladies who before had kept away in consideration of my business now came in crowds,' she complained, 'believing I had nothing to do but chat with them.' The days passed quickly, she was so busy that she hardly had time to say her prayers, and when the King went back to Holland at the end of the fortnight, the whole visit seemed, in retrospect, to be nothing more than a dream.

CHAPTER 26

THE SECOND SUMMER

IN SPITE OF the dangers of the time, the King was still inclined to be merciful. He reviewed the evidence which Preston had given in order to save his life and took little action except to exonerate Carmarthen, Dorset and Devonshire completely. He had accepted the fact, long ago, that many of his principal advisers were taking out an insurance policy with Saint-Germain, and he had adopted a merciful attitude towards such devious behaviour. One lesson he had learnt from his father-in-law was that bigotry engendered opposition where toleration bred loyalty. Besides, if he had dismissed all those who had from time to time made overtures to the exiled King he would have been left with few men of talent and ability.

The King was pleased with the way his wife had handled the difficult Preston affair, and during his stay in England, he pardoned both Preston and Croon, another Jacobite. The Queen was glad that they were to go free, but she had to admit that their subsequent behaviour proved that they did not really deserve such tolerant treatment.

Although the King's stay was short, the Queen was resolved to bring up a subject which was, to her, of the greatest urgency. It was in the good cause of the Protestant faith that she had overcome her scruples and consented to usurp her father's throne, and if William was now prepared to put Anglican matters to the back of his mind while he concentrated on his life's work of humbling the French, she was not. She had been disappointed and saddened by the behaviour of the non-juring clergy and the intransigence of Convocation; she longed to bring about an improvement in the situation, so that the Church could be free of schism and able to concentrate on its real work of pastoral care. The time limit for taking the new oaths had run out the previous August, with Sancroft and four hundred of the clergy still refusing to conform. The Archbishop was allowed to remain at Lambeth, although he was suspended from all his duties. The Queen had sent a message to the non-jurors to discover whether they would continue their work within the framework of the

Church, if an act of Parliament could be introduced exempting them from the oaths, but the response was far from encouraging. 'They would answer nothing and promise nothing' was the gist of their reply, and they expressed their intention of remaining 'wise in not answering such insidious questions but by a prudent silence as significant and loud as any vocal answer to let that unfortunate Princess and all the world know they scorned the baseness of her proposal.'

It was a further shock when the Bishop of Ely's letter to James assuring him of support, had been found among Preston's papers, and the Queen now told her husband that the time had surely come to fill the vacant Bishoprics with loyal prelates, and particularly the see of Canterbury on which all the others hinged. William would probably have been content to let Sancroft continue quietly at Lambeth for a while longer if the Queen had not pressed him to take action. To make an appointment was to show the world irrevocably where his sympathies lay, and to offend one political party or the other. And, as Burnet pointed out, the choice he eventually made revealed that he intended to pursue his original course of toleration, without making any concessions to the High Church party. Bishop Compton, in view of the service given by himself and his family in bringing about the Revolution, expected the plum to fall into his own lap. He had for months now been helping to carry out the duties which Sancroft had been unable and unwilling to perform since his suspension, and he had been chosen as president of the upper house of Convocation. Like the King, Compton had moved away from a complete dependence on the Whigs. The Northampton family, of which Compton was a member, inclined traditionally towards the Tories, and he had struck up a friendship with Carmarthen which helped to draw him still further away from the Whigs. Compton's militant approach did not appeal to the Queen or to her husband, whereas Tillotson, whom they had known well for only two years, had endeared himself to them by his 'soft and prudent counsels'. It seems that they had for some time been trying to persuade him to become the primate, but he had held back, for he was not an ambitious man, and he was getting on in years. Nor was he under any illusions about the difficulties he would have to face, for he had been in the Church long enough to know about the slander and jealousies which high promotion tends to bring in its wake. At last, however, he was unable to stand out any longer against the King's persuasiveness, and accepted the 'calamity', as he called it, that had come upon him. 'I am very sensible,' he told a friend, 'that I come into a difficult place in a very difficult time, and I shrink at the thought of the burden I stand under'.

Both the King and the Queen knew that a moderate unambitious man
was likely to lower the temperature, and from the ecclesiastical point of
view Tillotson was well fitted for the task. Birch maintains that he was
'ever in a good humour, always the same, both accessible and affable'.
At the same time he did not lack bite and he often had the last word, for
example when Sir John Trevor remarked loudly, as he passed by him in
the House of Lords, 'I hate a fanatic in lawn sleeves,' and Tillotson
replied, less loudly, 'and I hate a knave in any sleeves'.

The appointment of the Archbishop was less important to the King
than the attempt to leave the Queen, in this her second summer on her
own, with an administration trustworthy and efficient enough to keep
the wheels of government in motion. William always favoured the idea
of working with a coalition made up of the more moderate men of both
parties, but the English political system being what it was, he might have
done better to throw in his lot with the party which had a parliamentary
majority. In trying to please both sides, he often ended by offending both.
On the night after his arrival in England, the King went to an informal
dinner given by Montagu at which many important men were present.
Looking round at the paucity of talent available, the King could hardly
feel optimistic. There were some men of ability it is true, but whether
they were trustworthy or not was another matter.

A few days later the King lunched with Rochester, a sign that he was
hopeful of persuading more High Churchmen to join the administration.
Afterwards he went down to Hampton Court to view the works and to
discuss the placing of the Raphael cartoons. His time was limited; where-
ever he went his visits were short, and when he went back to Holland he
had made no progress in his attempt to consolidate the administration.
There had been strong rumours that Sunderland would be called back,
for that Lord when in exile had renounced all Catholic leanings and all
connection with his old master. William knew him to be a King's man, who
could adapt his ideas to suit the monarch in power, and he also knew that
Sunderland would always owe him a debt of gratitude. Lady Sunderland,
pining away in sordid surroundings in Rotterdam, had feared that she
would never see their home at Althorp again, but they were back there
now, and it would be difficult for them to forget the mercy the King had
shown. But Sunderland was not ready yet; he knew that he was still
unpopular, and he thought the King had not given enough care and
thought to the lesser government appointments. So he did not answer the
summons, and Rochester also failed to respond to any overtures. The King
had no option but to leave the Queen with virtually the same Council as

before. She still had Nottingham, whom they had both come increasingly to like and respect, and Lady Nottingham had been appointed to the Queen's Bedchamber. Sidney had become the second Secretary of State, and Godolphin was reinstated at the Treasury. Marlborough and Monmouth were omitted from the Council, their places being taken by Godolphin and Prince George of Denmark, and as far as the Queen was concerned, they were no loss.

The days went by all too quickly. As the end of the visit drew nearer, the Queen implored God to support her as he had so often done in the post. Two days before the King left, on April 29 which was a fast day, William and Mary attended a service at Whitehall and heard one of Burnet's most eloquent sermons, in which he brooded on the vanity and wickedness of the age. 'That small but much boasted earnest of burning upon our coast last year,' thundered the Bishop

was the true sample of what we may then look for; wasting and destruction must walk over the land as a flood sweeping all before it. And as we have no defended cities, nor passes to stop the fury of our enraged enemies if they can but once break in upon us, so the interest they have to make this nation a heap of ruins . . . and the fury of their priests, the outrageousness of their soldiery, and above all the barbarity of their counsels that direct them give us the certainest grounds of apprehending bitter destruction.

These were hardly comforting words for a woman who was about to be abandoned by her husband and to be left in charge of the country in question.

William left England from Harwich, and Mary went with him to the coast. As they had had so little opportunity to discuss political affairs, he made her dry her tears so that he could talk to her of 'necessary business'. Among other things he told her that her sister's husband, Prince George, had become embarrassingly patriotic; this would not have mattered if he had been gifted with qualities of leadership and military acumen, but unfortunately he was as stupid as he was willing. His latest whim was to set off for Portsmouth with all his luggage; if his brother-in-law would not grant him a suitable military command, then, he declared, he would serve his wife's country as a humble naval officer. This, of course, was impossible, and William left his wife with the disagreeable task of telling the bucolic Prince that he must curb his enthusiasm and accept his limitations.

After William's departure, Mary spent two or three days at Kensington preparing for the Sacrament 'and indeed for the worst accident that might happen'. Sidney accompanied the King to the Hague and reported that they had a quick and pleasant voyage during which William 'was not in the least indisposed'. Preparations for the ensuing campaign were well forward, and it was thought that the King would be ready to take the field in Flanders again very soon. He was able to snatch a few days hunting at Loo, in the bitter spring weather, against the advice of his doctors. Had she known this, the Queen would have been more worried than ever; continual rumours of Jacobite plots and French invasion made Burnet's picture of wasting and destruction seem all too realistic. She tried to keep her fears to herself, but she was by now feeling thoroughly frightened, as her memoirs show:

I looked over all my meditations, and burnt most of them, fearing they might fall into hands I did not like. The journals I had kept, I put in a bag and tied by my side resolving if anything happened to have them ready to burn. I prayed constantly and heartily, and committed myself to God as into the hands of a faithful creator, and so went about my business thinking so long as I was careful to do my duty to God and man, I might rest satisfied that whatever happened to my body my soul would be happy; and thus I hasted to Whitehall, being so foolish as to fancy myself securer there than here, or at last thinking whatever happened I should have more company to suffer with me.

The Jacobite menace was made all the more terrifying on account of the fact that many people were convinced the Denmark household was becoming a focus of Jacobite opposition to the government. The very idea that her own sister could be involved in such matters upset the Queen. Some people were even suggesting that Prince George's apparently unpremeditated desire to go to sea without asking the King's permission was part of a deep-laid scheme to gain popularity for his wife and the Jacobites.

In accordance with the King's instructions, the Queen did her best to prevent Prince George from carrying out his noble, if misguided, intentions. If Lady Marlborough is to be believed, the Queen sent a 'great Lord', not to her sister, but to the lady in waiting, asking her to intercede with the Princess. Prince George, after all the 'noise' that had by now been made, thought he would look ridicuolus if he suddenly removed his luggage from the ship where he had so inadvisedly put it, and the Queen was forced to send Nottingham with a positive order, which, she thought, 'was desired by them as much as avoided by me, that they might have a pretence to rail, and so in discontent go to Tunbridge'.

After this outbreak the Queen and the Princess managed for a while to live on more or less friendly terms, but Anne was blind to her husband's limitations and she would have been happy to see him as supreme commander of the army or the navy, it did not much matter which. William, on the other hand, had no illusions about the Prince, who indeed was remarkable in little except his ability to absorb liquor. When George had joined the Irish expedition uninvited, William had snubbed him mercilessly. By rank the Prince was entitled to travel in the King's coach, but this would have been more than William could stand. He had no room for a heavy-weight when he was engaged in a busy campaign, and he simply left the Prince to fend for himself. 'The King never took more notice of him than if he had been a page of the backstairs nor he was never once named in any gazette, though I am apt to think the bullet that so kindly kissed the King's shoulder was as near to his Royal Highness,' wrote Sarah Marlborough in one of her unpublished versions of the *Conduct*. William was bored by his heavy in-laws, and he was only too aware that they were steered by Marlborough's practised hand. Princess Anne returned her brother-in-law's dislike in full measure. There was that famous occasion when she had sat by with her mouth watering while William devoured the entire helping of green peas at dinner, and there were other examples of his boorishness. Besides, it was delicious for the Princess and her set to while away the hours exchanging stories about the hated 'Dutch abortion' or 'Mr Caliban' as they were pleased to call him, and to feel as they were doing so that they were contributing to their country's well-being.

The great point of discussion in the town was whether Sancroft would ever move out of the Palace at Lambeth. Encouraged by the Marlboroughs, Compton now went into open opposition, and although he continued to preach at Whitehall on occasions, he never went to court. If circumstances and the intricacies of ecclesiastical preferment had not made it impossible, the Queen and the Bishop might have had some pleasant discussion arising out of their mutual love of gardening and exotic plants, for Compton had been called 'the Maecenas of Botany' and the famous George London had remodelled his garden at Lambeth. They were never to have any discourse again—neither about Anglican dogma nor about jasmines, myrtles or oleanders.

Tillotson was giving great thought and care to the question of the vacant Bishoprics, which he was determined to fill with moderate clerics like himself. But his task was to prove more difficult than he had envisaged, for those he nominated were hesitant of filling places vacated by nonjurors. Dr Beveridge had been chosen for Bath and Wells, but Sancroft advised him to say '*nolo*, and say it from the heart'. Dr Ken, who had been put out, was known to be well loved in his diocese, and trouble threatened, but Kidder was told to fill the place at once, without argument.

Before his departure, William had written to Ginckel, the large, good-humoured Dutchman he had put in charge in Ireland, assuring him of his complete trust and confidence. Ginckel's task was to complete the campaign left unfinished the previous autumn, and in particular to reduce the garrisons of Limerick, Athlone and Galway. His likeable temperament made him popular with the troops, and the King's only fear was that he might prove too gentle. He advised him to act with more severity than he normally would. 'You know what sort of people you have to deal with,' he wrote, 'people who do not wish to be governed by gentleness.' Ginckel was only too anxious to attack, but his army was in a poor condition, his soldiers without pay and on the verge of mutiny. The Queen knew that the Treasury was almost empty; the supplies that Parliament had so meekly granted in the autumn were not adequate for a campaign in Ireland as well as in Flanders. It was difficult to persuade enough officers to go to Ireland, and in any case there was no money to pay their expenses. Russell, who was now in charge of the fleet, was becoming increasingly suspect; his Jacobite leanings were no secret, and the Queen was convinced that it was due to his deliberate negligence that the French had been able to land reinforcements in Ireland. In early May, Nottingham received a letter from Ginckel, asking whether he should proceed into action, a difficult decision for the bewildered Queen, but she sent this reply, giving him the authority to proceed if he felt that he was in a position to do so:

We have considered your letter to our Secretary of State of the 2nd May and do think it of great importance to our service to make some speedy attempt upon the enemy and we approve of your proposal to begin with the siege of Athlone, but not knowing the condition of our army so exactly as you do, we cannot judge of the success of such an enterprise so well as yourselves and therefore do leave it to your discretion, with this assurance that we do not doubt of your zeal for our service and therefore shall be satisfied with that resolution which upon mature consideration you shall think most expedient. And that you may the better judge whether the siege of Athlone should be hastened or delayed or any other matter may or proper to be attempted, we have ordered our Secretary at War to transmit to you the state of all the preparations designed for Ireland by which you may make some probable conjecture when you may expect them there. Given at our Court at Whitehall this 8th day of May 1691 in the 3rd year of our reign.

M.R.

Ginckel could now attack when he felt it advisable, but he was still agitating for supplies, and on May 18 wrote to Nottingham from Dublin Castle, one of a series of desperate letters on this topic: 'The army had long since taken the field if arms, clothes, recruits, and horses had been here ... Above all the want of money is what presses us.'

By the end of the month reinforcements had arrived, and on July 30 Athlone was taken by storm; the guns of London thundered out when the news of the victory came through.

The Queen despatched Godolphin to tell William the good news and wrote Ginckel a letter in her own hand, congratulating him on the happy success it had pleased God to give him in Athlone. 'As for me,' she wrote, 'I understand so little of this kind of affair that I can only tell you that the praise which you give to the officers in particular and the soldiers in general, makes me hope that the good God continues to bless those who do their duty so well, and in this way will soon finish the war. When I see you here, I will thank you in person, and meanwhile I assure you, Monsieur, that I will never forget what you have done—Marie R.' So recently there had seemed to be little chance of success in Ireland, and now, as the Queen put it, 'the messengers of good news came almost as quick as Job's did with ill, till by the reduction of Limerick the whole kingdom was subdued'. William's choice of Ginckel was more than justified by his succession of victories. 'I have never doubted his good behaviour, any more than his loyalty,' the Queen told Mlle Obdam. She asked her friend to congratulate Ginckel's mother and sister who had just arrived at the Hague from the family seat at Ameroongen; 'If they were to know how much M. Ginckel is loved where he is, that will give them great pleasure,' she added.

Elsewhere, operations were progressing less satisfactorily. In Flanders and at sea, the French amused themselves and tantalized their enemies by refusing to go into action. Russell had not as yet been given a chance to prove his loyalty, for he had not been vouchsafed so much as a glimpse of the French fleet. In desperation he went over to the French coast to look for it, and ran into a storm which, as the Queen put it, 'might have been fatal, had not the same Providence preserved the fleet, which has still watched over us, and that in small as well as great things, so that I can never enough praise my God for it'. In Flanders it was the same story, of marches and counter-marches, a few skirmishes, but never the large-scale battle which might have affected the outcome of the war. William found the stalemate infuriating; he was eager for action, and did all he could to court danger. He had, it seemed, learned nothing from the missile which had 'so kindly kissed' his shoulder in Ireland, though as the summer went on there were continual rumours of attempts on his life. A further anxiety was the fear of a descent on Scotland, or even England, during his absence, and this seemed such a real danger to William that he went so far as to borrow £200,000 in Amsterdam on his personal credit, in order to be able to pay the troops on the continent if cut off by a French descent on England.

As soon as William left, the usual problems began to arise, some trivial, some of great importance. Towards the end of May the Queen received a visit from the Spanish Ambassador, Ronquillo, who had risen from a bed of sickness and struggled three miles to Whitehall to lodge a complaint. One of his servants, it seemed, was indebted to an Irishman, but the Ambassador claimed diplomatic immunity for him, and was angered when the Privy Council in general, and Nottingham in particular, refused to let him go free, as the Irishman was thought to be in league with the Jacobite cabal. Ronquillo was so incensed that he was crying with rage, but the Queen greeted him sympathetically and he was very impressed with her winning manner.

The Queen found plenty of domestic matters to attend to; there were appointments and warrants, and requests such as the one she addressed to the Wardens of New College and Winchester to admit a child in whom she was interested. She recommended a Master for an Oxford College and wrote a letter to the Vice-Chancellor of the University with a rather different request:

Whereas some of the company of comedians have humbly besought us to recommend them to you for permission to act in our university . . . we being pleased to grant their request, have thought fit to recommend it to you, to permit the said comedians to act there with such liberty as they formerly enjoyed.

In his sermon of April 29 Burnet had remarked:

by the prodigality and luxury, the gaming, the playhouses, and the other extravagant expenses that are still among us one would conclude that men are not much pinched, when there is so much left for vanity and pleasure. A moderate frugality would do more than pay for their taxes.

The Queen was in complete agreement with this observation. She had from the first felt appalled by the immoral lives of her countrymen which compared so unfavourably with the frugal and godly existence of the Dutch. Tillotson was of the same mind, and although in the summer months he was busy with improvements at Lambeth, where he was building a large new apartment to house his wife, as well as doing many repairs and altering the windows, he began to take an active interest in the Queen's campaign for moral improvements as soon as he had moved from the Deanery of St Paul's into his new residence. He was extremely pleased to find the Queen 'incessantly employed in possessing her mind with the best schemes, that were either laid before her by others, or suggested by her own thoughts, for correcting everything, which was amiss, and improving everything, that wanted finishing'. On July 9 she issued directions to the magistrates, reminding them that it was their duty to execute the laws against drunkenness. This declaration set the pattern of the English Sunday for many years; foreigners from Catholic countries were to complain about the dreariness of a day on which no music was played, no hackney coaches were allowed to run, and the constables were ordered to take away pies and puddings from anybody they met carrying such un-sabbatical objects in the streets. The new Archbishop suggested to the Queen, who readily agreed, that Burnet should be engaged to write a tract 'to prepare the scene for many noble designs for the perfecting of our ecclesiastical constitution'. Burnet set to work at once, but it was not until the following spring that his masterly *Discourse of the Pastoral Care* was ready for publication.

The Queen saw to it that her own household was not immune. The officers of the Guards were told that it was 'Her Royal Pleasure that they strictly enjoin all the soldiers under them to refrain from swearing and drunkenness'. She was also known to 'mulct' those who failed to attend church services. It was observed that, after the issue of the declaration, the churches were certainly, for a few weeks at any rate, far fuller than usual, but it was also noted that the excise was bound to suffer, as people generally drank more on a Sunday than any other day—'but never mind,' wrote one commentator, 'the Queen has done well.' The more cynical were inclined to believe that it was an 'outward' reformation only, and that it could be carried too far. The Queen was persuaded to extend the time of the Bartholomew Fair which had been cut down to prevent 'lewdness', and some over-zealous informers brought the whole movement for reform into disrepute. All the same, a number of societies were formed as a result of the Queen's lead, which helped to put right many abuses, and gave help to the poor and the sick.

Although the Queen did not suffer the acute fear of imminent invasion which had troubled her the previous summer, she still had to face many worrying decisions; should she, for example, send a squadron to guard the mouth of the Shannon? She was as anxious as ever about William's safety, and she still had to undergo all the tedious formalities of court life and the endless requests of importunate place-hunters. She became increasingly afflicted with sleeplessness as the summer went on, and the nights seemed unbearably hot. 'You are very much in the right to believe I have cause enough to think this life not so fine a thing as it may be others do,' she confessed to Lady Russell. 'But I see,' she added, 'one is not ever to live for one's self. I have had many years of ease and content, and was not so sensible of my own happiness as I ought, till I lost it.'

One day in June Lord Preston came to Whitehall. He publicly kissed the Queen's hand, and thanked her profusely for the mercy she had shown him. The courtiers were interested to meet the man they had not expected to see again, except on the scaffold. His appearance, for the Queen, aroused unhappy memories of Ashton, who had gone to his death for crimes of lesser importance than Preston's.

The Queen was seeing less of Shrewsbury than before, for he still declined to take any responsible part in State affairs, but she was on good terms with Godolphin who had to a certain extent taken Shrewsbury's place. On one occasion he talked to her for half an hour, though they were surrounded by hundreds of people, and it was noticed that he laughed two or three times, in his case a very rare occurrence. She had struck up a real friendship at last with one of her Ladies, Lady Dorset, and she also liked Lady Nottingham very well. But this summer, Lady Dorset died, to her great sorrow, leaving an infant son, Lord Buckhurst, who was put in the care of his grandmother, the Dowager Lady Northampton. He was frequently brought to Kensington, and the Queen took a great interest in his development. She also had a fondness for the Bentinck children, who had grown up attractive and well-behaved. Portland's son was particularly lovable, and so good-looking that although he was so young, he was allowed to carry the Sword of State in front of the Queen when she came ceremonially from church. He carried it with such confidence that he might have been doing it all his life, and 'the Queen laughed heartily when she saw him'.

The Queen tried to appreciate all God's mercies; after the victories in Ireland she poured out her soul in thanksgiving—'What thanks must I give, oh my soul, to your Lord for all his goodness!' But she found it impossible to overcome her melancholy. To Mlle Obdam she confessed that it was not only pressure of affairs which prevented her from writing, but also certain *inquiétudes* which she was unable to master. 'Since you have so much tenderness for your friends, it will not be difficult to persuade you that when one is full of pain for those one loves, it is not easy to do what one wants.' But she was able to escape to Kensington for a few days of fresh air and greater leisure, where she found the opportunity to write to her friends. Her mind was too tortured and her body too tired for her to spend those quiet days in early August in a spirit of resignation.

In moments of anxiety and exhaustion, old griefs, long-buried, often come to the surface. It had taken her many years to accept the fact of her childlessness, and now, in her loneliness, she felt the longings which she had so resolutely pushed to the back of her mind. All at once she found herself repeating the words of the angel to Zacharias: *Thy prayer is granted and thy wife Elizabeth will bring forth a son.* Once again her reason had to wrestle with her emotion. 'Why art thou so troubled, O my soul?' she asked. The Lord is just, she told herself:

Although I have been married nearly thirteen years I know that the Lord can give me one or several if he finds it *à propos*, and meanwhile I must have patience, I must even consider that humanly speaking there is no appearance and that I should be blessed indeed after such a long sterility.

She went on to remind herself that it would have been almost unbearable to have been in constant anxiety on account of her children, as well as being ceaselessly concerned for the safety of her husband. It was for this reason, in all probability, that God had denied her children. 'Learn to resign thyself more to the will of God,' she wrote, with severity, though she was forced to add, 'Alas! that is said so easily, but not so easily done!' The letters she received from William gave her little comfort, for she could see that he was chafing at the inactivity in Flanders.

September came, and no battle had been fought. It was time for the armies to go into winter quarters. Another summer campaign was over, and the King was safe. He went to Loo for a few days' hunting, and then on to Dieren. In Ireland the war was over; Limerick, the last of the enemy strongholds, had fallen. Even so, there was still need for vigilance at sea, and on October 17 the Queen sent instructions to vice-Admiral Callenburgh to join Sir Ralph Delaval at Torbay or Plymouth, in order to ensure that the fleet, would be strong enough to oppose the French once the Dutch men-of-war, not designed for winter service, had gone home. She had to write a friendly letter to Sophia of Hanover who was playing a double game at this time, much to the delight of James, who congratulated her on withdrawing troops from the confederates, and expressed the hope that other Princes would follow suit and would no longer 'contribute to support the vampire who had brought nothing but ruin and desolation over all Christendom'.

In October the news that Limerick had fallen began to circulate 'among the gentlemen who went out into the park twice a day to hear all the news'. The official notification was brought by Ginckel's son, who arrived one evening as the Queen was playing bassett. The good news was passed on to William, whose return everyone was impatiently awaiting. On October

19 he sailed swiftly across in twenty-four hours with a favourable wind, arriving at seven o'clock on Sunday at Margate. His guards and retinue had gone to Harwich to meet him, expecting him to land there, and so he was obliged to rely on the local gentry for transport, and the country people for an escort. A gentleman's coachman turned over the vehicle in which the King was travelling with Portland, Marlborough and Over-kirk. Portland's ample weight landed on top of the King, who suffered a bruised arm which he bore without complaint. In the mêlée Marlborough cried out that his neck was broken, but the King dryly remarked there was little danger of that, in view of the fact that he was able to speak.

The party arrived in London late in the evening; bells were ringing, guns firing, bonfires blazing and candles flickering in every window. Although the King had come back without a marked victory to boast about, he at least had not suffered a defeat, and the London mob made this an excuse for rejoicing. A crowd followed his coach, and those who had already gone to bed leaned out of windows in their nightclothes to cheer him on his way. At last he reached Whitehall, and when his coach stopped at the Palace, he asked if the Queen was inside. The courtiers who were waiting to help him from his coach assured him that she was there and had been waiting for a long time. William went in at once and walked quickly past all those who were lined up hoping to 'wear out his hand with kisses'. He reached the Queen's apartments, and when he saw his wife, he kissed her twice in front of all her Ladies, and although it was past midnight, took her off to Kensington, where supper was waiting.

CHAPTER 27

THE QUARREL

'ALL MY FEARS AND TROUBLES vanished by the King's return on the 19th October being Monday,' the Queen wrote in her memoirs. 'I was truly thankful to my God for that new mercy, and must not forget to observe how kind the King is, how much more of his company I have had since he came home this time, than I used to have.' William became involved with affairs of State as soon as he came back, but the Queen's responsibilities were lifted from her shoulders overnight, and her health was restored at once.

All through the summer the joiners had been busy at Kensington, with the wainscots, the 'shashes' and shutters, the shelves and picture frames. The well-proportioned wooden staircase to the Queen's apartments was now finished, and the walls were clad with oak panelling of a deep warm reddish tone, the wood probably imported from Norway and specially cut to show off the pattern of the grain. For the Queen's Gallery, Wren had designed a chimney piece in marble veined with blue-grey, but in general the interior designing had been given over to the carvers, to Grinling Gibbons, William Emmett and an assistant, Nicholas Alcock. Now the house was free of workmen and the sound of hammers, and the Queen could arrange and rearrange the furniture and plan her collection of books, prints and porcelain.

The King's first day at home was more exhausting than any he had spent during the campaign. He went to Whitehall for a meeting of the Privy Council and then on to the opening of Parliament, where he gave a *belle harangue*, requesting large subsidies for the army and navy and to pay arrears in Ireland. At the Lord Mayor's Show he appeared on the balcony at Whitehall, and large crowds waited to see him. The river was so full of boats that the barges of the Corporations which followed the Lord Mayor had great difficulty in positioning themselves under the balcony where they made 'their discharges of cannon and their acclamations'.

In mid-November a ball was held to celebrate the King's birthday and his safe return. The drapers said that they had not known such an increase in trade for over thirty years, and, with all the ladies in their new dresses, the occasion was splendid if a trifle crushed.

'But of how little continuance are all worldly contentments,' the Queen reflected as those few weeks of happiness passed quickly by. The King's health soon declined in the damp air of London, and before the month was out she had been punished for her house-proudness. The fire at Whitehall she told herself, should have shown her the vanity of precious possessions. It might also have warned her against the folly of leaving them unprotected. In Holland, the King had seen to it that all his property was looked after by a firm which specialized in fire-fighting equipment and which had evolved a water-pump of its own design. But in England the attitude to fire was more casual, and no ladders, pumps or fire buckets had as yet been installed at Kensington.

At three-thirty on the morning of November 13, the King and Queen were woken by several musket shots. The King, who was perhaps less impervious to threats on his life than he liked to make out, immediately seized his sword, and the Queen was alarmed and said something about treason. The King smiled, 'cheered her Majesty up' and was preparing to go back to sleep again when the Earl of Essex, first gentleman of the Bedchamber, rushed into the room saying that fire had broken out in the south wing of the Palace. The King looked out and decided that the fire was not likely to be serious providing it was dealt with at once. Having said this he discovered that the nearest pumps and ladders were at Whitehall.

He told the Queen to dress and they went out into the garden. The fire, which had broken out in a servant's room, was affecting the apartments of Devonshire and Dorset, who were not in residence at the time. Portland was sent to Whitehall to wake people there and to ask for help, but it was six hours before water and the machine arrived. Fortunately the new road through the Park, well lighted to deter footpads, was now completed, otherwise help would have taken even longer to arrive. Soon a crowd began to gather, and indeed the whole scene seemed a strange sight to the onlookers. A touch of fog added to the weirdness of the spectacle, with a King and a Queen standing in the garden in dishabille, ladies in waiting *en chemise* rushing about in a state of panic, and all the valuable furniture, pictures and porcelain arranged neatly on the path.

The carriages which arrived from Whitehall for the King and Queen were sent back again. By eight in the morning the Foot Guards, with a crowd of willing helpers, had succeeded in putting out the fire, and by noon the King and Queen were back in residence. Although all the porcelain had been taken out into the garden, nothing was broken. Much of the south wing had been burnt down but nobody had been hurt and nothing of value damaged, so there was plenty to be thankful for, and much to enjoy in retrospect. People said they had never seen the King and Queen laugh so much as they recounted the events of the night, recalling the ladies running about in their nightgowns, and the Dutch cheeses laid out on the grass, all seen by the light of flames and torches. 'This had truly I hope, weaned me from the vanities I was most fond of, that is ease and good lodgings,' wrote the Queen in a more serious vein.

A few days after the fire, the King and Queen went down to Hampton Court. The treadways in the new building had been made good for them to walk on as they inspected the work. The main block was now well advanced, and Emmett had already carved in Portland stone six of the round windows in the Fountain Court, which were ornamented with lions' skins, laurels and berries bound with a fillet. Caius Cibber, Emmett and Grinling Gibbons were all working at the Palace and had completed an impressive amount of work between them, and the masons were busy on the outside of the building, fixing in position the trophies and festoons, the coats of arms, crowns and cyphers. In the archways of the Fountain Court cloisters were forty-six carvings, with all the familiar Gibbons motifs, flower baskets and cornucopiae, peapods and acanthus, cherubs and trumpets. Cibber was responsible for the 'great frontispiece with iconographical figures' on the east front. Inside the house Gibbons was busy with his magnificent door frames, and, urged on by the Queen, was drawing innumerable designs each one becoming more fantastic than the last, to display tier upon tier of fine porcelain. William may have felt she was going too far with some of these, for many of them never went beyond the drawing and none was made except in a toned-down version.

The garden, too, was progressing well. Marot had designed the great fountain garden with its thirteen fountains, and the King himself helped to work out the system of pipes and canals which was to feed them, estimating the dimensions of the *jets d'eaux* and how much water they would throw up. The English were on the whole impressed by Marot's parterres with their 'fine scrolls and brodure', though Switzer thought the gardens were 'stuffed too thick with box' and would have preferred to see more use made of good English grass and gravel. Princess Anne was evidently of the same opinion for as soon as she became Queen she rooted out all the box; she said she did not like the smell.

The Queen had not only acquired a taste for porcelain during the Dutch years; she had also developed a great interest in flowers of all kinds and particularly exotic plants. Dr Plunket, a distinguished herbalist, was appointed her head gardener at a salary of £200 a year, and he shared her enthusiasm for tropical exotics. So greenhouses were constructed with stoves under them to keep up a continual heat, and Plunket succeeded in raising exotics from seed in the hothouses and the old melon ground which was situated between the Tennis Court and the old moat. A gardener was sent to Virginia to make a collection of plants—his expenses came to £234 11s 9d—and two more were despatched to the Canary Islands. Some of these plants were still alive two centuries later, for example the Agave *americana variegata*, which according to Law in 1889 suddenly grew sixteen feet and burst into thousands of yellow flowers all dripping nectar, having never bloomed before within living memory. Besides these plants, the Queen specialized in orange trees, which had for her a political and emotional meaning. The catalogue of her collection mentions such exotic trees and shrubs as mangoes, jasmine, Java bean-trees, dogwood of Jamaica, cinnamon from Barbados, the perfuming cherry of Arabia and a silver lotus, as well as a crystal rose, *Acacia gloriosa* and apples of love. Orange-trees were brought over from Loo and two thousand gelders' worth of plants had been ordered from Holland that June—laurels, yew-trees and bulbs—for Hampton Court and Kensington.

Pearce and Cibber designed great 'vauzes' in white marble, more magnificent even than the urns in the gardens at Loo and certainly more expensive, for they cost anything from two hundred to five hundred pounds. Defoe was greatly impressed by two which he said were of ex-quisite workmanship; he believed that Pearce and Cibber had carried them out as 'a kind of trial of skill between them', and he thought they managed to prove, if nothing else, that they were both masters of the art.

The Water Gallery was now virtually finished, and Kneller had been busy painting the Beauties, chosen, so most people thought, for their good morals rather than their ravishing appearance. The finished pictures were nothing like as enchanting as Lely's roomful of less virtuous ladies; all the same, the portraits were much admired at the time, and Kneller was knighted for his pains; he also received a medal and a chain worth £300. 'Pray, Madam,' Catherine Sedley was reputed to have enquired of the Queen, 'were his Majesty to order portraits of all the clever men in his dominions, would not the rest consider themselves treated as blockheads?'

The autumn was fine and warm, without frosts, 'like a new spring', Evelyn observed. Once again the relief of having William home unharmed brought the Queen great happiness, and he was particularly kind and considerate at this time. But it had become an accepted fact that as long as the war continued he would have to divide his time between England and Flanders. Once the welcoming formalities were over he turned his mind at once towards obtaining supplies for the following spring, and did his best to ensure that the Queen would be left with an efficient and harmonious Council during his absence. He was pleased with the way she had managed affairs during the previous summer; she had worked well with Nottingham, and had behaved with the right mixture of firmness and malleability. The politicians had learnt, during the summer of the Irish campaign, that the Queen was more than a figurehead; she was sure in her own mind of the difference between right and wrong, and she had an eye for hypocrisy and greedy ambition in others. She was also sternly loyal to her husband, and, being gifted with humility, she was well aware of her own limitations. Given an administration of moderate men she could hold the reins of government well in William's absence, with only a light pull on the snaffle from time to time. But Carmarthen's coalition of men of the centre was becoming increasingly impracticable. Dominant characters in both parties were clamouring for admission. 'Good God!' exclaimed Archbishop Sharp in his lengthy Christmas sermon at Whitehall, 'whither will interest and zeal for a party transport a man!' For the King, this was more than a rhetorical question. Tory zeal, if driven to extremes, could transport a man straight into the arms of the Jacobites, and a discontented Whig was only one step away from the conclusion that Kings and Queens as a race were expendable. Of the two alternatives, William on the whole preferred the former, but where possible he shunned violent men of either party. There were plenty of trouble-makers in Parliament that session, and there were some eloquent opposition speeches, but somehow the money was voted. The King could still, with an effort, command the support of Parliament, but his administration was weak and lacking in men of talent. As for the Whigs and Tories, it was remarked that it would be more difficult to make a peace between them than it would to make one with the Turks.

'This year began,' wrote the Queen at the beginning of 1692, 'with family troubles of mine; where they will end God only knows.' From all sides she was hearing bad reports of her sister's behaviour. It was thought that Anne had by now made her peace with James, having written to him requesting forgiveness. Lady Fitzharding often went to the Princess's drawing-room at this time, and took back reports of the conversations being carried on there by the indiscreet Lady Marlborough—'*cet ingrat*' as one observer called her (one hopes that the masculine gender was not inten-

tional). Elizabeth Villiers, who had served William before in the capacity
of a society spy, now did him some further service, in this, if in no other
respect.

Throughout the year Jacobite agents had been busy sounding out many
influential men and stirring up latent sympathy for the deposed monarch.
Though on the surface men like Godolphin were 'shy', they were often
not above admitting that they would like to crave James's forgiveness.
This was considered a wise precaution in view of the instability of the
times, and the not altogether remote possibility that William, in his turn,
might vanish from the scene. Marlborough was among those who certainly communicated with Saint-Germain that year. He was not alone;
there were others, including the level-headed Godolphin, and Russell,
who felt that he was not receiving his due reward for the part his family
had played in the Revolution. But of all those who kept in touch with
Saint-Germain, Marlborough was the most dangerous. His wife's sister
was Tyrconnel's widow, and it was easy for him to communicate with
Saint-Germain through her. It was suspected that in one of several
letters he had written to the exiled King in 1691 he had promised to bring
Anne 'back to her duty'. There is little doubt that the Marlboroughs had
infected the Princess with their discontent. Marlborough had coveted the
command in Ireland which had been given to Ginckel; he had expected
to receive the Garter and a cherished and well-paid post as Master-
General of the Ordnance, but was denied these honours which in his
opinion were due to the conqueror of Kinsale. 'I cannot believe anybody
will be so unreasonable to be dissatisfied when it is known you are pleased
to give it him on the Prince's account and mine,' the Princess had written
the previous August. But the King was not a man to welcome pressure
being exerted by a female relation, and the association with the Denmarks
did nothing to increase his love for Marlborough. In any case the King's
fear of the man went far deeper; he knew that his whole position rested on
the fact that he himself was in real command of the land forces. For his
commander-in-chief he must have a man whom he could trust absolutely.
He could afford to ignore Jacobite leanings in others, but not in his General.
John Marlborough had turned traitor once, in 1688, and William had no
intention of giving him the chance to lead the army back to James again.
His military ability was not in question; he had already risen rapidly to a
position of power, and, given the chance to prove his skill and loyalty a
little further, would undoubtedly become supreme commander in the
fullness of time. But he was ambitious, and fond of financial gain; he did
not want to wait, and he was jealous of Ginckel. The King knew that he

was inciting the English to complain about the promotion of Dutch officers in the English forces.

As more detached commentators than the Marlboroughs themselves have noted, William did not have to look far to find excuses for refusing Marlborough's request to be put in command of the English army in Flanders. There were other Englishmen who had a good claim, Tollemache for example, or the Duke of Ormonde, son of the much-lamented Ossory. The King was inclined to trust men who had served as officers in the Dutch regiments before the Revolution, and Marlborough was not one of these. He also lacked noble birth, which was important in the European context, where princely commanders did not readily confer with commoners. Ginckel was more experienced than Marlborough and had acquitted himself well in Ireland. There were other familiar names—Solms, Overkirk, Nassau, Waldeck—which could not be easily overlooked.

The King could reasonably refuse Marlborough's demand, but when he dismissed him, suddenly, and without explanation, this naturally caused talk and speculation. One morning in January, Marlborough, as Gentleman of the Bedchamber, handed the King his shirt according to the usual routine. Only a few hours later, having received a letter to this effect, delivered by Nottingham, Marlborough learnt that his military career was at an end. He was ordered to sell all his offices and to keep away from Court.

The King's action was understandable, but its suddenness was not. There was a theory that William had been handed an intercepted letter which proved that Marlborough was sending secret information to the French. The reasons were probably far more complex than this and it may have been that William feared an immediate *coup*, and knew that any delay or rumour of his impending dismissal might have given Marlborough time to mobilize his forces. Unfortunately the Queen tried to make use of this opportunity to free her sister from the bad influence of Sarah Marlborough. But Anne could be stubborn when she chose and the Queen was not the last person to be angered by her obstinate refusals. She frankly refused to part with Lady Marlborough, the Queen lost her temper and an undignified argument ensued. The elder sister taxed the younger with the fact that she had given Lady Marlborough an annuity of £1,000 from her parliamentary grant, and insinuated that public money should not be spent on subsidizing the wife of a man suspected of treachery.

This distressing scene took place on the night before Marlborough was dismissed. The two sisters were not alone at the time, and the news that they had quarrelled was soon about the town. Unhappily for the

King, Marlborough's dismissal was seen by the uninitiated as the consequence rather than the cause of this family fracas. It was easy, after this,
for the Princess to attract sympathy, for inevitably she was pregnant and
the Queen's behaviour was seen as a cruel attack by a jealous woman
hoping that her sister would suffer a miscarriage. When, a few weeks later,
the Princess appeared at court with Lady Marlborough ostentatiously
in tow, the courtiers watched closely to see what would happen; but
disappointingly there was no public scene. The Queen waited until the next
day, which was February 5, before she wrote this firm letter to her sister:

Having something to say to you, which I know will not be very pleasing, I
choose rather to write it first, being unwilling to surprise you; though I think
what I am going to tell you, should not, if you give yourself the time to think,
that never anybody was suffered to live at court in my Lord Marlborough's
circumstances. I need not repeat the cause he has given the King to do what he
has done, nor his unwillingness at all times to come to such extremities, though
people do deserve it.

The Queen added that as Lady Marlborough had actually been brought
to Kensington the previous night, there was no alternative but 'to tell
you, she must not stay: and that I have all the reason imaginable to look
upon your bringing her, as the strangest thing that ever was done'. The
sight of Lady Marlborough had hardened her attitude, for up to that
moment she had hoped there might be some hope of a reconciliation, or
at least of a quiet talk. '[I] will always do my part to live with you as
sisters ought. That is, not only like so near relations, but like friends.' The
Queen intended to go herself to the Princess's drawing room the following
day, to find out whether, on reflection, her sister had changed her attitude.
'At some other time,' she added, 'we shall reason the business calmly:
which I will willingly do, or anything else that may show, it shall never be
my fault if we do not live kindly together.'

The Princess and her friend did not greatly care for the tone of this
letter. Lady Marlborough thought it was written as if it had been the
Queen's pleasure 'to remind her sister of the distance between them and
of what was due from the Princess of Denmark to the Queen of England'.
With Sarah no doubt at her elbow, Anne rushed to the writing-desk and
composed an answer which she asked Rochester to deliver. He refused to
handle such an inflammatory document, and it had to go by one of her
own servants. 'Your care of my present condition is extremely obliging,'
wrote the Princess. 'And if you would be pleased to add to it so far, as
upon my account to recall your severe command ... I should ever
acknowledge it as a very agreeable mark of your kindness to me. And I

must freely own, that as I think this proceeding can be for no other intent than to give me a very sensible mortification, so there is no misery that I cannot readily resolve to suffer, rather than the thoughts of parting with her.' This produced a curt message forbidding Lady Marlborough to stay at the Cockpit any longer, an unwise move on the Queen's part, for the King had no power to remove anybody from his sister-in-law's house, nor from any house on that side of the Park. Her lodgings had been settled on her and on her heirs by Charles II. She was being deprived, Lady Marlborough said, of the right she had in common with every other subject, 'of being mistress in her own house'.

Determined not to be defeated, the Princess asked the Duchess of Somerset if she could borrow Sion, her Richmond house. The Duke came later to tell the Princess 'in a very respectful manner, that Sion was at her service'. The King tried to dissuade the Duke, but, Sarah Marlborough was able to report triumphantly, 'his Grace had too much greatness of mind to go back from his promise; so there was an end of that matter'. Before leaving the Cockpit, Anne paid her sister a last visit, but the Queen remained distant—'as insensible as a statue'. The Princess persisted in her passionate attachment to her friend and showed the Queen nothing but indifference and coldness.

'In all this,' wrote the Queen, 'I see the hand of God, and look upon our disagreeing as a punishment upon us for the irregularity by us committed upon the Revolution.' It is impossible to pretend that the Queen was blameless. Family quarrels go deep, and she never mellowed towards her sister after the incident at Kensington. She visited her once more, when the Denmarks were still at Sion and Anne had just given birth to a dead child. Simple condolence was called for, but the Queen could not resist mentioning the subject of Lady Marlborough's dismissal to the bereft woman who had only just given birth. Anne was left white and trembling, and the sisters never met again. After this the King and Queen showed their disapproval in a number of petty ways. The Guards were removed from the Princess's household. She was no longer saluted. At St James's Church it had been customary for the Princess to find the text of the sermon on her cushion, and a decree went out that she should no longer do so. When she went to Bath, the mayor received official orders to avoid accompanying the Princess ceremonially to church. Seeing all this, people began to say that the Queen was devoid of natural feelings towards her relations; first she had driven her father out of the country and taken his throne for herself, and now she had turned her sister out of her lodgings and had cast her out of her life.

CHAPTER 28

LA HOGUE

WILLIAM left for Flanders early, at the beginning of March. It had been a cold season, with more people dying of apoplexy than usual. The King himself was in a poor state of health, his cough was bad, and just before he went he spat blood for a night and a day. The Queen parted with him sorrowfully. She was uneasy about his health and she knew that his absence was likely to be longer than ever. 'I had nothing to hope, much to fear,' she wrote.

As usual Mary took sanctuary in God, and as soon as William left she went to Whitehall for a course of devotion, being 'blessed with a more than ordinary fervour' in her preparations for the Sacrament at Easter. William had gone straight to Loo, and as long as he was there, she was happy, for she knew he was not in any immediate danger. On Easter Day, John Sharp, the Archbishop of York, preached a reassuring sermon:

Let us not faint. Let not our hearts be troubled; let us not despair of anything. *Our Saviour is risen.*

The threat of invasion soon became even more alarming than it had been two years before, and she knew that there were many 'dreadful designs' against herself. She met these with her usual courage. 'I am naturally extremely fearful,' she wrote, 'and now found, I had so much reason for it, that had I not been supported by God's special grace, I had died almost with the apprehensions.' She tried to put her trust implicitly in God, believing that she was ready to die if need be, secure in the knowledge that her husband would take care of the Church, and reminding herself that she had 'no children to be in pain for'.

Soon after Easter, the Queen was struck down with a feverish cold, and was so unwell that she felt unable to go to church on the Sunday—the first time she had missed a service since 1680. Tillotson went to visit her, taking a copy of Burnet's newly completed *Discourse of the Pastoral Care* for her to read. 'It would do anyone good,' he told Burnet, 'to see with what a grace and cheerfulness she plays off so great an illness. But

I hope the worst is over, and that God hath designed her for a long blessing to us.' Burnet had included a eulogy of the Queen but this, Tillotson reported, 'she will by no means allow; nor anything more than a bare dedication. She says, she knows you can use no moderation in speaking of her. So resolute and unaffected modesty I never saw'.

The Queen was anxious to announce a Fast day as soon as possible, for with William away, Louis was casting a greedy eye on the unprotected and Jacobite-infested island just across the Channel. His War Minister, Louvois, had always parried the idea of an invasion attempt, but Louvois was now dead. In England feeling was running high against the Dutch and against the King himself. Louis felt that his opportunity had come. He rallied the exiles, gathered up his fleet and assembled a large number of transports and store-ships in the Channel ports. Papers found on a French vessel in mid-April confirmed that the enemy was in earnest. 14,000 English and Irish with 3,000 French were to sail from Cherbourg and La Hogue, land in Sussex and then march with all haste for London. At the same time Louis intended to mount a strong attack in Flanders. He was feeling extremely confident, especially as Marlborough was at large and Russell, whose affinities were now doubtful, was in charge of the English fleet. The English intelligence system was so bad that nobody really took the possibility of an invasion seriously until mid-April, and, as Burnet put it, 'if the winds had favoured the French, they themselves would have brought us the first news of their design'. By good fortune, the winds were not favourable. It was a cold, late spring, not a leaf on the trees in late April, with a strong wind keeping the French in port. Fully awake to the danger at last, the English began to prepare for the invasion; the home fleet was assembled and Dutch reinforcements came over. The few troops available were sent to the coast.

Everyone was in a state of great alarm, and Proclamations were being read out all the time to secure dangerous Jacobites. Marlborough was among those who were taken up and sent to the Tower. The details of his supposed plot were found hidden in a flower pot in the house of the Bishop of Rochester.

The Queen had barely recovered from her illness and at the beginning of May she managed to snatch a few days' convalescence at Hampton Court. In the peace of the Thames Gallery she took the opportunity of writing a letter in answer to one of Mlle Obdam's of 'an ancient date'. The Queen assured her friend that 'a gazetteer like yourself brings me great pleasure'. Letters were the one link she had with the country she loved so much and she never tired of having news of it. In return she sent her

Dutch friends news of the expatriates in London. Ginckel, it seemed, had visited her in the new year, looking as plump as ever; nobody would think, to look at him, that he had just been through a strenuous campaign. 'I beg you to tell Madame his wife, that it is not my fault that he is not with her already.' And while they were on the subject of Ginckel, the Queen felt bound to observe that men were incapable of keeping their mouths shut; it was a fallacy to say that it was only women who were guilty of this fault, and here was an example of it—Ginckel himself had prattled to Mlle Obdam, reporting every word the Queen had said about her. As for Mlle Obdam, the Queen teased her gently: 'They tell me that you are working hard at your sewing, and that there are no young men around handsome enough to please you. What a change we have here! I pray you, don't change towards your friends in this way. All the time that I used to be at Dieren, I never saw you touch a needle once.' As she wrote this, so many memories came flooding into her mind that she felt unable to write any more; all she could do was to finish off the letter, enclosing another for her friend at Rosendaal. 'Between ourselves,' she concluded, 'I will say to you that I wish I was in that neighbourhood myself.'

Soon after her return to London, the Queen was presented with a list of dangerous people who were to be arrested. At the top she saw the name of her childhood friend, the Earl of Ailesbury. She told Nottingham that she thought his name should be omitted, since he had been through this two years before and all for nothing. Nottingham fell back on the usual expedient of saying that these were the King's orders. 'My Lord, show me your orders,' said the Queen. Nottingham was nonplussed; he replied, weakly, 'Madam, we have received orders to clap up a certain number.' At this she remarked that she thought people were taken up for crimes, 'and not to make up numbers, as they empanel jurymen'. At that Nottingham accepted defeat and produced another list, headed by Lord Scarsdale's name. 'Stop there, my Lord,' she told him. 'Since you will have your number, put in that Lord's name instead of my Lord Ailesbury's, and if titles please you, there is an Earl for an Earl. What is sauce for one is sauce for another.' The story is Ailesbury's and it could be apocryphal, but the proclamation which was issued on May 9 did include a list of names headed by Lord Scarsdale.

Ailesbury says that he heard the Proclamation being read outside as he lay in bed. Two years before, he had gone into hiding when he knew that his name was on the list, for he did not relish the idea of being shut up in the Tower in hot weather. But he had given himself up in the end, and this time he knew there would be no escape. He suspected a trick when he heard his name was not included, and it was not until later that he was told the part the Queen had played. She had taken the decision on her own, for there was no time to consult the King, and the arrests had already been carried out by the time a copy of the Proclamation reached Holland.

James had not learnt even in exile the hard lesson that tact can sometimes be as powerful a weapon in a monarch's hands as a large army. He was in a confident, even exultant mood; his wife, as he had informed Sophia of Hanover that spring, was quick, and he had already invited prominent English politicians to be present at the birth. At this auspicious moment he chose to publish a declaration of his intentions, in which he threatened vengeance on all his enemies if he regained the throne. Wisely the Queen agreed that this declaration should be printed and circulated. Had it been suppressed many people would have bought it secretly, but once it was openly on sale it lost its attraction. Lloyd wrote an introduction pointing out its follies, and James did more harm to himself by producing such a document, than he did to his daughter.

The most urgent question of all was the loyalty of the English fleet. Were all English ships riddled with Jacobite officers, as some averred, and would they, with Russell's connivance, turn the whole of the British naval power over to the French without a shot being fired? The Queen showed great insight when she openly refused to believe such assertions. She had been advised to take many commissions away, but she felt that an upheaval of this kind could prove fatal in the circumstances. An appeal to the honour of her sailors seemed a far better and more positive approach. So on May 13 Nottingham went down to the fleet and read a letter to the officers on board the *Brittannia*:

I do not know but the reports of the town may have reached the officers of the fleet that many of them have promised to desert, and upon this suspicion they were ordered to be turned out; I am confident these rumours are spread on purpose to create a distrust in the Queen of the officers, and in the officers of the government, for I can trace these reports to some here in town that I am sure wish the destruction of it . . . No such proposal has ever been made to the Queen, or mentioned at the cabinet but as a thing which our enemies maliciously wish, so the Queen commands me to tell you that nothing of this nature can make any impression on her, but that she reposes an entire confidence in them all, and will never think that any brave English seamen will betray her or his country to the insolent tyranny of the French; and as it is their duty and their glory to defend the government, it shall be her part to reward their service. This she would have you communicate to them all with the first opportunity.

Two days later a reassuring reply was received with sixty-four signatures attached which expressed the officers' desire to 'undeceive the world

in these false and malicious reports' and gave a promise that they would
venture their lives in her Majesty's service 'with all imaginable alacrity
and resolution'. Reinforced by the Dutch it was now possible to confront
the enemy with nearly a hundred ships. Fifty surgeons had been despatched to Portsmouth, and there was little to be done except to wait and
pray. And pray the Queen did. She was more than usually devout on the
day that the French, as she put it, 'fell into the mouths' of the English
ships.

On May 20, Princess Anne chose to write from that inappropriately
named house, Sion, reopening the wound that had not been given time to
heal, and asking whether she was to be allowed to pay her respects to her
sister now that she had recovered from her accouchement. She promised
to hide her feelings and she also declared that she would never attempt
to live at the Cockpit again unless the Queen 'would be so kind as make it
easy', that is allow her to take Lady Marlborough with her. It was this
last comment which made the Queen reply in her coldest vein:

I have received yours by the Bishop of Worcester and have very little to say to
it, since you cannot but know that as I never used compliments, so now they
will not serve. 'Tis none of my fault we live at this distance, and I have endeav-
oured to show my willingness to do otherwise. And I will do no more. Don't
give yourself any unnecessary trouble, for be assured it is not words can make
us live together as we ought. You know what I required of you. And I now tell
you, if you doubted it before, that I cannot change my mind but expect to be
complied with, or you must not wonder if I doubt of your kindness. You can give
me no other marks that will satisfy me. Nor can I put any other construction
upon your actions than what all the world must do that sees them. These things
don't hinder me being very glad to hear you are so well and wishing you
may continue so, and that you may yet, while 'tis in your power, oblige me
to be your affectionate sister,

Marie R.

The Queen had spoken; if the Princess had nursed any illusions before,
she could not have them now. There was more involved than family
affection, and had the Queen showed any softening she might have been
open to the charge of endangering the nation.

The allied fleets had stationed themselves at St Helen's, and at a
council of war it was decided not to proceed until definite news had been
received that the French were approaching the English coast. Meanwhile enemy agents had sent messages warning the French that the
English ships greatly outnumbered theirs. Orders were immediately sent
to Tourville advising him not to seek battle, but these came too late to
deter him. He was anxious to cover himself in glory and would not listen

to his experienced flag officers who advised him to retreat. He had only forty-four ships at his disposal, while Russell could call on ninety-nine. Tourville sailed on, driven by a light westerly wind, and Russell allowed his enemy 'to come within half musket shot of him'. It was a bad moment for the English fleet, in view of the rumours there had been about Russell's disloyalty; for a moment the captains wondered whether this was all a prearranged plot. Was it possible that Russell was meeting Tourville by appointment and that at any moment their fellow officers might rise against them? The moment passed, and if Tourville had expected a friendly reception, the guns of the flagship soon taught him his mistake. The engagement went on all day until a thick fog settled over the scene in the afternoon; when it lifted the English could see that the French had decided to retire. Russell ordered his ships to give chase, and a part of the French fleet was pursued into the deep bay at La Hogue, where the English took to their boats and boarded and burned the French ships under the very eyes of King James who was watching the action from the cliffs. As he saw his countrymen swarming aboard the French ships he is reported to have cried out, 'Ah! none but my brave English could do so brave an action!' A cannon ball from one of the burning ships landed among the onlookers, killing some who stood near the exiled King. He then said that 'Heaven fought against him' and retired to his tent, subsequently returning slowly and sadly to the convent of La Trappe, to brood over his former greatness, and to comfort himself with the thought that the battle showed plainly 'a particular Providence to punish the English by apparent successes, and to sanctify the King by continual suffering'.

The invasion threat was now over, Beachy Head was redeemed and the English had established mastery of the seas. When the news was finally confirmed in London the city broke into an ecstasy of bonfires and bell-ringing. But the Queen made her first mistake when she failed to order a public thanksgiving. The reason, she sadly admitted, was that she was hoping to hear at any time that William had won a great victory in Flanders. 'I thought, and so did several Bishops, we must stay for that, and so we did for, I believe, a fortnight together at least, every hour expecting to hear of a battle.' The desire that her husband should gain glory was, she admitted, one of her greatest sins, and one of which she found it impossible to cure herself. The sea victory had, in any case, as she told Sophia, surpassed anything they had dared to hope for, and Portland, Rochester and Sidney went to Portsmouth to congratulate the Admiral, carrying £50,000 with them. Every sailor was to receive a month's pay for his service, and the Queen proclaimed that the old Palace at Greenwich would be rebuilt as a hospital for disabled sailors.

In Flanders three salvoes were fired when the news of the victory came through. Louis, who was with his besieging army at Namur, heard them and was told the reason. 'They make a strange noise about the burning of a few ships,' he said, hating to admit defeat. For William the victory was the one piece of good news in a bad summer. His health was uncertain from the start, and the cold weather, continuing well into May with a bitter north wind and frost at night, did little to improve it. The doctors with their endless remedies could give him little relief, and he was continually troubled by headaches. He remained near the coast as long as possible, ready to go back to England at once if the French carried out their invasion threat, but on May 23 he told Portland that the French armies were on the march, destined probably for Namur or Charleroi. If it proved to be the former, he said that he intended to go to its aid *coûte que coûte* for he believed it to be vital for the defence of the Netherlands. He added a postscript saying that he had not had time to write to the Queen, and he asked Portland not to mention this news to her for it could only make her anxious.

As soon as the King knew for certain that the French had invested Namur, he set out to its relief, but his march there was beset with difficulties. First of all the weather was so hot that men were dying of heatstroke, and torrential rain followed, making the roads difficult. A flooded river held the allied forces up for several days, and even when the torrent receded and the troops were able to cross, they found the enemy so well entrenched in front of the city that it was impossible to discover any way of reaching it.

On June 24 Namur fell. When she heard the news, the Queen was 'troubled and disappointed'. The excitement of the sea victory had now worn off, leaving an unpleasant aftermath of bickering and jealousy. Nottingham and Russell were continually quarrelling and the Queen noticed that the Admiral seemed curiously dissatisfied and did nothing but speak of retiring. 'People all talked according to their several humours or inclinations and partiality, but none seemed sensible as they ought of the great mercies of God,' the Queen observed.

Before leaving for Flanders the King had pressed a plan to make a direct descent on France. Nottingham had also favoured the scheme; early in his career as William's Secretary of State he had assumed responsibility for naval affairs, and he believed that a successful attack on the French coast might help to still the criticism which was being increasingly levelled at him. But as soon as William left for Holland, Nottingham began

to meet with opposition, and several of the Council said they did not
intend to proceed until further confirmation had been received from the
King. Now that the English fleet was in the ascendant, it would have
been possible to cause a distraction on the French coast, thus helping the
allied forces in Flanders. But Russell, in particular, had lost all enthusiasm
for the scheme. He was on such bad terms with Nottingham that he auto-
matically opposed anything the Secretary favoured. He was convinced
that Nottingham was sowing discord among his flag officers. The Queen
felt herself unable to smoothe over their differences, or to act authori-
tatively enough to over-ride her councillors and ensure that the victory
at La Hogue was properly followed up. 'A woman is seldom good for
anything and here it was plainly seen, and that vexed me too much,'
she confessed.

Meanwhile Princess Anne and Lady Marlborough had moved to
Berkeley House in Piccadilly, where they were pleased to entertain anyone
out of favour with the King and Queen. There were whispers that the
Prince and Princess had dined with the Marlboroughs at St Albans, in the
company of the Bishop of London. Godolphin too was behaving strangely.
He had been seen out walking in St James's Park with a well-known
Jacobite in full daylight, and had dined openly with Marlborough.
Anne's court at Bath was well attended, and there even seemed to be a
danger at this time that the violent Whigs might join with the Jacobites
to overthrow the ministry.

While she awaited news of a battle in Flanders, the Queen withdrew
to Kensington, but the rest did her little good. She was advised to drink
Spa water, which she disliked, for it made her 'neglect all things else' for
the sake of her health. 'When I reflect on the 19 days of folly I spent
there, I hate myself for it,' she wrote. She was continually worried by
reports of assassination plots, and she was afraid that at anytime she
might hear that William had been murdered or killed in action. A
Frenchman named Grandval had been apprehended and brought to trial
for a supposed plot, but the Queen suspected that there were still many
assassins at large.

The Queen was still at Kensington when she at last heard that the
allied armies had gone into action. The first message came at noon; in
the evening there was further news, but it was not until late that night
that a letter arrived from the King himself. He had come to grips with
Luxembourg at Steinkerk, but although a surprise attack had been planned,
the French had been given just enough time to organize themselves.
Unfortunately Solms failed to bring up the Dutch infantry to support

the British troops who were exposed to an attack in which they suffered appalling casualties. They fought bravely, and for a moment it seemed that they might carry the day, and indeed they might have done so, had not the French reinforcements under Boufflers arrived just in time.

Steinkerk was not a defeat. Nothing had been lost or won in terms of strategic positions, but many good men had been killed. The foreign commanders, and especially Solms, who was related to the King, were bitterly criticized. Peace was now farther away than ever, and William disliked the thought of returning to England a disappointed rather than a conquering hero.

It was a relief to the Queen to know that her husband was safe, and her thoughts immediately went to those who had received no such reassuring news. At midnight, after hearing about the battle, she wrote to Lady Scarborough saying that as her husband had not been mentioned in any of the lists of casualties it was probable that he was safe. 'I thank God the King is so, though we have got no victory, yet the French have had an equal loss, so that they need not brag.'

William had, as usual, taken no care of his own life, and had been at the heart of the battle. His troops had inflicted such heavy losses that the French army was now forced to go into winter quarters, for it was in no state to continue the campaign. Louis had certainly intended to carry on late into the autumn, adding other towns to the treasured Namur, and in particular he would have liked to secure Liège, the most vital of all, which would have put him in a strong position for the following year. But in England, few people were ready to concede that William had won even a partial victory; they were far more eager to grumble about foreign commanders and the bad harvest. The Queen found this depressing, and she was further discouraged when she read the printed version of Grandval's trial, which proved indisputably that her father had known about, and even encouraged, the murder plot. ''Tis impossible for me to express what I then felt,' she wrote in her diary. 'I was ashamed to look anybody in the face. I fancied I should be pointed at as the daughter of one who was capable of such things, and the people would believe I might by nature have as ill inclinations. I lamented his sin and his shame; I feared it might lessen my husband's kindness to me. It made such impressions upon me that I was uncapable of comfort.'

All through the summer, and for the rest of her life, the Queen was tormented by the thought that she had forgotten to order the general thanksgiving for the naval victory, and she believed that both she and the nation were under the displeasure of the Almighty as a result. This was confirmed for her when an earthquake lasting three or four minutes was felt in England and the Netherlands on September 8. Far away in Jamaica there was an earth tremor which almost wiped out the biggest town on the island, but this was not known for some time. 'These were very extra-ordinary things, which made those who studied apocalyptical matters, imagine that the end of the world drew near. It had been happy for us,' Burnet pontificated, 'if such dismal accidents had struck us with a deeper sense of the judgments of God.'

In spite of her failure to order a thanksgiving service, the Queen had, in the opinion of many, outshone her husband in the achievements of that summer. She had remained calm in the face of all the dangers that had threatened the country since William's departure; she had trusted her navy and it had won her a memorable victory. In every crisis, where others had vacillated, she had remained firm. When the sailors' wives from Wapping, fearful that their husbands would not receive arrears of pay, had marched on Whitehall and staged a noisy demonstration outside the Palace, the Queen, magnificent in ermine and jewels, had emerged from a Council meeting and received their leaders. She put them at their ease with her friendly, humane manner, and sent them home peacefully with promises of payment which she later made sure the Treasury honoured.

William in general had created a far less favourable impression. The year had started badly with the massacre at Glencoe, and it had seemed that nothing would go right for him. 'Will should have knotted and Moll gone to Flanders,' ran a comment in one of the broadsheets, and there was little doubt that he was in for a great deal of criticism on his return.

CHAPTER 29

AN UNFORTUNATE ADMINISTRATION

To MATCH the general dissatisfaction, it was a cold September, with a
strong north-east wind blowing for days on end. Evelyn complained that
this usually pleasant season was very uncomfortable; 'no fruit ripened
kindly,' he reported.

The King, after spending a few days at Loo, returned to England in
October, after a very rough crossing. The Queen feared that his ships
might be scattered and fall into the hands of the Dunkirk privateers
which had been shadowing him all the way. Although when she met him
at New Hall, she was overjoyed to welcome him safely home, she had to
admit that they were both 'melancholy at the ill prospect of things'. She
was afraid that William would tax her with her failure to press on with the
plan to attack Dunkirk or Saint-Malo, or that he would love her less as a
result of her father's folly and the revelations of the Grandval trial. He
looked ill, and he was obviously disappointed by the summer campaign;
but all the same he was in a kindly, even charming mood, and he comforted her, showing her greater tenderness than ever. The day after his
arrival at Kensington he held a court and treated everyone affably. He was
particularly kind to Admiral Russell who was still feeling disgruntled,
although the Queen had offered him a title which he had refused. 'I find
he is resolved to be Mr Russell still,' the Queen told Lady Russell. 'I
could not press him further in a thing he seemed so little to care for, so
there is an end of that matter . . . it is not in my nature to compliment,
which makes me always take people at their words.'

The King and Queen had a few quiet days at Windsor, while William
hunted and worked at his speech for the opening of Parliament. As always
when he returned the Queen's health improved at once—he could do her
more good in a week than a whole course of Spa waters. 'I immediately
gave myself to my own ease and carelessness for business, believing it very
unnecessary for me to meddle, or trouble my head, when the King was
here.' She would have more time now, she assured Lady Russell, to talk
to her friends and help with their problems—'it is easier to say many

things than to write them.' There was time, too, to attend to the re-furnishing of the rooms restored after the fire, and to go out and inspect the gardens. She began to enjoy walking again, almost as she had done in Holland, and she was to be seen sometimes striding along the new road from Kensington to Whitehall, her guards following at a respectful distance. She had instructed one of her godchildren in the catechism. Early in October she presented a sword to her nephew Gloucester. She also had the satisfaction of rewarding a woman who had dressed up as a man and joined the fleet, and who now came to Whitehall bearing a certificate signed by the captain of the *St Andrew* testifying to her bravery at La Hogue.

With William at home, Mary was able to spend more time on the welfare of the Church, and on the preferments which he was inclined to think of as her particular responsibility. In consultation with Tillotson, she was able to ensure that all vacancies were filled by men who were sincere, tolerant and lacking in High Church tendencies. Burnet's *Pastoral Care* was now being distributed among the clergy; it had been discussed at a meeting of eight Bishops who, to Tillotson's surprise, debated the matter 'very calmly' and 'without the least clashing'. Its sound advice to pastors, urging sincerity, wide and balanced reading, and zeal for the faith tempered by reason, could only have a good effect on those clergy who chose to read it. The Irish Church was not forgotten and the Queen con-tinued to press William to fill the Bishoprics, which had been left vacant by James in order to weaken the establishment there. The non-jurors continued to criticize the Queen for her adherence to men such as Tillot-son, and in particular they blamed her for succumbing to the influence of Burnet who in their eyes was only one step away from a Scottish Covenanter. Had she not fallen under his spell in Holland, they considered, she might never have been persuaded to supplant her father. 'A daughter once poisoned with the principle,' wrote Dr Hicks, 'is more than half parricide already, and will like Absolom be ready to grasp at any occasion to ravish the crown from her aged father's head under the fine pretence of subversion whenever the Achitophels and Shimeis would say that this was the time.' But even the most rabid non-jurors conceded that the Queen was noble by nature, though she had fallen under alien influences, among whom her husband could be counted the most powerful. Dr Ken had forfeited the see of Bath and Wells in 1690, feeling unable to take the oaths, but he maintained the admiration he had always felt for Mary in the Dutch days. In April of this year, when invasion had seemed so imminent, he had drafted a letter with the intention of sending it to the

Queen by Mrs Jesson whom he had known in Holland. 'Madam, I most humbly, I most importunately beg of you to consider ... that if King James once sets up his standard in his kingdom, the arguments now urged against him will then all turn for him, and be generally urged on his side, that you yourself will tremble at the thoughts of drawing the sword against your own Royal Father and against God's anointed.' There was little chance of shaking the Queen's convictions, and she was not afraid to show where her sympathies lay. Tillotson, who had to face many attacks from non-jurors, was deeply grateful to the Queen for her open support, which was revealed for all to see and appreciate when she suggested that he should stand as co-sponsor to the Marquis of Winchester's child.

On November 4 the King opened Parliament. His carefully prepared speech was one of the best he had ever made. The same evening his birthday ball was held with great splendour. Princess Anne was conspicuous by her absence, though Prince George made the effort to attend, and even, as was customary, had a new suit made for the occasion, though it was suspected that he had not spent as much money on it as he might have done. The Queen did not take the floor, for, as she told Sophia, she had given up dancing, and the Prince found the party very tiring on top of the State opening of Parliament.

William and Mary paid several visits to Hampton Court and felt more than usually happy in each other's company. It was as well that they were contented in their private lives, for public affairs were giving William an increasing amount of trouble. The noticeable lack of applause after the King's speech in Parliament was an indication of the temper of the House. Wishing to be conciliatory, William had asked for the help and advice of Parliament, and members proceeded to give advice all too readily and help very grudgingly. The quarrel between Russell and Nottingham continued publicly in Parliament, and an unnecessary amount of energy was expended on the task of deciding who was to blame for the mistakes that had been made during the summer. Nottingham's enemies were anxious to lay at his door the failure to carry out the descent on France, while Nottingham and his allies counter-attacked by saying that Russell had failed to follow up the advantages gained at La Hogue, so that as a result the Channel was full of French privateers. In the Lords, Nottingham justified himself at length; 'he aggravated Russell's errors and neglects very severely,' according to Burnet. In the Commons, however, after a close vote, the responsibility for the miscarriages of the previous summer were attributed to the Council, which everyone really knew to be, by implication, Nottingham, and complaints were again made about the dangers of closet government.

In such a troubled atmosphere it was evident that the King would not obtain his supplies for the forthcoming summer without a struggle. There was an increasing restlessness as William became more involved in the European quarrel. The Land Tax was now standing at four shillings in the pound and the country gentlemen felt they had a right to grumble if the money so raised went to finance expensive military operations on the continent, and thus putting money into the pockets of City business men who were landing the army contracts. William's coalition was now facing strong opposition voiced by the New Country Party, an alliance of landed gentry of Whig and Tory hue—Harley and Foley, for example, were 'old Whigs', while Musgrave and Clarges were typical Tories, but all were ready to join together in defence of the landed interest. They demanded a careful scrutiny of all the estimates, and the Bill of Supply had a stormy passage; 'those who could not oppose them yet showed their ill humour in delaying them and clogging them with unacceptable clauses all they could.' In addition, criticism of foreign officers in the army was growing loud and unpleasant, and Solms in particular came in for criticism on account of the part he had played at Steinkerk. Next, a bill calling for triennial parliaments was introduced. The King, who was beginning to run out of patience, was bitterly opposed to this, believing it to be levelled against himself and his prerogative. The Place Bill, which was very nearly carried in the Commons, aimed at excluding from Parliament all those who held offices of trust or profit, and this was also prompted by a desire to limit the King's power. There was a genuine fear that if too many army officers sat in Parliament, the King could control affairs by force, and the instigators of the two bills took as their slogan the danger of the country becoming governed by a standing army and a standing parliament.

In spite of his attempts to be polite and sociable, William's popularity was declining rapidly. He had done his best to pacify his critics by promising a large-scale descent on France in the summer, but in spite of this the Money Bill was still delayed, and the King feared that when supplies were finally granted they would come too late and in any case prove inadequate. Towards the end of the year the King received a personal blow in the death of Waldeck who, though not an attractive man or a particularly successful general, was an experienced soldier and an old friend.

As the end of the year approached the Queen embarked on her annual stocktaking. She remembered the comfort she had increasingly found in the sacrament, though she was ashamed to have to admit that in the last

months, just when she should have devoted more time to them, she had
slackened a little in her 'holly duties'. The comfort she had found in
William's presence had been balanced by the increasing difficulties which
had arisen in public life, but she had observed before that the Lord seldom
sent either happiness or sorrow 'without allay'. When William was at
home, she tried to keep out of public life as much as possible, but she
could not avoid hearing what was going on in both Houses:

I saw parties so much increase and a kind of affectation to do all that was
insolent to the King without fear of punishment, that he could not govern his
own servants, nay that he durst not punish them, but was obliged to keep those
in his service who least deserved it, and who he might be pretty sure would not
really serve him.

The King realized that he would have to make some attempt to streng-
then the administration before he left for Flanders once again. He would
perhaps have been wise to take the advice of Sunderland and put himself
in the hands of the Whigs. But William still could not trust a party
which seemed to him to have dangerous republican tendencies. Nor could
he bear to part with Nottingham, to whom both he and the Queen remained unwaveringly loyal throughout the whole winter, supporting him
when he was under attack and refusing to listen to his calumniators. It was
difficult for the Queen to forget how kind 'Lord Nott.' had been during the
dark days of the Irish campaign.

The quarrel between Russell and Nottingham was impossible to resolve. In January 1693 Evelyn reported that it was still 'undetermined'.
The whole controversy came to a head when Russell announced that he
refused to serve if Nottingham remained Secretary of State during the
summer campaign, whereupon the King dispensed with his services and
appointed three admirals in his place—Killigrew, Delaval and Shovel.
Shovel was able enough, a good and loyal seaman, but some said the other
two were Jacobite sympathizers. Nottingham had no intention of sur-
rendering the Seals, even if he had given the Queen the impression that
he might, but he was pressing now for the post of second Secretary of
State, left vacant since Sidney's departure for Ireland, to be filled. The
work and responsibility was too much for any one man, he considered,
and he liked the idea of 'sharing the public hate'.

The King was determined to keep Nottingham, but he was wise enough
to see that it would be courting disaster to bring in any more Tories at
this stage. A year before the King had appointed the young Whig,
Montagu, to the Treasury, but this concession was not likely to satisfy
the party for long. Sunderland was still reluctant to return to the forefront

of politics, but he was already exerting his influence in the background, and this could be traced in the appointments made by the King before he departed to Flanders. He handed the Great Seal, which had been in commission for some time, to Sir John Somers, a brilliant lawyer, gifted with a patient, balanced nature. The vacant Secretaryship went to Sir John Trenchard, whom Burnet described as 'a calm, sedate man', not at all the kind of person he would have expected to find in the Whig ranks.

Neither the Whigs nor the Tories were satisfied with these new appointments. It seemed to the Queen that there was unrest everywhere. The bad harvest of the previous year had sent up the cost of living; crimes of violence were on the increase, and the Queen's pleas had done little to improve morality. Just before Christmas Lord Mohun, a corrupt and drunken peer, had murdered in the street an actor named Mountford,who was his rival in the affections of the actress Mrs Bracegirdle. Although Mohun was found guilty by the Grand Jury of Middlesex, he was acquitted in the Lords by a large majority. This blatant travesty of justice shocked the Queen, and furnished her with further evidence of the universal corruption which had now apparently spread to almost the entire nobility. In April a proclamation was printed prohibiting 'prophane swearing, cursing, drunkenness, idleness and unlawful gaming, and all manner of prophaneness whatsoever', encouraging Sunday observance, and requiring the Justices and Sheriffs to be more diligent in enforcing the law. The reform societies which were being founded with the Queen's approval were doing what they could to trace murderers, discover houses of ill fame and bring offenders to justice; all the same, the Queen was none too sanguine about the situation in this troubled spring of 1693.

The King's influence in Parliament was now so weak that he was unable to prevent the passage of the hated Triennial Bill. It was passed by both Houses, although the King did his best to avoid the issue by letting it lie on the table for some time. Even the King himself was beginning to realize that he must take Sunderland's advice and work hard at lobbying peers if he wished to control the Lords, but William had little time or patience for such a task, and he had no 'managers' to do the work for him. So, before he left for Holland, he exercised the royal veto, which, though a right of the Crown, was one which was seldom exercised. His action put Parliament in a very bad humour, and William prorogued it in March.

The weather had so far been mild, in February there was a week when the sun shone as if it were summer, but at the end of the month it suddenly turned colder, with deep snow. The King, knowing that France was already mobilizing her forces, was anxious to be away, and restless because he could not hear any news of the situation in Flanders.

At last, towards the end of March, the weather improved, and William was able to set sail for Holland, leaving the Queen to deal with the most divided Council she had yet been called upon to control. The old-stagers resented the presence of the newly appointed Whigs, who for their part, knowing that the Queen inclined towards Nottingham and the Tories, treated her with what she described as 'a great coldness and strangeness'. She had been rash enough to depart from her usual custom of keeping well out of politics when the King was at home. Lord Bellomont, who as Lord Coote had first joined her household in Holland, and had served her faithfully ever since, had behaved, in her opinion, 'impertinently'. In spite of her express orders to the contrary, he had abstained from voting on the Triennial Bill, so she had dismissed him, though knowing him to be as much without means as he had been when he first joined her, she had granted him a generous pension. She was surprised and vexed by the censure which her action aroused. 'I could not be convinced,' she wrote, 'that I was in the wrong, yet was sorry 'twas so understood.'

The Queen told Sophia that everyone now had too much on their mind to give any time to their pleasures. She would still be prepared to dance herself—although, as she confessed, she no longer had the figure for it— if by doing so she could put every one around her in a good humour, but she was beginning to despair of doing that, and she expressed envy of Sophia who was apparently in an easier situation. It was a pity, she said, that Sophia could not come to England to judge things for herself, in case the Prince of Denmark, whom she knew well, had given her a biased version of the family dispute. The Queen said she, herself, had no desire to lengthen out the quarrel with her sister, and if only Anne were as anxious to end it as she was, they would be able to live in harmony well enough. All she hoped was that she was not being misrepresented in this, as in so many other matters.

Marlborough, having been released on bail soon after his committal to the Tower, had now been cleared and was free to make trouble where he liked. Shrewsbury had gone into an alliance with the Marlboroughs, and Godolphin was not above fraternizing with them, perhaps as an insurance for the future, or possibly out of respect for an old friendship; but whatever his motives, his behaviour was bound to arouse uneasiness in the Queen's mind. Suspicion about his loyalties may have influenced the King, and induced him to take less notice than he should have done when Godolphin warned him of the excessive cost and impracticability of the projected descent on France.

Almost as soon as the King left England a controversy arose concerning the appointment of a new Attorney-General. The Whigs thought that this post had been promised to Sir Thomas Trevor, but it now seemed that Nottingham had persuaded the King to change his mind at the last minute in favour of Edward Ward. The Queen was faced almost immediately with a Cabinet crisis, and Somers threatened to resign. 'Thus,' wrote the Queen sadly in retrospect, 'I entered into my administration which was all along unfortunate, and whereas other years the King had almost ever approved all was done, this year he disapproved almost everything.'

Meanwhile the King had gone to Loo to inspect the progress of the work on the garden and house. Unlike Louis, who had suspended all building operations for the duration of the war, William had given orders that Loo must be finished. The main buildings were now complete, and it was time to think about furnishings—tapestries, pictures, 'beds, mattresses, blankets and other furniture'. Marot and Romeyne de Hooghe were busy with decorations, the murals, mirrors, carved mantelpieces, garden urns, ceilings, doorways. Robert Duval had been appointed as 'art-keeper' to look after the pictures of Honselaersdyck, Loo and Ryswick. Marot had now produced designs for murals on the famous staircase; like those in the gallery at Honselaersdyck they were to deceive the eye, and give the impression that real people were standing above the stairs— a group of exotic eastern figures looking over a balcony.

At home the Queen concentrated on her houses and furniture if only to take her mind off her loneliness. Evelyn was impressed by the progress she had made:

I saw the Queen's rare cabinets and collection of china, which was wonderfully rich and plentiful, but especially a large cabinet, looking-glass frame and stands, all of amber, much of it white, with historical bas-reliefs and statues, with medals carved in them, esteemed worth £4,000, sent by the Duke of Brandenburg, whose country, Prussia, abounds with amber, cast up by the sea; divers other china and Indian cabinets, screens and hangings. In her library were many books in English, French and Dutch, of all sorts; a cupboard of gold plate; a cabinet of silver filigree, which I think was our Queen Mary's, and which in my opinion should have been generously sent to her.

It was some solace to walk through the rooms at Kensington admiring all the works of art she had collected, but it was impossible to find any real comfort in this, the most difficult of all the summers she spent on her own.

The Queen hoped to spend six weeks at Kensington; she did not dare go farther away for fear of missing important news from Flanders. Sophia, whose husband had recently been admitted to the Electoral College, had two sons taking part in the campaign and the Queen expressed sympathy for her, although she said she herself was a bad judge of maternal affection since she had never had children. It was a pity, she thought, that she and Sophia had never had the chance to meet; even if they had nothing else in common they were both great walkers. 'A thousand times I have wished myself with you,' she wrote, 'and why should I yet despair of that satisfaction, at least let me please myself sometimes with such thoughts, you will easily believe I have vexing ones enough to fill my mind, to divert which I go sometimes to Hampton Court, a place I don't doubt but you have heard named, where the King had begun a great building and large gardens, 'tis at so convenient a distance from this place, I go to it with ease in two hours time.' Kensington, she explained, was more convenient still, within walking distance, about as far from Whitehall as the House in the Wood was from the Hague.

It was difficult for anyone on the allied side not to be alarmed by what the Queen described as the 'prodigious' preparations being made by the French. William was sure that with the vast army they now had in readiness, they would try to take the vital stronghold of Liège. He had encamped at Park where there was an old abbey with fishponds and delightful gardens, but he had chosen the site not for its beauty but because it was strategically placed, guarding the approaches to the coveted city. Louis, who had arrived with Madame de Maintenon to watch the fortress fall, was disgusted when his commander-in-chief, Luxembourg, refused to proceed against an enemy so well placed. Luxembourg wished to draw the allies into a battle which he had every chance of winning, and then, having overcome the opposition, he intended to march on to Liège. Louis, however, was not interested in battles; he had come to see a city surrender, and being denied this immediate satisfaction, he retired to Paris with all his train.

Bad news was delivered to William at Park. A rich fleet of English merchantmen, bound for the Mediterranean, had been waiting for months for a convoy. The navy, which had gained the supremacy of the seas at La Hogue, should have been able to ensure the safe passage of the Turkey fleet, or the Smyrna fleet, as it was sometimes called. The French fleet, depleted as it was, had been split into two, one part being based on Toulon, the other at Brest. The English merchantmen set out, believing that it would be some time before the Brest fleet would be ready to sail.

The main convoy put back to base very soon, since no danger was visualized, and the Turkey fleet sailed on with a small escort under the command of Rooke. Meanwhile a message had been received at the Secretary's office, imparting the information that the French fleet had already sailed from Brest, but Rooke, driven by a near gale, sailed swiftly on towards the unknown danger. The French had already reached the great bay of Lagos in Portugal, without waiting for the provisions and men which were to be sent after them. Rooke's only fear was that, at a later date, he might encounter the Toulon squadron, and he was as incredulous as those at home when he learned that the Brest fleet had sailed already and was now lying in wait for him. Had the main fleet not returned, his plight would not have been serious; as it was, he was almost within view of the French ships before he realized what had happened. There was little he could do except to retreat, which he did, accompanied by a number of merchantmen, until he reached the safety of the Canaries. The French fleet pursued those that had reached Gibraltar, where the merchants scuttled their ships to prevent them falling into enemy hands. About fifty were lost in this way and a further thirty were captured, but many others managed to escape with Rooke.

The first reports spoke of a complete disaster, which caused consternation in the City, and made William fear that just at this crucial time, when he was expecting to fight a major battle at any moment, he might find himself deprived of further financial aid or supplies of any kind. Credit revived when it was realized that the merchant fleet had not been completely wiped out; all the same the sense of anger and shame in the merchant community and in the nation as a whole was naturally great. In the Cabinet Council the already unhappy atmosphere deteriorated still further; there were bitter recriminations, and Nottingham's position was now worse than ever. Although nobody was prepared to admit it, the King had foreseen a possible disaster, having urged the Admiralty for months to send a squadron to the Mediterranean to look after English trading interests and to guard the Turkey fleet. The Queen watched with mounting anger as all those who had ignored the King's warning, now greeted the news of the disaster with 'a sort of malicious joy'. She was as sensible as anybody of the shortcomings of the English intelligence, of the honour lost and the wealth squandered, and all this when the English had won the naval superiority a year ago; 'no orders being obeyed, no faults punished, everyone glad to lay the blame on another, and it may be sometimes contributing on purpose to have others blamed,' the Queen wrote furiously adding, 'all this I saw, was vexed and troubled and much more because I could not help it'. It was difficult for her to control her temper, hearing the insolence and stupidity of her so-called councillors, but she managed somehow to keep her feelings to herself. It was one of Tillotson's written Resolutions, which he read over to himself every morning, 'not to be angry with anybody upon any occasion, because all anger is foolish, and a short fit of madness; betrays us into great indecencies; and whereas it is intended to hurt others, the edge of it turns upon ourselves'. The Queen, in a similar vein, wrote in her diary, 'I am always apprehensive of letting myself grow angry, especially where it will signify nothing.'

Nottingham was under no illusions. He knew that he had many enemies all too ready to apportion blame. This disaster—more justly than some others—would be laid at his door. There had been confusion in the Secretary's office, and for this only he could shoulder the full responsibility. He was perhaps as much to blame as anybody, but the whole affair was the culmination of a long history of muddle and delay. The fact that the report of the French fleet's departure from Brest never reached the English admirals was due to a misunderstanding, and in fact the cumbersome nature of the whole system militated against success. The responsibilities of the two Secretaries of State were not clearly defined, and those of the three admirals the King had left in charge of the fleet even less so. The fact that the King was in Flanders and unable to give orders himself was an added consideration. The Queen felt that she could not escape blame herself. 'You spare the sea matters as much as you can,' the Queen wrote to the Electress Sophia, 'tho' the little you say is enough; I wish I could differ from you in that, but there is one of the misfortunes of the King's long absence, that he cannot at a distance take the necessary care of so great a concern, and a woman is but a very useless and helpless creature at all times of war and difficulty. That I find by my own sad experience, that an old English inclination to the love and honour of the nation signifies nothing in a woman's heart without a man's head and hands.' She added that as the English prided themselves particularly on their naval genius, perhaps they needed humbling. 'I think they have had it,' she said.

In the bitter aftermath of the Turkey fleet's disaster, the Cabinet Council was more divided, more exasperating than ever. Burnet tried to intercede with some of its members on her behalf, but he was told that she and the King had been invited to come to England to take orders, not to give them. Only Nottingham remained as staunch and loyal as ever, and the Queen to him—that spring she had become godmother to his fourteenth child—but the others hated him and made no secret of the fact.

The news from Flanders did nothing to lighten the gloom. Throughout the early weeks of July the two armies watched each other until Luxembourg, at the end of the month, moved towards Huy, apparently making the first step in the direction of Liège. He succeeded in luring William away from his strong position at Park, but the King was too late to save Huy, and on July 28 he heard that he was within a league of the French Army at Landen, which numbered 80,000 men. William had only 50,000. It would have been impossible for him to win a pitched battle against such tremendous odds, but in the action which was to take place on July 29 the English fought bravely, while the King himself was like a man inspired. Even the French were full of admiration, and the Prince de Condé remarked that 'so much valour very well deserves the possession of the crown he wears.' He had three lucky escapes when musket shots went through his peruke, the sleeve of his coat and the knot of his scarf. Solms was less fortunate; he had his leg shot off by a cannon ball and died soon after.

It took the French all day to dislodge the allies, but when they brought up reinforcements in the evening, William had to accept defeat and withdraw his troops. The French, too, were exhausted and unable to follow up their victory. English casualties ran into thousands, but when the final count was made, it was realized that the French had lost twice as many. The French, in theory victorious, had suffered a loss both of men and morale, as well as a shock from which they did not recover that summer. Charleroi fell to Luxembourg's forces, but Liège was safe. Thus far William had achieved his aim. He had the satisfaction of knowing also that the French nation was growing tired of a war that was draining its resources without bringing it any spectacular gains, while two successive years of bad harvests and a poor vintage had led to real hardship. The battle of Landen was a blow for the allies; that it had been a blow too for the French was proved by the fact that gradually and tentatively Louis let it be known that he was ready for peace.

As soon as the fighting was over the King wrote to his wife telling her that he was well. Stories of his own bravery, and of the terrible losses his small army had inflicted on the French, brought him, in the Queen's words, 'honour enough to flatter and please the vainest humour'; but a victory, which he might have gained had Parliament been more generous in the matter of supplies, would have been preferable.

The Whigs had been busy all the summer preparing for the forthcoming session, some of them sacrificing several weeks of the country air by staying in London to organize support. After the battle of Landen their activities were intensified, and there were strong rumours of an important conference of leading Whig members assembling at Althorp, Sunderland's country seat. It was clear that Sunderland would no longer tolerate the King's policy of 'patching' the ministry with frequent re-shuffles and the occasional introduction of a Whig candidate.

A bitter east wind blew for nearly a month from the end of September. Everybody was impatient for the King's return, nobody was satisfied with the political situation and they knew that nothing could be settled or thrashed out until he came. The Queen, like many other people, was suffering from a bad cold; she was sure that she would not be able to breathe properly until the wind changed. William finally arrived on October 29, and the next day the wind veered to an unfavourable quarter; if he had stayed in Holland for twenty-four hours longer he might have been delayed for weeks. This fact the Queen described as one of God's mercies, but the King was in such a bad humour on his return that it might have been better for everybody if he had stayed in Holland. For the first and only time he showed the Queen no tenderness and seemed critical of everything she had done during his absence. He realized now too well that he must throw in his lot with the Whigs and rule with the help of men whom he and the Queen found personally obnoxious. Sunderland, in the Queen's opinion, was insupportable; he was just the kind of hard, sarcastic man she could never bring herself to like. The King, she complained, 'was forced to part with Lord Nottingham to please a party whom he cannot trust'. It would have been easier if the Secretary had offered to resign of his own accord, but he refused to do so, thinking that such an action would seem like an admission of guilt. When Trenchard was sent to demand the Seals, he refused to deliver them up, saying that he would only give them into the hands from which he had received them—the King's. Lady Nottingham retained her position as maid of honour to the Queen, and both she and Nottingham talked of the dismissal without bitterness. Nottingham said he would always be at hand to give help where he could.

The weather was wet and cheerless as it had been all the summer, 'if,' as Evelyn said, 'one might call it a summer'. Although there was little to be thankful for, a day of thanksgiving was held early in November and the Lord Mayor and Court of Aldermen waited on the King and Queen, to congratulate the King on his happy return and 'wonderful preservation in that signal providence, that had protected him in the greatest of dangers, to which he had exposed his royal person for our safety'. Archbishop Sharp preached the sermon at Whitehall. 'All is well, and all [will] be well for ever to them that love God,' he asserted.

Certainly as the year drew to its close the situation began to improve. Parliament was less intractable than usual, for the Whig 'managers' had been at work, ready to bring their party in behind them to support the King, now that he had dismissed Nottingham, reinstated Russell and promised more Whig appointments. Five million pounds was voted for the next campaign without too much delay, the Triennial Bill was thrown out, and, as the Queen put it, 'to make us end an unfortunate year well', several corn ships which might have helped to relieve the famine in France, were taken by English ships. It was remarkable, too, looking back on it, how in spite of the disappointments of the summer, the people had remained in good heart, God having supported them 'by the goodness of the season and the fruits of the earth'. At the beginning of the year the French had seemed to possess overwhelming supremacy, and yet they had still failed to gain a victory or make any great progress. The Queen could only thank God for making her husband the instrument of their disappointment. She could not resist comparing the two Kings—Louis who had returned in a sulk to Versailles, and William who had remained with his troops and covered himself in glory.

As for her own spiritual development during the year, she had meditated, read the word and heard it preached, prayed perhaps more fervently than usual and kept 'in a pretty even course'. She found herself in a good frame of mind, able to look forward with confidence to another year, a year which everyone hoped might prove to be the last of the war:

I continue still in an earnest desire of doing good, but alas! I do not find I have made any great progress therein. Oh my God, if it be my fault, pardon me . . . Pardon, oh my God, all my sins and infirmities, increase in me all Christian graces, that if it be thy will to add any days or years to mine, I may spend them entirely in thy service and to thy glory.

And thus in a very good disposition of mind I bless my God and end the year 1693.

CHAPTER 30

THE DEVILISH PARTY

ALTHOUGH unofficial peace moves were already being made, it seemed likely that the war would go on for at least another year, and the King would once again call on the Queen to reign without him. In previous summers she had always turned to Nottingham for help, but it was unlikely that she would find a congenial adviser among the worldly ambitious Whigs who were now in the ascendant. For the time being, the King found that he could work with Somers, but his eventual aim was to bring in Shrewsbury, whom the Queen liked and trusted, and who had kept his affiliations with the Whig party in spite of strong pressure from his Catholic mother.

Almost immediately after his return, William called for Shrewsbury and was disappointed to find the Earl in an unco-operative mood. The two men parted on such bad terms after the interview that the King felt unable to approach Shrewsbury again direct, and delegated the task to Elizabeth Villiers, who was a close friend of Shrewsbury's mistress, Miss Lundy, daughter of the former Jacobite governor of Londonderry. But she proved equally unsuccessful, and by now Shrewsbury was becoming thoroughly peevish. He explained once again that he felt himself unfit by nature to serve the King; in any case, he had decided to go to Spain. 'When you, madam, have attempted to persuade, and have failed, you may conclude the thing is impossible,' he told Elizabeth Villiers.

We do not know whether the Queen had been aware of the means her husband had chosen to win Shrewsbury; in view of her tranquillity at the end of the year, one suspects that she did not. At the beginning of December she had been confined to her room for over a week with a discharge from her ear but the in new year she was again in good health and spirits.

Wren, who had agreed to undertake the work at Greenwich gratis, often came to consult her about the plans. The hospital which she intended to found was designed for the support of veteran seamen, for the relief and maintenance of their widows, and for educating the orphans of men who had died defending the nation at sea. The Queen had been down several times to view the site. She was unwilling to demolish the Queen's House, or King's Pavilion, and in the final design this remained intact, framed by the two domed pavilions of the new building. She planned to use the house herself at a later date and wished to be able to reach it by water; it was also intended that Ambassadors should stay there before making their State entry up the river. Wren eventually accepted this limitation on his design, and proceeded to plan the large building with its great painted hall and chapel, its school and living accommodation.

The Queen was interested in another project. James Blair, a clergyman from New England, had come over from America with plans for starting a college in Virginia, half way between the southern and northern plantations, to give the English settlers the educational opportunities which at present they lacked. Blair had started a voluntary subscription list which had already brought him a large sum of money, though there was a great deal of opposition from those with a vested interest in plantations. It was maintained by some that Blair's college would take the planters away from their mechanical employments, and make them grow 'too knowing to be obedient and submissive'. The Queen, who believed that the foundation of the college might prepare people to spread the gospel among the natives, was unmoved by these prophecies of student revolt, and she supported the idea with such determination that eventually all obstacles were removed. The college was founded by royal charter and built to a design provided by Wren.

The King had apparently recovered from his bad humour of the autumn before, and, with Parliament in a better mood, and supplies granted with comparative willingness, he was able to look ahead and plan for the future. Childless though they were, both he and the Queen were fond of children and took an interest in the offspring of those who had been luckier than themselves. Lady Northampton often brought the two-year-old son of the Queen's much-lamented friend Lady Dorset, to see the King and Queen at Kensington. It was when Lord Buckhurst was there one day, playing in the gallery with his new cart, that he heard the Queen express impatience because the King went on working in his study and would not come to tea. The little boy on his own initiative went to the monarch's door and banged on it, something which his closest advisers would never have dared to do. The King asked irritably who was there. 'It's Lord Buck,' came the reply. 'And what does Lord Buck want with me?' inquired the King as he opened the door. 'You must come to tea immediately' said Lord Buckhurst firmly. The King put down his pen, put the boy into the cart and pulled him to the drawing room, then succumbed to a bad attack of coughing, which alarmed the Queen and scandalized Lady Northampton, who threatened to take the boy away. But the King, so well known for his dour nature, intervened on his behalf.

The King and Queen were equally fond of William, Duke of Gloucester, the Denmark's child. The little Duke had never been strong; he had to be carried upstairs, and if he fell over he was unable to rise without assistance. To compensate for these handicaps he had developed a passion for the military art; his thoughts ran almost entirely on martial themes, and his favourite pastime was to play soldiers. The Duke could muster two companies of boys recruited in Kensington, and on several occasions the King and Queen were summoned into the garden at Kensington where the miniature army marched past them in style. The King gave twenty guineas to be distributed among the boys, and took special notice of one six-year-old, who was almost as skilful as the best adult drummer.

In the spring of 1694 the Duke had an ague, which was cured with the help of Jesuit's powder, but it returned on April 17, and no more powder was given 'for fear of clogging him'. The child was therefore given a mixture of brandy and saffron which made him vomit, but even when he was in the last extremity of sickness he had his cannon drawn up as in a fight, and those who tended him were made to stand at his door like sentinels in a garrison.

The Denmarks hoped that when a riband of the Order of the Garter became vacant on the death of the Duke of Hamilton, the King would bestow it on Gloucester, and he was sent pointedly to see his aunt with a blue bandolier over his shoulder. But William had already decided to bestow the honour on Shrewsbury, together with a dukedom, for the Earl had at last capitulated and agreed to become Secretary of State. The Duke of Gloucester had done something to bridge the gap between the two households, but the sisters still would not meet.

The King was unable to leave for Holland as soon as he would have liked, as the parliamentary session in England dragged on into the spring. For once he was at home to share her birthday celebrations at the end of April. The year before, Purcell's Ode had been sung to the lute by one of the Queen's ladies, with the composer accompanying on the harpsichord, and afterwards the Queen had asked them to play 'Cold and raw the wind doth blow'. This melody was now incorporated into the birthday ode, and sung by Mr Gostling, a tenor who had once performed duets with Charles II to James's guitar accompaniment. The Duke of Gloucester came to wish her joy as usual, where he pleased the King and Queen very much with his 'pretty jocular sayings'. There were carpenters working in the Queen's Gallery at Kensington, and the Duke asked what they were doing. The Queen told him that they were mending the gallery, otherwise it would fall down. 'Let it fall, let it fall,' replied the boy, 'and then you will scamper away to London.'

A few days after the birthday William was ready to go. It was said that when the Duke of Gloucester came to say goodbye, he offered the King his two companies, although L'Hermitage had the story that he added they were only to fight the Turks or the French, and not his grandfather James II.

The Queen went with William to Gravesend, but on her return to London she heard that he had been forced to put back owing to strong winds. She rejoined him at once, and while they waited for the weather to improve they went together to Canterbury as they had done on their first journey to Holland. The Queen had only Lady Derby and one other lady with her, but they made for the largest and grandest house in the town which happened to belong to a lady who was not a great admirer of the King. Having heard that she might expect the royal visitors, she had taken care to be away. The Queen was then told that the Deanery was the next largest house. 'Oh, that is Dr Hooper's house I will go there,' said the Queen, and arrived before her ex-chaplain or his servants had been given time to light the fires or prepare a reception. Dr Hooper himself was at Lambeth and did not hear about his visitors until they had already left.

William's stay was short, for as soon as the wind moderated he was anxious to be away. The Queen told Hooper on her return to London that his was the cleanest house she had ever stayed in, and that the people of Canterbury had been very 'solicitous to see her'. The only drawback was that the windows of his house were so high, and such a large walnut tree grew in front of them, that it had been difficult for her to be seen by the crowd outside. On Sunday morning she went to the cathedral where she heard an excellent sermon and to the parish church in the afternoon where she listened to another. 'I thought myself in a Dutch church,' she told Hooper, 'for they stood up upon the communion table to see me.' A little while later she sent for Hooper and took him into her dressing room where she showed him some silver material and purple flowered velvets, and told him that if he approved of it, she would give it to the Cathedral, for she had noticed that some of the furniture there was in need of replacement. There was not quite enough of the figured velvet, so she tried to match it up in Holland, and took a great deal of trouble over such details as the tapes, rings and gilt rails. She even sent down one of her pages of the backstairs, who understood such matters, to see that the work was carried out satisfactorily. Besides providing two footstools padded with curled hair, she gave an altar cover of figured velvet with a panel of gold with silver flowers, and had the Archbishop's throne re-covered in plain velvet with six swan's down cushions; both were finished off with a tufted fringe in gold, silver and purple which alone cost £500. She told Hooper that she had enjoyed her stay at Canterbury so much that she would certainly want to go there again. He set to work at once to alter the offending windows, putting sashes in, and making some of the rooms larger with the help of folding doors; he also furnished a wing of the house which had not been used before, and promised to cut down the walnut tree which Tillotson had planted many years before.

The Queen returned sadly to London after the pleasant interlude at Canterbury. Her partings with William never became any easier. 'It is the one thing in the world to which I shall never accustom myself,' she told Mlle Obdam. Although she was sympathetic when Sophia had to endure a parting of six weeks, she could not help wondering what the Electress would think of one that lasted for as many months:

There has never been a year yet since the first I came into England in which the King has not been longer away, I think almost 8 months in the year he is from home. That is one of my crosses, which it seems I was born to, and indeed that which is the worst to be borne, but I learn patience whether I will or no.

The King's journey to Holland was hazardous, for the wind changed when he was within sight of the shore and he had to be rowed to land in an open boat, a prey to enemy privateers. As usual he went first of all to Loo, and his retainers found him in a sour temper after the journey; his cough was bad, and Portland was being difficult, for he was growing jealous of Keppel who was superseding him in the King's affections. The news that the French King was already gathering his forces together was a further irritation, for it confirmed that the extra length of the parliamentary session had given the enemy a good start, 'the loss of which,' he told Shrewsbury, 'we shall have cause to regret this whole campaign'.

This year it had been definitely resolved before the King's departure that a direct attack on France should be carried out to help draw troops away from Flanders. Plans had been laid to make a landing at Brest; men and ships had been assembled, but so far a westerly wind had prevented them from setting out. The French intelligence, always more efficient than the English on account of the many Jacobite sympathizers

in England, had obtained accurate information about the scope and destination of the project. When Tollemache finally set out with 6,000 men,
the French were already well prepared. Camaret, a neck of land jutting
out into the river, had been fortified with numerous batteries, and many
men had been brought in, about double the invading force. But Tollemache over-rode the officers who at a council of war counselled him to
call off the attempt. Almost all those who went ashore were killed or taken
prisoner, and Tollemache himself died from a wound in the thigh.
Nothing was gained, and the King was robbed of a gallant commander,
who had been with him since the days of the English regiment in Holland.

The fleet returned to Plymouth and subsequently occupied itself
bombarding French ports and spreading terror among the inhabitants.
William had ordered Russell to the Mediterranean, but this admiral,
who was conservative by nature and did not like new theories of naval
strategy any more than he appreciated long absences from his native
country, procrastinated as long as he dared. 'God grant that Russell
may soon arrive in the Mediterranean, as from that alone we expect
success in this campaign,' the King wrote to Shrewsbury on June 18. In
Flanders neither side was prepared to risk an engagement. As Shrewsbury put it, 'I should think the loss of a battle so much more dangerous
for our affairs, than the gaining of one would be advantageous'. The French
forces remained firmly on the defensive and both sides played the waiting
game.

For the Queen there was no guarantee, however, that there would not
be a battle. She had received the news of the Camaret Bay disaster from
a Captain Green, who had insisted on putting the despatch into her own
hands; she had been alone at the time with nobody else there except
Shrewsbury. At any moment she could receive a similar message from
Flanders, bringing news of William's death. In early July, when there
seemed most likelihood of an engagement, both armies being encamped
very near each other, she felt so anxious that she was unable to settle to
anything. For days strong contrary winds were blowing so that it was
impossible for any news to come; a battle could have been fought while
she knew nothing about it. This kept her in a 'perpetual expectation and
a thousand fears of what might have happened'. She told Sophia that a
good peace grew more and more desirable, but, as she sadly added, 'I am
so little used to have what I wish that I dare not flatter myself with any
hopes of it, though one would think war could not last much longer'.

Apart from her anxiety, the Queen found the summer rather less
trying than usual. Having at last persuaded Shrewsbury to take office,

the King had put complete confidence in him; for these few months the Duke worked hard without complaining about his health, and his tact kept everyone in a good humour.

The Queen saw him almost every day, and his pleasant sympathetic manner made life tolerable. Sunderland, fortunately for the Queen, spent most of the summer at Althorp, making plans to marry his son Lord Spencer to Lady Arabella Cavendish and arguing about the dowry. Godolphin seemed out of humour, and there was a violent quarrel when he refused to accept a list of candidates for the new commission of custom and excise drawn up by his colleagues, Somers, Trenchard and Shrewsbury. In July the scheme for the first national bank met with a great deal of opposition, especially in the Lords, but it was passed and established by an Act of Parliament and put under the direction of men whom Evelyn considered to be 'the most able and wealthy citizens of London'.

Tillotson was in the country for six weeks in July and August for his wife's health, but on his return he and the Queen were in consultation again about Church matters and particularly discussing preferments. By now everybody knew that the Queen was far less likely to bestow places on those who asked for them on their own account, than on those who were recommended by other people. She looked for talent outside the court, and often took advice from the impartial Tillotson. Burnet thought that their policy would produce a great change in the Church and the quality of the clergy, but Tillotson was often bitterly criticized for his lack of bias. The Queen took just as much care over the Irish Bishops as she did over the English, and it was thought that Bishops as a breed showed a marked improvement during her reign. They visited their dioceses more often, confirmed more frequently and preached a great deal; they also kept a good eye on the behaviour of their clergy. They were gentle to dissenters, and did not 'rail' at them, although this fact was not appreciated in all quarters and some said they were undermining the Church's authority.

With the Queen's approbation Tillotson worked hard to eradicate some of the worst abuses of the clergy at that time, particularly trying to ensure that they were resident in the parishes supposed to be under their care. In the later summer of 1694 he called the Bishops to Lambeth with the aim of working out new regulations which were to be published as a royal injunction. The Queen, however, would not allow anything to go out under the King's name unless he had seen it first, and she advised Tillotson to hold it over until his return so that it should not appear to be 'contrived' in his absence. 'Your Lordship sees,' Tillotson wrote to Dr

Stillingfleet, Bishop of Worcester, 'how her Majesty's great wisdom looks on every side of a thing ... The alteration of the clause of encouragement to the clergy, is, I think, much for the better; and, which is more, so doth the Queen, who also approves of the article concerning family devotion.'

On the whole the summer passed pleasantly enough, with 'glorious steady weather, corn and all fruits in extraordinary plenty generally'. The Queen had some opportunities to enjoy herself, and on August 9 she wrote to Lady Nottingham who was pregnant again; 'You were mightily wanted at Lord Ranalagh's, but I believe it was well for you, for everybody lost, except Lord Bradford, who went back by water, as soon as the tide served, which was a pretence to rise a winner.' Her account book shows that she had spent unstintingly buying gauze, lace, painted fans, lace tippets, pieces of 'nonpareille', some lengths of new Italian flowered lutestring, diamond 'yeare rings' price £135, and crystalline bottles for her Hungary water. She had purchased this year a pocket glass with a gold frame and a filigree back, also a gold patch-box with an agate-stone cover (and this in spite of the fact, that the Bishop of Gloucester boasted that she did not support 'such childish vanities as spotted faces'). She was reorganizing her winter wardrobe, and preparing for the cold weather with a rich sable muff and a petticoat lined with 'choyce squirril bellys [sic]'.

The campaign in Europe finished without a pitched battle or the loss of many lives. An allied force under the command of the Duke of Holstein recaptured Huy, and there was less talk now of peace and more of the next year's campaign and the possibility of regaining Namur. The King's reluctant swing towards the Whigs had bought him some peace at home, and there were even signs that Marlborough was becoming more amenable. Surely, before long, the pathetic little Duke of Gloucester would help to repair the rift between Kensington and Campden? He always behaved very prettily with the Queen, and she was growing increasingly fond of him. She offered him the present of one of her beautiful birds, but he 'excused himself from accepting of it, by saying, Madam, I will not rob you of it'.

The King had at last achieved his aim of sending an English fleet to Mediterranean waters. The problem now was to ensure that Russell agreed to winter where he was, but in the King's opinion the orders which the Queen had signed, telling him not to return, were not sufficiently strongly worded. He was afraid that Russell, whose homing instincts were strong, would find an excuse to sail back before a firmer message could reach him; if this were to happen, the King told Shrewsbury, it would be worth sending a ship to Cadiz to intercept him. But on October 12 the King wrote from Dieren, rejoicing that Russell had obeyed his orders and was preparing to stay, not without complaint, at Cadiz until the spring.

The King was now preparing to return. Shrewsbury wrote begging him to cross to England in a man-of-war rather than a yacht. Besides the danger of encountering the privateers, there were other accidents, such as 'night, mists, or storms, may occasion,' and Shrewsbury thought William owed it to England and to Europe as well to take good care of himself. As it turned out he had one of the best crossings he had ever experienced. He landed at Margate and spent a night at Canterbury. The Queen, who had been suffering from a cold, met him at Rochester, and she found him looking very thin and weak. But at least he was safe and had no military defeat to explain away.

When they drove into London, they received an ecstatic welcome; the usual bonfires and illuminations were better than ever; it was almost a victor's welcome. And although both of them felt unwell at the moment, this could be remedied, for all they needed was rest. There was plenty to live for and look forward to—the new Palaces finished and fit to live in during the years of peace that surely lay ahead.

CHAPTER 31

THE INEXORABLE DISTEMPER

SOON AFTER William's return, Mary lost a ruby from the ring which William had given her three days after their wedding. Although the stone was soon found, its loss upset her disproportionately. She saw it as some kind of an omen; she had several times during the year been troubled by grim premonitions and fears of illness. To avoid further accidents, she put the ring away, with a paper giving its history.

The King found Parliament in a good mood and generous supplies were voted for the next campaign, but his health did not help him to enjoy this situation. A week after his arrival he went down with a chill accompanied by a bout of fever. The Queen nursed him faithfully herself and fed him on a diet of apples and milk. Her devotion astonished those around her. William took massive doses of quinine, but did not begin to feel better until well on into December.

The Queen's cold seemed to be worse rather than better, and as there was smallpox in the town, some feared she might be sickening, as she had never had the disease. Within a few days she was better, to everyone's relief, but towards the end of the month she suffered a grievous shock. It was a Sunday, and during the service at Whitehall, Tillotson began to feel ill. Not wishing to interrupt the divine service, he said nothing, but people could tell there was something wrong from the expression on his face. In a few minutes he suffered a severe stroke which soon turned, in the medical parlance of the time, 'to a dead palsy'. His speech was affected, but his understanding remained clear, and he seemed serene and calm. Brokenly he managed to say that he thanked God he was quiet within, and had nothing then to do, but to await the will of heaven. Five days after he was taken ill he died in the arms of a friend. It was on this day, by a strange coincidence, that Hooper cut down the tree Tillotson had planted outside the Deanery at Canterbury, and which had prevented the crowd from seeing the Queen.

Both the King and the Queen were stricken by the loss of this gentle and tolerant man who, in spite of all the attacks of the calumniators, had

persisted in his conciliatory policy, and had managed to keep the worst
passions of the churchmen in check. The King had read all his works, and
described him as 'the best man, that I ever knew, and the best friend, that
I ever had'. Burnet, who preached his funeral sermon, broke down in the
middle, and his tears were seen by his audience, who accompanied them
'with a general groan'. As for the Queen, she wept when she heard the
news, and for several days was unable to speak of the late Archbishop
without tears. She had seen so much of this considerate, saintly man,
who had written down in the *Resolutions* which he read over every day that
he was 'not to trouble the Queen any more with my troubles . . . Not to
disturb the Queen on the Lord's day, or, if I speak with her, to speak only
on matters of religion . . . Never to mention anything said by me to the
King or Queen, or by them to me; but to thank God every day for the
great blessing of the King and Queen, and for their admirable example'.
The Queen knew that she would never find anyone else to measure up to
him, for as Burnet put it 'he had a clear head, with a most tender and
compassionate heart; he was a faithful and zealous friend, but a gentle
and soon conquered enemy; he was truly and seriously religious, but
without affectation, bigotry, or superstition; his notions of morality were
fine and sublime; his thread of reasoning was easy, clear and solid'.

The appointment of a successor was no easy task. If the Queen favoured
anyone, it was Dr Stillingfleet, a close friend of the late Archbishop, a
learned man cast in a similar mould. He was, however, inclined to press
High Church principles in his excellent sermons, and this did not please
William or the Whigs. His health was not good, which provided an excuse
for appointing Dr Tenison, the Bishop of Lincoln, 'who had a firmer
health, with a more active temper'. The Queen put her point of view
earnestly to Shrewsbury and her husband, but William was more intent
on pleasing the Whigs than on pacifying his wife. In any case, although
the Queen was disappointed, Tenison was in many ways the more suitable
candidate; he was learned if a trifle dull, and he possessed a certain insen-
sitivity which made him better able to deal with the difficulties of his
position than the over-vulnerable Tillotson. In the past, the Queen had
championed Tenison when he was criticized for preaching at Nell
Gwynne's funeral; she said it was a sign that the unfortunate woman
had died penitent, for such a distinguished clergyman would never have
spoken well of her unless she had made 'a pious Christian end'.

The building at Hampton Court was going well, and a week before
Christmas the Queen went down to start ordering the furniture. The
weather was very cold and there was a great deal of illness about. William

had caught another chill while out hunting and Shrewsbury was suffering from gout; 'for want of legs' he had to send a messenger to the King with a letter that had come from Russell. The smallpox epidemic was increasing every day, and was proving a very virulent strain.

The Queen had already caught two colds this autumn, and she had told Mlle Obdam earlier in the year that she was beginning to feel old. The King was working very hard, sometimes so late into the night that he was unable to come back to Kensington and had to stay at Whitehall. The strain of nursing him through his illness, her continuing worry about his health and the shock of Tillotson's death, had brought her into a low state. Burnet saw her on December 18 and thought she was not as cheerful as she usually was when she had William at home. A day or two later, she felt unwell, but took no notice and went out and about as usual, telling nobody. That evening she was worse and could no longer hide the fact that she was ill. All the same she did not send for the doctors, but shut herself into her closet at Kensington, putting her papers in order, probably burning all her letters from William and her diary for the year that was just finishing; the previous ones, fortunately, were at Whitehall. She wrote out instructions that at her funeral there should be 'no extraordinary expense' and that her body should not be examined for poisoning. She also mentioned the few small debts outstanding at the time, which included sums expended on the two children she had 'adopted'—three hair-cuts for the boy at sixpence a time, laces for the girl, a 'cosy winter coat' (price twelve shillings), a new frock and breeches for the boy, the apothecary's bill, two pairs of shoes and a fan. She also wrote a letter to William which she put in a locked desk by her bed. Hardwicke, who later saw the letter, said that it contained 'a strong but decent admonition to the King, for some irregularity in his conduct. The expressions are so general that one can neither make out the fact or person alluded to'. Dalrymple did not consider the letter proper for inclusion in his book, and it is no longer in existence. Posterity has assumed that she was referring to Elizabeth Villiers, but there is no proof that this was so.

Only when she had put her affairs in order did the Queen tell her husband that she felt ill. She guessed that she had caught smallpox and the doctors immediately assumed the same. William abandoned hope at once; fourteen years before, his mother had died of 'the inexorable and pitiless distemper' in London at Christmas time, and as he had also lost his father from the same disease, it was not surprising that he felt pessimistic. All those who had not already had smallpox were sent away from the Palace. The Queen had been treating herself with the remedies she usually took for a bad cold, but nine doctors were now summoned. On Sunday, December 23 there were signs of a rash.

On the second day of her illness the King attended to business; the Triennial Bill had come up in Parliament and this time it was going through, but what had once seemed so important now faded into insignificance. Perhaps if he had not been so preoccupied, the King would have exercised the royal veto once again. He was by now in such a state of despair that he was unable to deal with anything coherently. He called Burnet into his closet, and burst into tears, sobbing out that there was no hope for the Queen; 'from being the happiest, he was now going to be the miserablest creature upon earth.' He said that during the whole course of their marriage, he had never known one single fault in her; 'there was a worth in her that nobody knew besides himself.'

The news had now spread beyond the Palace. 'Never was such a face of universal sorrow seen in a court or in a town as at this time,' Burnet wrote; 'all people, men and women, young and old, could scarce refrain from tears.' The ante-room was crowded with people waiting for news. On Christmas day the rash subsided and there was universal rejoicing; the doctors began to think that she after all had been only suffering from measles. She seemed now to be quite herself, but the doctors still made her undergo some bleeding and purging; they also applied leeches to her neck. Jenkin Lewis, Gloucester's servant, who was sent down to enquire about the Queen's health from her laundress, was 'transported' when he heard that she had rested well. He said there was 'abundance of joy to all people; for she was beloved by everybody; she had found the method of pleasing people, by her obliging easy deportment', although he added that in his opinion her money proved 'a powerful persuasive'. He went back to Campden, and threw his hat into the air saying 'O be joyful', and when the little Duke heard the reason why, he said, well pleased, 'I am glad of it with all my heart'.

The King, who had ordered a camp-bed to be set up in the Queen's room so that he did not have to leave her, agreed that this should be moved next door. But by evening the mood of hope had faded. So often, with smallpox sufferers, there appeared to be a slight improvement on the third day, but this could mean that the poison, instead of breaking out into a rash, had turned inwards, and this was the most dangerous symptom of all. On Christmas evening the doctors realized that the spots had 'sunk' and that there was no hope of raising them. The King poured out his troubles in a letter to Vaudemont. 'You can imagine the state I am in, loving her as I do,' he wrote. 'You know what it is to have a good wife. If I were so unhappy as to lose mine, I should have to withdraw from the world, and though we have no monasteries in our religion, one can always find somewhere to go and spend the rest of one's days in prayer to God.'

The King's camp-bed was now moved back into the sick room, and he refused to do any business or to see anyone except Burnet or Portland. He managed to control his cough, so much so that Mary thought he had left the room and asked where he was. From time to time he wept, as did others who were standing in the room. 'Why are you crying? I am not so bad,' she said. She was not in any pain, but she seemed drowsy and gradually became more and more breathless. The doctors were unable to control the bleeding in her throat; she was spitting blood, and there was also blood in her urine. It was sad that she could not have her friend Tillotson at her side, but Tenison was attentive and talked to her. When it became evident that there was no more hope, he told the King that he could not do his duty faithfully, unless he told her the danger she was in. The King agreed, for he felt that even if she were to be upset, he did not want her deceived. The Archbishop began his unpleasant task carefully and gently, to avoid giving her a shock, but she helped him out by guessing what he was trying to say before he had finished. She said, in Burnet's version, that 'she thanked God she had always carried this in her mind, that nothing was to be left to the last hour; she had nothing then to do, but to look up to God, and submit to his will; it went further indeed than submission; for she seemed to desire death rather than life'. She had told Mlle Obdam only this September, when writing to condole with her on the death of her mother, that it is more difficult for these who have children to die, for they are 'attached by so many affections to the earth; this must render death more easy to those who have none'.

The doctors continued to administer the remedies they knew, but everyone realized at heart that all hope had gone. 'Because her Majesty's time had come all was useless', wrote one Dutch observer. She was strangely composed and indeed it was hard for her to believe that she was going to die, for she hardly felt ill; moreover she was able to sit up with some support and feed herself with water gruel. On the morning of December 27 she received the sacrament from the hands of Archbishop Tenison, and all the other Bishops who were in the Palace were invited in to receive it with her. 'We were, God knows, a sorrowful company,' Burnet recorded. The Queen followed the whole service, repeating it after the Archbishop, and was a little upset when they told her she might not be able to swallow the bread. The Queen said that her last letter to her husband lay in the little desk by her bed, and as she wished to avoid upsetting him further by having a parting scene, she spent most of her time in prayer. Once the sacrament was over, she 'composed herself solemnly' to die. She asked the Archbishop to read her suitable extracts from the scriptures, and once or twice tried to speak to the King but felt unable to.

William now broke out into passionate weeping, astonishing to those who thought of him as a cold, reserved, unemotional man. The Queen herself was distressed; she asked him 'not to make her suffer the pangs of death twice' and begged him to take care of himself for the sake of the nation. He replied 'that if God caused this blow to fall upon him everything would be over for him'. The doctors led him away to the ante-room, where he fainted with exhaustion and grief. Still further remedies were tried—Sir Walter Raleigh's cordial, King Charles's drops, and other cordials—but nothing could touch the poison in the blood stream. The rash had never come out and her skin remained 'as smooth as glass'.

When she realized that she had dozed off while prayers were being read, Mary roused herself and asked that they should continue all the same. 'Others have need to pray for me seeing I am so little able to pray for myself,' she said. Dr Radcliffe, who had been called in on Christmas Eve, offered her further medicines which she refused. 'I believe I shall now soon die,' Tenison heard her say, and she added something that sounded like 'a better way'. Stimulants were administered, but her mind was wandering; she called Tenison to her side and asked him to look behind the screen at the head of her bed. He did so, and told her there was no one there, but she insisted, telling him that Dr Radcliffe had brought in a Popish nurse—her mind had wandered back to the time when Anne had been ill with smallpox and Lake and Compton had been so concerned about her Papist nurse.

Under bitter black skies and in scurries of snow the crowds stood outside in the Kensington road waiting for news. Anyone who could find an excuse to come into the stifling sick room to join in the sighing and groaning did so.

At Campden House, Princess Anne, who had, on the advice of her physicians, spent the last few months lying on a couch to avoid a miscarriage, heard of her sister's danger, and sent one of her ladies of the bedchamber with a message saying that she was prepared to run any hazard if the Queen would give her the happiness of waiting on her. Lady Derby received the message and she later replied that the King and Queen both thanked the Princess for offering to come but, since it was thought so necessary to keep the Queen as quiet as possible, they hoped she would defer the visit. Such a civil answer, in Lady Marlborough's opinion, could only mean that the disease was mortal; this good lady also concluded that the refusal was just another excuse to lengthen out the quarrel; surely if the Queen were well enough to take the sacrament she was well enough to see her sister?

The Queen was now beyond the reach of petty feuds and quarrels. On December 27 she slipped into unconsciousness. William, leaning on the arm of Portland, was brought back into the room. When he saw his wife he broke into weeping again and had to be taken away. Rumour had it that his own life was in danger, and that he had already lost his sanity. When he was told that Mary's pulse was failing, he collapsed. At a quarter to one on December 28, after what Tenison described as 'two or three small strugglings of nature', and without such agonies as were expected, she died peacefully.

She was only thirty-two, and although at times she felt old and tired, she had still retained something of the bloom of her youth. Grief was universal, not only in England, but also on the continent, and in Holland the bells tolled three times a day. The complete overthrow of the soldier King made everyone realize at last how much he had loved her. The loud lamentations which had amazed the onlookers at the Queen's death-bed were now stilled, and William had fallen into a state of numbed depression; he lay on his bed, motionless and without speaking, and those about him feared that he, too, was going to die. He could not bear to have anyone near him who reminded him of the Queen. After her death, Portland had picked him up in his arms and carried him out of the room, where the Archbishop tried to comfort him. Tenison stayed at the Palace day and night consoling him and giving him what comfort he could. He refused to see anyone else, except Portland, Keppel and his page La Fontaine. When a delegation came from the two Houses of Parliament on the last day of the year, its members were shocked by his appearance. He broke down in front of them and was incapable of uttering more than a few broken sentences. Shrewsbury found it impossible to conduct any business; 'the affliction his Majesty has been under, and still expressed, to a passionate degree, has hindered me from making any steps towards what you commanded me,' he wrote to Russell. Huygens, who arrived faithfully at Kensington, after leaving a decent interval of a few days, in the hope of taking down some letters, found the King closeted in his bedchamber. The Queen's body had by this time been embalmed, and an attendant told Huygens he had opened one of the windows a little to let out some of the bad air. Huygens came back several times but found little improvement, and Keppel, who was now the only person allowed in the Bedchamber, was finally moved to exclaim, 'What is that old man here for every post day, the King will still see nobody, when he is seeing people again he will send for them.'

Within a few days William felt able to go out into the garden, but he was so weak that he had to be carried in a chair. One of the first people the King agreed to see was Prince George, who came on his own. Anne had already sent him a respectful letter expressing her condolences, and although the two sisters had not met again, it was generally believed that there had been a last-minute reconciliation. On January 12 the Princess managed to visit the King in person and they talked together amicably. Subsequently the King restored her guards and granted her the use of St James's Palace. All the Queen's jewellery became hers, the rubies and emeralds, the diamond collars, the pearl and diamond loops, the buckles and rings, 'twelve diamond taggs for bodies', one pair of diamond shoe-buckles, a 'conceited ring' of small diamonds, and 'the great diamond ear-rings with their drops'.

A few hours after the Queen's death, Parliament met and made plans for the lying-in-state and the funeral. The Queen's letter requesting that the ceremonies should be kept simple and inexpensive was not found until too late. Her bowels were removed at once and deposited, according to custom, in King Henry VII's Chapel. The embalmed body was removed to Whitehall; as it was being carried away from Kensington several of the stairs were damaged and later had to be repaired. All the rooms leading to the Banqueting Hall were re-decorated, and Wren was commissioned to design an elaborate catafalque. On the day of the Queen's death all the Seals were broken, but Parliament hastened to show its loyalty to William, to disappoint any hopes the Jacobites might have of bringing back King James now that his daughter was dead. At Saint-Germain the exiled King forbade any mourning and showed no signs of personal sorrow. The *bonnes dispositions* of the two Houses of Parliament and of the whole populace of London showed that there was to be no disturbance in the State. Parliament was even promising to increase the subsidies and to despatch them more quickly to help the progress of the war. The reconciliation with Anne ensured that there was no hope of making further trouble by means of the Denmark household.

Although William regained his strength every day, it was weeks before he could bring himself to attend to business. On January 24 he agreed to see Burnet, but even as he was thanking the Bishop for his devotion to the

Queen he broke down again, and they wept together for about an hour. He still found it hard to realize that the Queen had left him for ever, and he told Portland that sometimes he imagined that things were just as they had always been and that he must go down to have supper with her as usual. At the end of the month, while Kensington was being hung throughout with black, Portland insisted that the King should go away to Richmond so that he would not hear the sound of hammering. All the month, the country had been in the grip of a cold spell; the Thames was frozen over and the smallpox epidemic continued, with, it was rumoured, over five hundred deaths in one week. It was still very cold when the King was at Richmond, but he managed to go out and do some shooting on horseback. In February he had to steel himself to return to Kensington, which he dreaded. 'I think the stones fly against my head,' he told Heinsius. In the Banqueting Hall the lying-in-state had begun, and the King could watch the people filing respectfully past from an alcove hung with purple velvet under the royal arms with *Je Maintiendrai* embroidered on it. He was excused from attending the funeral, and little by little he regained his strength, though in the spring his cough was bad and he was spitting blood. He threw himself into his work, trying to forget his sorrow in plans for a campaign that might bring nearer the peace his wife had longed for but now would never see. For months he was unable to talk about her without weeping, and once, months after her death, when at supper some small thing reminded him of her, he was overcome and had to be carried up to his bed. He continued to talk to Tenison, and in general became more religious—he had tended to leave the practice of religion to his wife—going to prayers twice a day rather than once, and spending more time in private prayer. It may have been her last letter that prompted him to cut himself off completely from Elizabeth Villiers; he settled estates on her worth £30,000 a year, in recognition of the services, of various kinds, that she had done him and in November 1695, having received clear evidence that she could be of no further use to the King, she married Lord George Hamilton, who was later created Earl of Orkney.

William remained faithful to the Queen's memory and never married again, though it was rumoured in 1696 that he had designs on the Elector of Brandenburg's daughter, whom Matthew Prior described as 'a tall miss at a boarding school with a scraggy lean neck'. She was no substitute for the beautiful Mary, and the King turned more and more to his men friends and particularly to Keppel.

From February 21 the public were admitted to the Banqueting Hall. Hundreds were turned away, many were injured in the crush and pickpockets did good business. The Queen lay with her hands crossed on her breast, with a crown and sword at her head and at her feet a sword and shield. At each corner of the coffin stood a lady in mourning clothes, in a rota that changed every half-hour. Twelve gentlemen at arms were also in attendance, dressed in black satin. The room was lit by candles in black glass chandeliers with silver fittings, which flickered over the symbolic empty throne and the pictures depicting St George chasing away spirits and the Queen being carried off by angels.

The funeral took place on March 5. It was a raw, cold day with snow and an icy wind. The route from Whitehall to the Abbey was lined with three regiments of Guards. In the procession were heralds carrying the banners of Wales, Chester and Cornwall. The Duchess of Somerset was the chief mourner, and Catherine Sedley ironically enough, was among the six gentlewoman who accompanied her. Sir Edward Villiers led the Queen's charger. As the coffin was lowered the officers of the household broke their staves and flung them into the grave. Sixty cannon sounded from the Tower and sixty from St James's Park. Tenison delivered a sermon, and a boy's voice sang Purcell's Elegy 'O Dive Custos Auricae Domus, Maria Maria'. Four hundred poor women and all the members of Parliament had been issued with black cloaks, and the streets were hung with black cloth. And when all the pomp and ceremony was over, the ladies walked home through the falling snow 'draggling their trains' in the slush.

It was said that Parliament had cheerfully voted the £50,000 needed for all the expenses. The coffin alone cost £850, and the enormous baroque catafalque was another costly item. Grinling Gibbons carved for it three boys three foot high, with lions and unicorns, and the cornice measured seventy-three feet. Gibbons, who had served Mary so well in life, had the sad task of carving the inscription on the coffin, for the lordly sum of one pound. The English, whose politicians had often spurned her in life, and whose courtiers had never treated her with great friendliness, gave her magnificent treatment in death. She would certainly have disapproved of the pompous ceremony which her corpse was afforded. Her virtues, as she knew so well herself, were of a homely nature; she disliked pomp and show, and could never accustom herself to the artificiality of court life; flattery had always sickened her. She herself spoke of her 'simplicité Hollandoise' which made her neither expect compliments nor bestow them on other people. Dartmouth said that until her Grace the Duchess of Marlborough thought fit to publish her Conduct he had never 'heard an ill character of her Majesty given by anybody'. Although the majority of her countrymen had never seen her, since she had scarcely ever left

London, the fame of her piety and charm had spread to all corners of the land. Few people had anything but good to say about her, and there was little need to gloss over her faults. The Bishop of Lichfield and Coventry told Evelyn about the pious behaviour of the Queen in her last sickness, and spoke of her impartiality; 'she never inquired of what opinion persons were, who were objects of charity.' As Evelyn put it himself, 'in sum, she was an admirable woman, abating for taking the Crown without a more due apology, as does, if possible, outdo the renowned Queen Elizabeth'. Ailesbury talked of her as an incomparable Princess and a perfect wife, whose humanity was unsurpassed. As to her fate, which drove her to supplant her father, he said that she submitted to it, 'but God knows what she suffered inwardly and to a high degree'. Burnet confessed that he had never admired anyone so entirely as he did her:

In the course of above eight years' very particular knowledge of her I never saw any one thing that I could have wished to be otherwise than it was in her. The more I knew her, I still saw the more reason to admire both her understanding, her piety, and her virtue, without discovering the least defect or fault in her. The purity and sublimity of her mind was the perfectest thing I ever saw; I never felt myself sink so much under anything that had happened to me as by her death; it is a daily load upon my thought, and gives me great apprehensions of very heavy judgments hanging over us, for I am afraid that in losing her we have lost both our strength and our glory.

In the many funeral sermons which were preached from pulpits all over the country, the clergy talked of her goodness and benignity, her cheerfulness and good humour, her sweetness of expression, and it was generally considered that her death was a judgment on the nation, an example of the 'awful divine dispose'. Proverbs XXXI, 29, provided a suitable text—'Many daughters have done virtuously, but thou excellest them all.' Her good example, authority and zeal were held up to view, and one preacher in Rotterdam pointed out that although 'the devouring grave' had swallowed up her bodily beauty, the memory of her virtues would live on.

Elegies and odes were plentiful:

> First, she loved God, not like the Pharisee,
> In ostentation and hypocrisy;
> But even with her heart and all her soul,
> She secretly did raging sin control . . .
>
> She was a pattern of humility
> And therefore ladies now of high degree,
> Her good example imitate, and try,
> To live like her, that you like her may die.

Some poets mourned her in the pastoral mode, reviving the mourning shepherds and dying shades of her youth. At the Hague, Matthew Prior, the poet and diplomat, had been charged with the task of breaking the news officially to the Dutch; the long mourning cloak which he put on for the occasion was 'slubbered' with his tears, and it trailed in the thawing snow in the streets. His grief was genuine; he owned that he was dazed into a colic. 'I have lost my senses and a £100 a year,' he wrote, referring to the small pension granted to him by the Queen. He was surprised to see how deeply the phlegmatic Dutchmen were affected by the news. 'Marble weeps,' he wrote laconically. He found it very mournful writing official melancholy letters, and listening to 'the dismal sound of bells, and more dismal chimes of many bad poems on too good a subject'. His own poem was, he thought not much better than the rest—'God preserve it from singeing pullets, or being laid under pies.' Probably his best effort was the verse he wrote spontaneously in the sand at Scheveling, where he was wandering after hearing the news of the Queen's death:

> Number the sands extended here;
> So many Mary's virtues were:
> Number the drops that yonder roll;
> So many griefs press William's soul.

After her death the King did his best to continue supporting all those charities in which the Queen had been particularly interested, such as those which aimed at helping Protestant refugees, or 'encouraging a pious and a laborious clergy'. But without her active sympathy and encouragement, many reform societies died out. Even when she had come over to England, Mlle Obdam, whom she had deputed to keep an eye on the French Society, often asked for her opinion on difficult matters.

The King could not bring himself to finish the building and furnishing at Hampton Court. The houses he had planned with the Queen held too many memories; he could not enjoy lingering in them or giving his mind to their improvement. Greenwich Palace rose as a fit memorial to his beloved Queen, but for the time being he left the other buildings as they were. The collections of porcelain and books, which had been her especial interest, languished now, without her guiding inspiration; the books were dispersed and all the porcelain eventually went with Keppel to Holland. At Kensington Gibbons carved a picture frame with melancholy doves and sorrowing cherubs, perhaps commissioned by William after the Queen's death to house her portrait. In 1700 William, who was in Holland, sent orders for the Water Gallery at Hampton Court to be pulled down. The Queen had always known that it was to be a temporary building, but it was six years before the King could bring himself to destroy the little refuge that was so particularly hers, and he made sure that he was far away when the demolition took place.

'I often flatter myself,' the Queen had written to Mlle Obdam in 1692, 'with the thought of one day being able to see Holland again, one of these days, if God preserves my life long enough.' She was never to achieve this ambition, never to see Loo in its finished state—never to see the fountains play, or lose herself in the labyrinths, or watch the wild animals wander in the park. Her life had been cut off when she was still in her prime, and she could have accomplished much if she had survived her husband and ruled on her own. As it was, she had failed in the most important task of all, for she had never solved the problem of the English succession by providing the Stuart family with a healthy Protestant heir. Her children had been her houses, and her contribution to the English people and its landscape the homely buildings in soft-coloured brick with their sash windows and slate roofs, restrained in outline and in perfect taste, built in imitation of her own unpretentious palaces in the simple Calvinistic spirit of the Dutch.

Her virtues, like her houses, were homely and unspectacular, and the dour and warlike William has for too long taken the centre of the stage, overshadowing his graceful wife. Her rare achievement was that she remained simple and unassuming though she lived in high places and wielded great power. To the end of her life, she retained the common touch and her servants loved her. When she stayed at the Deanery in Canterbury she particularly noticed 'a very good old woman with whom she had a great deal of discourse', and she always took an interest in the children of her friends and servants. She was, as Lady Russell put it, a 'ready writer', though like so many other people, she found it hard to settle down to her correspondence. Her letters and diaries, sometimes poignant, sometimes witty, provide the unique record of a woman who looked at great affairs with the simple unaffected gaze of one who is in touch with higher realities. She had no ambition to be a Queen, and yet she filled that position with a quiet dignity which remained a legend for many years after her death.

BIBLIOGRAPHY

ABBREVIATIONS used in the notes are shown in parentheses; in general references are to the first word shown in the list below.

MANUSCRIPT SOURCES

England: Bodleian Library—Carte MSS, Rawlinson MSS, Tanner MSS.

British Museum—Additional MSS (Add MSS), Egerton MSS, Bathurst MSS.

Chatsworth MSS.

Public Record Office—State Papers Foreign, Holland (PRO SPF Holland), Works 5/55, Kensington Pay Books.

Walton—Manuscript Memoirs of Bishop Hooper by his daughter Mrs Prowse (Walton Hooper MSS). Extracts from these are printed in Trevor's *Life of William III*, appendix to vol. II.

Victoria and Albert Museum: Forster MSS, George Chalmers Collection (V and A, Forster MSS).

Holland: Koninklijk Bibliotheek (KB).

Koninklijk Huis Archiev (KHA).

Algemeen Rijksarchiev, Nassau Domeinen Ordonnanties (RA Nass Dom Ord).

PRINTED SOURCES
Contemporary Letters and Memoirs

Historical Manuscripts Commission (HMC) in particular the following volumes: Bath II, Buccleuch II, Dartmouth, Finch II, Foljambe, Hope-Johnston, Le Fleming, Stopford-Sackville, Report II, Report VII.

Public Record Office: State Papers Domestic (SPDom)

AILESBURY, THOMAS EARL OF: *Memoirs*, ed. W. Buckley, vol I (1890).

ANON: *A Brief History of the Pious and Glorious Life of Mary II* (1695).

— *A Pindarique Ode to the Memory of the Late Queen Mary* (1695).

— *Life and Death of her Royal Majesty* (1695).

— *Poems on the Death of Queen Mary* (1710).

— *The Mourning Poets* (1695).

BATHURST, THE HON. BENJAMIN: *Letters of Two Queens* (1924).

BENTINCK, WILLIAM: *Correspondentie van William III en van Hans Willem Bentinck*, 2 vols. (1927, 1937).

BOURDON, DANIEL DE: *Mémoires*, ed. F. J. L. Kramer (1898).

BOYER, ABEL: *The History of King William III* (1702-3).

BRAMSTON, SIR JOHN: *Autobiography*, ed. Lord Braybrooke, Camden Society (1845).

BULSTRODE, SIR RICHARD: *Memoirs of the Reign of Charles II* (1721).

BURNET, BISHOP GILBERT: *History of His Own Time*, 6 vols. (1833).

— *Supplement*, ed. H. C. Foxcroft (1902).

— *Original Memoirs*, ed. H. C. Foxcroft.

— *A Discourse of the Pastoral Care* (1692).

— *Funeral Sermon* (1695).

CALAMY, EDMUND: *An Historical Account of my own Life 1671-1731*, ed. J. T. Rutt, 2 vols. (1829).

CAMPANA DE CAVELLI, E.: *Les Derniers Stuarts à Saint-Germain en Laye*, 2 vols. (1871).

CIBBER, COLLEY: *Poem on the Death of Queen Mary* (1695).

— *An Apology for the Life of Mr. Colley Cibber* (1740).

CLARENDON, EDWARD HYDE, EARL OF: *Life and Continuation*, 3 vols. (1759).

CLARENDON, HENRY HYDE, EARL OF: *Correspondence*, ed. S. W. Singer, 2 vols. (1828).

CLARKE, J. S., ed.: *The Life of James II collected out of Memoirs Writ of his own hand*, 2 vols. (1816).

COKE, ROGER: *A Detection of the Court and State of England*, 3 vols. (1719).

A Collection of Ordinances and Regulations for the Government of the Royal Household made in Divers Reigns from King Edward III to King William and Queen Mary also Receipts in Ancient Cookery (1790).

COXE, ARCHDEACON W., ed.: *Private and Original Correspondence of Charles Talbot, Duke of Shrewsbury* (1821).

CROWNE, JOHN: *Dramatic Works*, ed. James Maidment and W. H. Logan, 3 vols. (1875).

DALRYMPLE, SIR JOHN: *Memoirs of Great Britain and Ireland*, 3 vols. (1790).

D'AVAUX, COMTE: *Négotiations en Hollande 1679-1688*, 6 vols. (1752-3).

DEFOE, DANIEL: *A Tour through the Whole Island of Great Britain*, ed. G. D. H. Cole and D. C. Browning, 2 vols. (1962).

DE GOURVILLE, JEAN HERAULT: *Mémoires*, 2 vols. (1724).

D'ESTRADES, COMTE: *Memoirs and Letters*, 8 vols. (1743).

DOEBNER, DR R.: *Memoirs of Mary Queen of England 1689-1693* (1886).

DRELINCOURT, C.: *A Christian's Defence Against the Fears of Death* (1701).

DROSTE, CONRAD: *Overblyfsels van Geheugchenis der bisonderste Voorvallen* (1728).

ECHARD, LAURENCE: *The History of England*, 3 vols. (1718).

ELIZABETH, QUEEN OF BOHEMIA: *Letters*, ed. L. M. Baker (1953).

ELLIS, H., ed.: *Original Letters Illustrative of English History*, 4 vols. (1846).

EVELYN, JOHN: *Diary*, ed. de Beer, 6 vols. (1955).

— *Life of Mrs. Godolphin* (1904).

FANSHAWE, LADY: *Memoirs*, ed. Beatrice Marshall (1905).

FIENNES, CELIA: *The Journeys*, ed. Christopher Morris (1947).

FOXCROFT, H. C.: *The Life and Letters of George Savile 1st Marquess of Halifax*, 2 vols. (1898).
— ed. *A Supplement to Burnet's History of My Own Times* (1902).
— *A Life of Gilbert Burnet*, vol. II (1907).
FULLER, WILLIAM: *The Whole Life of Mr. Fuller Impartially Written by Himself* (1703).
GRAMONT, ANTHONY HAMILTON, COMTE DE: *Memoirs*, ed. Peter Quennell (1930).
GREY, LORD: *The Secret History of the Rye-House Plot and Monmouth's Rebellion* (1754).
HARRIS, WALTER: *A Description of the King's Royal Palace at Loo* (1689).
— *A Short Account of Holland* (1689).
— *A New History of the Life and Reign of William-Henry* (1749).
Hatton Correspondence, 2 vols., Camden Society (1878).
HUYGENS, CHRISTIAN: *Correspondance, Œuvres Complètes*, vols. VIII and IX (1901).
HUYGENS, CONSTANTINE the elder: *Briefwisseling*, vol. VI (1917).
— *Mémoires*.
HUYGENS, CONSTANTINE the younger: *Journal*, 4 vols. (1676–81).
JAMES II: *Papers of Devotion*, ed. Godfrey Davies (1925).
— *Memoirs of his Campaigns as Duke of York 1652–1660* (1962).
JAPIKSE, N., ed.: *Correspondentie van William III en van Hans Willem Bentinck*, Part I, 2 vols., Part II 3 vols. (1927–35).
JURIEU, PIERRE: *Histoire du Calvinisme et celle du Papisme*, 4 vols. (1683).
— *The Groans of France in Slavery* (1689).
KENNET, WHITE: *History of England, Charles I–William III*.
KRÄMER, F. J. L., ed.: *Archives ou correspondance inédite de la Maison d'Orange Nassau 1689–1702*, 3rd Series (1907–9).
LAKE, DR EDWARD: *Diary*, Camden Society (1847).
Lettres et Mémoires de Mary II, ed. Countess Bentinck (1880).
Leven and Melville Papers, Bannatyne Club (1843).
LEWIS, JENKIN: *An Account of the Duke of Gloucester* (1789).
Lexington Papers, ed. H. M. Sutton (1851).
LISELOTTE, ELIZABETH CHARLOTTE, PRINCESS PALATINE AND DUCHESS OF ORLEANS, 'MADAME': *Letters 1652–1722*, translated Maria Kroll (1970). See also 'Madame'.
LUTTRELL, NARCISSUS: *A Brief Historical Relation of State Affairs*, 6 vols. (1857).
MACPHERSON, JAMES: *Original Papers*, 2 vols. (1775).
'MADAME' ELIZABETH CHARLOTTE OF BAVARIA, PRINCESS PALATINE, DUCHESS OF ORLÉANS: *Letters*, ed. G. S. Stevenson, 2 vols. (1924). See also Liselotte.
MARLBOROUGH, SARAH, DUCHESS OF: *An Account of the Conduct of the Duchess of Marlborough from her first coming to Court to the Year 1710*, ed. Hooke (1742).
MIDDLEBUSH, F. A., ed.: *The Dispatches of Thomas Plott and Thomas Chudleigh: English Envoys at the Hague* (1926).

MONSIEUR DE B.: *Mémoires*, ed. F. J. L. Krämer (1898).
MÜLLER, P. L.: *Wilhelm II von Oranien und Georg Friedrich von Waldeck* (1873).
OLDMIXON, T.: *History of the Stuarts* (1730).
PATRICK, SYMON, BISHOP OF ELY: *Autobiography* (1839).
PEPYS, SAMUEL: *Diary*, ed. H. B. Wheatley, 3 vols. (1946).
POMPONNE, ARNAULD NICOLAS SIMON, MARQUIS DE: *Relation de mon Ambassade en Hollande*, ed. R. H. Rowan (1955).
PRINSTERER, GROEN VAN: *Archives ou Correspondance inédite de la Maison d'Orange-Nassau*, Series II, vol. V (1861).
RALPH, JAMES: *The Other Side of the Question* (1742).
— *The History of England during the Reigns of King William, Queen Anne and King George I*, 2 vols. (1744–6).
RERESBY, SIR JOHN: *Memoirs*, ed. A. Browning (1936).
RONQUILLO, DON PEDRO: *Correspondencia entre dos Embajadores 1689–91*, 2 vols. (1951–2).
Royal Diary or King William III's Interiour Portraicture (1705).
RUSSELL, LADY RACHEL: *Letters*, ed. Lord John Russell, 2 vols. (1853).
SAINT-SIMON, CLAUDE HENRI ROUVROY, DUC DE: *Mémoires*, 5 vols. (1950).
SAVILE, HENRY: *Correspondence*, Camden Society (1871).
SIDNEY, HENRY: *Diary of the Times of Charles II*, ed. R. S. Blencowe, 2 vols. (1843).
SOPHIA, ELECTRESS OF HANOVER: *Memoirs 1630–1680*, trans. H. Forester (1888).
— *Correspondance avec son Frère Charles Louis, Count Palatine of the Rhine* (1886). Referred to in the notes as *Letters of Sophia*.
SWITZER, STEPHEN: *The Nobleman, Gentleman, and Gardener's Recreation* (1715).
TEMPLE, SIR WILLIAM: *Works*, 4 vols. (1770).
— *Memoirs of the Life, Works and Correspondence*, ed. Thomas Courtenay, 2 vols. (1836).
VERNEY: *Memoirs of the Verney Family*, ed. Margaret M. Verney, vol. IV (1899).
WELWOOD, J.: *Memoirs of the Most Material Transactions in England for the Last Hundred Years Preceding the Revolution in 1688* (1820).
WHITE, IGNATIUS, MARQUIS D'ALBEVILLE: *Memorial* (1688).
WILLIAMSON, SIR JOSEPH: *Letters*, Camden Society, 2 vols. (1874).
WREN, CHRISTOPHER, JNR.: *Parentalia* (1750).
ZOUTELANDT, MADAME DE: *Mémoires* (1709).

Secondary Authorities

ASHLEY, MAURICE: *John Wildman: Plotter and Postmaster* (1947).
— *The Glorious Revolution of 1688* (1966).
BAXTER, STEPHEN: *William III* (1966).
BEATTLE, JOHN M.: *The English Court in the Reign of George I* (1967).
BIRCH, T.: *Life of Tillotson* (1752).
BLOK, P.: *History of the People of the Netherlands* (1907).
BOWEN, MARJORIE: *The Third Mary Stuart* (1929).
BRIGGS, MARTIN SHAW: *Wren the Incomparable* (1953).

BROWNING, ANDREW: *Thomas Osborne Earl of Danby and Duke of Leeds*, 3 vols. (1944–51).

BRYANT, A.: *Samuel Pepys: The Years of Peril* (1948), *The Saviour of the Navy* (1949).

— *King Charles II* (1955).

CARPENTER, EDWARD: *The Life and Times of Thomas Tenison* (1948).

— *The Protestant Bishop* (1956).

CARSWELL, JOHN: *The Descent on England* (1969).

CARTE, THOMAS: *The Life of James, Duke of Ormonde* 1851).

CHAPMAN, HESTER W.: *Mary II Queen of England* (1953).

CHENEVIX-TRENCH, CHARLES: *The Western Rising* (1969).

CHURCHILL, SIR WINSTON S.: *Marlborough, his Life and Times*, 2 vols. (1947).

CLARK, SIR G. N.: *The Dutch Alliance and the French War 1688–97* (1923).

— *The Later Stuarts 1660–1714* (1934).

COURTENAY, THOMAS: *Life of Sir William Temple*, 2 vols. (1836).

CUNDALL, H. M.: *Bygone Richmond* (1925).

CUNNINGHAM, ALEXANDER: *The History of Great Britain from the Revolution in 1688*, 2 vols. (1787).

DAVIDSON, L. C.: *Catherine of Braganza* (1908).

D'OYLEY, ELIZABETH: *James, Duke of Monmouth* (1938).

EHRMAN, JOHN: *The Navy in the War of William III 1689–1697* (1953).

EVERY, G.: *The High Church Party 1688–1715* (1956).

FEILING, SIR KEITH: *A History of the Tory Party 1640–1714* (1924).

FOX, CHARLES JAMES: *A History of the Early Part of the Reign of James II* (1808).

FRANSEN, J.: *Les Comédiens Français en Hollande* (1925).

GEYL, P.: *The Netherlands in the Seventeenth Century* (1964).

— *History of the Low Countries* (1964).

GREEN, DAVID: *Grinling Gibbons* (1964).

— *Sarah, Duchess of Marlborough* (1967).

— *Queen Anne* (1970).

GREW, MARION E.: *William Bentinck and William III* (1924).

HALEY, K. D. H.: *William of Orange and the English Opposition 1672–4* (1953).

HAMILTON, ELIZABETH: *The Backstairs Dragon* (1969).

HART, A. TINDALL: *The Life and Times of John Sharp, Archbishop of York* (1949).

— *William Lloyd 1627–1717* (1952).

HARTMAN, C. H.: *Charles II and Madame* (1934).

— *Clifford of the Cabal 1630–73* (1937).

HORWITZ, HENRY: *Revolution Politicks, the Career of Daniel Finch Second Earl of Nottingham 1647–1730* (1968).

JAMES, F. G.: *Conflict in Stuart England: Essays in Honour of Wallace Notestein*, 'The Bishops in Politics 1688–1714' (1960).

JAPIKSE, N.: *Prins Willem III de Stadhouder Konig* (1930).

JESSE, JOHN HENEAGE: *Memoirs of the Court of England during the Reign of the Stuarts*, 4 vols. (1843).

JUSSERAND, J. J.: *A French Ambassador at the Court of Charles II* (1892).

KEMBLE, JOHN M.: *Papers and Correspondence Illustrative of the Social and Political State of Europe from the Revolution to the Accession of the House of Hanover* (1857).

KENYON, J. P.: *Robert Spencer, Earl of Sunderland 1641–1702* (1958).

KLOPP, ONNO: *Der Fall des Hauses Stuart*, 14 vols. (1875–88).

KRÄMER, F. J. L.: *Maria II Stuart* (1890).

LAW, ERNEST: *Hampton Court* (1924).

— *Kensington Palace* (1929).

LEVER, SIR TRESHAM: *Godolphin: his Life and Times* (1952).

LINGARD, JOHN: *A History of England*, 8 vols. (1819–30).

LISTER, T. H.: *The Life and Administration of Edward First Earl of Clarendon*, 3 vols. (1838).

MAZURE, F. A. J.: *Histoire de la Révolution de 1688 en Angleterre*, 3 vols. (1825).

MCINNES, ANGUS: *Robert Harley, Puritan Politician* (1970).

NICHOLSON, T. C. and TURBERVILLE, A. S.: *Charles Talbot, Duke of Shrewsbury* (1930).

NYEVELT, BARONESS VAN: *Court Life in the Dutch Republic 1638–1689* (1906).

OGG, DAVID: *England in the Reign of Charles II*, 2 vols. (1934).

— *England in the Reigns of James II and William III* (1955).

OMAN, CAROLA: *Mary of Modena* (1962).

PERKINS, JOCELYN: *The Crowning of the Sovereign* (1953).

PLUMPTRE, E. H.: *Life of Ken*, 2 vols. (1860–1).

RANKE, L. VON: *A History of England principally in the Seventeenth Century*, 6 vols. (1875).

RENIER, G. J.: *William of Orange* (1932).

— *The Dutch Nation* (1944).

ROBB, NESCA A.: *William of Orange*, 2 vols. (1962–6).

SANDERS, MARY: *Mary II* (1913).

SHARP, THOMAS: *The Life of John Sharp, D.D.*, ed. T. Newcombe, 2 vols. (1821.)

SITWELL, SACHEVERELL: *The Netherlands* (1948).

SOMERVILLE, DOROTHEA: *The King of Hearts* (1962).

STRAKA, GERALD M.: *Anglican Reaction to the Revolution of 1688* (1962).

— *The Revolution of 1688: Whig Triumph or Palace Revolution* (1963).

STRICKLAND, AGNES: *Lives of the Queens of England*, vol. X (1847).

THOYRAS, RAPIN DE: *The History of England*.

— and N. TINDALL: *The Continuation of Mr. Rapin's History*, 21 vols. (1757–9).

TREVOR, THE HON. ARTHUR: *The Life and Times of William the Third*, 2 vols. (1835–6).

TURNER, F. C.: *James II* (1948).

WATERSON, N. M.: *Mary II* (1928).

WHITING, C. E.: *Nathaniel Lord Crewe, Bishop of Durham 1674–1721* (1940).

WREN SOCIETY: Vols. IV and VI.

ZUCCOLI, VITTORIA CAPECE GALEOTA: *Maria di Modena, Regina di Inghilterra* (1940).

NOTES

CHAPTER 1 DAUGHTER OF YORK

2 *Une aversion horrible*: Mademoiselle de Montpensier, fille de Gaston duc d'Orléans, III, 140, quoted Nyevelt, 173.
3 *Character of Morley*: Clarendon, *Life*, I, 49–50.
4 *Anne Hyde*: Lister, I, 393; Pepys, July 27, 1665.
William and Liselotte: Kroll, *Liselotte*, 230, November 26, 1720.
The Princess Royal's visit to Paris: James, *Memoirs*, 219.
James's 'stirring nature': quoted Turner, 27.
Charles's laziness: Lister, I, 388.
5 *James and Anne*: Clarke, I, 387; Burnet, I. 302.
6 *The Restoration*: *Letters of Elizabeth*, 309; Lady Fanshawe, *Memoirs*, 121.
7 *Anne Hyde's supposed infidelity*: Gramont, 158–63.
Hyde's reaction: Clarendon, *Life*, II, 50 et seq.
8 *James's version of the marriage*: Clarke, I, 387.
9 *The birth of Anne's child*: Clarendon, *Life*, I, 62–3.
The Scandal at Breda: *Letters of Elizabeth*, 332.
The death of the Duke of Gloucester and of Princess Mary: *Letters of Elizabeth*, 327, October 4, 1660, 334, January 17, 1661; Evelyn, December 21, 1660.
The Duke of Gloucester and Anne: Burnet, I, 307; D's note.
William's reaction to his mother's death: Robb, I, 102.
10 *'The Duchess of York; there she stands'*: Gramont, 163.
Anne's character: Clarke, I, 388; Gramont, 103; Jusserand, 107; Pepys, April 20, 1661, April 13, 1662.
The Birth of Mary and of her brother: Pepys, May 1, 1662, July 13, 1663; Family Notebook of James, Duke of York, at Windsor Castle.
11 *Mary and her father*: Pepys, September 12, 1664.
The Duke and Duchess: Pepys, January 6, 1663.
The Duchess and the snake: Reresby, 55.
11–12 *The Duke's mistresses*: Burnet, I, 304–6; Pepys, January 4, 1664, June 10, 1666; (in Dublin) Madame, I, 97.
12 *Catherine of Braganza*: Gramont, 102–3; Evelyn, June 2, 9, 1662.
Castlemaine and Stewart: Pepys, February 23, 1663, January 20, 27, 1667.
13 *The Duchess and Sidney*: Reresby, 55.
14 *The fall of Clarendon*: Evelyn, December 9, 1667; Reresby, 53.
14–15 *Lady Mary dances*: Pepys, April 2, 1669.
15 *The Duke's conversion*: Clarke, I, 440.
16 *The Duchess at Dover*: SPDom, May 29, 1670.
Her appetite: Gramont, 277.
16–17 *Her death*: Evelyn, *Life of Mrs Godolphin*, 9; Clarke, I, 452–3, V. and A., Forster MSS 48.c. 8, 27.

CHAPTER 2 AN ARTIFICIAL DAY

18 *The Duke's character*: Burnet, I, 304–6; II, 3, 40.
The consequences of his apostasy: Evelyn, March 30, 1673.
19 *Colonel Villiers*: SPDom, July 1660.
20 *'You have played the fool'*: Burnet, II, 16.
20–1 *The Duke's marriage*: Russell, *Letters*, I, 13; Campana, I, 64 *et seq*; Halstead, *Genealogies*, 415–32; Family Notebook of James, Duke of York at Windsor Castle.
22 *The new Duchess's melancholy*: Campana, I, 132.
Character of the King: *Letters of Elizabeth*, 309, June 7, 1660.
'pretty entertainments': Green, *Duchess of Marlborough*, 32.
23–8 *Calisto*: Crowne, *Dramatic Works*; text of *Calisto* with author's introduction and dedication, Evelyn, *Life of Mrs Godolphin*, 66.

CHAPTER 3 AURELIA

29 *The birth of Catherine Laura*: Campana, I, 145–6.
29–30 *The Duke's behaviour*: Campana, I, 149.
30 *The Countess Vezzani-Prateroni*: Campana, I, 154.
31 *James's theories about reading matter*: *Papers of Devotion*, 17.
31–3 *The correspondence with Frances Apsley*: Bathurst, 31–78.
32 *Guts or bowels*: Bathurst, 50.
The humble trout: Bathurst, 60–1.
The melancholy qualm: Bathurst, 44.
The Cornelian ring: Bathurst, 54.
33 *'Have some pity'*: Bathurst, 71–2.
Near discovery: Bathurst, 64.
34 *Une generosa risolutione*: Campana, I, 167–8.
Henry Compton: William Bingham Compton, *History of the Comptons of Compton Wynyates*, 122 *et seq*; Evelyn, April 17, 1673; F. L. Colvile, *The Worthies of Warwickshire*, 145.

CHAPTER 4 THE PRINCE

37 *The disposal of his charming self*: Strickland, X, 265.
37–8 *The visit of Arlington and Ossory*: Gloucester County RO, William Blathwayt letter to ? from the Hague, December 13, 1674; Burnet, II, 63; Temple, *Memoirs*, III, 81–2.
38 *Temple*: Oldmixon, 600; *Memoirs*, II, 165.
39 *Possible marriage with the Dauphin*: Turner, 128–9.
The States' disapproval of the marriage: HMC Rutland, II, 34.
40 *William's little tour*: Bentinck, *Correspondentie*, I, 4–5.
41 *Discussions of Mary's charms*: Huygens, *Journal*, III, 184.
The yachts: Japikse, II, ii, 208; William to Arlington, October 14, 1677.
The hasty lover: Temple, *Memoirs*, II, 292.
41–3 *The marriage negotiations*: Burnet, II, 120–3; Clarke, I, 508–10.
43 *The Prince's express to the States*: *The Life and Death of Her Royal Majesty*, Bodleian Pamphlet no. 247.
The French King's disapproval: Burnet, II, 132.
44 *The Lord Mayor's Show*: Oldmixon, 606; Bowen, 43–5.

44-5 *William's character and appearance*: Pomponne, 55-6; Baxter, 51; Temple, *Memoirs*, II, 236; Courtenay, I, 286; Verney, IV, 237.

45-6 *The wedding*: Lake, 6; Family Notebook of James Duke of York, Windsor; *Hatton Correspondence*, I, 154, V. and A. Forster MSS. 48. c. 8, 55.

46 *Celebrations in Edinburgh*: Strickland, X, 255.
Frances Apsley: Bathurst, 81.
The birth of the Duke of Cambridge: Campana, I, 203.

47 *The smallpox danger*: Lake, 6-7.

47-8 *The Princess's appointments*: HMC Bath, II, 158-9; HMC Rutland, II, 42.

48-9 *The departure*: HMC Rutland, II, 42; HMC Bath, II, 158-9; Lake 9-10; Campana, I, 204; BM Add MSS, 28040, 40-1.

49-50 *The stay at Canterbury*: Birch, 49-52.

50 *The yachts*: Prinsterer, V, 356-7; Huygens, *Correspondance*, VIII, 82.
The walk in the frost: HMC, Rutland II, 43.

CHAPTER 5 MARY OF ORANGE

51 *William's letter to Waldeck*: Müller, II, 351; December 9, 1677.

51-2 *Honselaersdyck*: D. P. Snoep, 'Honselaersdijk—restauraties op papier', *Oud Holland*, Nr 4, Jaargang LXXXIV, 1969, 270-94.

52 *Cleanliness of the Dutch*: Temple, *Memoirs*, II, 358, 360.
'Le feindre est défendu': KB, 48, *Discours sur la Nourriture*.

53 *'Ce précieux enfant'*: Huygens, *Mémoires*. 97.

54 *William's dislike of his guardians*: d'Estrades *Letters*, IV, 242-3, April 22, 166.

55 *William the hero*: *Letters of Sophia*, Sophia to Karl Ludwig, December 19, 1674.
De Witt: Courtenay, I, 285-6.

56-7 *The State entry*: *Royal Diary*, 31-2; Harris, *History of William Henry*, 137.

57 *Letters of Congratulation*: KHA, Mary, A16, XV, b17.
Two nightgowns: PRO SPF Holland, 84/207, 15, Hague, January 1/11, 1678, Roger Meredith to Williamson.
Huygens: *Briefwisseling*, VI 400, April 20, 1678.

57-8 *Waller*: *The Poetical Works of Edmund Waller*, Cooke's pocket edition, 72-3; Bath, II, 158.

58 *Valconier*: Sidney, I, 66.
Nobility and the office holders: Nyevelt 363, *Letters of Sophia*, 309-10, January 5, 1678.

59 *Incident in the Voorhout*: PRO SPF Holland, 84/706, 297, 300, July 7, 8, 1678.

60 *Bentinck*: Temple, *Memoirs*, III, 98.

60-1 *Overkirk and Odyck*: *Mémoires of Monsieur de B*, 94-5.

61 *Ossory*: Temple, *Memoirs*, 75.

61 *William's dining habits before his marriage*: de Gourville, *Mémoires*, II, 2.

62 *The Dutch air*: Harris, *An Account of Holland*.
Correspondence with Aurelia: Bathurst, 82-6.
Death of Duke of Cambridge and recovery of Anne: Lake, 11, 14; HMC Rutland II, 42-4.
The Prince at Soestdyck: PRO SPF Holland, 84/207, 15.

63 *William's character*: *Royal Diary*, 11-12, 19, 41.

64 *The fear of war*: Reresby, 134.
The parting scene: Clarendon, *Correspondence*, I, 11.

CHAPTER 6 THE WAR

65 *Letter to Frances*: Bathurst, 88–9, March, 3 1678.
66 *The Prince and the peace*: Letters of Sophia, 308, November, 24, 1677.
His unpopularity: Letters of Sophia, 277.
The Princess's departure: PRO SPF Holland, 206, 91, March 12/21, Meredith to Williamson.
66–7 *Her visit to Antwerp*: Letters of Sophia, 96–129; Robb, II, 109; Huygens, Journal, III, 237, March 29; Evelyn, November 11, 1677.
67 *Sylvius*: Temple, Memoirs, II, 132.
The miscarriage: PRO SPF Holland, 84/206, 129–51, April 12/22–18/28, Meredith to Williamson.
67–8 *The doctors*: I am indebted to Dr A. M. Luyendijk-Elshout of the Rijksmuseum voor de Geschiedenis der Natuurwetenschappen at Leyden for information and advice in this connection.
68 *Hyde and the French*: Clarendon, Correspondence, I, 17.
His wife's crossing: Clarendon, Correspondence, I, 17.
The massing of French troops: Clarendon, Correspondence, I, 16.
69 *Holland and the Hague*: Harris, A Short Account of Holland, 30.
69–70 *Dr Hooper*: Walton (Hooper) MSS, Trevor, II (Appendix).
70–1 *The Princess's finances*: Princess Mary's Account Book, Windsor Castle.
71 *The Earl of Orrery's letter*: KHA A16, XV a2, Castle Martyr, April 15, 1678.
72 *William, Temple and Arlington*: Temple, Memoirs, II, 80; Courtenay, I, 436.
73 *The swallow*: Temple, Memoirs, II, 330.
water and wine: Letters of Sophia, 330, June 30, 1678.
Desolation at the Hague: Clarendon, Correspondence, I 22.
Letter to Frances: Bathurst, 91.
74–5 *The Princess's pregnancy, illness and threatened miscarriage*: Huygens, Correspondance, VIII, 95; Bathurst, 95; PRO SPF Holland, 84/208, 49–67, September 13/23, 17/27, Meredith to Williamson.

CHAPTER 7 DEAR LEMON

76–7 *The visit of Anne and the Duchess*: Campana, I, 225 et seq; PRO SPF Holland, 84/208, 102–10; Huygens, Correspondance, VIII, 109, 121; Clarendon, Correspondence, I, 28; Oman 26.
77–8 *The Popish plot*: Burnet, II, 152–79; Reresby, 152–5; Campana, I, 226–9; Dalrymple, I, Appendix to Chapter III of the Review, 257–9.
78 *James's advice to William*: SPDom, May 21, 1678.
William's letter to Hyde: Clarendon, Correspondence, I, 32.
79 *Temple's opinion of the Prince*: Clarendon, Correspondence, I, 37–8.
Organization of the Prince's property: Th. H. Lunsingh Scheurleer, 'The Living Quarters in Amalia van Solms' Huis in het Bosch', Oud Holland, Nr I, Jaargang LXXXIV, 1969, 29–66; RA Nass Dom Ord (Soestdyck), 789,355 (Charles Gerbay), 741,180 (Charles de Buisson) 789,348 (flowers in the house), 741,190–1.
79–80 *The cold winter*: Temple, Memoirs, II, 378.
80 *William on the subject of marriage*: Temple, Memoirs, II, 150–2.
James's exile: Burnet, II, 197–8; Campana, I, 245–6.

81 *The Princess's confinement*: HMC Ormonde, IV, 329, Ossory to Ormonde, February 22, 1679; HMC Dartmouth, 30, James to Legge, March 28, 1679; Huygens, *Correspondance*, VIII, Susanna to Christiaan Huygens, February 16, 1679.
   William's impotence: Letters of Sophia, 363, June 22, 1679.
81–2 *Mary's illness*: HMC Foljambe, 129: Campana, I, 253.
82 *The French comedians*: Fransen, 135 *et seq.*
83 *The Kermesse*: Huygens, *Correspondance*, VIII, 165, Susanna to Christian Huygens, May 11, 1679.
   The Hague in summer: Sidney, I, 55.

CHAPTER 8 SUMMER AT DIEREN

84 *Ossory*: Clarendon, *Correspondence*, I, 19.
   Sidney's opinion of Dieren: Sidney, I, 43.
   William's court: Sidney, I, 54.
85 *Sir Leoline Jenkins*: Sidney, I, 303–4n.
   The Princess's illness: HMC Foljambe, 132; HMC Verney, Report VII, Appendix, 473.
   The King's illness: Sidney, I, 99, 122, 141; HMC Foljambe, 137.
86 *James's gloom*: HMC Foljambe, 129, 131.
   The Duchess: Campana, I, 250.
   The Princess's projected visit to Brussels: Sidney, I, 145–6.
87 *James and Monmouth*: Clarke, I, 551–2.
87–8 *Monmouth at the Hague*: d'Oyley, 140–5; d'Avaux, I, 59–62; HMC Dartmouth, I, 33 *et seq*; Sidney, I, 154–6; Grew, 59.
89 *Mary's letter from her father*: HMC Foljambe, 139.
   James in Holland: Sidney, I, 162–4.
   The Duke and Duchess go to Scotland: Campana, I, 307–8.

CHAPTER 9 THE TWO DUKES

90–1 *Soestdyck*: Huygens, *Briefwisseling*, VI 403.
91 *Amalia of Solms*: Temple, *Memoirs*, III, 122–3; Sophia, *Memoirs*, 27.
92 *Sidney and the Prince*: Sidney, I, 193–5.
   D'Avaux and the English: Sidney, I, 155.
93 *The Prince's possible visit to England*: Sidney, I, 150.
   Fitzpatrick: Sidney, I, 179; Baxter, 167.
94 *Mary's character*: Burnet, *An Essay on the Memory of the Late Queen*, 194; Nyevelt, 311–13; Huygens, *Correspondance*, VIII, 255.

CHAPTER 10 FAMILY FRICTION

95 *The ball at Odyck's*: Huygens, *Correspondance*, VIII, 255.
96 *Adam Loofs*: Huygens, *Correspondance*, VIII, 261.
   Letter to Frances: Bathurst, 118–19.
   Sidney: Sidney, I, 212, 214–15.
   Improvements at Honselaersdyck: Japikse, *William III*; RA Nass Dom Ord 790,300.
   The caged birds: Account book, Windsor Castle.

97 *The new chapel*: Walton (Hooper) MSS, Trevor, II Appendix 466–7.

97–8 *The departure of the Hoopers*: Walton (Hooper) MSS.

98 *Dr Ken*: Plumptre, 139–41.

98–9 *The Princess's illness*: Sidney, II, 19–20, 27; Huygens, *Journal*, III, 14; Prinsterer, Series II, vol. V, 387–91.

99 *The Duke's behaviour*: Sidney, II, 25, April 6, 1680, Prinsterer; Series II, vol. V, 392–3.

The King's illness: Prinsterer, Series II, vol. V, 391, 400; Sidney, II, 57, May 18.

The war of nerves: Prinsterer, Series II, vol. V, 34, 46

100 *William's illness*: d'Avaux, V, 174; Sidney, II, 16–17; Prinsterer, Series II, vol. V, 412, July 23, 1680.

The visit to England: Sidney, II, 84, July 16, 1680.

101 *The Death of Ossory*: HMC Ormonde Report, VII, Appendix 741–2; Prinsterer, Series II, vol. V, 414.

Dr Ken: Plumptre, I, 146–7.

101–3 *The conversion of Fitzpatrick*: Bathurst, 124, Plumptre, I, 148 *et seq.*

103 *The Prince's visit to Germany*: Huygens, *Journal*, III, 12 *et seq.*

Mary at Soestdyck: Bathurst, 124–5.

Lady Sunderland and the Prince's visit to England: Sidney, II, 125, November 16, 1680.

104 *The Duchess of York's condition*: Prinsterer, Series II, vol. V, 423.

104–5 *The English Parliament and the Exclusion question*: Prinsterer, Series II, vol. V, 429, 437, 440–3; Sidney, II, 124.

104 *James and William*: Prinsterer, Series II, vol. V, 457; Campana, I, 344; Burnet, II, 251.

105 *William's readiness to leave for England*: Sidney, II, 156.

The King's attitude: Reresby, 209, January 4, 1681.

106 *'He spoke admirably'*: Sidney, II, 120, November 3, 1680.

French tyranny: Savile, *Correspondence*, 169.

106–7 *D'Avaux visits the Princess*: Sidney, II, 141–2, December 3, 1680.

107 *Prince George of Hanover at the Hague*: Sidney, II, 145–6; Strickland, X, 313.

The meteor: Huygens, *Correspondance*, VIII, 312–13; Evelyn, December 12, 1680.

CHAPTER 11 A DARK NEW YEAR

108 *The death of the dwarf*: Huygens, *Correspondance*, VIII, 315.

108–9 *The opera*: Fransen, 166; Huygens, *Correspondance*, VIII.

The visit to Amsterdam: Savile, *Correspondence*, 182, Savile to Sir Leoline Jenkins, February 7/17, 1681.

109–10 *The Zuylestein affair*: Plumptre, I, 142 *et seq*; Sidney, II, 162; de Bourdon, 95–6; Huygens, *Journal*, III, 72.

110 *Miss Gibsone*: Huygens, *Correspondance*, VIII, 315.

111 *Dieren and Hummeling*: Huygens, *Correspondance*, VIII, 326, 338; Account Book, Windsor.

James in Scotland: Prinsterer, Series II, vol. V, 498, May 7, 1681.

The Oxford Parliament: Prinsterer, Series II, vol. V, 490 495,; Clarendon, *Correspondence*, I, 56.

James and the prorogation: Clarendon, *Correspondence*, I, 49; Campana, I, 357–8; Prinsterer, Series II, vol. V, 483.

112 *Sidney's recall*: Sidney, II, 181–205; Prinsterer, Series II, vol. V, 502, 505, Hyde to William, May 31, June 7, 1681; Japikse, II, ii, 391–2, William to the King, June 25, 1681.
    The subsidy from France: Clarendon, *Correspondence*, I, 59.
113–14 *William's visit to England*: Sidney, II, 205; Prinsterer, Series II, vol. V, 511–13; Clarke, I, 690; Campana, I, 377–8; Robb, II, 167–8; Grew, 65; Burnet, II, 415.
114 *James's letter to Legge*: Campana, I, 363, July 16/26.
    James to William: Prinsterer, Series II, vol. V, 510–13.
    The drought: Prinsterer, Series II, vol. V, 503.
    Hyde: Prinsterer, Series II, vol. V, 529, November 4, 1681.

CHAPTER 12 THE ATTACK ON ORANGE

116 *The visit to Aix*: Prinsterer, Series II, vol. V, 514.
116–17 *Lady Ogle*: Sidney, II, 224; Bathurst, 141, November 20, 1681.
117 *The kidnapping plot*: Prinsterer, Series II, vol. V, 536, 538; Clarendon, *Correspondence*, I, 64; Robb, II, 171–2; Fransen, 144–52.
118 *Sidney's visit*: Japikse, II, ii, 426, van Beunighen to Bentinck, January 27, 1683; Sidney, II, 224–6, January 9, 1682.
    Mary Beatrice's accident: Prinsterer, Series II, vol V, 538, James to William, December 17, 1681.
    New Year's gifts: Account Book, Windsor.
    The floods: Prinsterer, Series II, vol. V, 540–544.
119 *Van Beunighen*: Japiske, II, ii, 426.
    James and Sidney: Prinsterer, Series II, vol. V, 545, March 20, 1682.
    The Kermesse: Prinsterer, Series II, vol. V, 549, April 24, 1682.
120 *Visit to the opera*: Fransen, 165.
    The King's illness: Reresby, 252; Prinsterer, Series II, vol. V, 551, James to William, May 30, 1682.
    The boating accident: Prinsterer, Series II, vol. V, 551.
    The visit to Brussels: Bathurst, 144; Baxter, 187.
120–1 *The marriage of Frances Apsley*: Bathurst, 147–50.
121 *Soestdyck*: Prinsterer, Series II, vol. V, 556.
    The shipwreck: Campana, I, 397, June 10, 1682; Burnet, II, 324.
122 *Anne's romance*: Bathurst, 151, August 14, 1682; 154–5 November 27, 1682; Luttrell, I, 236; Reresby, 281.
    Birth of James's daughter: Campana, I, 390, August 27, 1682.
122–3 *The attack on Orange*: Prinsterer, Series II, vol. V, 561–4; Clarendon, *Correspondence*, I, 79; Huygens, *Journal*, III, 62–3, September 2.

CHAPTER 13 PROTESTANT CHAMPIONS

124 *Cornbury's visit*: Huygens, *Journal*, III, 62–3.
125 *The chocolate pot*: Loofs' inventory KHA Mary, A16, VII, 18.
    Halley's Comet: Huygens, *Correspondance*, VIII, 388–95.
    The Princess's purchases: Account Book, Windsor.
125–6 *Lady Bathurst's child*: Bathurst, 156–7.
126 *Van Beunighen*: Sidney, I, 112; Burnet, I, 604; Temple, *Memoirs*, II, 119.
    News from Paris: d'Avaux, I, 285.
    At Dieren: Huygens, *Journal*, III, 83.
127 *Letters to Lady Bathurst*: Bathurst, 160–1, 168, 172.

127 *The Rye House Plot*: Japikse, II, ii, 552; Reresby, 304; HMC Report, VII, 363, June 21; Bathurst, 172; Prinsterer, Series II, vol. V, 578–9.

127–8 *Bentinck's visit to England*: Grew, 68–74.

128 *The lock of hair*: Japikse, I. i, 11, July 19, 1683.
The garden at Dieren: Japikse, I, i, 11, July 27, 1683.
Hunting at Zuylestein: Japikse, I, i, 11, August 2, 1683.
The King's letter to William: Prinsterer, Series II, vol. V, 581–2.

129 *William's letter to Rochester*: Clarendon, *Correspondence*, I, 90, August 16, 1683.
The scene in the Dutch Assembly: d'Avaux, I, 374–81.

130 *Fagel*: BM Add MSS 32094, 327.
Letter to Lady Bathurst: Bathurst, 176–7.

130–1 *Princess Anne and her marriage*: Prinsterer, Series II, vol. V, 575; Bathurst, 167, 174; HMC Report, III, 289.

131 *Books and accounts*: Bathurst, 160–1, 174; Account Book, Windsor.
Persecution of the Protestants: Chatsworth, 37.1, 38.0, Letter from Trumbull, December 8/18, 1685; Burnet, III, 80.2.

132–4 *The French Society*: *Bulletin de la Société de l'Histoire du Protestantisme Français*, Tome xxvii, 315, 'Société des Dames Françaises de Haarlem'; Mélanges, *Eigen Haard*, 1885, 616, L. Ph. C. van den Bergh, *'s-Gravenhaagsche bijzonderheden*, II, 47 *et seq*; *Lettres et Mémoires* 137–45.

CHAPTER 14 MONMOUTH IN HOLLAND

135 *Monmouth*: Burnet, II, 411–14; Reresby, 320–1; HMC Graham, Report VII, Appendix, 363.

136 *The cold weather*: Bathurst, 178–80.
Van Beunighen: HMC Graham, Report VII, Appendix, 363.
The Duke's haughtiness: Reresby, 329, January 30, 1684.
William's outburst: quoted Grew, 77.
Ces coquins d'Amsterdam: Nyevelt, 301.

137 *William's treatment of Chudleigh*: d'Avaux, IV.
His departure: d'Avaux, III, 27.

137–8 *James to William and Mary*: Dalrymple, I, Appendix to Part I, Book I, 118–19.

138 *William's second departure*: Bathurst, 181.
William hears about the truce: Müller, I, 279, William to Waldeck, June 12, 1684; Robb II, 195.

138–9 *Anne's child*: Prinsterer, Series II, vol. V, 586, May 13, 1684; Bathurst, 181; Burnet, II, 391–2.

139 *James to William*: Dalrymple, I, Appendix to Part I, Book I, 118.
The Seal: Burnet, II, 416.

140 *William's movements*: Huygens, *Correspondance*, VIII, 523.
The eclipse: Huygens, *Correspondance*, VIII, 512.
The grotto at Dieren: Huygens, *Correspondance*, VIII, 540, 542
The Princess and Henrietta Wentworth: d'Avaux, IV, 118.
'*I could say more to you*': Dalrymple, I, Appendix to Part I, Book I, 123–5.

140–1 *The King and van Citters*: Japikse, II, ii, 681, December 16/26.

141 *Monmouth*: Dalrymple, I, Appendix to Part I; d'Oyley, 257–9.
'*Farewell to all modesty*': BM Add MSS 38847, 123, December 15/25, 1684.

141–2 *The conversation with the Princess of Anhalt*: d'Avaux, IV, 131–2.

142 *The visit to Amsterdam*: Burnet, II, 448.

143–4 *The Princess and Monmouth*: d'Avaux, IV, 211–12, 217.
144 *Jurieu*: d'Avaux, IV, 217–18.
    The evening of January 30: d'Avaux, IV, 262–3.

CHAPTER 15 A QUARREL FOR THE CROWN

145–6 *The death of the King*: Burnet, II, 466–8; Evelyn, February 4–6, 1685; d'Avaux,
    IV, 265; Wellwood, 123–5.
    James's letters to William: Dalrymple, II, Appendix to Part I, Book II, 11, Feb-
    ruary 6, 1685.
146 *James's accession*: Reresby, 352.
    The Queen's illness: Campana, II, 35.
    The new King's letters to William and Mary, and William's reply: Dalrymple, II,
    Appendix to Part I, Book II, 13–15.
147 *Monmouth's whereabouts*: Dalrymple, II, Appendix to Part I, Book II, 16, April
    14, 1685; Clarendon, *Correspondence*, I, 123–4.
    The officers: d'Avaux, IV, 314–15.
    The coronation: Reresby, 362; Verney, IV, 342–3.
147–8 *Monmouth*: Welwood, 152–3; Dalrymple II, Appendix to Part I, Book II, 20–1,
    Grey, *Secret History*, 84–104; V. and A., Forster MSS 48. c. 8. 68–70.
148 *Skelton*: Dalrymple, II, Appendix to Part I, Book II, 18.
149 *The banners*: d'Avaux, V, 21.
    The Regiments: Evelyn, July 18, 1685.
    Bentinck's visit to England: Grew, 86; Clarendon, *Correspondence*, I, 130.
    Monmouth's pocket book: BM Egerton MSS 1527, 148.
150 *The execution of Monmouth*: Walton (Hooper) MSS, Hall Lloyd 89; Evelyn, July
    15, 1685; Dalrymple, II, Appendix to Part I, Book II, 26.
    The kneeling pages: *Mémoires de Monsieur de B*, 87.

CHAPTER 16 THE PALACE AT LOO

151–3 *The garden at Loo*: Walter Harris, *A Description of the King's Royal Palace at
    Loo*.
153 *The stag-hunt*: Huygens, *Correspondance*, IX, 33.
    James's attitude to William: Clarke, II, 24.
    His speech to Parliament: Wellwood, 140.

CHAPTER 17 A MALICIOUS SPY

155 *Letters from the Princess, summer 1685*: Bathurst, 184.
    The Wissing portraits: Huygens, *Correspondance* IX, 23, August 24, 1685.
155–6 *Elizabeth Villiers*: *Mémoires de Monsieur de B*, 84–6; Swift, *Journal to Stella*
    (1948 ed.), II, 558, 570.
157 *Covell's letter*: Clarendon, *Correspondence*, I, 165, October 5/15, 1685.
158 *Covell to Compton*: Bodleian Rawlinson C83.97, August 14/24, 1685.
    William to Rochester: Clarendon, *Correspondence*, I, 164.
158–9 *Mary's letter to Lady Bathurst*: Bathurst, 189, December 11, 1685.
159 *William and Skelton*: Japikse, II, ii, 721–2, October 28 and November 1, 1685.
    Hugyens's opinion: Huygens, *Correspondance*, IX, 34.

159 *Bentinck to Sidney*: Sidney, II, 255, October 22, 1685.
160 *The Princess's purchases*: Bathurst, 186, 189, 190.
    Lady Mary Forester: HMC Stopford Sackville (Forester), 29–30.
    John Horne: Bodleian Rawlinson C982,39, November 27, 1685.
161 *Mary's fall from her horse*: Chapman, 126.
    Persecution of the Protestants: d'Avaux, V, 218–20.
    James's complaints and his attitude to the Prince: d'Avaux, V, 226–7; Dalrymple, II, Appendix to Part I, Book II, 49, February 17/27, 1686.
162 *Orange*: Dalrymple, II, Appendix to Part I, Book II, 54; Japikse, II, ii, 727; Clarendon, *Correspondence*, I, 169, February 12, 1686.
    The Elector of Brandenburg: Japikse, II, ii, 738; Clarendon, *Correspondence*, I, 170.
    The Queen: Campana, II, 89; Evelyn, January 19, 1686.
163 *Compton's suspension*: Clarke, II, 91; Burnet, III, 110–12; Bodleian Rawlinson C983,107.
    Stanley to Compton: Burnet, III, 111–12.
    Welwood: Welwood, 201.
    Petre: Campana, II, 125–7.
    Lady Mary Forester: HMC Stopford-Sackville, I, 31.
    '*En qualité d'architecte*': Huygens, *Correspondance*, IX, 90.
165 *The Chinese cabinet*: Huygens, *Briefwisseling*, 456, September 27, 1685.
    The portrait of Charles V: Huygens, *Briefwisseling*, 422, August 24, 1679.
    Dr Stanley and the Princess: Bodleian Rawlinson C983,106, December 22, 1685, 99, January 1, 1686.
166 *Dr Burnet and the Princess*: Burnet, III, 133–9; Burnet, *Supplement*, 194–6; Foxcroft, *Burnet*, 205, 221.
    Huygens and Burnet: Huygens, *Correspondance*, IX, 90.
167 *The Prince*: Bodleian Rawlinson C983,99.
    His religious practices: Bodleian Rawlinson C983,99, May 3/13, 1686.
    The plot on the Prince's life: Burnet, III, 133.
168 *Burnet's conversation with the Princess*: Burnet, III, 137–9.
    James and the Papists: Evelyn, December 29, 1686, January 3–17, 1687.

CHAPTER 18 IMPORTANT VISITORS

170–1 *Penn's visit*: Burnet, III, 139–40; Baxter, 217.
171 *The Princess's debts*: Account Book, Windsor.
    The Portraits: Bathurst, 193–4.
    Letter to Lady Bathurst: Bathurst, 198.
171–2 *The Ball at the House in the Wood*: BM Map Room, 14C 9 'E', engraving by Daniel Marot.
172 *Dyckevelt's visit*: Japikse, II, ii, 746, James to William, March 1, 1687.
    The Edict of Toleration: Kenyon, 152–3.
173 *The conversion of Anne*: Baxter, 219; Campana, II, 130, April 3.
    Stanley and Burnet: Bodleian Rawlinson C983,110–11, March 21/31, 1687.
174 *Lady Sunderland*: Sidney, II, 261, March 7, 1687.
    James to Sophia of Hanover: Doebner, 69, May 23, 1687.
174–5 *Fagel and Stewart*: Welwood, 196–8.
175 *The pincushions*: Bathurst, 195 *et seq*.
    Zuylestein's visit: Dalrymple, I, Appendix to Book V, 74–85.
    James's tour: Carswell, 102.
    His visit to Coventry: *Heraldic notebook to John Dugdale at Merevale* (typed list 73), September 1, 1687.

175–6 *His visit to Oxford*: Bramston, 287; SPDom, September 9, 1687 (seen in proof).
  Fitzpatrick's letter: Japikse, II, ii, 761.
  The improvement in the Queen's health: Campana, II, 122.
  Letter to Sancroft: Strickland, X, 354–5,
177 *Huygens and Stanley*: Huygens, *Correspondance*, IX, 206.
177–8 *Mary's letters to her father*: *Lettres et Mémoires*, 4–17.

CHAPTER 19 THE BIRTH OF THE PRINCE

179 *Despondency in England*: Campana, II, 154, V. and A., Forster MSS 48. c. 8,
  78–9.
  New year spending: Account Book, Windsor.
  Mary's letter to her father: *Lettres et Mémoires*, 18.
180 *Verace*: *Lettres et Mémoires*, 66.
181 *Lord Coote*: *Lettres et Mémoires*, 69; Bodleian Rawlinson C983,123, April 20.
182 *Danby's letters*: Japikse, II, iii, 7, March 27, 29.
183 *The Princess's reply*: Japikse, II, iii, 7(n), April 29, 1688.
  Lady Mary Forester: HMC Stopford-Sackville, I, 31–2.
  The Elector of Saxony: *Lettres et Mémoires*, 70.
  Letters from Anne: Dalrymple, II, Appendix to Book V, 176–7.
184 *The Queen's threatened miscarriage*: Clarendon, *Correspondence*, II, 169.
  Suspicions about the Queen's condition: Dalrymple, II, Appendix to Book V, 171
  et seq.
  The petition: Clarendon, *Correspondence*, II, 170–3.
185 *The Bishops*: Clarendon, *Correspondence*, II, 175; Reresby, 499.
  Stanley's letter to Sancroft: Strickland, X, 371.
185–6 *The birth of the Prince*: Evelyn, June 10, 1688; *Lettres et Mémoires*, 74 *et seq*;
  Clarendon, *Correspondence*, II, 176; Campana, II, 213–30; Dalrymple, II,
  Appendix to vol. V, 162, 185.
186 *The Queen's 'upsitting'*: Evelyn, July 17, 1688.
187 *Herbert's visit*: Dalrymple, II, Appendix to Book V, 228–32.
  Other visitors: Dalrymple, II, Appendix to Book V, 20; Burnett, III, 274–6.
187–8 *Letter of the Seven*: Dalrymple, II, Appendix to Book V, 107–10.
188 *The Queen's letter*: BM Birch. Add. MSS 4163, vol. I.
  D'Albeville's party: Campana, II, 240.
189 *The acquittal of the Bishops*: Reresby, 501; Evelyn, June 29, V. and A. Forster
  MSS 48. c. 8, 81.
189–90 *The questionnaire*: Dalrymple, II, Appendix to Book V, 177–84.
190 *Letters from the King and Queen*: BM Birch Add MSS 4163, vol. I.
191 *The King's suspicions*: Doebner, 70, July 31, 1688.
  The Report from Rotterdam: SPDom, September 30, 1688.
  Clarendon and the King: Clarendon, *Correspondence*, II, 189, September 24, 1688.
192 *The Queen's letter*: BM Birch Add MSS 4163, vol. I.
  Events in September: *Lettres et Mémoires*, 78–80.
192–3 *The emotional thumbscrew*: Strickland, X, 376.
193 *The King's concessions*: Campana, II, 290–2.
  Doubts about the Prince's birth: Doebner, 71, September 28, 1688, Chatsworth,
  54.0, Anne Newport to Lady Cavendish, October 23, 1688.
194 *William takes leave of the States*: RA, *Proceedings of the States of Holland and West
  Friesland*, October 1688.
194–5 *Parting scenes*: *Lettres et Mémoires*, 80–2.

CHAPTER 20 GOD'S WEATHER

196 *Lady Sunderland to Evelyn*: Sidney, II, 279, October 11, 1688.
James's confidence: Campana, II, 300.
196–7 *William in the storm*: *Royal Diary*, 64.
198 *Mary's feelings during the storm*: *Lettres et Mémoires*, 83–4, *Royal Diary*, 9.
197–8 *Last days before the expedition sailed*: *Lettres et Mémoires*, 84–7.
199 *D'Alonne's letter*: KHA Mary A16, XV, 3, November 9/19, 1688 (copy).
200 *The death of Anne Bentinck*: *Lettres et Mémoires*, 88–9.
201 *Huygens's letter*: Huygens, *Correspondance*, IX, 304.
William enters London: Campana, II, 466.
The escape of the Queen and the Prince: Reresby, 536.
The King captured: Reresby, 539.
202 *The Princess receives news from England*: *Lettres et Mémoires*, 91–2.
The end of the year: *Lettres et Mémoires*, 192.

CHAPTER 21 THE RETURN TO ENGLAND

203 *The King's flight*: Clarendon, *Correspondence*, II, 234.
Self-love: Doebner, 4.
Muddled accounts: Account Book, Windsor.
203–4 *The visit of the Elector of Brandenburg*: Doebner, 4–5; Nyevelt, 348.
204 *The Earl of Arran*: Dalrymple, II, Part I, Book VII, 266.
A possible Regency: Dalrymple, II, Part I, Book VII, 271.
Danby's letter to Mary: Dalrymple, II, Part I, Book VII, 283.
204–5 *William and the apron-strings*: quoted Grew, 152.
205 *Herbert's gout*: Grew, 151.
Mary's agitation: Doebner, 7–9.
206 *Desolation at the Hague*: Huygens, *Correspondance*, IX, 309.
207 *Mary's arrival in England*: Doebner, 9–10.
Lady Churchill's opinion: *Conduct*, 25–6.
208 *Evelyn's opinion*: February 21, 1689.
The ceremony in the Banqueting Hall: Reresby, 554; Russell, *Letters*, I, 270; Dalrymple, II, Part I, Book VII, 290.
209 *'My heart is not made for a kingdom'*: Doebner, 11.
Her father's mistresses: Churchill, *Marlborough*, I, 115; Dalrymple, II, Part I, Book VII, 271.
210 *The Bishops*: Dalrymple, II, Part I, Book VII, 285; Clarendon, *Correspondence*, II, 242; Carpenter, 141; Evelyn, January 15; *The Autobiography of Symon Patrick*, 143.
210–11 *William's advisers*: Foxcroft, *Halifax*, II; Clarendon, *Correspondence*, II, 239, 241.
211 *The Dutch in London*: Reresby, 545.
Huygens: *Correspondance*, IX, 309.
211–12 *Further appointments*: Foxcroft, *Halifax*, II, 202–5.
212 *Hampton Court*: Burnet, IV, 2–3.
213 *Burnet's appointment*: Burnet, 13–14; Huygens, *Journal*, I, 92–3.
213–15 *The coronation*: Carpenter, *The Protestant Bishop*, 150–2; Perkins, *The Crowning of the Sovereign*, 89–90; Clarendon, *Correspondence*, II, 273; Reresby, 571–2; Doebner, 12; Hart, 119; Evelyn, April 11, 1689, Yorkshire Archaeological Society, DD 5 XII, *Order of Proceedings at the Coronation of William and Mary*.

215 *Pomp and ceremony at the Sacrament*: Doebner, 13.
   Consecration of Burnet: Foxcroft, *Burnet*, 266–7.
   William and Mary's difficulties: Doebner, 13–14; Foxcroft, *Halifax*, II, 206–7.
215–16 *Temple's suicide*: Clarendon, *Correspondence*, II.
216 *The Duke of Venice*: Foxcroft, *Halifax*, II, 203.
   'The world is a beast': Foxcroft, *Halifax*, II, 288.
   The King's state of health: Huygens, *Journal*, I, 112–13.
   His nostalgia: Huygens, *Journal*, I, 122.
217 *Kensington*: Doebner, 17; Foxcroft, *Halifax*, II,   .

CHAPTER 22 THE NEW HOUSEHOLD

218–20 *The new household*: *A Collection of Ordinances and Regulations for the Government of the Royal Household*, 380–422.
220–1 *The building at Hampton Court*: PRO Works 5/55, 1689.
221 *Public fasting*: Doebner, 14.
   Tenderness in the French: Foxcroft, II, 221.
   The birth of Anne's child: Doebner, 15.
222 *The King's depression*: Foxcroft, *Halifax*, II, 222–8.
222–3 *Shrewsbury's threatened resignation*: Coxe, *Shrewsbury*, 6–17, August 27, 28, September 1, 1689.
224 *The King and the Church*: Burnet, IV, 11, 27; Huygens, *Journal*, I, 103; Foxcroft, *Halifax*, II, 222, 230, 232.
   The Queen to Sophia: *Lettres et Mémoires*, 105, May 23, 1689.
   Sickness payments: *A Collection of Ordinances*, 393.
   Help for the Protestants: SPDom, April 26, 1689.
224–5 *The Queen's homesickness*: *Lettres et Mémoires*, 116.
225 *The birthday ball*: Huygens, *Journal*, I, 202–3.
   Holland House: Doebner, 15.
225–6 *The accidents at Kensington and Hampton Court*: Doebner, 17; Briggs, *Wren the Incomparable*, 187.
226–7 *The quarrel with Anne*: *Lettres et Mémoires*, 118–19; Evelyn, July 19, 1689; *Conduct*, 25–32.
227–8 *Thoughts at the end of the year*: Doebner, 19–21.

CHAPTER 23 MARIE R

229 *Winter weather*: Evelyn, January 11, 1689.
   Kensington: Huygens, *Journal*, I, 219; Evelyn, February 25, 1689.
   Dutch women's opinion of England: Huygens, *Journal*, I, 167.
230 *Burnet and Lloyd*: Doebner, 21.
   William's intention of going to Ireland: Foxcroft, *Halifax*, II, 244.
231 *The proroguing of Parliament*: Japikse, I, i, 70.
231–2 *The Queen's distress*: Japikse, I, i, 70.
232 *The Leonardo drawings*: Kenneth Clarke, *A Catalogue of Drawings of Leonardo da Vinci at Windsor Castle*, 1935.
   Possible Scottish expedition: Doebner, 21–3; Foxcroft, *Halifax*, II, 248.
232–3 *The Queen's Council*: Foxcroft, *Halifax*, II, 245; Doebner, 22–3.
233 *William and his troops*: Dalrymple, II, Book II, Part II, 59.

233 *The new Parliament*: Dalrymple, III, Part II, Book V, 2.
Wren: Huygens, *Correspondance*, IX, 356.
233-4 *The quarrel continues*: Doebner, 24.
234 *The Queen's illness*: Doebner, 25-8.
235 *The Act of Grace*: Dalrymple, II, Part II, Book V, 3.
The Regency Bill: Ronquillo, II, 189.
The Council: Foxcroft, *Halifax*, II, 247, 251; Doebner, 28-30.
Shrewsbury's resignation: Doebner, 28.
236 *William's concern for the Queen*: Burnet, IV, 82.
237 *His departure*: Huygens, *Journal*, I, 281-2; HMC Finch, II, 290; Doebner, 28.

CHAPTER 24 THE NINE

238 *The reprieve of M'Guire*: Dalrymple, III, Appendix to Book V, 69-70.
239 *The Queen and the Dowager*: Dalrymple, III, Appendix to Book V, 70-3, June 21, 22, 1690.
240 *The French fleet*: Dalrymple, III, Appendix to Book V, 73-5, July 2, 4, 1690.
Pembroke: Doebner, 30.
241 *The Privy Council and the disaffected persons*: Dalrymple, III, Appendix to Book V, 74-5.
242 *Building at Hampton Court*: Dalrymple, III, Appendix to Book V, 76.
242-3 *The Nine*: Dalrymple, III, Appendix to Book V, 78-80; Doebner, 30.
243-4 *Scotland*: Dalrymple, III, Appendix to Book V, 77.
244 *The Queen Dowager*: Dalrymple, III, Appendix to Book V, 80, PRO E 101, 541/11, Letter signed by Feversham, August 12, 1690, another from the owner of the barge, and one from Henry Thynne, the Queen Dowager's Treasurer.
244-6 *Beachy Head*: Dalrymple, III, Appendix to Book V, 84; Ehrman, 344-6, Waterson, 65.
246 *General alarm*: Chatsworth, 44, 2.
The Queen's imperturbability: Burnet, IV, 87, 98-9.
The trained bands: Chatsworth, 44.2.
Letter to Evertzen: Dalrymple, III, Appendix to Book V, 87.
247 *The loan*: Horwitz, 121.
William's narrow escape: Dalrymple, III, Appendix to Book V, 89, 92; HMC, Report IV, Coningsby, 317.
248 *The Lieutenancy*: Chatsworth, 44.2.
248-50 *The naval appointments*: Dalrymple, III, Appendix to Book V, 104-24.
250 *Shrewsbury*: Dalrymple, III, Appendix to Book V, 87, 101, 107.
The Queen's outburst: Dalrymple, III, Appendix to Book V, 127.
Her conversation with Devonshire: Dalrymple, III, Appendix to Book V, 110.
251 *Devonshire's loyalties*: Chatsworth, 51.3; White's *Funeral Sermon*, quoted Francis Thompson, *A History of Chatsworth*.
Churchill: Dalrymple, III, Appendix to Book V, 123-5.
252 *Monmouth's bid for a new Parliament*: Dalrymple, III, Appendix to Book V, 117-18.
The Scottish conspirators: Leven and Melville Papers, 525.
253 *The Church in Ireland*: Dalrymple, III, Appendix to Book V, 93.
'*I must laugh and talk*': Dalrymple, III, Appendix to Book V, 127.
254 *Her pity for Lady Marlborough*: Dalrymple, III, Appendix to Book V, 128.
Reunion: Doebner, 33.

CHAPTER 25 THE RETURN OF THE HERO

255 *Kensington*: Dalrymple, III, Appendix to Book V, 100, 106.
   The King's plans: Dalrymple, III, Appendix to Book V, 129.
256 *Gaiety*: Doebner, 33.
   The Queen's visit to the theatre: Cibber, 107-8.
256-7 *Dinner at Woburn*: HMC, Rutland, II, 131.
257 *Tillotson's eulogy*: Birch, 240.
   Burnet's sermon: Bodleian C2.21.
   The reform of manners: Burnet, *Memorial*, 52.
257-8 *James in France*: Liselotte, 57, October 20, 1690, Liselotte to Sophia of Hanover.
258 *Liselotte and William*: Liselotte, 57, August 20, 1690.
   Kensington: PRO Kensington Pay Books for 1690-1, Derek Hudson, *Kensington Palace*, 8-10; Law, *Kensington Palace*.
258-9 *Wren's opinion of the Queen*: Parentalia, 326.
259 *Wren's plans*: Wren Society, IV, Plate 13; Briggs, 182-7.
259 *Hampton Court*: PRO Works, 55/5; Hugh Murray Baillie, *Archaeologia*, vol. CI, 1967, 'Etiquette and the planning of the State Apartments in Baroque Palaces,' 169-80.
260-1 *The Water Gallery*: PRO Works, 55/5; Defoe, *Tour* I, 175; C. H. de Jonge, *Apollo*, November 1964, 386 'Delft Ware at Vught'; Fiennes 59-60; Green, *Grinling Gibbons*.
261 *The Queen reads aloud*: Burnet, *Funeral Sermon*, 38.
262 *The King's taste*: Wren, *Parentalia*, 326.
   The Queen's love of Holland: Lettres et Mémoires, 124.
   The King's apprehension: Huygens, *Journal*, I, 340.
   The journey: *A Late Voyage to Holland*, Harleian Miscellany, II, 591; Burnet, IV, 129.
263 *'Where they give one shout for me'*: Echard, 118.
   Mary entertains: Doebner, 36; SPDom, March 17, 1691; HMC, Le Fleming, 320, March 17, 1691.
   Clearing the staircases at Hampton Court: PRO, Works, 5/55.
   De Marot's shed: PRO, Works, 5/55.
   Irregularities in hospitals: SPDom, 1690-1, 241.
   The Queen's way of life: Bishop of Gloucester, *Memoirs*.
264-5 *Blancard's calumnies*: HMC Denbigh, 83 *et seq*.
265 *Keppel*: Huygens, *Journal*, I, 401.
265-6 *The Queen's difficulties*: Doebner, 36.
266 *Ailesbury's admiration*: Ailesbury, I, 269.
   The Preston plot: Doebner, 40; Burnet, IV, 123-6; Dalrymple, III, Book VI, 148; HMC Le Fleming, 310-321.
266-7 *Ashton and the young apprentice*: Doebner, 40.
268 *The fire at Whitehall*: Doebner, 37; Bramston, 365; Evelyn, April 10, 1691.
269 *The Queen's visitors*: Doebner, 37.

CHAPTER 26 THE SECOND SUMMER

270 *The King pardons Preston and Croon*: Doebner, 40-1.
270-1 *The Bishops*: Doebner, 41; Waterson, 145-6; Bodleian Rawlinson, 68, 55-7.

271-2 *The appointment of Tillotson*: Burnet, IV, 72-3, 134-5; Birch, 252, 322, 337; H. P. Turner, *Five Studies of the Aristocracy* (unpublished M.Litt. dissertation 1965, Cambridge University Library sub. *Northampton*).
272 *Difficulties with the administration*: Baxter, 295; Huygens, *Journal*, I, 428; Grew, 194-5; Luttrell, II, 215.
273 *Burnet's sermon*: Bodleian C2.21 Linc., April 29, 1691.
The journey to Harwich: Doebner, 38; Huygens, *Journal*, I, 430; SPDom, May 5/15, The Hague.
274 '*I looked over all my meditations*': Doebner, 38-9.
275 *Prince George's ambition*: Doebner, 38; *Conduct*, 39-40.
Prince George in Ireland: Blenheim MSS, quoted Churchill, *Marlborough*, I, 342(n).
The Bishop of London's love of gardening: H. P. Turner (see note 369-70); HMC Denbigh Report, VII, Appendix 198.
Sancroft and Beveridge: Evelyn, May 7, 1691.
276 *William's warning to Ginckel*: Japikse, II, iii, 234-5, May 1/11, 1691.
Worries about the Irish campaign: Doebner, 39.
The Queen's letter to Ginckel: copy at the Bentinck Archives, Ameroongen.
277 *Her letter of congratulation*: copy at the Bentinck Archives, Ameroongen, in her own hand to 'Monsieur de Ginckle'.
Ginckel's letter to the Queen: SPDom, May 18, 1691.
Ginckel's victories: Doebner, 42; *Lettres et Mémoires*, 126-7.
The French fleet: Doebner, 41.
278 *William's loan*: Baxter, 296.
Ronquillo: HMC Denbigh Report, VII, Appendix, 197.
278-9 *The reform of manners*: Bodleian C2.21 (Linc); Birch, 242, 263-4; SPDom, July 9, 1691; Burnet, IV, 182(n); J. E. B. Mayor, *Cambridge under Queen Anne*, 348-53.
279 *A squadron to the Shannon*: SPDom, August 28, 1691.
279-80 *Her letter to Lady Russell*: Russell, *Letters*, II, 89.
280 *Preston at Whitehall*: HMC, Denbigh Report, VII, Appendix, 199.
The Queen and Godolphin: HMC, Denbigh Report, VII, Appendix, 200.
Death of Lady Dorset: Doebner, 43.
Young Bentinck: HMC, Denbigh Report, VII, Appendix, 191, June 19, 1691.
The Queen's prayer of thanksgiving: *Lettres et Mémoires*, 102, July 18, 1691.
281 *Her longing for children*: *Lettres et Mémoires*, 92-3.
Her instructions to Callenburgh: SPDom, October 17, 1691.
The capture of Limerick: HMC Denbigh Report, VII, Appendix, 203.
282 *William's return*: HMC Denbigh Report, VII, Appendix, 204; SPDom, October 20, News Letter; Ronquillo, II, 464; Robb, II, 329.

CHAPTER 27 THE QUARREL

283 *The Queen's thankfulness at the King's safe return, his good health and hers*: Doebner, 43; Ronquillo, II, 464.
Kensington: Green, *Grinling Gibbons*, 67-8; Law, *Kensington Palace*, 71 *et seq*; Wren Society, VII, 135, 157, 160, 178.
Lord Mayor's Show: HMC Denbigh Report, VII, Appendix, 205.
283-4 *The ball at court*: HMC Denbigh Report, VII, Appendix, 205.
284-5 *The fire at Kensington*: HMC Denbigh Report, VII, Appendix, 196-7, 207; Defoe, II, 10-11; Doebner, 44.

285 *Hampton Court*: Green, *Grinling Gibbons*, 69 *et seq.*; Law, *Hampton Court Palace*, 28 *et seq.*; Wren Society, IV, 50; Celia Fiennes, 353–7; Defoe, I, 174–6.

286 *Plants for Kensington and Hampton Court*: RA Nass Dom Ord, 740.234; BM Sloane MSS 2928, 3343.

    The weather: Evelyn, November 8–30, 1691.

287 *Sharp's Christmas sermon*: Bodleian C2.21 (Linc).

    Whigs and Tories: HMC Denbigh Report, VII, Appendix, 203.

288–91 *The quarrel with the Marlboroughs*: HMC Denbigh Report, VII, Appendix, 220; Green, *Duchess of Marlborough*, 61–8; *Conduct*, 41; Doebner, 45; Clarke, II, 444, 477; Churchill, I, 343–4.

291 *The Queen's letter*: Conduct, 45–7.

CHAPTER 28 LA HOGUE

292 *William's departure*: Doebner, 46.

    Sharp's Easter sermon: Bodleian C2.21.

292–3 *The Queen's illness*: Doebner, 47; Birch, 266–7.

293 *The Fast day*: Doebner, 267.

    Invasion threats: Churchill, I, 350–1; Evelyn, April 24, May 5, 1692; Burnet, IV, 165–7.

293–4 *Letters to Mlle Obdam*: *Lettres et Mémoires*, 127–32.

294 *The list of dangerous persons*: Ailesbury, I, 93, 298; SPDom, May 9, 1692.

295 *The Queen's letter to the fleet*: Dalrymple, III, Part II, Book VII, 238; HMC, Finch, II, 335.

296 *Letters to and from the Princess*: Churchill, I, 355–6.

296–7 *The battle of La Hogue*: Burnet, IV, 167–8; Dalrymple, III, Part II, Book VII, 238–46; Clarke, II, 166; Waterson, 100–1; Russell, *Letters*, II, 98; Guizot, *Mémoires de Jaques II*, IV, 505; Sandars, 338.

298 *William in Flanders*: Japikse, I, i, 169–171.

    The situation in England: Doebner, 52–3.

299 *The Nottingham-Russell dispute*: Horwitz, 132.

    The Bishop of London: Luttrell, II, 525; Carpenter, 177–8.

    Godolphin: Baxter, 307.

    Rest at Kensington: Doebner, 53.

299–300 *The battle of Steinkerk*: Burnet, IV, 175; Grew, 208; Doebner, 53.

300 *Letter to Lady Scarborough*: BM Add MSS 20731.6.

    Grandval's trial: Doebner, 54.

301 *The earthquake*: Burnet, IV, 181; Robb, II, 346; Evelyn, September 15, 1692; Huygens, *Journal*, II, 124–5.

    The sailors' wives: Luttrell, III, August 31, 1693.

CHAPTER 29 AN UNFORTUNATE ADMINISTRATION

302 *William's return*: Doebner, 55.

    Russell's title: Russell, *Letters*, II, 109, October 18, 1692.

302–3 *A time of ease and rest*: *Letters*, II, 109; Doebner, 55–6.

303 *Gloucester's sword*: Luttrell, II.

    The Pastoral Care: Birch, 292; Foxcroft, *Burnet*, 310.

    Dr Hicks: Bodleian Rawlinson D841.83–5.

303–4 *Dr Ken*: Plumptre, II, 304–9.

304 *The birthday ball*: Doebner, 95.
305 *The stormy session in Parliament*: Burnet, IV, 183–92, R. A. Heinsius MM.SS, 348.
Party pettiness: Doebner, 58.
306 '*The public hate*': Ranke, *History of England*, VI, 215, quoted Horwitz, 141.
307 *Trenchard*: Burnet, IV, 141.
Lord Mohun's trial: Doebner, 59.
Reform of manners: Proclamation in the Library of Congress, Washington, D.C., quoted Waterson, 182.
Sunderland: Kenyon, 255.
308 *Lord Bellomont*: Doebner, 59.
Letters to Sophia: Doebner, 96–100, January 13, February 12, 1693.
The sisterly quarrel continued: *Conduct*, 100–2.
309 *Cabinet crisis*: Doebner, 59; Horwitz, 143.
Progress at Loo: RA Nass Dom Ord. 741, 194, 195, 198, 212, 218, 240, 249; 742.32, 75, 95, 193, 202, 208.
The Queen's collection of china: Evelyn, July 13, 1693.
310 *Letter to the Electress*: Doebner, 103.
310–12 *The Smyrna fleet*: Burnet, IV, 205–9; Baxter, 312; Doebner, 60, 108–9; Waterson, 110–13.
313 *The Battle of Landen*: Doebner, 60; Burnet, IV, 202–4; Baxter, 312–15; Robb, II, 349–52.
313–14 *Sunderland and the Whigs*: Kenyon, 259–63; HMC Denbigh Report, VII, Appendix, 214.
314 *The King's return*: Doebner, 61.
Nottingham's dismissal: Doebner, 61; Horwitz, 145–6; Hatton, II, 198.
The weather: Evelyn, November 12, 1693.
Sharp's sermon: Bodleian C812 Linc.
315 *The Queen's thoughts at the end of the year*: Doebner, 61.

CHAPTER 30 THE DEVILISH PARTY

316 *Shrewsbury*: Coxe, *Shrewsbury*, 18–30; HMC, Buccleuch, II, 58–60.
The Queen's cold: *Lettres et Mémoires*, 140.
Greenwich: *Parentalia*, 328.
317 *William and Mary College, Virginia*: Burnet, IV, 215.
316–17 *Lord Buckhurst*: Robb, II, 357; Sackville West, *Knowle and the Sackvilles*, 158.
317–18 *The Duke of Gloucester*: Lewis, 40–7.
319 *Gloucester says goodbye*: Lewis, 48; Baxter, 317; RA Heinsius 348.
320 *The stay at Canterbury*: Walton (Hooper) MSS, 11–12; Trevor.
320 *The Cathedral furnishings*: Walton (Hooper) MSS, 11–12; BM Add MSS 5751 (A), 171
320 *The King's journey and his stay at Loo*: Grew, 226; Coxe, *Shrewsbury*, 32–3.
320–1 *Camaret Bay*: Burnet, IV, 232–5. Churchill's defence of Marlborough, who was said to have given information to the enemy, is to be found in *Marlborough*, I, 368–86, 'The Camaret Bay Letter'.
321 *Russell and the Mediterranean*: Coxe, *Shrewsbury*, 32, 44.
The risk of a battle: Coxe, *Shrewsbury*, 52.
The Queen's fears: Doebner, 11–112.
Sunderland's match-making: Kenyon, 262–3.
322 *The Queen and the clergy*: Burnet, IV, 211–12.
322 *Tillotson*: Birch, 307–8.

The Bishops: Birch, 309.
323 *Evening at Lord Ranalagh's*: BM Add MSS 20,731,8.
    Jewellery and clothes: BM Add MSS 5751 (A), 98–185.
    The cage bird: Lewis, 46.
323–4 *Russell's plans for the winter*: Coxe, *Shrewsbury*, 69, 72–5.
324 *William's return journey*: Coxe, *Shrewsbury*, 77.

CHAPTER 31 THE INEXORABLE DISTEMPER

325 *The ring*: this ring, with the paper written in the Queen's hand, went into the
    collection of the Dukes of Portland.
    The King's illness: Baxter, 319; HMC Buccleuch, II, 102; Japikse, II, iii, 345;
    Huygens, *Journal*, II, 437, 440; KHA, William, C. XI, 899.
    The death of Tillotson: Birch, 315–18; 424; Burnet, IV, 241–4.
    The tree: Walton (Hooper) MSS, Trevor, II, Appendix I, 475.
326 *The appointment of a new Archbishop*: Trevor, II, Appendix I, 476.
    The Queen visits Hampton Court: Baxter, 319.
327–332 *et seq. The Queen's illness and death*: Burnet, IV, 245–50; BM Add MSS 5751
    (A), 180; Japikse, II, iii, 346; KHA, A16 XV, a letter from Van Hulst (clerk to the
    King's Secretary), *Royal Diary*, 10–11; *The Life of our Late Gracious Queen Mary*,
    71–4; HMC Hope-Johnstone, 69–70; Lewis, 454; Huygens, *Journal*, II, 440–53;
    Lexington, 31, 36–52., V. and A., Forster MSS 48. c. 8, 223 et seq.
327 'the inexorable and pitiless distemper': *The Life and Death of her Royal Majesty*,
    Bodleian Pamphlet, 247, 1695.
328–30 *The King's affliction*: Burnet, IV, 249–50; Grew, 234–5; Robb, II, 364–6;
    Japikse, II, iii, 346; Coxe, *Shrewsbury*, 78; Heinsius, I, 377, RA Heinsius 402,
    HMC Hope-Johnston, 72.
330–1 *Reconciliation with Anne*: *Conduct*, 105–11; Evelyn, January 13, 1695; KHA
    Mary, A16, XV, a1; Letter from l'Hermitage, January 8/18, 1695.
332 *Parliamentary arrangements*: KHA Mary, A16, XV, a1.
    The jewellery: KHA Mary, A16, XV, a1.
    The stairs at Kensington: PRO Kensington Pay Books.
    James's reaction: Kemble, 175.
333 *The King at Richmond*: Heinsius, I, 378.
    Burnet's visit: HMC Hope Johnstone, 72.
333–4 *The lying-in-state and funeral*: Bodleian Rawlinson B138–66; Evelyn, February
    27–March 5, 1695, V. and A. Forster MSS 48 c. 8. 223 et seq.
334 *The catafalque*: PRO Works 5/47; Green, *Grinling Gibbons*, 73.
    La simplicité Hollandoise: Doebner, 96.
335 *The Queen's character*: Ailesbury, I, 298–9; Evelyn, March 8, 1695.
    Funeral sermons: Bodleian Pamphlet, 220.
335–6 *Elegies*: 12 *Pamphlets of Poems*, Hill's Reprints.
336 *Prior*: HMC Bath, III, 46; Lexington, 63.
    The Queen's charities: Burnet, *Supplement*, 406.
    The Gibbons frame: Green, *Grinling Gibbons*, 68.
337 *The old lady at Canterbury*: Walton (Hooper) MSS 11, Appendix 47, Trevor, II.
    Lady Russell: Russell, II, 122.

INDEX

Carlingford, Nicholas, 2nd Earl of, 154
Carmarthen, *see* Danby
Castlemaine, *see* Cleveland
Catherine, Lady, daughter of the Duke of York and Anne Hyde, 17
Catherine Laura, Lady, daughter of Duke of York and Mary Beatrice, 29
Catherine, Queen, Princess of Braganza, 12, 13, 14, 22, 23, 48, 78, 146, 239–40, 244
Cavendish, Lady, 208
Cavendish, Lady Arabella, 322
Cavendish, Lord, 251
Chambrun, M, 197
Charles I, 1, 5, 23, 105
Charles II, in exile, 1–5; restoration, 6; Catholic leanings, 15; his character, 22; at Mary's wedding, 45–6; his broken promises, 66; his illness, 85; recalls Sidney 105, 112; sees William at Windsor, 113; writes unpleasant letters, 139; death of, 144–6; mentioned, 7, 8, 14, 16, 20, 21, 29, 30, 37, 40, 41, 42, 43, 44, 45, 47, 48, 49, 68, 75, 77, 78, 80, 87, 89, 92, 93, 99, 100, 108, 111, 116, 118, 119, 121, 124, 126, 127, 129, 135, 140, 142, 268, 291, 318
Charles, Stuart, Duke of Cambridge (1660–61), 8, 10
Charles Duke of Cambridge (born and died 1677), 46, 62
Charlotte, daughter of the Duke of York, 122, 125
Chatsworth, 251
Chesterfield, Countess of, 11
Chiffinch, William, 159
Chudleigh, Thomas, 137, 140, 142, 148, 157
Churchill, Arabella, 12, 30
Churchill, John, *see* Marlborough, Duke of,
Churchill, Lady (Sarah Jennings), *see* Marlborough, Lady
Churchill, Winston, 268
Cibber, Caius, 285, 286
Cibber, Colley, 256
Clarendon, Edward Hyde, 1st Earl of, 2, 3, 6, 7, 8, 9, 14
Clarendon, Henry Hyde, 2nd Earl of, 172, 184, 185, 191, 203, 209, 210, 212, 213, 214, 241, 267
Clarges, Sir Thomas, 305
Cleveland, Lady Castlemaine, Duchess of, 12, 14, 16, 25
Clifford, Lord and Lady, 164
Coleman, Edward, 78
Compton, Henry, Bishop of London, 34, 45, 47, 78, 101, 102, 158, 163, 165, 168, 174, 179, 181, 182, 187, 210, 213–14, 215, 223, 271, 275, 299, 330
Condé, Prince de, 313
Congreve, William, 256
Coningsby, Thomas, 1st Earl of, 247
Coote, *see* Bellomont
Cornbury, Lord, *see* Hyde
Cornwallis, Mistress, 33
Covell, Dr, 157–60, 264
Crewe, Nathaniel, Bishop of Durham, 46, 163, 210

Cromwell, Oliver, 1, 209
Crowne, John, 23, 24

D'Albeville, Ignatius White, Marquis of, 162, 170, 173, 174, 179, 181, 188, 192, 196, 199
D'Alonne, Abel Tessin, 157, 158, 199, 229
Dalrymple, Sir John, 327
Danby, Thomas Osborne, Earl of, Marquis of Carmarthen, Earl of Leeds, 41, 181, 182, 183, 187, 204, 212, 214, 235, 240, 242, 243, 244, 248, 249, 250, 252, 254, 267, 270, 271, 287
Dartmouth, George Legge, 1st Earl of, 105, 114, 197
D'Avaux, Jean Antoine, Comte, 80, 88, 92, 93, 94, 96, 106, 123, 126, 129, 130, 136, 137, 142, 143, 144, 161, 162, 171, 193
Davies, Mrs, 25
Dawson, Mrs, 189–90
De Brécourt, William Marcoureau, Sieur, 117
Defoe, Daniel, 286
De Hooghe, Romeyne, 309
Delaval, Sir Ralph, 281, 306
De Marais, M, 151
Denham, Lady, 11, 13
Derby, Countess of, 224, 266, 319, 330
D'Estrades, Godefroi, Comte, 59, 85
Devonshire, William Cavendish, 1st Duke of, 187, 227, 235, 250–1, 267, 270, 284
Dieren, 79, 83, 84, 85, 100, 101, 111, 113, 118, 119, 121, 124, 126, 128, 139–41, 147, 151, 157–9, 163, 192, 217, 224, 294
Dolben, Archbishop, 70
Dorchester, Catherine Sedley, Countess of, 104, 162–3, 209, 286, 334
Dorset, Charles Sackville, 6th Earl of, 235, 267, 270, 284
Dorset, Countess of, 280, 317
Doughtie, Dr, 18, 34
Drelincourt, Charles, 67, 197
Dryden, John, 23, 31, 32, 36
Dumblane, Viscount Osborne of, 181–2
Dundee, Viscount, 222
Duval, Robert, 309
Dyckvelt, 172–3, 194, 199, 210, 264, 265

Edgar, Duke of Cambridge, son of the Duke of York and Anne Hyde, 17
Elizabeth Charlotte, 'Liselotte', Duchess of Orleans, 4, 12, 257–8
Ely, Bishop of, 184, 266–7
Emmett, William, 283, 285
Essex, Arthur Capel, 2nd Earl of, 284
Evelyn, John, 1, 9, 11, 25, 67, 96, 108, 146, 149, 169, 188, 191, 196, 208, 214, 229, 268, 286, 302, 309, 314, 322, 335
Evertzen, Admiral, 246
Exclusion Bill, 103, 104

Fagel, Gaspar, 126, 130, 136, 138, 140, 167, 172, 194
Fatio, Mr, 167
Fell, Dr John, Bishop of Oxford, 101, 167
Fenwick, Sir John, 268
Feversham, Louis Duras, 1st Earl of, 239
Fitzharding, Lady, 287

et Hofhuijs. 2 K. Maj: Vertrek. 3 de Kerck. 4 de Keüken 5 Wachthüijs. 6 Orangerie. 7 Thüijngereetschap